Theories of Concepts

Theories of Concepts

A History of the Major Philosophical Tradition

Morris Weitz

R

Routledge
London and New York

First published in 1988 by
Routledge
11 New Fetter Lane, London EC4P 4EE

Published in the USA by
Routledge
in association with Routledge, Chapman and Hall, Inc.
29 West 35th Street, New York, NY 10001

Set in 10/12pt Times
by Witwell Ltd, Southport
and printed in Great Britain
by Biddles Ltd, Guildford

Library of Congress Cataloging in Publication Data
Weitz, Morris.
Theories of concepts: a history of the major philosophical
    tradition/Morris Weitz.
      p.   cm.
    Bibliography: p.
    Includes index.
    1. Concepts — History.   I. Title.
    BD181.W384   1988
    121'.4 – dc 19   87-31663

British Library Cataloguing in Publication Data
Weitz, Morris
    Theories of concepts: a history of the
    major philosophical tradition.
    1. Concepts
    I. Title
    121'.4   BD181

ISBN 0-415-00180-3

CONTENTS

Professor Morris Weitz died before publication of this book and the final editing and preparation of the manuscript was done by Professor Margaret Collins Weitz.

For Richard, David and Catherine

FOREWORD

Morris Weitz spent most of his academic life working in the fields of analytic philosophy, aesthetics, and philosophy in literature. His studies in analytic philosophy were everywhere recognized as models of clarity and incisiveness. The publication of his study, 'Oxford Philosophy'[1] was a major event in that it brought to American students of philosophy one of the first comprehensive analyses and explications of the movement that had come to dominate philosophy in England in the years just before and after World War II. As early as 1944 Weitz had published his comprehensive study of the development of the philosophical thought of Bertrand Russell from its earliest stages to the time of writing.[2] A steady stream of articles and books dealing with these areas of aesthetics, literature, and analytic philosophy continued to appear until the very end of his life.

In the course of his philosophical work Weitz became progressively more interested in the problem of the nature of concepts. He became convinced that this was one of the most fruitful areas of philosophical reflection, and one that was only beginning to be properly explored. His later work was devoted in considerable measure to this topic. One result of that effort is the companion volume to the present book.[3] The second is this volume which Weitz prepared fully for publication prior to his death.

This study is not quite like anything else that Weitz wrote, but it followed naturally from his philosophical interests and from his own

[1] *Philosophical Review*, 62 (1953): 187–233.
[2] 'Analysis and the Unity of Russell's Philosophy,' in Paul A. Schilpp, ed., *The Philosophy of Bertrand Russell* (Northwestern University Press, 1944).
[3] *The Opening Mind: A Philosophical Study of Humanistic Concepts* (University of Chicago Press, 1977).

unwavering scholarly integrity. In the course of his work he came to the conclusion that contemporary discussions of the problem of concepts were seriously limited by the fact that we have no history of the theory of concepts. He searched the literature thoroughly and was astonished to discover that so basically important a piece of work had never been done. It was at that point that he determined to do it himself, and thus to pioneer in an area of the history of philosophy that had been neglected by others.

Once he decided to undertake the project, it was characteristic of Weitz that he would bring to it the highest level of scholarly responsibility and philosophic judgment. He quickly became convinced that to produce the kind of book that he wanted and that was required by the subject it was essential for the author to have a sound mastery of Greek as well as Latin. Under the tutelage of a Brandeis University colleague, Professor Douglas Stewart, Weitz devoted himself intensely to this project and emerged as a thoroughly respectable scholar of Greek. (He knew Latin already.) It is fair to say that he took special delight in an achievement which helped him to master still one more area of scholarship. The historical learning in this book may seem to be rather far removed from the interests and the scholarly work which occupied Weitz throughout his adult life. For those who knew him well it will be readily apparent that he was simply extending himself to an area of philosophy which he discovered to be a necessary foundation for further contemporary work on the theory of concepts.

With the requisite linguistic tools firmly in hand. Weitz set himself the task of restudying the history of western philosophy. He did an extremely careful rereading of the main works of that history beginning with Plato and ending with some main figures of the twentieth century. He accompanied his study of the primary texts with a close examination of the most important works of commentary and exegesis on the philosophers that concerned him. His goal was to free himself from established views so that he could gain his own understanding through his own perspective.

Although his main interest was in discovering what the philosophers who constitute the canon of the western tradition had to say about concepts, he knew that one had to see their treatment of this particular subject in the context of their total philosophic systems. Weitz was much too intelligent and sophisticated a thinker and reader to make the elementary mistake of isolating the theory of concepts from the rest of a philosophic system. However, once he had done his work, he set himself the task of dealing in this book with just that one topic, being fully and justifiably confident that his treatment of concepts would reflect his deep and thorough understanding of the complete thought of each individual philosopher whose views he set forth. In this book Weitz has given us his mature study of a topic which had hitherto been largely neglected.

Weitz was astonished to discover that while practically every modern philosopher talks about concepts, and almost all contemporary students of philosopy take for granted that some use of concepts and some theory of concepts is present in every philosophical system, hardly anyone had paid serious attention to a number of key questions. Just what does each individual philosopher mean by 'concept,' and what account does he give of concepts? What is the epistemological and ontological status of concepts within a given philosophic system? How shall we understand the various terms used for 'concept' both in a given language and in diverse languages? If a philosopher has no term for 'concept' in his system, does that mean that he makes no use of concepts or that he has no theory of concepts? How have earlier theories of concepts affected the thinking of later philosophers? Is there, in fact, a history of such theories, and if there is what light will it shed on our understanding? These are some of the main questions that concerned Weitz, questions which he discovered had evoked little interest and even less serious study. Above all he realized that no one had ever undertaken to provide a complete historical account of this subject, and it was his decision to write the book which would fill this remarkable gap in the literature of the history of philosophy.

His purposes, as he himself makes clear, were not purely to fill a need of historical scholarship. Important as this is, and granted its intrinsic interest and value, this by itself would not have been sufficient to move Weitz to undertake this massive work. He never lost sight for a moment of the very important philosophical consequences of such a study. First, clarity about a given philosopher's theory of concepts is essential for a correct grasp of his whole philosophical system. As Weitz expresses it, 'the basic reason why a survey of theories [of concepts] is required – certainly the reason why I have devoted this book to it – is that a philosopher's theory of concepts is not simply incidental to his work but fundamental in his philosophy in that it determines the overall condition or criterion of what he takes to be the correct statements and solutions of his problems.'[4] Second, he sought to correct the basic misunderstanding of some major philosophers by those who affirm that because a philosopher has no term for concepts he therefore has no theory of concepts. Weitz finds this to be a very serious error, since it leads to basic mistakes in our understanding of the views of these philosophers. Every philosopher employs concepts, and every serious philosopher must have a theory of concepts, whether it be explicit or implicit. In the case of those philosophers who do not use the term 'concept' or who seem to have no term for it, Weitz set for himself the task of uncovering the theory that is hidden in each system. His prime examples of such philosophers are Plato and Hume, and of them and others like them Weitz says, 'that their views about their concepts – what they are, what roles they play, the conditions for playing these roles, and the logical character, closed or open, of these conditions – are to be found in and to be elicited from their employment of the concepts they employed.'[5] His third objective, which is ultimately the most important, is to elucidate the notion of 'concept' by seeing the range of views that great philosophers have held over the centuries. Weitz was not so overawed by the great philosophical names of the past that he thought we had to submit to their views at all costs. On the contrary, he approaches each philosopher critically, seeking not only to understand him but also to evaluate the soundness of his teachings. He was convinced, however, that in coming to understand the history of theories of concepts from Plato to such twentieth century figures as Ryle and Geach, we would open ourselves to a deeper grasp of the problems and possibilities implicit in the very notion of a 'concept.' This could only mean that contemporary thinkers would now be in a position to reflect on concepts and to elucidate them in a way that is more perceptive and philosophically sound than was possible for those philosophers who preceded them. Some of the results of his own reflections on the subject are contained in *The Opening Mind.* The present book is the study of the historical background and philosophical development of the idea of a 'concept' from which contemporary thought about the problem might begin anew.

[4] See below, Introduction.
[5] See below, Introduction.

Morris Weitz spent his entire professional life teaching philosophy and writing philosophy. He was a member of the faculty of philosophy at the University of Washington, Seattle, at Vassar College, at The Ohio State University, and at Brandeis University. His students admired him both for the lucidity of his teaching and for the model he provided them of the truly and totally dedicated philosopher. Those of his colleagues who knew how to appreciate him (and they were all but a very few over a long career) took delight in the precision and incisiveness of his mind, in the kindness but sharpness of his criticism, and in the originality and depth of his thought. As a friend he was unfailing in his loyalty, deep in his devotion, and totally undemanding. His death was a loss to our profession, but even more a great personal loss to his family, his students, his colleagues and his friends. This last book which he wrote with so much care and thought is the most fitting of all memorials to a distinguished philosopher and an exemplary man.

Marvin Fox
Brandeis University

ACKNOWLEDGMENTS

Any publication – but particularly one of this nature – is based upon the help and assistance of others. A Senior Fellowship from the National Endowment for the Humanities enabled the author to devote a full academic year, as a resident at the Camargo Foundation in Cassis, to writing this book. Cassis had been a mecca for some of the members and intimates of the Bloomsbury Circle. Morris Weitz liked to think that their historical presence inspired him as G. E. Moore had, in ways he could never fathom, inspired them.

His late colleague Henry David Aiken helped immeasurably by conversing with him over the years about the language of philosophy itself. Another Brandeis colleague, Douglas Stewart, introduced Weitz to the riches of the Greek language: he also helped verify the Greek references. Marvin Fox of the Department of Near Eastern and Judaic Studies of Brandeis University kindly consented to write a preface. Israel Scheffler of the Education and Philosophy Departments of Harvard University was instrumental in seeing that the volume was published. The editors at Routledge, particularly Stratford Caldecott, provided valuable assistance as the manuscript made its way to publication.

Finally, Theodore Uehling of the Philosophy Department of the University of Minnesota and their press granted permission to reprint the chapter on Descartes which first appeared as an article in their journal, *Midwest Studies in Philosophy VIII*. To them and to all those who contributed to the publication of this volume I would like to express my deep gratitude.

Margaret Collins Weitz
Professor/Chair
Humanities and Modern Languages
Suffolk University

INTRODUCTION

Having already canvassed open concepts, both contemporary formulations of them and some of their variety, most recently in *The Opening Mind: a philosophical study of humanistic concepts* (1977), it seems to me that absolutely basic to further exploration in the area of conceptualization is a thorough inquiry into the history of traditional theories of concepts. Such an inquiry would be valuable if only to test the accuracy of contemporary criticisms of these theories as a series of mistaken views about concepts as entities, or concepts as erroneous readings of the meanings of words, or concepts as unintelligible abstractions, or – my own view – concepts as closed in their definitive properties, conditions or criteria. Many contemporary philosophers, whether they subscribe to open concepts or to concepts as dispositions, not entities, have offered one or other wholesale doctrine about traditional theories of concepts. The doctrine, as attribution and as condemnation, in this regard, much resembles recent attempts to foist mistaken naming theories of words or denotative theories of meaning and language on traditional philosophy, to be contrasted with some modern, correct theory of naming and meaning, put forth by the particular philosopher-historian in question. Because much evidence by way of historical analysis of traditional theories of language and meaning has accompanied and supported this contemporary critique of them, one would naturally suppose that similar evidence is available to vindicate the wholesale condemnation of traditional theories of concepts.

To my amazement and incredulity, I could find no book on the history of philosophical theories of concepts. There are, of course, Encyclopedia articles on CONCEPTS; however, these are, without exception, either too brief, too general or delinquent, contain too many inaccuracies and, on the whole, simply repeat the historical clichés of their predecessors. Dictionaries, too, are unhelpful, as are the more detailed Etymologies and Lexicons. What, then, of independently written essays or chapters of books on the different philosophers? Here, one finds a great deal on Kant's or Frege's theory of concepts, and much on Aquinas' or Leibniz'. But there is nothing, except paragraphs in chapters of books or in essays, on Plato's theory of concepts and, even more surprising, on Descartes', since he is preoccupied with what he refers to as 'concepts' when he turns from *Meditation* to *Reply*, for example. And the little that there is on these two philosophers – that, for example, Plato's theory of concepts is that concepts are forms among the forms; or that Descartes means by a concept a variant of an idea – it soon became apparent to me is incorrect.

To one, like myself, who is not a specialist in the history of philosophy, this whole business of an individual philosopher's theory of concepts and of the history of theories of concepts, from Plato on, became confusing. The hope persisted that somewhere, someone – surely some German scholar, whose colleagues had devoted their lives to Plato's theory of justice or to the etymology of *arete* – had written a long, accurate history of philosophical theories of concepts.

That I could find no such survey dictated the writing of this book, entirely concerned with the history of philosophical theories of concepts. If I am right in claiming that such a survey does not exist, then this history of philosophical theories of concepts is the first. And in this regard, it will have realized one of its aims even if, disagreed with, in its parts or as a whole, it only provokes others to do the history better or differently.

But, it may be asked, is this history needed? Obviously, it seems so to me, first, because any important idea and related set of doctrines about it that have a history enjoin and invite meticulous delineation of them. Second, no contemporary criticism of traditional theories of concepts nor, I think, any putatively original and true theory of concepts and the having of them can long ignore the competing theories of the past. Recent claims about the modernity of the dispositional theory of concepts are falsified and the truth of many variants of this theory are challenged by Plato's theory which, if my interpretation of it is correct, is not only the first dispositional theory of concepts as abilities to move about intellectually and morally in the world, but also the first to imply that concepts are such abilities only on the condition that these are closed, ultimately beholden to the forms or definitions of the forms or of certain classes of things. However, the basic reason why a survey of theories is required – certainly the reason why I have devoted this book to it – is that a philosopher's theory of concepts is not simply incidental to his work but fundamental in his philosophy in that it determines the overall condition or criterion of what he takes to be the correct statements and solutions of his problems.

Why such a theory is needed perhaps also suggests why it has not yet been done: because such a survey, at least as I have conceived it, as a history of the nature and role of concepts, not simply of their ontology, depends on the recent shift in philosophy itself from analysis to the elucidation of concepts. For it is only when elucidation replaces analysis that one can generalize from the elucidation of particular concepts to the overall elucidation of theories of concepts, both past and present. Thus, I have tried to understand the different theories of concepts, not to analyze or to recast the concepts dealt with in the history of philosophy. What do philosophers say or imply concepts are in the concepts they employ? Do they subscribe to the doctrine that all concepts, hence their conveying words, are governed by necessary and sufficient conditions or criteria? How do their theories play the roles they do in their philosophies? These are the questions I have set myself.

But, it may also be asked: Is there a history of theories of concepts? Negative answers range from the denial that there are concepts and therefore any theory of them, let alone a history of such theories, to the acceptance of at least concept-talk in the history of philosophy, some articulate theories of concepts, but the rejection of anything as grand as a history of theories of concepts.

If we distinguish, as we must, between Are there concepts? and What are concepts? the affirmative answer to the first, that concepts are neutral intermediaries between words and things, irreducible to anything else, commits us to no affirmative answer to the second, as to what they are, whether sensible, supersensible or neutral entities or dispositions. However, my answer and argument for it (given in Chapter 1 of *The Opening Mind*) are not relevant to the argument of this book: that there *is* a history of theories of concepts; that this history encompasses both explicit and implicit theories; and that these theories, different as they are in their ontological answers to what concepts are, concur in the major doctrine that all concepts are and must be governed by definitive sets of properties or criteria.

That there have been explicit theories of concepts cannot be denied, however these theories are assessed, as fabrications or as ontological truths. Surely, Aquinas, Kant, Frege, and Moore, among many others, both affirmed concepts and theorized about their status and roles. What can be questioned and denied is that these articulated theories point to a history of a single subject rather than, say, to the ambiguity of a 'concept,' in one language or another.

If this objection to a history of philosophical theories stands, it rules out not only my proposed history but all the Encyclopedia articles as well that attempt to trace the history of the words for concept and explicit theories of them, which I question on grounds of inadequacy, not of dubiety. What these articles show is that though 'concept' is ambiguous, theories of concepts are more multiple than ambiguous.

Indeed, this query about the history of philosophical theories of concepts as a single subject much resembles similar worries expressed by those who question the very possibility of a history of (philosophical) theories of tragedy or morality. Here, too, the argument has been that there can be no such history because there is no single subject. Tragedies differ and moralities are too diverse to yield any univocal meaning of 'tragedy' or 'morality.' All the historian can do is to trace the diversity. It is therefore a conceptual illusion to suppose, for example, that Greek tragedy or Aristotle's theory of tragedy and, say, modern tragedy or Schopenhauer's or Nietzsche's theory of tragedy, are historical points in the same continuum, that can then serve as a single subject for the philosophical elucidation of tragedy. So, too with, say, Plato's theory of morality as against, say, Kant's. Here, too, critics of any putative history of philosophical theories of morality stress that since Plato meant by 'moral' something entirely different from what Kant meant by 'moral,' there cannot be any univocal history of the subject of philosophical theories of morality.

Like all writers of books on the history of tragedy or theories of tragedy or on the history of ethics or theories of morality, I do not find this scepticism persuasive. For the multiplicity of use of 'moral,' 'tragic,' or, in my case, of 'concept,' need not capitulate to the despair of ambiguity. Instead, this multiplicity itself offers a single subject of the enfolding of a concept in all its challenging disparateness of conflicting criteria for its correct use, whether that concept be that of tragedy, morality or concept itself.

What, now, about implicit theories of concepts? Throughout this book, I repeat the refrain that doing philosophy (and not just being a philosopher in the possible variant of immersing oneself in the Sea of Ineffability) is, whatever else it is, conceptualizing in language; and that the concepts the individual philosopher employs is the source of his theory of concepts. This is not to say or to imply that a necessary condition for doing philosophy or even for conceptualizing is having a theory of concepts, on an absurd par with saying that doing sawing is to have a theory of saws, that doing some punctuation is to have a theory of punctuation, or even doing some referring is to have a theory of reference.

'A is a philosopher and has no theory of concepts' is not a self-contradiction or incoherent. But 'A philosophizes about x (justice, knowledge, morality, truth, etc.), yet employs no concept of x, conveyed by the word "x" in the particular language he uses to express his concept of x; and does not employ his concept of x in accordance with certain criteria that govern what he regards as the correct use of his concept of x and his word "x," where these criteria are neither a definitive nor a less than definitive set,' is, I think, incoherent. To say, then, as I do, that Plato or Hume, among others, has a theory of concepts, even though Plato had no word for concept and Hume did not use the word, is only to say that their views about their concepts – what they are, what roles they play, the conditions for playing these roles, and the logical character, closed or open, of these conditions – are to be found in and to be elicited from their employment of the concepts they employed. Both of them, though neither had an explicit theory of concepts, have an implicit theory, as indeed do all philosophers as they conceptualize in language, whether they articulate an explicit theory of concepts as well.

A theory of concepts, then, is not the doctrine that there are concepts; such a doctrine affirms no things, rather that talk about concepts is not reducible to talk about words or things. A theory of concepts is a statement about the nature and role of concepts. This statement may be explicit; in any case, it must be implicit in the language of philosophy. A particular philosopher's theory of concepts is what he says or implies they are or what they do in what he says or implies about the things he discusses in his philosophy. What renders his theory of concepts fundamental in his philosophy –

and why I think a book on the history of philosophical theories of concepts is imperative – is the logic of the set of properties, conditions or criteria that he invests in the concepts he employs as these are conveyed by the words he uses to make his doctrinal pronouncements about knowledge, reality, truth, morality, and so on, or, as the case may be, to demolish these pronouncements when put forth by others. The assumption or affirmation that all concepts are and must be closed may not determine his specific doctrines or scepticism about their truth; as we shall see, the history of philosophy shows that the univocity of the closure of all concepts is compatible with a multiplicity of divergent metaphysical, moral, epistemological, or theological views. This assumption that all concepts are and must be closed goes much deeper, for it determines that *the* definitive answer is forthcoming to whatever question, however the individual philosopher formulates it, whether about essences, meanings or necessary and sufficient conditions, he raises in his philosophy. The criteria of this definitive answer correspond to and are guaranteed by the definitive criteria of the postulated closed concept. Indeed, the theory that all concepts are and must be closed, governed by definitive sets of necessary and sufficient criteria, a theory as old as Plato and Aristotle and as up-to-date as Frege and the Wittgenstein of the *Tractatus*, is itself the putatively definitive answer to the putatively definitive question, What is a concept?

There are, then, philosophical theories of concepts, some explicit, all implicit. And, more to my immediate purpose, there is a history of these theories, inviting its delineation and, if I am right about the centrality of implicit theories of concepts in individual philosophers, enjoining an elucidation of this history. Russell's great insight into the history of philosophy was that, according to his understanding of it, the assumption of a subject-predicate logic had been the driving force in the development of western metaphysics with its incipient, yet inevitable Monism of One Substance and its attributes. In this book, I make a similar claim about the hegemony of the doctrine that all concepts, to be concepts at all, in philosophy or anywhere else, must be closed; that this doctrine or assumption has been as much of a driving force in the course of western philosophy. Whether my claim is also an insight, I leave to the Reader to judge.

My aim is to provide a history of philosophical theories of concepts; my major theme is the historical unfolding of the pervasive assumption or doctrine that all concepts are and must be closed. The fifteen chapters speak for themselves. Each, with the exception of the last, I hope, is an original reading of the philosopher or philosophers in question; in which I have tried to formulate his explicit or implicit theory of concepts in order to test it against the actual major concepts he employs in his work. Most of these readings are unorthodox in that they oppose traditional commentaries and interpretations. If they infuriate specialists, I hope the reason they do is that my accounts are incorrect rather than merely eccentric. I have not tried to make friends with my interpretations and history, only to influence people, and not only philosophers, to come to see the important, perhaps centrality, of theories of concepts in philosophical doctrine and disputation; and also to see just how pervasive the assumption that all concepts are closed has been in western philosophy and thought. As I understand the history of theories of concepts, this assumption and its ubiquity have been more fundamental in traditional notions of conceptualization than the doctrine that all concepts are entitities of one sort or another.

In my separate accounts of the major philosophers' theories of concepts, there is little overt quarrel with competing readings. I do single out, for example, Wolfson on Philo, or Gilson on Augustine, but only because their views are so immediately contrary to mine that they must be met head on. However, it must not be inferred from my lack of overt controversy that I have ignored the great commentaries. I have, I hope, read most of them. But I realized fairly soon in working up this history that most of the commentators, when they do introduce the problem of concepts or of theories of them held by the philosophers they are commenting on, bring to their interpretations their own theories of concepts, that they can invest in the putative theories of their subjects. As a consequence, I have not been overimpressed or overwhelmed by the commentators in this area of philosophical investigation. Nevertheless, I must not be allowed to renege on any responsibility to have read the great historical interpretations of philosophers from Plato to Moore. The fact remains, though, that I have obtained little enlightenment from them on the problems I have set myself: What does each of the great philosophers say or imply concepts are? What does each say or imply about the roles and conditions of these roles of their concepts as these are exemplified in the concepts employed by the philosopher? Perhaps I should also add that I have not used footnotes to inveigh against traditional interpretations of the tradition; instead, I have kept the footnotes to a minimum, and almost without exception, they are mere references, with no substance that properly belongs in the text itself.

One result of my history is unorthodox; that the major tradition does affirm concepts as entities. However, the varieties of the entity theories yield no easy formula about sensible versus supersensible entities; and, most important, neither the entity theory nor its variants encompasses Plato's theory which, I argue, is dispositional and, therefore, he, not Berkeley, Hume or Kant, is the first to intimate such a theory of concepts. And, in this connection, I also argue that neither Berkeley, Hume nor Kant – the supposed founders of the dispositional theory – formulated or implied such a theory. A related, again unorthodox, claim I make is that Aristotle, not Plato, first formulated the entity theory of concepts; that they are definitional entities; from which it follows that if platonism is the view that concepts are entities or supersensible entities, Aristotle, not Plato, is its father.

In the case of Augustine, I try to show that, contrary to Gilson's thesis that Augustine has no, and needs no, theory of concepts, he does have such a theory and, for the most part, an entity theory. With Aquinas, the burden shifts from what he says concepts are to whether his theory covers the concepts he employs and discusses in his work. My answer is that it does not. Moving on to Descartes, I attempt to prove that concepts are, for him, ontological entities, on a par with God, mind and matter, in their irreducibility. Spinoza and Leibniz, too, affirm concepts as entities, the first as conceptions among the modes of substance, the second, as innate ideas. With Hobbes, I argue that he, too, is stuck with an entity theory of concepts, specifically, as definitions; and, consequently, recent attempts to interpret concepts in Hobbes as revolutionary contrary to fact conditionals or fictions, will not wash. Locke, Berkeley and Hume are special problems since their epistemological or ontological views seem to leave no room for concepts, only for sensations and ideas or notions in the mind. In the case of each, I argue that a ground of coherence of their individual sets of doctrines is a realm of concepts that is not reducible to ideas or notions. I also argue that Locke, not Wittgenstein, is the first to challenge the assumption that a necessary condition for sorting (classification) is an ontology of real essences and their apprehension. I follow with a long chapter on Kant's theory of concepts which (heresy of heresies!) because it rests on concepts as entities or objects, cannot secure a coherent place in his Transcendentalist Idealism. The next two chapters on nineteenth and twentieth century theories are necessarily selective. My main purpose here is to delineate the platonic strain in Frege, Russell and Moore as a conflation of Plato's theory of concepts with his theory of forms; a subordinate aim is to sum up traditional theories as well as to introduce very recent dispositional approaches to concepts and the having of them in Ryle and Geach. One of the delights (for me) of the penultimate chapter was to refocus Ryle's contributions to theories of concepts; from our traditional meadowland picture of him as a logical geographer mapping ordinary concepts – suggested by his *Concept of Mind* – to a new vision of him as a logical explorer engaged in the discovery of the varieties of logical types of concepts – impressed upon us by his entire *oeuvre* – where he stands, joined by his pioneers, Frege, Russell and Wittgenstein, on the white peaks of philosophical logic. The emphasis, then, of my history, as I summarize in the final chapter, is on the whole tradition, with all its variety, but with an especial accent on the assumption that all concepts are and must be closed; governed by definitive sets of properties, conditions or criteria.

Note: To facilitate printing, the original Greek of the manuscript has been transliterated, and hence accent marks omitted.

CHAPTER I

Plato

That Plato employs certain concepts in his dialogues can no more be questioned than that he uses language. Although he discusses many things – he even devotes one dialogue, the *Cratylus*, to the origin and nature of language – he never discusses concepts as such, only particular concepts: piety, justice, knowledge, pleasure, love, beauty, dialectic, being, and the like.

From Aristotle on, commentators have written about Plato's doctrines. Often they talk about his particular concepts. Plato analyzes justice, among other things, without at the same time talking about the concept of justice, albeit not without using the concept and its corresponding Greek word. But can commentators write about Plato's concept of justice without saying something about his theory of concepts? It seems to me that both Plato and his commentators can talk about justice and can use the concept without further analysis of the concept of a concept. However, commentators cannot talk about Plato's concept of justice, or of his doctrine or theory of justice that in any case converges on his concept of justice, without saying what Plato means by a concept. For a condition of the intelligibility of any account of Plato's various doctrines is a reasoned statement of his theory of concepts.

Basic, then, to both Plato's employment of particular concepts and the commentator's interpretations of them is Plato's theory of concepts. Nevertheless, it is a fact, deplorable as it is, that among the volumes of explication of Plato's doctrines, there is no full study of his conception of concepts. To be sure, there is much talk about Plato's concept of this or that as well as a tradition from Aristotle to Shorey and Ryle according to which platonic forms are timeless, immutable concepts that have an independent existence as super entities. But there is next to nothing on Plato's theory of concepts (which is not to say there is little on Plato's theory of forms as hypostasized concepts – indeed, there is too much!). So far as I have been able to determine, there is no discussion of Plato's theory of concepts that compares at all with the extensive treatment of practically everything else in Plato's philosophy. And the little there is – that Plato identifies concept with *noeton, logos, eidos, ennoia or noema*, according to the individual commentator – is not only incorrect but inadequately supported, almost brought in by the interpreter as an afterthought about that which is relatively unimportant in relation to what the concept is a concept of.

It is because I think that Plato's theory of concepts is fundamental in his philosophy, as indeed a theory of concepts is basic in any individual philosophy, that I must now try to formulate Plato's theory. Plato has no explicit theory of concepts; nor has he a word for concept in the sense that, say, Sextus Empiricus or Abelard has both. His theory, therefore, must be implicit, to be elicited from the way or ways in which he employs the particular concepts he deals with in his writings.

Consider, then, to begin with, one of his early dialogues, the *Euthyphro*. At the end of that dialogue, Socrates says to Euthyphro: 'For if you had not clear knowledge of holiness and unholiness, you would surely not have undertaken to prosecute your aged father for murder for the sake of a servant' (15d).

This summative rejoinder to Euthyphro suggests the possibility that to Plato a necessary condition for being ϕ (when ϕ is a virtue) or of saying that 'P is ϕ' is knowing what ϕ is, and that knowing what ϕ is is being able to define ϕ: to state its necessary and sufficient properties. Thus, in order for Euthyphro to be pious or holy, or to claim that his father's action of murder is impious while his ensuing prosecution is pious, presupposes that Euthyphro knows what piety is. Since Euthyphro is not able to define piety and holiness, Socrates shows, Euthyphro is not pious or holy, nor can he meaningfully and correctly assert his claims about his and his father's actions.

In the dialogue, Euthyphro utters words such as 'pious,' 'holy' and 'murder.' There is no hint that unless he knows what murder is, he cannot say 'X is murder.' But Socrates does imply that unless Euthyphro knows what piety is – can define it – he cannot intelligibly say 'X is pious.' Euthyphro says that what he is doing is pious.

2

Socrates counters that Euthyphro does not know what he is talking about because he does not know what piety is. In short, Socrates implies that Euthyphro has the word 'piety' but not the concept of piety; and unless he has the concept he cannot use the word correctly. All he can do and does is to make verbal noises.

However, it is not clear in this early dialogue whether knowing what piety is is identical with having the concept; or is rather a presupposition of having the concept. Nevertheless, the answer to this question is crucial in the understanding of Plato's theory of concepts. It is my hypothesis that Plato does not identify the concept of piety with its definition; nor the having of the concept with knowing what piety is. Rather that for Plato a necessary condition for having that concept is knowing what piety is and that knowing what piety is is knowing piety: being directly acquainted with it.

As a first step in the clarification of this hypothesis that for Plato the having of the concept of ϕ presupposes but is not identical with clear knowledge (*eidestha sophos*) of ϕ, I turn to the seventh *Letter*. Genuine or a forgery, the *Letter* suggests a theory of concepts that may be Plato's. I quote the relevant portion:

> For every real being, there are three things that are
> necessary if knowledge of it is to be acquired: first, the
> name; second, the definition; third, the image; knowledge
> comes fourth, and in the fifth place we must put the object
> itself, the knowable and truly real being. To understand
> what this means, take a particular example, and think of
> all other objects as analogous to it. There is something
> called a circle, and its name is this very word we have just
> used. Second, there is its definition, composed of nouns
> and verbs ... Third is what we draw or rub out, what is
> turned or destroyed; but the circle itself to which they all
> refer remains unaffected, because it is different from them.
> In the fourth place are knowledge (*episteme*), reason (*nous*),
> and right opinion (which are in our minds, not in words or
> bodily shapes, and therefore must be taken together as
> something distinct both from the circle itself and from the
> three things previously mentioned); of these, reason is
> nearest the fifth in kinship and likeness, while the others
> are further away. The same thing is true of straight-lined as
> well as of circular figures; of colour; of the good, the

beautiful, the just; of body in general...of all living beings...of all actions and affections. For in each case, whoever does not somehow grasp the four things mentioned will never fully attain knowledge of the fifth (342; Morrow tr.).

If genuine, this quotation can be read as Plato's genetic and logical account of knowledge. Both are parts of the orthodox reading, according to which Plato lays down four necessary conditions for attaining true knowledge of a real thing, like a circle: learning its name; defining it; instancing it; and making true judgments about it. Unless and until we satisfy these conditions, we cannot and do not know the circle. ('And we must apprehend Name, Definition, Image and Knowledge ("the first Four") before we attain to the Real ("the Fifth"),' Bury, in his introduction to the seventh *Letter*, Loeb edition). The concept of the circle is the same as the real circle; the having of that concept is identical with grasping the circle; both the concept and the circle are logically dependent on naming, defining, instancing, and opining about circles. These latter activities are also genetically necessary as preliminary steps to the ultimate apprehension of the concept-being of the circle.

Now, whatever plausibility there may be in the genetic account of learning about the circle vanishes in the logical account. If the seventh *Letter* is suspect on stylistic grounds or on the doctrinal ground that it distorts Plato's theory of ideas, it is equally suspect in its theory of concepts. For if anything is clear in Plato's implicit theory of concepts – through all the dialogues – it is that naming, defining, instancing, and truly opining about circles are not necessary conditions of knowledge of the real circle. Indeed, it may be the other way round: that a necessary condition for naming, defining, instancing, and opining truly about circles is a prior grasp, intuition, direct apprehension of the circle. For unless and until we grasp the form of the circle – its *eidos* or *noēton* – we cannot name, define, instance, or make true judgements about circles.

This is the logical relation Plato affirms stright through his writings, with serious reservations in the *Phaedrus* and *Philebus*, and is garbled by the author of the genetic-logical account in the seventh *Letter*. Moreover, it is a logical relation that yields a completely unorthodox interpretation of concepts in Plato's philosophy, since they are no longer to be sought in apprehended forms but rather in those activities and procedures that presuppose this apprehension. Thus, to have the concept of a circle is to have intuited the circle and to be able to use this knowledge in naming, defining, instancing, and judging truly about circles. Concepts, therefore, are not entities – subsistent or mental – but skills, such as being able to name and identify objects, recognize and discriminate among them, to say what counts as an object of a certain kind, and to define and make true statements about objects. In short, the conceptual life for Plato encompasses that enormous range of activity which centers on our intelligent moving around and about in the world. A necessary condition of such activity is the prior grasp of the realm of forms, because it is in this realm that the criteria and standards of the success of these activities can be secured and measured.

Plato, it seems to me, has a dispositional, not an entity, theory of concepts. A concept, thus, if a Greek word is required, is more like a *techne* than it is like a *logos, noeton, eidos, noema*, or *ennoia*. This dispositional theory is not only implicit in the dialogues; it is also basic in Plato's philosophy since it underwrites all his views, including those about the forms and their corresponding concept of *eide*.

By way of confirmation of my hypothesis about Plato's theory of concepts, I turn to the dialogues. As everyone knows, in his early dialogues – the *Euthyphro, Lysis, Laches, Hippias Major, Charmides*, and *Republic*, Book I – Socrates raises as a fundamental question, 'What is piety, friendship, courage, beauty, temperance, or justice?' Later, in the *Protagoras* and the *Meno*, Socrates asks, 'What is virtue?' as basic to 'Is virtue one?' and 'Can virtue be taught?' In the *Theaetetus*, 'What is knowledge?' becomes central. In the *Symposium*, 'What is love?' and in the *Philebus*, 'What is pleasure?' are focal. Similar 'What is x?' questions, some raised by Socrates, others by different speakers, run through most of the dialogues.

The centrality of this 'What is x?' question; its meaning, even its cogency; its bearing on the methods of the *elenchus*, dialectic, and division; and the linguistic as against the ontological character of this question have been much discussed and debated by the commentators (as well as by Plato in some of his dialogues). Rather than enter into this controversy, important as it is, I wish instead to ask, 'What is the role of concepts in the posing and answering of this "What is x?" question?'

Both asking and answering 'What is x?' employ the concept of x, expressed by its corresponding Greek word 'x'. Answering this question surely involves being able to define x, unless x is a simple, such as Plato's Good. Consequently, answering 'What is x?' is one manifestation of having the concept of x. Other manifestations are: Answering 'x' to 'What is that called?' Pointing to x when asked 'What is an instance or example of x?' Saying of x, 'It is better than y' or 'It is hard to find an x,' when the question, 'What are some true opinions about x?' arises. All of these questions and replies are conceptual activities for Plato; each activity is a different manifestation of the same concept of x. Answering the 'What is x?' question, thus, is a conceptual activity in which the concept is not a form-entity that the word 'x' names or means but is rather an ability to provide the requisite definition. And, on the hypothesis I propose, this kind of definitional conceptual activity entails a prior apprehension of the appropriate form.

If, however, *answering* 'What is x?' questions, along with naming x, instancing x, and making true assertions about x, support the dispositional theory of concepts as founded on prior acquaintance with the forms, does *asking* 'What is x?' also confirm this theory?

Asking belongs to that group of activities which include inquiry, scrutiny, the *elenchus*, dialectic, and division cell – all central to Plato's Socrates. My question about the role of concepts in the asking procedures, consequently, becomes a crucial one in that the answer to it seems to challenge my hypothesis that Plato's is a dispositional theory of concepts, in which concepts depend for their intelligibility upon the prior grasp of forms.

To be sure, asking, like answering, 'What is x?' involves skill, if only the ability to use language to ask questions. But if asking, like answering, is a conceptual activity, to be added to the list given in the seventh *Letter*, we must ask, How can a necessary condition for *asking* 'What is x?' be a prior grasp of the form x, since such a condition forecloses on the very activity itself? That is, if I can give a definition of piety – an answer to 'What is piety' – because I have apprehended piety, I can ask for or seek such a definition without having grasped piety as such. So, too, I can give an instance of piety, hence employ the concept of piety in this way, but only if I have known piety itself – the form piety (*to hosion auto/auto*). Surely, one wants to say, I can ask for an instance of piety or whether this particular action is an instance or not without having known piety in this absolute sense. Thus, the thesis that the apprehension of forms is a necessary condition of the having of concepts as dispositions is in seeming fundamental conflict with a whole range of skills and abilities having to do with asking rather than answering questions.

Does, then, the logic of questioning differ from the logic of answering in Plato? Do the necessary conditions of both differ? If they do differ, then dialectic as the method of question and answer must be recast in the account of Plato's use of that method, since asking and answering are heterogeneous activities, not homogeneous, as the tradition holds. Whether concepts are form-entities or, as I maintain, dispositions, the concepts employed in questioning cannot function under the same necessary condition which governs the concepts present in answering.

The method of question and answer in Plato's conception of dialectic raises the larger problem of the logical differences between inquiring and proclaiming. A necessary condition of the second but a self-contradictory or at least self-defeating condition of the first is knowledge of a form. Of course, one can neither proclaim nor examine unless one has something to proclaim or examine; in both the concept (as skill or as entity) is present. But there can be no apprehension of what the concept is a concept of in examining as there must be in the proclaiming. The conditions of trying to find cannot be those of having found.

Is this admission – it cannot be denied – that no form need be apprehended when I ask what piety is? What is piety? Is this pious? Why is this pious? Is piety better than impiety? fatal to the theory of concepts as abilities founded on prior intuitions of forms – the view I attribute to Plato?

It is a difficulty; and I have no desire to minimize it. But it is not fatal because the necessary condition of a prior grasp of the *eidos* is present in a weaker form of a prior assumption that there is such a form which the questioner has not yet grasped and is groping for. This, I think, is for Plato the necessary condition of the life of examination: that whole range of conceptual activities that revolve around asking, seeking, examining, scrutinizing, inquiring. Euthyphro, we recall, does not know piety, so he does not have the concept; that is, he is not able to name, instance, or speak truly about pious acts; nor is he able to define piety, to give the *logos* of its *eidos*. Neither can Socrates do what Euthyphro cannot do. But Socrates (and, one hopes, you and I) can ask about piety and pious acts. Socrates has the concept even though he has not (or so he intimates) apprehended the form; hence, he is not able to name pious acts, discriminate them from other things, speak truly about them, or define piety. He has the concept because he is able to ask what piety is, how to recognize it, how to talk about it, what a reason for something being pious would be? He can wield the concept in these ways, but only because he assumes that there is a form which can be defined, even though he does not know, has not grasped, that form. Asking about piety, then, is not a necessary preliminary to getting to know piety. It is rather a conceptual activity, as intelligible as any other, that can persevere only on the assumption that asking has an answer.

Of course, there is much asking in the dialogues that is conceptual and does presuppose prior knowledge of a form as a necessary condition of its intelligibility. 'Should I escape?' and 'Is it ever right to disobey the laws of one's country?' in the *Crito*; 'Is it better to suffer than to commit injustice?' in the *Gorgias*; 'Is the just man happy?' in the *Republic*; 'Can one be overcome by pleasure?' in the *Protagoras*; 'Is the soul immortal?' in the *Phaedo* – each of these questions, asked or repeated by Socrates, presupposes an appropriate form and acquaintance with it that govern its *logos* and the doctrines derived from this *logos*, given in Socrates' answer. Here both asking and answering serve as conceptual analysis in which logical entailments among the constituents of certain forms are articulated. Thus, asking whether it is better to suffer than commit injustice is asking if the definition of justice – the *logos* of an *eidos* – contains doing harm as a constituent. To have the concept of justice is in part to be able to see that doing harm contradicts being just; and without the prior grasp of the form justice, neither its definition nor this particular entailment could be conceptualized.

There is a further difficulty about concepts as abilities governed by apprehension or assumption of forms. In the *Symposium*, 'What is love?' is asked and putatively answered by a number of speakers. In the *Philebus*, Socrates raises the question, 'What is pleasure?' In both dialogues, the final definitions yield a startling conclusion, that these definitions constitute *logoi* all right, but not of any *eide*, because there are none of love and pleasure. Love and pleasure are not forms as their objects beauty and the good are. In the *Symposium*, for example, all the speakers have the word 'love.' But only Socrates possesses the concept of love that he claims the word 'love' correctly expresses. And he has the concept not because he has grasped the form of love but because he can provide a true definition of love: the common denominator in all cases of love which, he says, is the progressive desire to possess, generate and ultimately to contemplate the beautiful. In the sense that love may be said to rest on the form of beauty, love does not rest on the form of love, since there is no such form. Socrates has the concept of love because he can name and instance examples of love, say why they are such examples, and distinguish these cases from other things. (So, too, we may say that Plato has the concept of love as he dramatizes its various but one-sided facets in each of the five speakers who precede Socrates' magnificent synthesis and in Socrates' rejection of Alcibiades as one who is incapable of love, that ends the dialogue. The *Symposium*, one is tempted to say, becomes another manifestation, along with those involved in asking and answering, naming and instancing, already canvassed, of conceptualization in Plato: as the ability to dramatize the search for and the attainment of the definition of love.)

Both Socrates and Plato have the concept of love: Socrates defines it, Plato dramatizes it. Love has an essence (*ousia*). The *logos* of love supplants the *eidos* of love as a necessary condition of the possession of the concept.

The *Philebus*, complex as it is, also shows how one may have a concept, in this case of pleasure, without any prior apprehension of a corresponding form. To have the concept of pleasure is, among other things, to be able to name pleasure, to discriminate it from other things and, most importantly, in the *Philebus*, to distinguish its pure from its mixed varieties. But none of these activities is possible without a definition of pleasure, a definition that analyzes the properties of an essence, not a form. As in the *Symposium*, *logos* replaces *eidos* as a necessary condition of having the relevant concept.

It should also be noted as a further qualification of my hypothesis that asking and answering in the dialogues are conceptual activities which rest on prior apprehensions of forms, that many of the putative answers – those that are refuted, succumbing to the *elenchus* – cannot meet this necessary condition. Like intelligent asking, these answers depend rather on the assumption that there is a form which the putative definition-answer fails to explicate. For example, in the *Theaetetus*, neither Theaetetus nor Socrates knows the *eidos* or the *logos* of knowledge. But both have the concept in that they can ask 'What is knowledge?' and can offer answers to the question and agree on the inadequacy of the three answers proposed, on the ground that none of these answers satisfies the criterion (never stated) that knowledge is a certainty about forms, a criterion derived from their joint assumption but not apprehension that there are these forms as the stable elements without which neither reality nor knowledge is possible.

For Plato, the conceptual life, I am contending, centers in the middle range of human activities between pure, direct knowledge or assumption of the forms or definition of the essences of things and ignorance about things and forms. These activities include the abilities to learn and teach, name and recognize objects, describe and evaluate, explain and interpret phenomena in the world, and to ask and answer questions about different aspects of reality, knowledge and morality. That Plato promotes such an implicit dispositional theory of concepts as skills and abilities, not as entities or capacities, to move about in the world, intellectually and morally, where a condition of the intelligibility and correctness of such moving about is an ontological order that secures and corresponds to the conceptual and in which this order of forms and definitions of them is the guiding principle of thought and action is, I think, directly confirmed by many of the dialogues.

In the *Phaedo*, for example, Socrates offers our ordinary perceptions of objects and comparisons of them as examples of our employment of some of the forms. We say of two things that they are equal or unequal. To be able to do this, he insists, we must have the concept of equality; and to have this concept, we must already have apprehended the form of equality. To be sure, he reaffirms his doctrine of knowledge as recollection as an explanatory hypothesis about the origin and formation of the concept of equality; but this hypothesis is independent of his claim that concepts are non-empirically derived constituents of perceptual experiences. We cannot, Socrates says, even see two things as unequal or as equal (which they never are) unless we conceptualize them. And we cannot conceptualize them unless we already possess the form of equality. This passage (72eff) of the *Phaedo*, thus, beautifully illustrates his implicit theory of concepts as skills founded on, but not identical with, prior apprehension of forms.

In the *Cratylus*, Socrates compares naming to weaving, names to shuttles. Names are best construed as instruments 'of teaching and of separating reality' (388b–c). Although naming is distinguished from conceiving and naming well is tied to conceiving correctly (436b), naming is affirmed as a skill which, if done well, is dependent upon a prior apprehension of the forms. Names (and language) are no clue to the nature of things or to the forms. Nor is naming a conceptual activity on a par with dialectical division. Indeed, if we must choose between language and direct apprehension in seeking knowledge of the world, '... no man of sense can put himself and his soul under the control of names, and trust in names and their nature to the point of affirming that he knows anything' (440c). This dilemma, however, does not require the rejection of naming and using language if we opt for knowledge as direct apprehension of the forms. All it entails is that language by itself provides no knowledge, not even of the changing world. Without the forms and knowledge of them, we have no criterion for measuring the correctness of language and the place of naming in it. Both naming and using language remain as conceptual skills, no more to be rejected than the weaver's shuttle in making cloth, each governed by prior apprehensions of relevant forms.

Parmenides also supports the hypothesis that concepts are skills or abilities, not entities or capacities, where a necessary condition for the possession of these skills – the having of concepts – is a prior grasp of the realm of forms.

Part I of the *Parmenides* is a devastating critique of the theory of forms. How, then, can the *Parmenides* support this necessary condition of conceptualization? Parmenides himself provides the answer:

> ... If, in view of all these difficulties and others like them,
> a man refuses to admit that Forms of things exist or to
> distinguish a definite Form in every case, he will have
> nothing on which to fix his thought, so long as he will not
> allow that each thing has a character which is always the
> same; and in so doing he will completely destroy the
> significance of all discourse (135b–c; Cornford tr.).

What is challenged in the *Parmenides*, then, is not the reality of the forms, but rather Socrates' various views about their relation to particular things. That thought and discourse, including philosophy, are conceptual activities which rest on the forms and our apprehension of them as a ground of their intelligibility remains intact.

Phaedrus, too, in many ways, affirms that conceptualization is a skill, not a mental state, that involves, among other prerequisites, prior apprehension of the forms. In this dialogue, it is rhetoric, not thought or discourse (as in *Parmenides*) or naming (as in the *Cratylus*), that becomes focal. The sharp contrast between rhetoric and philosophy, between knackery and art, dominant in the *Gorgias*, is softened so that even rhetoric can serve as an art – *techne* – of persuasion, provided its practitioner first grasps the forms (as well as the nature of the soul).

In the *Gorgias*, Socrates rejects rhetoric as an art because it is irrational (*alogov*). In the *Phaedrus*, he provides it with a method of rationality, that of dialectic, which now becomes the technique of collection (*sunagoge*) and division (*diairesis*): 'Unless a man take account of the characters of his hearers and is able to divide things by classes and to comprehend particulars under a general idea, he will never attain the highest human perfection in the art of speech' (273e). Speaking, like writing (but with reservations), achieves respectability only when it is rooted in the forms and articulates collection and division of particulars and forms. Here, too, in the *Phaedrus*, neither the concept of rhetoric nor the concepts used in rhetoric are forms as entities but an assortment of skills from dialectic to naming, instancing, opining truly, and persuading, each of which presupposes that there are forms, already apprehended, requiring analysis and definition.

That dialectic as the method of collection and division is a conceptual activity which presupposes but is not identical with the apprehension of the forms is enlarged upon and reinforced in the *Sophist*, by the chief speaker, The Stranger:

> Dividing according to Kinds, not taking the same Form for a different one or a different one for the same – is not that the business of the science of Dialectic? . . . And the man who can do that discerns clearly *one* Form everywhere extended throughout many, where each one lies apart, and *many* Forms, different from one another, embraced from without by one Form; and again *one* Form connected in a unity through many wholes, and *many* Forms, entirely marked off apart. That means knowing how to distinguish Kind by Kind, in what ways the several Kinds can or can not combine (253d; Cornford tr.).

Five forms – 'the Greatest Kinds' – are illustrated: existence, motion, rest, sameness, and difference. Dialectic becomes the collection and division of them as well as discerning which combines with which. We may ask, is, for example, the concept of existence the same as the form of existence? It is not: the form is an entity, the concept is the ability to recognize existence, distinguish it from, say, motion, and to be able to perceive that it can mingle, for example, with motion. If dialectic is the mastery of these skills and if philosophy is dialectic, as it is in the *Sophist*, the concepts present in dialectic and philosophy – like the concepts of dialectic and philosophy themselves – are dispositions, not entities. They are not forms but they presuppose forms and the apprehensions of them. Dialectic and philosophy, both of which involve discourse, are like naming, instancing, and opining truly about objects, conceptual activities – particular manifestations or uses of concepts.

In the *Phaedrus*, Socrates follows his statement of the two principles of dialectic – collection and division – as they relate to rhetoric with a distinction between knowing how to do certain things and knowing the nature of certain things. One can know how to cure certain ills without knowing what medicine is. One can know how to write pitiful or terrifying speeches without knowing what tragedy is. One can know how to strike the highest and the lowest tones without knowing the nature of harmony. Instead of rebuking these practitioners, which is his usual procedure, Socrates allows that one can know 'the necessary preliminaries' of a subject without knowing the subject itself. Applying this concession to rhetoric, Socrates says:

> We ought not to be angry, but lenient, if certain persons who are ignorant of dialectics have been unable to define the nature of rhetoric and on this account have thought, when they possessed the knowledge that is a necessary preliminary to rhetoric, that they had discovered rhetoric...(269b; Fowler tr.).

In the *Philebus*, there is this exchange between Socrates and Protarchus:

> *Soc.* Now let us imagine a man who understands what Justice itself is, and can give an account of it conformable to his knowledge, and who moreover has a like understanding of all else that is.

Prot. Very well.

Soc. Will such a man be adequately possessed of knowledge, if he can give his account of the divine circle, and the divine sphere themselves, but knows nothing of these human spheres and circles of ours, so that, when he is building a house, the rules that he uses, no less than the circles, are of the other sort?

Prot. I am moved to mirth, Socrates, by this description we are giving of ourselves confined to divine knowledge.

Soc. What's that? Are we to throw in alongside of our other ingredients the art of the false rule and false circle, with all the lack of fixity and purity it involves?

Prot. We must, if we are going to find the way home when we want it. (62a–b; Hackforth tr.).

In the *Meno*, Socrates offers this counter-example to the suggestion that right guidance rests on knowledge and not just true opinion: 'If a man knew the way to Larisa, or any other place you please, and walked there and led others, would he not give right and good guidance?' (97a; Lamb tr.).

Other examples from the dialogues could be given. But these three are sufficient to call seriously into question my hypothesis regarding Plato's theory of concepts. For what they suggest, among other things, is that there are conceptual activities which do not presuppose forms or essences as a necessary condition for their success. On the hypothesis I have been applying to Plato, one either has a particular concept or he does not. One has the relevant concept if one can name or instance certain objects, or opine truly about them, ask and answer certain questions about these objects, or collect and divide them and their classes, and see whether their corresponding forms combine. But one can do none of these without first apprehending or assuming the relevant forms or common denominators of those classes that have no independent forms, such as love or pleasure. For example, Euthyphro, I have claimed, has the word 'piety' but he cannot name pious acts; nor can he give examples of them or make true judgements about them (nor, if we borrow from the *Phaedrus* and the *Sophist*, can he collect pious acts or distinguish them from other acts), because he has not apprehended the form of piety or made the assumption that there is one. In short, he has neither knowledge nor the concept of piety.

But now if we generalize from our three examples, it looks as if we are being too harsh with Euthyphro, for he may be said to know what piety is in the same sense as the man who knows the way to Larisa or who knows how to build a house or how to find his way home. In prosecuting his father for allowing the slave to die tied in a ditch, does not Euthyphro know how to be pious? Cannot we say then of Euthyphro that he does have the concept of piety because he understands, however incompletely, something about piety; and also that with the proper intellectual prodding, he can be taught more and more about piety?

That Euthyphro (or anyone else) can be said to have a particular concept if he is able, for example, to recognize and to discriminate among objects of a certain sort, without first satisfying the condition of apprehension or assumption of a corresponding form or definition of an essence when there is no form, is as attractive a doctrine as it may be sound. But is it Plato's?

It seems to me that it is Plato's; and that his implicit theory of concepts reflects the same tension as his explicit theory of knowledge: that knowledge is opposed to opinion, as he argues in the *Republic*; and that knowledge includes true opinion, as he concedes in the *Philebus*.

However, even in the *Republic* (475e–480, 509d–511e), it is not clear that the dichotomy between knowledge and opinion renders the first conceptual and the second non-conceptual. Socrates distinguishes between *noesis* (reason), *dianoia* (understanding), *pistis* (belief), and *eikasia* (conjecture or image-making). The first two he classifies as *episteme* (knowledge); the second two, as *doxa* opinion). Each, we are told, is a mental state with its own kind of object. Reason contemplates the forms and exercises dialectic upon them; understanding assumes certain principles and draws inferences from them; belief makes true or false judgments on things; and conjecture reports on appearances. Each of these states is best understood as a mental activity in which concepts are present. But it is not obvious from Socrates' description that belief and conjecture or even understanding are conceptual in the way in which the dialectic of reason is conceptual. The philosopher contemplates and defines the circle: he gives the *logos* of its *eidos*. He has the concept because he can state what a circle is; and he can do this because he has first apprehended circularity. The mathematician assumes there are circles but without assuming there is the form of the circle, draws examples of circles, and makes inferences from his assumption and examples. Does he have the concept of a circle? Socrates says the mathematician has understanding but not reason of the circle: he does not know the circle; he does not know what a circle is; he knows circles and he assumes without reason certain principles about circles. Given all this, it would not be far-fetched to say that for Plato, the mathematician does not have the concept. He cannot name, instance, opine truly about circles because he does not know what a circle is and he does not know because he has not yet apprehended the form of the circle.

And if *dianoia* is bereft of the concept, it follows that both *pistis* and *eikasia* are too. In which case we are left with seemingly conceptual activities that are not conceptual in the strong sense of *noesis*.

There is a further difficulty in the *Republic* (which is in other dialogues as well). The highest form of knowledge is contemplation of the forms. Here I do not only know what the circle is, I know the circle, I 'devour' it. How can this direct acquaintance be conceptual? Contemplation, unlike dialectic, is a mystical immersion in the forms, ineffable, therefore not conceptualizable. Whether this sort of contemplation without conceptualization is possible or even intelligible is problematic. However, even if it is possible, it does not rule out concepts as skills since no concept is present in this communion.

Finally, the *Republic* introduces the Form of the Good as a simple, indefinable form, one that underwrites all the other forms (504d–506d). Immediately relevant to Plato's theory of concepts is the introduction of the corresponding simple, indefinable concept of the good. It may be true, as Shorey says, that the Idea or Form of the Good is the hypostatization of the concept of the good ('Introduction' to volume 2 of his Loeb edition of the *Republic*, p. xxiii). But it is not true that the concept is the form. The form is an entity; the concept, the ability to relate all other ideas and all things to their origin and end – to see the world teleologically.

However we interpret the concept of the good, it remains simple, indefinable, as ineffable as its corresponding form. The search for the *logos* of its *eidos* is ruled out. What, then, are the criteria for its correct use? They cannot be the constituent properties invested in the form since, the form of the good being simple, it has none. That nevertheless the concept of the good and the word 'good,' in whatever language, are governed by definitive criteria that determine and measure their correct use, is a doctrine basic to Plato, as it is to G. E. Moore, twenty-five centuries later.

There are other facets of Plato's theory of concepts that deserve examination, for example, his views on the formation of concepts as they relate to *anamnesis* (recollection). But I hope that I have covered the main ones. Basic to Plato's philosophy, I have argued, is his theory of concepts. That is, implicit in all his talk about the forms, knowledge, the virtues, and the methods for securing truth are views about their corresponding concepts. Like any other philosopher, Plato cannot formulate theories or promulgate doctrines without employing concepts expressed in language to do so.

Since he does not do our work for us, we must seek his views in how he deals with the particular concepts he discusses. I have argued that there is a theory of concepts in Plato's philosophy which can be elicited from what he says is involved in an enormous range of activity from the perception of objects to the contemplation of the forms, including naming, discriminating, giving reasons, asking and answering, collecting and dividing, and defining.

Concepts for Plato, I have suggested, are best understood, as they are for any philosopher, in the context of having or possessing concepts. My major claim has been that concepts in this context are best construed as skills or abilities and not as mental or metaphysical entities, which is the traditional interpretation.

I further suggested that a necessary condition for the possession of a particular concept is the prior apprehension of its corresponding form; or, when that is lacking, the assumption that there is such a form; and, when that is lacking, at least the real definition of its corresponding essence. Concepts, thus, are tied to *eide, ousiai*, and *logoi*, but they are not identical with any of these.

The forms (except the simple ones, of which the good is Plato's supreme example) and the essences of things have properties which, as their definitions imply, are sets of necessary and sufficient properties. It is these sets that determine the necessary and sufficient criteria of our concepts and of the linguistic terms in which we express them. Concepts and their general terms are governed by these definitive sets of criteria that derive from their definitive sets of properties. Plato's ontology of forms and essences is closed in the sense of complexes of necessary and sufficient properties, all generated by the simple form of the good. These forms and essences serve as the overriding, second-order, necessary condition of the intelligibility of thought, discourse and action; from which it follows that all concepts are also closed, governed by sets of necessary and sufficient criteria.

Thus, if $\mathcal{Q}$ is a form, simple or complex, or is an essence, Plato's theory of concepts, I am claiming, is that the concept of $\mathcal{Q}$, hence the word '$\mathcal{Q}$' are governed by the nature of $\mathcal{Q}$. That nature establishes the standards of correct use of the concept and its corresponding word or term. The conceptual life, therefore, has as its fundamental principle of intelligibility an ontological principle of order: the concept of $\mathcal{Q}$ and '$\mathcal{Q}$' rest on the nature of $\mathcal{Q}$.

Even as skills, concepts are closed in Plato's scheme: there are necessary and sufficient criteria for naming objects, discriminating among them, giving reasons for something being what it is and not something else, asking and answering, collecting and dividing. Plato originated the doctrine that all concepts are closed, governed by definitive sets of criteria. This doctrine was not effectively challenged until Wittgenstein. If I am right in holding that a philosopher's theory of concepts is basic in his thought, then Plato's theory of closed concepts is his most influential contribution to the history of philosophy, so pervasive has it been from Aristotle to Russell and Moore, and even later.

Again, if my interpretation is correct, Plato is also the inventor of the dispositional theory of concepts, having developed it more than twenty centuries before its supposed founders, Berkeley and Kant. And if we include the *Phaedrus* and the *Philebus*, among others of his dialogues, as indeed we must in any complete account of his theory of concepts he also stands as the first to suggest the extremely contemporary view that there are sufficient but no necessary conditions for conceptualization. Plato's, thus, was no mean achievement.

CHAPTER 2

Aristotle

Certain key passages in Aristotle suggest and to some commentators actually state a theory of concepts. Let us look at these first and see whether they do clarify his theory; or, perhaps, reveal no more about it than a study of his verbs and nouns of conception.

On Interpretation 16a is traditionally singled out as Aristotle's first statement of his distinction between the simple apprehension of a concept and the true or false combination-judgment of two or more concepts. However, in this opening section, what Aristotle says is that spoken words are signs of affections (*pathemata*) of the soul. Written words, in turn, are signs of spoken words. Both vary among different peoples but the affections they symbolize as well as the objects the affections represent remain invariant among human kind.

He follows this with another, presumably related, idea that there are thoughts (*noema, noemata*), some of which are like nouns or verbs, each by itself neither true nor false; and others of which are like combinations of nouns and verbs, each combination being true or false.

In this passage, the relation between the affections of the soul and thought is obscure; it remains so throughout *On Interpretation*. As dubious as each of Aristotle's separate points may be, at least one thing is clear, that there is no compelling reason to read *pathemata* or *noema* or *noemata* as 'concept' and to interpret Aristotle's distinction of simple apprehension and complex judgments as one about concepts. His distinction may imply that there are concepts: how else could thought and judgment be explained? Nevertheless, Aristotle here does not say or even hint that there are concepts and that these are the same as mental affections or thoughts.

Another passage, often referred to as a source of Aristotle's theory of concepts, is the *Posterior Analytics*, Book II, chapter 19, 91a 13–100b 17. Having already explained the nature of science or absolute knowledge as syllogistic demonstration, which he claims rests on self-evident principles and axioms that cannot be proved, Aristotle asks how do we obtain knowledge of these ultimate, primary, necessary premises?

His answer is that they are acquired by intuition (*nous*). However, this does not mean for him that they are innate or recollected in Plato's sense. For intuition is a culmination of, albeit not identical with, any part of the empirical process from particular sense perceptions, memories of them, repetitions of these memories, to the planting of a universal (*katholou*) in the soul, which *nous* then apprehends. Aristotle calls this process of arriving at universals and knowledge of them by intuition 'induction' (*epagoge*) and compares it to an army regaining its original position of strength after a retreat:

> As soon as one individual percept has 'come to a halt' in
> the soul, this is the first beginning of the presence there of
> a universal (because although it is the particular that we
> perceive, the act of perception involves the universal, e.g.,
> 'man,' not 'a man, Callias'). Then other 'halts' occur
> among these [proximate] universals, until the individuals
> genera or [ultimate] universals are established. E.g., a
> particular species of animal leads to the genus 'animal,' and
> so on. Clearly then it must be by induction that we acquire
> knowledge of the primary premisses, because this is also the
> way in which general concepts (*to katholou*) are conveyed
> to us by sense-perception (100a 15–100b 4; Tredennick tr.).

Earlier in the *Posterior Analytics*, Aristotle describes the same process which, this time, ends in a definition, not an intuition:

> We must set about our search by looking out for a group
> of things which are alike in the sense of being specifically
> indifferent, and asking what they all have in common; then
> we must do the same with another group in the same
> genus and belonging to the same species as one another
> but to a species different from that of the first group.
> When we have discovered in the case of this second group
> what its members have in common, and similarly in the
> case of all the other groups, we must consider again

whether the common features which we have established have any feature which is common to them all, until we reach a single expression (*logon*). This will be the required definition (97b 8–14; Tredennick tr.).

Perhaps *nous* is involved in the apprehension and statement of a real definition of the sort Aristotle is talking about in this last quotation. But he does not say so; nor does he claim that it is in his final summary of induction and intuition (100b). His silence raises the question why we need intuition for primary premisses if we do not for real (not nominal) definition? The answer cannot be that definitions are demonstrable whereas the primary principles are not, because Aristotle has already argued in the *Posterior Analytics* 'that in no case is it possible to have both definition and demonstration of the same thing' (91a 9–10).

It is not *nous*, however, that is our immediate concern, since it is Aristotle's theory of concepts, not his conception of intuitive knowledge, that is at issue. Once again it seems to me that there is no warrant for translating *to katholou* as 'general concepts' or for reading this whole section as Aristotle's early attempt at a theory of concepts. For in this chapter he is discussing the formation of universals, just as he seeks the role of common denominators of species and genera in the earlier selection quoted above. It may be, as I think it surely is, that one cannot talk about universals or common denominators without employing concepts of them. But this particular use of concepts need not identify concepts with universals: we can talk about universals without talking about the concept of a universal or about concepts at all. This is what Aristotle does, with the exception of his revealing parenthetical remark that the act of perception, e.g., of seeing a man, Callias, includes the universal (*ton katholou*) man. Now, if seeing a man involves seeing him as an instance of man, the concept of man is a necessary ingredient of this particular act of perception. (Plato had already made this point in the *Phaedo*, 74dff.) Aristotle sees here that one applies the concept of man to Callias; one does not abstract it from him and other men and then apply it to Callias. Why he does not see that universals, like concepts, cannot be abstractions from similar particulars, since abstraction of any sort without the relevant concept as a principle of classification and abstraction is impossible, I do not know.

I conclude, then, that there is no evidence in the *Posterior Analytics* that Aristotle affirms or intimates a theory of concepts. He does claim that there are universals which arise in sense experience but are apprehended only by intuition; and that there are common denominators which are suggested by sense experiences but are defined by a process of intellectual abstraction. Both of these claims imply a theory of concepts that Aristotle requires in order to render his claims coherent. But he neither states this theory nor realizes that he is committed to it.

The *Topics* has one item (125b 28ff.) that is relevant to Aristotle's theory of concepts. It occurs in his discussion of the relation of belief and conception. Conception, he argues, is not the genus of belief, since it is possible for people to have the same conception without believing in it. This suggests that conception is larger than belief, that our conceptions exceed our opinions, and that belief differs from conception in some way but not in its being non-conceptual. Belief remains as conceptual as knowledge in Aristotle's discussion of the genus-species relation of knowledge and conception.

De Anima, especially Book III, chapters vi–viii (430a 26–422a 14), is the third traditionally ascribed source of Aristotle's theory of concepts. However, before he turns to thought, which is the main topic of these chapters, Aristotle has already treated us to his list of the operations of the soul, which include knowing, perceiving, opining, desiring, wishing, and the appetites; to his distinction between the nutritive, sensitive and thinking aspects of the soul; to the definition of the soul; and to lengthy analyses of sensation and imagination. In all of this, there is not a word about conceiving and conception as part of the soul's activity.

Does he remedy this in the appointed chapters by introducing concepts and conception, giving these a proper role among the soul's activities? He begins with his distinction between apprehension of indivisible objects of thought (*ton adiaireton noesis*), which cannot be false, and a compounding of thoughts into a fresh unity (*sunthesis tis ede noematon hosper hen onton*).

That this distinction is one of individual versus combined concepts, as it is often glossed, is as questionable as the thesis that Plato's *noeta* are concepts because they are supersensible, eternal objects of thought. Aristotle, like Plato, is simply formulating the duality of thought and its object. Conceptions and concepts of course are implied by this relation; but neither Aristotle nor Plato says so or intimates it; and neither identifies the *noeton* with a concept.

22

Aristotle goes on in these chapters to claim that knowledge, when actively operative, is identical with its object; that thinking always involves a mental image; and that the mind is capable of thinking of abstracted objects, such as snub-nosed, but is not able to think or conceive (*enoei*) snub-nosed apart from flesh, as it is able to think or conceive its hollowness apart from flesh. It is in this latter sense, Aristotle says, that we can think of the objects of mathematics: as separable objects though they are not.

As obscure as the first claim is, and as false as is the second, only the third is relevant to Aristotle's theory of concepts. What it suggests is that many of our thoughts, including all of mathematics, involve concepts – not things – that are formed by the abstraction of one *imaginable* constituent of an object from its other constituents. Thus, we cannot conceive the snub-nosed without flesh because we cannot imagine it ('the soul never thinks without a mental image'); but, presumably, we can conceive hollowness all by itself because we can imagine it. If this is what Aristotle means by the thought (or conception or concept) of hollowness, this thought and the thesis that supports it, that thoughts (conceptions, concepts) are mental abstract images, vulnerable as it is, shall have to wait until Berkeley for its refutation, so powerful was its hold on western philosophy. However, if Aristotle rather means that hollowness is a potentiality, not an actuality, then it follows that not all abstract objects are potential; some, such as snub-nosed with its flesh, are as actual as the whole face.

In the *Physics*, III, viii (208a 15–20), Aristotle adds this to his theory of concepts:

> It is futile to trust to what we can conceive (*noesei*) as a
> guide to what is or can be; for the excess or defect in such
> a case lies not in the thing but in the conceiving (*epi tes
> noeseos*). One might conceive (*noeseien*) any one of us to be
> many times as big as we are, without limit; but if there
> does exist a man too big for the city to hold, for instance,
> or even bigger than the men we know of, that is not
> because we have conceived him to exist, but because he
> does (*all hoti estin*); and whether we have or have not
> conceived him to exist is a mere incident (Wicksteed and
> Cornford trs.).

Another source of Aristotle's theory of concepts, not usually referred to in this context, yet as illuminating as any of the traditional ones, is his discussion of the intellectual virtues in the *Nicomachean Ethics*, Book VI. He lists five of these virtues or excellences. All belong to the rational as against the irrational part of the soul; three are concerned with the invariable; two with the variable; all aim at the attainment of truth. These five are: scientific knowledge, intelligence, wisdom, art, and prudence. All are contrasted with conception and opinion in that the latter two but not the former five are capable of error.

Now, given Aristotle's principle, which he reaffirms in this Book (1139ff.), that knowledge is based on a likeness of some sort between its subject and its object – a principle that holds for the five intellectual virtues and for opinion – it is surprising that Aristotle does not say that conception also has an object. He does not say that it does not; but it is not clear whether the reader is allowed to infer from the distinctness of conception Aristotle's principle of the duality of subject and object; and the explicit claim that since this duality is present in all the intellectual virtues as well as in opinion, that conception also involves both a conceiver and a concept that is conception's own object.

Although he does not say that conception has an object, he does say, in speaking of scientific knowledge, that it involves a conception and, more revealingly, that it is a mode of conception. This claim requires more detail: Consider the virtue of scientific knowledge (*episteme*). To understand its nature – to possess the concept of *episteme* – is, at least in part, to understand that which is necessary, eternal, invariable. 'We all conceive (*hupolambanomen*) that a thing which we know scientifically cannot vary... An object of Scientific Knowledge, therefore, exists of necessity. It is therefore eternal, for everything existing of absolute necessity is eternal' (1139b 20–24; Rackham tr.).

Aristotle of course does not talk of the concept of *epistémé*; he talks of its nature. But he does introduce a particular concept – of necessary, invariable, eternal truth – that is entailed by an understanding of *epistémé*. Without pushing Aristotle too far here, we can certainly say that he does recognize conception or conceiving, and its concept as something distinct from, perhaps even on a par with, knowledge. Conceiving that a thing which we know scientifically cannot vary is not a bit of *episteme*, since it is not demonstrable. Further, it does not seem to be one of *nous* primary principles. Why, then, does Aristotle leave this concept and its conception dangling among and yet outside the intellectual virtues?

Later, in distinguishing between *episteme, nous*, and *sophia*, Aristotle says: 'Scientific knowledge is a mode of conception dealing with universals and things that are of necessity; and demonstrated truths and all scientific knowledge...are derived from first principles' (1140b 31–35; Rackham tr.).

Now, *episteme* is not the same as *nous* or *sophia*, but it does include the principles derived by *nous*. Further, *sophia,* Aristotle says, is a combination of *episteme* and *nous*. If all this is so, it seems to follow that not only *episteme* is a mode of conception, which Aristotle admits, but also that *nous* and *sophia* are modes of conception as well. From which it is a further consequence – to use Aristotle's terminology – that conception is the genus of which *episteme, nous*, and *sophia* are its species!

That *nous* and *sophia* involve conception and concepts, however, can be argued for independently of their being modes of conception. Aristotle says that the wise man must have a 'true conception' (Rackham's translation of *aletheuein*, 1141a 19–20; literally, it means 'to speak truly') of the first principles of *nous*. Even if he does not mean that wisdom is a form of true conception, the apprehension of first principles is incomprehensible without the involvement of concepts. One cannot grasp, for example, that nothing can both be and not be at the same time, in the same respect, without grasping the concept of an individual; and one cannot intuit that equals subtracted from equals remain equal without apprehending the concept of equality. Thus, every first principle or axiom involves at least one concept. Yet Aristotle nowhere discusses the intuition of concepts, not even in those passages (*De Inter.* 16a and *De Anima* 430a–b) in which he distinguishes between simple and complex *noema. Nous* as intuition must include within its compass concepts as well as thoughts and judgements of the simple and complex. If this involvement is true of *nous*, it follows, once more, that *sophia*, as a combination of *episteme* and *nous*, is also a fundamental conceptual activity.

What about the practical intellectual virtues, art and prudence? Are they conceptual? Can we make objects for a certain purpose; can we deliberate well, become experts in handling particular facts (*ta kath hekasta*) without concepts? According to Aristotle, we cannot practice *techne* or *phronesis* without reason in the form of correct principles of procedure. To be sure, these are not enough, as Aristotle says; but they are necessary, if objects are to be made well and if actions are to be beneficial and advantageous. As necessary, these principles of art and prudence involve concepts, in the same way as perceiving a man, Callias, involves the concept of man.

Aristotle, I think, comes close to recognizing the role of concepts, conceptions and conceiving in his treatment of the intellectual virtues. His insistence that both *episteme* and *sophia* are forms of conception or involve concepts and the implications of his conceptions of *nous, techne*, and *phronesis* as involving concepts leave no doubt that his appreciation of the range of the conceptual life is much richer than his statements about conception, meagre as they are, lead us to believe.

Does Aristotle, then, state his theory of concepts? Our texts, especially Book VI of the *Nicomachean Ethics*, I think, do contain a number of intimations of a theory: that concepts are abstracted entities; that they differ from things that exist, indeed, that they encompass much more than the things that are real; and that they are constituents of many of our experiences, from sense-perception to intellectual activity, including the practical life.

These intimations raise the central question: Does Aristotle hint at or formulate the theory of concepts that is exemplified in or implied by his discussions of the many particular concepts in his work?

If we turn from the little he says about concepts to the way he employs the concepts he discusses, perhaps we may find his implicit theory of concepts. He talks, for example, about substance, using the word *ousia* to do so. But in talking about substance, in trying to state its nature, he necessarily employs the concept of substance in order to state the essence of substance. He could not – nor could any other philosopher – formulate the nature of substance or of anything else without employing a concept to do it. Hence, we can ask, without doing any injustice to Aristotle, what does all his talk about substance (or anything else) imply about the concept of substance (or any other relevant concept)? Since he thinks (and says so) that he knows what substance (or change or the good or tragedy, etc.) is, whereas his predecessors did not, what does he think or imply that having a particular concept amounts to? Throughout his work, Aristotle is acutely aware that the different theories of different sorts of things involve different, competing, true-false conceptions about these things. There can be many conceptions about some one thing;

but only one is correct: the one that has the concept right. In refuting his predecessors on any number of claims about the natures of things and in affirming his own theses about these, Aristotle must be implying that he has finally clarified the relevant concepts; this follows from his putatively true, real definitions, whether of substance, change, tragedy, or what not.

What, then, does Aristotle imply a concept is? What does he imply about having a particular concept?

Let us, by way of example, look at the concept of tragedy and Aristotle's definition of it; or, if that way of putting it begs the question, let us examine Aristotle's claims about the nature of tragedy in the *Poetics*:

> Tragedy, then, is an imitation of an action that is serious, complete, and of a certain magnitude; in language embellished with each kind of artistic ornament, the several kinds being found in separate parts of the play; in the form of action, not of narrative; with incidents arousing pity and fear effecting the proper purgation of these emotions (1449b; Butcher tr.).

This theory – it is a definition – Aristotle explicates in much of the *Poetics*. First, he states that tragedy is a mode or species of imitation which differs from the other modes or species of poetic imitation (comedy, epic, dithyramb, and music) in that it imitates the actions of men who are better than or like us; and that it imitates by means of language, rhythm, and harmony, in the medium of representation.

Aristotle, however, does not define 'imitation' (*mimesis*), the genus of tragedy. Its meaning has been much disputed: 'replica,' 'reproduction,' 'ideal representation,' 're-creation,' among others, have been offered. But the only meaning, vague as it is, that seems warranted by the *Poetics*, especially by the discussion of the origin of poetry in man's instinct to imitate, is that imitation is a creation of a likeness of something which is not necessarily an exact copy of it.

'Action' is not defined either. All that seems clear is that it implies personal agents with distinctive qualities of character and thought, and that it has to do with what men do and suffer. By 'serious action,' Aristotle means a passage, that is necessary or probable, from happiness to misery, and that is worth while; it is not an action that necessarily ends unhappily or in death.

27

'Action' leads to 'plot,' one of the central concepts of the *Poetics*, yet one that is not even articulated in Aristotle's explicit definition of tragedy. By 'plot' Aristotle means the arrangement of the incidents of the story. Fundamentally, plot is an imitation of the action. As such, it is central to tragedy, more important than the other generative or formative elements: character, thought, diction, melody, and spectacle. According to Aristotle, plot is the most important element of tragedy because (1) it imitates what in life is most important for tragedy, namely, the actions of men or the passage from happiness to misery; (2) it induces pity and fear and the tragic effect, purgation; and (3) it may contain (as the best tragedies do) the most powerful elements of emotional interest in tragedy, namely, reversal of the situation (*peripetaia*) and recognition (*anagnorisis*).

Neither 'pity' nor 'fear' is defined. All Aristotle says is that pity is aroused by unmerited misfortune, and fear, by the misfortune of one like ourselves. 'Reversal of the situation' denotes a change of the action into its opposite, as in *Oedipus Rex*, where the messenger attempts to cheer Oedipus and instead produces the opposite effect by revealing who he really is. 'Recognition' refers to the change from ignorance to knowledge. The best form of recognition is one that coincides with a reversal of the situation, again as in *Oedipus Rex*.

'Purgation' (*katharsis*) is the most debated term in the *Poetics*. Explanations range from expulsion of harmful emotions to purifications of them. Whatever the exact meaning of the term is to Aristotle, all that is clear is that the effect of tragedy on its audience becomes an intrinsic part of the definition of tragedy.

The best tragic plots are complete, whole, and of a certain magnitude. What this means is that a good plot has a causally related beginning, middle and end; and a length that allows the hero to pass, by a series of probable or necessary stages, from happiness to misfortune, or vice versa. Good plots also possess unity – a unity of action, not of the hero and not of time and place. Aristotle says nothing about unity of place and, insofar as time is concerned, he says only that tragedy, unlike epic, tends to confine itself within or nearly within a period of 24 hours. Further, good plots can indicate what may happen as well as what did happen. Indeed, this concern for the possible (provided the possible is probable or necessary) distinguishes poetry from history, making poetry more philosophical and elevated than history. For the statements of poetry are universal, that is, they are about what A or B will probably or necessarily do, rather than what A or B did do. Finally, the worst plots are episodic, that is, they are plots in which the sequences are not probable or necessary.

Character is subordinate to plot. Indeed, tragic plots determine their chief characters. Characters should manifest good, moral purpose, act appropriately (for example, men but not women should be valorous), be true to life, and be consistent. But in order that the tragedy may achieve the tragic effect, the tragic hero must also be highly renowned and prosperous, although not eminently good or just, and in fact must display some error of judgment or fault (*hamartia*) that causes his misfortune; however, he need not have any vice or depravity as the cause of his downfall. Hence, the tragic plot cannot present a virtuous man brought from prosperity to adversity, nor a bad man proceeding from adversity to prosperity, nor an utter villain being defeated, for none of these inspires pity or fear.

As his explication reveals, Aristotle not only defines tragedy, he offers two definitions: of tragedy and of good tragedy. Every tragedy is an imitation of the passage from happiness to misery and contains the requisite pity and fear, *hamartia*, purgation, thought, melody, representation, and spectacle. Every good tragedy has all these properties plus reversal and recognition (together); unity of action; good, appropriate, true, and consistent characters; and a fine use of language, especially metaphor. That Aristotle does offer two definitions, hence either two sets of criteria for the concept of tragedy or two different sets of criteria for two different concepts of tragedy, can be seen in the fact that, for him, a certain vehicle may be a tragedy even though it has no reversal, but it cannot be a tragedy if it has no pity and fear.

I have dwelt on Aristotle's theory of tragedy – he calls it 'the definition of its nature' (*horontes ousias*, 1149b 11) – because it illustrates beautifully the relation between theory, definition and concept in Aristotle. And it does this with a class and its term that has a history rooted in its institutional development. 'Tragedy,' that is, is neither technical nor stipulatory.

What, now, can we learn from the *Poetics* about Aristotle's implicit theory of concepts? Tragedy is a class of things for Aristotle. He attempts to ascertain the nature of that class by fixing its genus and differentiae. His definition is a summative enumeration of this genus and especially its differences from other species of the same genus. The essence of tragedy, stated in the definition of its nature, is all those constituents or properties that are common to the members of the class of tragedies and that are necessary and sufficient for these members to belong to this class. His definition constitutes his theory of tragedy. Questions, such as 'What is tragedy?' 'Why is *Oedipus Rex* tragic?' or 'Is *Medea* really tragic?' revolve around the definitive set of properties of tragedy; these properties serve as the criteria for Aristotle's tragedy-giving reasons. Without these properties and their definitive set, we simply do not know what tragedy is, why a particular X is a tragedy, or whether another particular, Y, is tragic? Thus, a necessary condition for intelligent discourse about tragedy is absolute knowledge – the true definition – of the nature of tragedy.

What, then, is the concept of tragedy and the having of the concept to Aristotle? It seems plain to me that this concept is the definition and that the having of this concept is the possession of the definition: the knowledge of the essence of tragedy. Thus, we can say that for Aristotle one has the concept of tragedy when one has and states (or can state in the sense of 'can, if asked to') the *logos* of *to ti en einai* (or *ti esti* or *ousia*) of tragedy: the formula of the essence (or the whatness or the substance) of tragedy. In Aristotelian terms, the concept of tragedy is a definitional entity, not a capacity or ability; the having of that concept, an actuality, not a potentiality.

If this is correct, that for Aristotle the concept of tragedy is a definitional entity, we confront immediately two problems: What sort of entity? and How is it known? In regard to the second, I have already mentioned the difficulties surrounding the relation between definitions and *nous* in Aristotle. Whether the concept of tragedy is a definition (as I propose) or not, he still has the problem of explaining how we apprehend definitions that are not nominal or primary principles or axioms; if he allows these real definitions to be intuited, then concepts (as definitions) can also be said to be intuited.

In regard to the first problem, what sort of entity is the concept of tragedy, if it is a definition? Two points are clear: (1) that not all concepts are abstractions, such as snub-nosed or hollowness; or involve mental images, such as mathematical concepts; and (2) that the concept of tragedy as a real definition is an entity at least in the sense that it does not depend for its being or truth on its being apprehended, no more than the visible (as Aristotle says) depends on the seer. Primary or first principles and axioms also do not depend on their being intuited; furthermore, they are ontological, not merely logical or linguistic, principles for Aristotle. If they are entities of some sort, to be intuited, but possessing an objectivity of their own, then my claim that the concept of tragedy is a (definitional) entity is sound Aristotle, however unsound it may otherwise be.

At least one concept, then, in Aristotle is a definitional entity – a *logos* – that can serve as an object of conception and is logically independent of the conceiver or his conception.

There is a further point: the concept of tragedy – the definition of tragedy – is governed by the necessary and sufficient properties of the class of tragedies, as they are stated in the definition. It follows that the concept of tragedy is closed in the precise sense of being governed by necessary and sufficient properties of the class. For Aristotle, tragedy has a number of necessary and sufficient properties: call them '1–5'; good tragedy has these plus four others as well ('reversal and recognition together', etc.), which nine are each necessary and all together necessary and sufficient. That one could have the concept of tragedy and *thereby* be able to name, recognize, or argue about tragedies without knowing the true definitions – the necessary and sufficient properties of the tragic – is unthinkable to Aristotle.

It is also unthinkable for Plato, at least in his major mood and with some qualms about tragedy as an imitation of an imitation in the *Republic*. If I am correct in my reading of Plato, he would leave out Aristotle's 'thereby' and restrict the concept of tragedy (or some more suitable concept) to the skills and abilities to name, recognize, and argue about tragedies, on the necessary condition that one had first grasped the form or assumed that there is one or, if there is none, at least apprehended the definition. It is only in the latter case that Plato comes close to Aristotle: that one must first grasp the definition before one can wield the concept. But on the major issue, their disagreement is vast: for Plato, the concept of tragedy (or, perhaps better, of justice) is never only a definition; for Aristotle, it always is. Nevertheless, in spite of this basic disagreement, both concur that the concept of tragedy, whether as a skill (Plato) or as an entity (Aristotle), is governed by a definitive set of criteria derived from the nature of tragedy. It is these criteria that determine the correctness of the use of *tragodia* for both.

Are all concepts *logoi* – definitional entities – in Aristotle? Can we generalize from the concept of tragedy to Aristotle's implicit theory of concepts as definitional entities? It seems to me that we can; that the hypothesis that Aristotle's major doctrines and his methods of arriving at them revolve around his perennial search for real definitions and statements of them as the essences of things best explains his philosophy. Implied in this search for and statement of real definitions is the doctrine that these definitions are concepts. Thus, his theories of substance, matter, form, essence, change, motion, potentiality, actuality, infinity, time, continuity, memory, recollection, imagination, void, place; or of knowledge, opinion, art, prudence, wisdom, deliberation; or of the moral virtues; or of the sciences of mathematics, physics and theology; or of cause, the good, the soul, tragedy; or of valid argument, truth, error; or of the necessary and the incidental; or of the predicables; or of God; or of the first principles and axioms of demonstrative knowledge – each of these theories, as a real definition, implies a concept as a definitional entity: a *logos* of *ti esti*, of *to ti en einai*, or of *ousia*. Basic, then, in Aristotle's philosophy is this implicit theory of concepts as *logoi*. They are the driving forces in his work. It is because he takes the concept as a formula or definition of an essence as his fundamental assumption that he perseveres in his search for a correct statement of these formulas. That there are concepts – *logoi* – and that these are governed by necessary and sufficient criteria derived from the necessary and sufficient properties of things, as embodied in their essences and, consequently, that our language, ambiguous, vague, or neither, must be tightened up to conform to these definitive criteria if it is to be a correct and useful instrument: this enormous assumption, I submit, is absolutely fundamental in Aristotle.

It is even more fundamental than his theory of substance, which for many is Aristotle's central doctrine. For his whole analysis of *ousia* is rooted in the presupposition that *ousia* is a closed concept, governed by the definitive set of criteria garnered from the definitive set of properties that constitutes substance. Aristotle never questions that *ousia* has a *logos*; his doubts rather centre on what exactly that *logos* includes: matter, matter and form, form alone, or some essence. In the end, in spite of his confidence about the reality and priority of substance, the attempt to state its exact nature – to secure the content of the *logos* of *ousia* – defeats him. He is left with a concept that he knows is a definitional entity but whose exact formula he does not know. In short, he knows that there is a concept of substance, but he does not quite have it. The bafflement he attributes to 'the question which was raised long ago, is still and always will be' (*Metaph.* 1028b 3–5) remains intact.

One final observation: It is often said that Aristotle's theory of substance precludes knowledge of an individual because an individual for Aristotle has no genus and species to be known. Now, if concepts are *logoi* and an individual has no *logos*, there is not only no knowledge of an individual but no concept of him either. That there is no such concept in Aristotle is both a confirmation of the hypothesis that concepts are definitional entities (to him) and a disconfirmation of the thesis that they are. If platonism in the history of philosophy is the doctrine that concepts are supersensible entities, Aristotle is its founder, not Plato.

CHAPTER 3

Augustine

Even if it is true, as historians of philosophy chronicle, that 'the battle of the gods and the giants,' as depicted by Plato in the *Sophist*, was followed by a greater struggle between the philosophies of Plato and Aristotle during the Hellenistic and Medieval periods, it is not true that there was warfare over their theories of concepts. Indeed, there was not even a contest, since Aristotle's theory, as I indicated in Chapter 1, won without a fight. Plato's implicit dispositional theory, fertile as it was, remained smothered, not least of all because of the ontological accretions imposed upon it by the Platonists and neo-Platonists who transformed Plato's lavish description of the conceptual life into their stringent conception of the noetic, with the disastrous consequence that concepts became equated with the highest entities, *ta noéta*.

The Stoics, the Epicureans, the neo-Platonists, and the Eclectics clung to the fundamentally Aristotelian doctrine that concepts are entities of one sort or another: either supersensible or mental. Only the Sceptic, Sextus Empiricus, suggested that concepts are metaphysically neutral intermediaries between words or competing conceptions and things. However, neither his insight nor Plato's had the slightest impact on the development of philosophy until at least the eighteenth century. The history of theories of concepts, whether explicit or implicit, from Augustine to Descartes – the period we must discuss next – is a history of variations on the entity theory.

In discussing this period, I cannot even begin to deal with it adequately, since such an enterprise would require a full history of the major figures of medieval philosophy. Each of these has a theory of concepts that he either articulates or implies in his work. And this theory is basic in each individual philosophy. For the most part, unfortunately, these two claims must remain just those. All I can do here is to say something, however inadequate, about two of these philosophers: St Augustine and St Thomas Aquinas.

Among the concepts Augustine introduces in his major works are those of God, creation, time, memory, good, evil, matter, happiness, wisdom, number, beauty, love, will, and the Trinity, divine light or divine illumination, faith, and beatitude. Although he says something about conceiving, conception and notion, his theory of concepts is best elicited from his treatment of the specific concepts that are central in his philosophy.

Are all of these concepts, or only those that are not matters of faith alone? Augustine does not say that they are concepts or, in his own language, that each is a *notio*. However, his *crede ut intelligas* and certainly his *intellige ut credas* leave no doubt that he enjoins us to seek understanding of what we accept on faith. Whether understanding is anterior or posterior to faith – both views are present in his work – his distinction between understanding and faith, however he articulates it, never renders faith conceptless.

Augustine is surely correct in implying that faith is as conceptual as understanding. For one can have faith in God and then seek the proof that He exists, and in this way understand what he has faith in; or one can have faith in the Trinity and understand it without being able to prove it. Not being able to prove or not being susceptible to proof does not render faith non-conceptual.

There cannot be faith without a relevant concept. But can there even be faith without understanding? Some theologians say there can be. Of course, understanding includes more than the having of a concept; in the case of understanding the Trinity, it may involve trying to relate certain concepts that resist our ordinary understanding of the relationship: how to relate three persons to one. But even in this example, and in understanding in any example, there must be at least one concept, so faith cannot be without understanding at least in the sense of possessing a concert. If one has faith, one accepts or believes in something. He may not be able to render his belief coherent or to prove it, but he cannot believe in something without believing that *that* something exists; and he cannot do this without the relevant concept exemplified in his belief. One cannot believe in God or accept Him or the Trinity on faith without understanding the concept involved in one's faith. Hence, there can be no faith without understanding. Nor, consequently, can there be any division of philosophy and religion or theology that rests on a distinction between the presence as against the absence of concepts.

To return to Augustine. An elucidation of his theory of concepts need not rule out any of them as concepts on the ground that it belongs to faith, not understanding. For Augustine would not tolerate such division nor, I think, is it tolerable. Neither religion nor theology can relieve its philosophical headaches by affirming or assuming that it transcends the conceptual, therefore, is not answerable to it.

God is central in Augustine's philosophy. Therefore, on my reading of the relation of ontology to concepts, the concept of God is his central concept. What, then, does Augustine take God to be? What is the concept of God to Augustine?

It is a concept of a being '... supreme, most excellent, most mighty, most omnipotent, most merciful and most just; most secret and most present; most beautiful and most strong; constant and incomprehensible; immutable, yet changing all things; never new and never old...' (*Confessions*, I. iv).

Less rapturously, God is ... *quo esse aut cogitari melius nihil possit* ... (*De Moribus Manichaeorum*, I. ii, xi) – '(a being) than which nothing better can be thought.' (The proper title of the work cited is *De Moribus ecclesiae catholicae et de moribus Manichaeorum*, twin treatises written by Augustine early in his career, between 388 and 390. It can be found in volume 32 of Migne's *Patrologia Latina*.) This is not quite Anselm's 'something than which nothing greater can be thought;' nor is Augustine's argument for God derived from his thought of God, as Anselm's argument is from Anselm's thought of God. Nor is there anything short of a being who is absolutely simple, omnipotent, omniscient, immutable, eternal, and benevolent involved in Augustine's concept of God.

What is the status of this concept in Augustine? What is involved in the having of this concept according to him? Is it an entity, mental or ontologically independent of the human mind? Is it a definitional *logos* or an *eidos* – an idea in the mind of God, that is reflected by the divine light in the human image of it?

God, for Augustine, is an entity that exists independently of the human mind and all else. He is no *logos, eidos* or *notio*. He is not an idea. He is a divine light illuminating the world, including our human minds. All this, and much more, is clear from Augustine's voluminous talk about God and his proofs for His existence. However, none of this clarity is possible unless Augustine has the concept of God in order that he can provide an account of His attributes.

Given what he says about God, the concept of God for Augustine cannot be a definitional entity, an eternal idea, an image, or God Himself. All eternal ideas and truths are in God; all real definitions are among the eternal ideas and truths; and to reduce the concept of God to an image of Him or to elevate the concept of God to God Himself would be to violate the nature of God.

What, then, is the concept of God according to Augustine? One possible answer to this crucial question is suggested by his discussion of notions and truth in *De libero arbitrio voluntatis*, Book II. Reason (*ratio*) is able to grasp numbers, number series and mathematical truths. It does this independently of the senses; and what it grasps it recognizes as immutable, necessary, eternal. It can grasp also certain relations of and operations upon numbers, for example, addition and subtraction. How does reason do this? By man's inner light which, presumably, reflects the divine light. Reason also apprehends the notions of wisdom and happiness and their definitions and interrelation. Both these notions, Augustine says, are impressed upon our minds before we are wise or happy, and they direct our pursuit of a happiness that achieves wisdom, which is God's truth. Without the notion of wisdom, impressed upon us, we would not, could not, want to be wise or know we ought to be wise. This notion of wisdom (*notio sapientiae*) is, Augustine says, inherent in the human mind, a gift from God.

What Augustine says of the notions of number, wisdom and happiness – not what he says about mathematical, moral and religious truths – provides the clue to the status of the concept of God in his philosophy that is consistent with his other doctrines: that it, too, is a *notio*, impressed on the human mind, discovered by our reason, through our inner light as reflecting God's light. In short, the concept of God is an innate idea, implanted in us by God. It is an innate idea, not an eternal idea, hence is not part of God's mind as, for example, the definition of God as a Supreme Being is of God's essence, therefore, of His mind. The eternal truths that flow from the concept of God are in God's mind; but the concept of God is not. It is in our minds, put there by God. Divine illumination does not give us the concept or *notio* of God; rather it allows us to see all the truths about God – the true definition of Him. Since Augustine cannot deny that he has the concept of God because he talks about God, I am at a loss to suggest any alternative to the entity theory I attribute to him.

That a concept as a *notio* is an inherent entity, implanted in the human mind by God, covers Augustine's concepts of number, addition and subtraction, happiness, and wisdom. What about the others on our initial list? Are Augustine's concepts of time, memory, will, matter, evil, sensation, love, beauty, good, creation, the Trinity, and so on, also innate entities? Some, such as the concepts of the will, freedom, good, beauty, and love, I think, can be read as inherent ideas or notions impressed on the mind by God, independently of any aid from sense-experience. Each is an entity lodged in human reason, waiting to be discovered by the 'inner man' who then, with the help of divine illumination, can spell out the truths invested in and implied by his innate idea.

This leaves the others. Let us first consider Augustine's concept of time, as he employs it to talk about time, in *Confessions*, Book XI. Our question, to repeat, is not what does Augustine say time is but what does he imply about the concept of time in saying (or trying to say) what it is? We may as well start with his famous question: 'What is time then? If nobody asks me, I know: but if I were desirous to explain it to one that should ask me, plainly I know not' (xiv).

I have the concept of time, Augustine implies, because I am able to employ it correctly, but I cannot define it. There is a whole book here, in this confession, most of it in the *Philosophical Investigations*, which we must refrain from opening now. What is immediately relevant, however, is that Augustine commits himself to his having the concept of time even though he cannot define it, with the possibility that it is definable and can be defined. There is no suggestion that the concept is simple, therefore indefinable.

It is also undeniable that Augustine affirms the objective reality of time: that is, temporal phenomena of all sorts that do not depend on their being experienced by human minds. How else, he asks, can we make intelligible (a) his entreaty to God, in spoken, silent and written language, to tell him what time is; (b) the everyday occurrences of the passage of time – the ceaseless coming into being, changing, and passing away of persons, animals and things; (c) certain locutions, such as 'long' and 'short,' applied to duration; (d) our measurements of this duration; and (e) the creation of a world that is mutable, contingent and, as Scripture declares, dependent on God, its Creator.

We know there is time – the temporal – but we experience only the non-temporal present; it is here that we measure time by sight (*contuitus*), memory, and anticipation, that give sense, if not reference, to the concepts of present, past, and future.

As fraught with difficulties as these reflections on time are – Augustine is aware of them – they do not detract from their dominant theme, that the concept of time is an empirical, not an apriori concept or innate idea, such as the concept of God. Thus, Augustine seems to be claiming, I have the concept of time – I know what time is – because I know the temporal in the five ways listed above. I form the concept by reflecting on these undeniable facts. The concept of time, then, is some sort of abstract idea in my mind, derived from certain phenomena involving passage.

Can this be the correct reading of Augustine's concept of time? The obvious objection to its being an empirical concept he offers himself, that we do not observe or sense the temporal, even though it is present in all the five sets of phenomena he lists. If the concept of time is empirical – an abstraction from similar sets of phenomena – then we ought to be able to experience the temporal in them which, he says, we do not and cannot do. The concept of time is rooted in objective facts but it is not abstracted from them, hence it is not an empirical concept. If it is an entity, it is not an abstract idea.

Here is another possibility: that the concept of time is derived (not abstracted) from the concept of God *together* with the fact of creation. Neither alone can yield the concept of time since the first entails eternity, not temporality, and the second reduces to the non-temporality of the present as we experience creation.

The concept of God is innate. The necessary truths about God are constituent eternal ideas of His mind, to be comprehended by our minds through divine illumination. Among these necessary truths are that God is eternal and the creator.

God created the world – the fact of creation. That He did may be a necessary truth, an eternal idea, in and to Him, but it is not to us. The concept of the creation of the world is not innate as the concept of God is. Nor does divine illumination guarantee as a necessary truth that the world is created as it does that God is a creator.

How do I get the concept of the creation if I do not get it from God as an innate idea or as a necessary truth? From myself. I am certain (Augustine says) that I exist. I am further certain that I am not a necessary being since I am not God. Hence, I am certain that I am contingent, created, not my creator. I am, however, but a tiny part of the fact of creation: my contingency, mutability and dependence are

shared by all that is created. I know that I am a created being –
dependent, mutable, contingent – because I know that I exist and
that I am not God – the creator, eternal, necessary, independent.
Knowing that I am a created being among other contingent beings,
all dependent on God, is, in its mutability, the source of the temporal
in the world. The concept of time is derived from this omnipresent
feature of the world, created by God and contingent upon Him.
Derived, not abstracted, from creation, because it is an inferred
concept, constructed by man to explain and reconcile God the
Creator and the world the creation. The concept of time, therefore, is
a relational concept, not because time is relational, which it is, but
because the concept relates the mutable to the immutable, the
contingent to the necessary, the temporal to the eternal, the world to
God. As a relational, inferred concept, the concept of time is neither
wholly innate nor wholly empirical. It is rather a notion which in
man combines the innate notion of God with the inner-empirical
notion of man; and which in God must be among His eternal ideas,
even though it is an idea of change.

I come now to Augustine's concept of divine illumination.
Historically, it has been the most difficult of all his concepts to
explicate. For some commentators – Gilson is one of them – there
can be no concept of divine illumination in Augustine because the
doctrine obviates the need for concepts altogether. However, since
Gilson conflates abstractions of intelligibles from the sensibles with
the having of concepts, even though he argues convincingly that
divine illumination renders abstraction unnecessary, the problem of
concepts that are not abstractions in Augustine remains. One of these
is the concepts of divine illumination. What is that concept? What
role does it play in Augustine's philosophy? The main issue seems to
converge on whether it is a concept about the content of eternal ideas
and necessary truths or about the criterion of necessary truths in
human judgments. Most commentators reject the first and affirm the
second in the attempt to avoid what they call 'ontologism:' the
doctrine that we intuit God's essence by divine illumination.

What is Augustine's doctrine of divine illumination? It is a
metaphor that Augustine employs in many of his writings, but
especially in *De Trinitate* 9.6.9 and in some of his soliloquies.
Inspired by Plato's idea of the good as the source of intelligibility in
comparison with the sun as the source of visible light and by
Plotinus' One as the source of all radiation, Augustine, borrowing

also from the Gospel of St. John, enlarges the metaphor to make God the ultimate fount of all spiritual and physical light. God, therefore, not only created the world; His divine light also illuminates the visible, presented to the sense, and the invisible, given to the intellect.

The intellect is acquainted with both notions and necessary truths. These are related to God's eternal ideas and essence. Sometimes Augustine talks of this relationship as one of direct participation; when, for example, I know what justice is and that it is better than injustice; or what 2, +, =, and 4 are and that $2+2=4$, I am directly acquainted with certain ethical and mathematical ideas and truths in God's mind.

Such an interpretation of the relation between the human and divine intellect entails direct knowledge of God by saint and sinner, Christian and pagan alike; and at the same time renders otiose any attempted proof for the existence of God. Because of these embarrassing consequences, the relationship between the human and divine intellect, it is suggested, is not one of direct acquaintance but that of indirect divine illumination: God does not share His ideas and truths with human intellects; rather, God gives us divine illumination as a criterion for determining the truth of certain necessary judgments. Thus, divine illumination, so this interpretation holds, provides neither concepts nor truths, but instead only a test for the necessity of certain truths.

Suppose we grant that divine illumination does not yield direct acquaintance with God when we apprehend eternal ideas or necessary truths; and that all it provides is the criterion for testing whether a particular truth is necessary or not. Does it follow from this restricted assigned role to divine illumination that divine illumination is a doctrine only of the truth of judgments and not the content of concepts? Consider a concrete example: $5+2=7$. If, according to the restrictive interpretation, I need divine illumination to tell me that this is a necessary truth and I do not need it to tell me what 5, 2, 7, addition, and equality are, can I test the necessity of the judgment that $5+2=7$ without grasping something about the content and relationships of the individual concepts or eternal ideas? How could I possibly determine this arithmetical judgement as a necessary truth without first apprehending the entailments among these concepts of individual numbers, addition, and equality? That divine illumination concerns the truth of judgments, but not the content of concepts, collapses in the necessary truth that necessary truths or judgments presuppose concepts and their specific contents and entailments.

Divine illumination, then, must be a doctrine about concepts as well as about necessary truths which, for Augustine, are exfoliations of concepts. That the human intellect is illumined by God as to its concepts and their conceptual entailments that give rise to necessary truths – whatever such illumination implies about our knowledge of God – must be the final verdict on divine illumination as a conceptual activity in Augustine's philosophy.

If divine illumination involves the having of concepts in the determination of the necessary truths invested in conceptual entailment, and if the concept of divine illumination is itself a concept, not to be ruled out as a concept on the false claim that divine illumination replaces conceptual activity in Augustine, what sort of concept is it? Does God impress on our minds the notion that we can determine conceptual entailments, thereby necessary truth, by His Light? However vacuous this concept may be, since God's Light serves as a mere superfluity on conceptual entailment, Augustine's implied answer to What sort of Concept is the concept of divine illumination? must be that it is innate, like the concept of God.

These examples of concepts in Augustine, which do not even begin to penetrate the depth and brilliance of his philosophical contributions, I hope, at least suffice to illustrate my claim that Augustine has an implicit theory of concepts in his work, best exemplified in the way he employs the concepts he deals with. This theory is that concepts – at least some of them and certainly his main, focal one of God – are innate mental entities, implanted in our human intellects by God and illumined by Him in such a manner that we can determine conceptual entailments expressed by necessary truths. These concepts – if the concept of God can serve as the paradigm – are also closed, being governed by definitive sets of criteria, derived from the definitive sets of properties of the realities they relate to and, in turn, determining the definitive sets of criteria for the correct use of the linguistic terms that express the concepts. God is the supreme being and all that this implies; the concept of God is governed by these implicative criteria; the word 'God' is correctly employed only be adhering to these same criteria. Augustine, too, never wavers from the classical thesis that all concepts are closed.

CHAPTER 4

Aquinas

With Aquinas, we come to a philosopher who formulates a theory of concepts. He not only employs certain concepts in his works and a vocabulary of conception, concept and conceiving, he also states what concepts are, how they are formed, and what their role in knowledge and philosophy is.

Our question, after elucidating his theory of concepts, shifts to whether his stated theory adequately explains and covers the use of the concepts he employs.

From John of St. Thomas and the earliest commentators to Peifer, Gilson and Copleston, among the contemporary commentators, there is unanimity on the basic texts of Aquinas' theory of concepts. These include: *De Potentia*, 8, 1; *Summa Contra Gentiles*, I, 53; *Compendium Theologiae*, 1. 38–39; *De Veritate*, IV, 2 *ad* 3; and *Summa Theologiae*, Ia, 85.

I am neither qualified to question this authority, nor wish to; further, I shall proceed on the assumption, shared by all, that the *Summa Theologiae* represents his maturest views, and concentrate on that work. There may be differences of doctrine between this late work and his earlier ones but, so far as I am able to ascertain, none of any significance regarding Aquinas' theory of concepts.

What, then, does Aquinas say concepts are? In *De Potentia*, he distinguishes conception (*conceptio*) of the intellect from the thing understood, the intelligible species, and the act of understanding:

> Now this conception differs from the three forementioned
> things. *From the thing* understood, because the thing
> understood is sometimes outside the intellect, but the
> conception of the intellect is only in the intellect; and again

the conception of the intellect is ordered to the thing understood as to an end: for the intellect forms a conception of the thing in itself for this reason, that it might know the thing. It differs *from the intelligible species (specie intelligibili):* by which intellect is in act, is considered as the principle of the action of the intellect, since every agent acts according as it is in act, but it is in act through some form, which must be the principle of the action. It (i.e. the concept) differs *from the action* of the intellect: because the conception is considered as the term of the action, as something constituted through it. For the intellect by its own action forms a definition of the thing, or also an affirmative or negative proposition. This conception of the intellect is properly called a *word (verbum)*: for this is what is signified by an exterior word: for the exterior word does not signify the intellect itself, nor the intelligible species, nor the act of the intellect, but the conception of the intellect by whose mediation it is referred to the thing.[1]

In the *Summa Contra Gentiles*, Aquinas writes:

An external thing which comes to be an object of our understanding does not thereby exist in our understanding according to its proper nature; but the species of it must be in our intellect, through which the latter becomes actually understanding. The intellect actualized and informed by the species, as by a proper form, understands the thing itself; not, however, by an act passing outward to the thing known, as heating passes into the thing made hot, but in such a way that the act remains in the intelligence, and bears a relation to the thing which it understands, because the afore mentioned species, which is the principle of the act of thought, as its form, is a likeness of the thing known.

Now it must further be realized that the intellect, informed by the species of the thing (impressed species), in the act of understanding forms within itself a certain *intention (intentionem)* of the thing understood (expressed species, conception, concept) which is the *ratio* of the thing, which the definition signifies.

And this concept is indeed necessary, because the intellect

understands indifferently an absent thing and a present thing. In this the intellect is like the imagination. But the intellect has this further feature, not shared with the imagination, that it understands the thing as separated from the material (individualizing) conditions, without which the thing does not exist in nature. This can happen only because the intellect forms this aforesaid *intention*.

This concept which is known (*Haec autem intentio intellecta*), since it is as the *term* of the intellectual act, is different from the intelligible species, which actualizes the intellect, and which must be regarded as the *principle* of the intellectual act; yet, both (the impressed and the expressed species) are likenesses of the thing itself, which is the object of the understanding.

Because the *intelligible species*, which is the form of the intellect and the principle of the act of understanding, is a likeness (*similitudo*) of the external thing, it follows that the intellect forms an *intention* like unto that thing, for as a thing is, so it acts. And since this intention, which is known, is like unto the thing, the consequence is that the intellect, by forming this intention, understands the thing itself.[2]

In the *Compendium Theologiae*, Aquinas compares the formation of a concept to the conception of a child; the concept is a child of the mind:

When the intellect understands something other than itself, the thing understood is, so to speak the father of the word conceived in the intellect, and the intellect itself rather resembles the mother, whose function is that conception takes place in her.[3]

As these quotations show, Aquinas variously construes concepts as expressed species, terms, intentions, words, and likenesses – all in the mind as entities that through their representations of things aid in the knowledge of things.

In *De Veritate*, Aquinas maintains that the concept is both knowledge and the means by which knowledge is obtained: it is not only 'that which' is understood, but also that 'by which' the thing is understood:

The conception of the intellect is a medium between the intellect and the thing understood, because by its mediation the operation of the intellect attains the thing, and so the conception of the intellect is not only *that which (id quod)* is understood, but also that *by which (id quo)* the thing is understood; and so that which is understood can be said to be both the thing and the conception of the intellect.[4]

Gilson adds a further text from the *Summa Contra Gentiles* (IV, 11):[5]

I call the idea or mental image that which the mind conceives within itself or of the one thing understood. With us this is neither the thing itself nor the substance of the mind, but a certain likeness conceived in the mind from the thing understood and signified by external speech, whence it is called the inner word. That this concept is not the thing understood appears from the fact that one activity is required to understand the thing and another to understand the concept, as happens when the mind reflects on its processes. On this account the sciences that treat of things are distinct from the sciences that treat of concepts. That the concept is not the mind itself appears from this consideration, that the being of a concept consists in being understood, which is not the case with the being of the mind (Gilby tr.).

Gilson comments on this passage: 'The name "concept" is given to what the intellect conceives in itself and expresses by a word . . . The concept is the similitude of the object which the intellect brings forth under the action of the species.'[6]

In the *Summa Theologiae*, Aquinas relates the concept as a word to the Word in God. He argues that the Word in God is the Person of the Son in the Trinity, and says: 'Now *word* is taken strictly in God, as signifying the concept of the intellect . . . *Word*, according as we use the term strictly of God, signifies something proceeding from another' (I*a*, 34, 1). The Word in God is not a metaphor of the word in man, Aquinas insists, since words in man signify interior concepts. Words are the meanings of vocal sounds or signs, not simply vocal sounds or signs by themselves. As such, they embody interior concepts. 'For the Father, by understanding Himself, the Son, and the Holy Ghost, and all other things comprised in this knowledge, conceives the Word; so that thus the whole Trinity is *spoken* in the

Word, and likewise also all creatures, just as the intellect of a man by the word he conceives in the act of understanding a stone, speaks a stone' (I*a*, 34, 1, *ad* 3). Here, in this passage and context, Aquinas takes a concept to be a word – the meaning of a sound or inner sign. It is something that man shares with God, univocally, not analogically, as he does, for example, wisdom.

Another unlikely place where Aquinas discusses conceptualization is 'The Knowledge of the Angels' (I*a*, 54). (Indeed, one learns more about Aquinas' views of man's cognitive nature from his talk about the angels than one does from his discussion of man or of God!).

> The necessity for admitting a possible intellect in us is derived from the fact that we sometimes understand only in potentiality, and not actually. Hence there must exist some power which, previous to the act of understanding, is in potentiality to intelligibles, but which becomes actualized in this regard when it apprehends them and furthermore when it considers them. This is the power which is named the *possible intellect*. The necessity for admitting an agent intellect is due to this, that the natures of the material things which we know are not immaterial and actually intelligible outside the soul, but are only intelligible in potentiality so long as they are outside the soul. Consequently it is necessary that there should be some power capable of rendering such natures actually intelligible, and this power in us is called the *agent intellect* (I*a*, 54, 4).

'The Mode and Order of Understanding' (I*a*, 85) is Aquinas' most detailed and maturest account of conceptualization. First, Aquinas argues that the human intellect, because it is a power of the soul which itself is the form of the body, properly knows the forms existing in corporeal matter. This kind of knowledge is proper to the intellect because it satisfies the criterion that in all knowledge, whether of God, the angels or man, the object of knowledge is proportionate to the power of knowledge. Thus, the human intellect can

> know a form existing individually in corporeal matter, but not as existing in this individual matter. But to know what is in individual matter, yet not as existing in such matter, is

to abstract the form from individual matter which is
represented by the phantasms. Therefore we must needs say
that our intellect understands material things by abstracting
from phantasms; and that through material things thus
considered we acquire some knowledge of immaterial
things, just as, on the contrary, angels know material things
through the immaterial (I*a*, 85, 1).

Second, Aquinas says that abstraction can occur either by
composition and division or by simple consideration of one thing
without considering another. The latter mode of abstraction, unlike
the former, when what is abstracted is not really a separate entity,
does not yield falsehood. Thus, we cannot abstract colour from a
coloured body; but we can abstract – consider – the colour of an
apple without considering a coloured apple,

for an apple is not essential to colour, and therefore colour
can be understood independently of the apple. In the same
way, the things which belong to the species of a material
thing, such as a stone, or a man, or a horse, can be
thought without the individual principles which do not
belong to the notion of the species. This is what we mean
by abstracting the universal from the particular, or the
intelligible species from the phantasm (I*a*, 85, 1, *ad* 1).

He immediately adds to this:

The intellect therefore abstracts the species of a natural
thing from the individual sensible matter, but not from the
common sensible matter. For example, it abstracts the
species of *man* from *this flesh and these bones*, which do
not belong to the species as such, but to the individual,
and need not be considered in the species. But the species
of man cannot be abstracted by the intellect from *flesh and
bones* (I*a*, 85, 1, *ad* 2).

Mathematical species, however, Aquinas says, can be abstracted
from individual sensible matter and from common sensible matter:
from this flesh and these bones and from flesh and bones.

But they cannot be abstracted from common intelligible
matter, but only from individual intelligible matter. For
sensible matter is corporeal matter as subject to sensible

qualities... while intelligible matter is substance as subject to quantity... Quantity is in substance before sensible qualities are. Hence quantities... can be considered apart from sensible qualities, and this is to abstract them from sensible matter. But they cannot be considered without understanding the substance which is subject to the quantity, for that would be to abstract them from common intelligible matter. Yet they can be considered apart from this or that substance, and this is to abstract them from individual intelligible matter (Ia, 85, 1, *ad* 2).

Being, unity, potency, act, and the like, Aquinas further adds, unlike both natural and mathematical species (and their concepts) can be abstracted – considered apart – from common intelligible matter, such as immaterial substances. Elsewhere (in discussing the Trinity), he says this about abstraction:

Abstraction by the intellect is twofold. One takes place when the universal is abstracted from the particular, as animal is abstracted from man; the other, when form is abstracted from matter, as the form of a circle is abstracted by the intellect from all sensible matter. The difference between these two abstractions consists in the fact that in the abstraction of the universal from the particular, that from which the abstraction is made does not remain; for when the difference of rationality is removed from man, the man no longer remains in the intellect, but animal alone remains. But in abstraction in terms of form and matter, both the form and the matter remain in the intellect; as, for instance, if we abstract the form of a circle from brass, there remain in our intellect separately both the understanding of a circle and the understanding of brass (Ia, 40, 3).

Third, Aquinas clarifies the phantasm and its role in conceptualization. Phantasms are images of individuals and exist in corporeal organs. Unlike colours, for example, which can impress their images on the eye, phantasms cannot impress the possible intellect without the agent intellect:

Through the power of the agent intellect, there results in the possible intellect a certain likeness produced by the turning of the agent intellect toward the phantasms. This likeness represents what is in the phantasms, but includes only the nature of the species. It is thus that the intelligible species is said to be abstracted from the phantasm (I*a*, 85, 1, *ad* 3).

Fourth, the agent intellect not only illumines the phantasms, it abstracts from the phantasms intelligible species (I*a*, 85, 1, *ad* 4).

Having established that the intellect abstracts intelligible species from the phantasms, Aquinas next asks whether these species alone are understood or whether they are used as likenesses to understand things? He claims that the intelligible species is that *by* which the intellect understands: '...the intelligible species is secondarily that which is understood; but that which is primarily understood is the thing, of which the species is the likeness' (I*a*, 85, 2).

Before we begin to try to pull all these strands together into a coherent, unified theory of concepts, there are a number of other passages in the *Summa Theologiae* that must be cited, since no consideration of Aquinas' consummate theory can survive without including them.

Throughout the *Summa Theologiae*, and in other works as well, Aquinas reaffirms the thesis he attributes to Aristotle that knowledge arises from sense experiences (e.g., I*a*, 1, 9; 85, 3). However, that knowledge includes more than sense-perception is clear from what he says about our knowledge of immaterial things and from what is implied by the kinds of concepts involved in all knowledge, including sense-perception (see, e.g., his argument for the presence of the concept – species – of the stone in our ordinary perception of a stone, I*a*, 14, 7, *ad* 1).

It is also clear that Aquinas does not restrict knowledge to universals. To be sure, only these can be known directly by the intellect. 'But indirectly, however, and as it were by a kind of reflexion, it can know the singular' – by turning to the 'phantasms in which it understands the species...' (I*a*, 86, 1). Human knowledge, thus, not only arises in the senses but returns to it, that is, the phantasms:

> In the state of the present life, in which the soul is united to a corruptible body, it is impossible for our intellect to understand anything actually, except by turning to phantasms ... When we wish to help someone to understand

something, we lay examples before him, from which he can form phantasms for the purpose of understanding.

Now the reason for this is that the power of knowledge is proportioned to the thing known. Therefore the proper object of an angelic intellect, which is entirely separate from a body, is an intelligible substance separate from a body. Whereas the proper object of the human intellect, which is united to a body, is the quiddity or nature existing in corporeal matter; and it is through these natures of visible things that it rises to a certain knowledge of things invisible (Ia, 84, 7).

Much has been made by his followers of Aquinas' insistence on the empirical origin of our concepts. It remains to be seen just how empirically founded his concepts are.

It is time now to tie these pieces together. Here again, we have in the commentators our work purportedly done for us. Let us, therefore, look at some of them.

The simplest exposition I am acquainted with is Copleston's statement of Aquinas' theory of concepts; and Copleston's most concise statement is in his *History of Philosophy*, Volume 2, Part II. Like everyone else, he places Aquinas' theory of concepts in Aquinas' larger theory of knowledge. Knowledge begins with sensation, an act of the *compositum*: body and soul. The senses perceive the material object, represented by its phantasm or image that arises in the imagination. Both the sensation and image are particulars. It is therefore the intellect that apprehends the universal, the form of the material object in abstraction. We perceive particular trees or men, form particular individual or composite images of them, but we conceive the general idea of tree or man: the concept that is the universal or form abstracted from the particular objects.

Neither material things nor phantasms can effect the transition from sensation and imagination to thought. The concept needs the active intellect in order to illumine the phantasm and to abstract from it the intelligible species. The active intellect, through this abstraction, produces in the passive intellect the *species impressa*: 'The reaction of the passive intellect to this determination by the active intellect is the *verbum mentis (species expressa)*, the universal concept in the full sense.'[7] The function of the active intellect is to abstract the universal from the particular phantasm. 'To abstract means to isolate intellectually the universal apart from the particularising notes.'[8] The concept, as produced, is the means, not the object, of cognition: *id quo intelligitur*, not *id quod intelligitur*.

For Copleston, all knowledge according to Aquinas begins with and is dependent upon sense-perception. Further, we cannot think without a phantasm. This raises the problem of how we can obtain knowledge of immaterial things, including God? Copleston gives Aquinas' answer that we can achieve a kind of indirect knowledge. But he does not raise the more basic question. How can we form the concept of that for which there is and can be no sensuous criterion? Nor does Aquinas raise it. But it must be raised; for I cannot ask, how do or can I know God? until I ask and answer, how do or can I form the concept of God? If the concept of God neither arises in nor is dependent on the senses, it seems erroneous to relate our knowledge of God to anything sensuous.

Peifer also finds a unified theory of concepts in Aquinas. In the main, his interpretation is similar to Copleston's, with the addition, which he attributes to the early followers of Aquinas, John of St. Thomas and Cajetan, that for Aquinas '...the concept, physically considered...is a thing or spiritual quality, and...formally considered...is a similitude of the things known, an interior image, a formal sign representing the object of knowledge to the understanding.'[9] As such, '...the concept is...a unique reality; it is a vital image or intentional similitude produced by the mind to represent to itself something outside the mind.'[10] In short, it is a thing or an image.

In a later *New Catholic Encyclopedia* article, 'Concept,' Peifer claims that 'a concept is a representation that the mind forms within itself, in which it simply apprehends the nature of something without affirming or denying anything of it.' It is thus a mental entity, recognized already by Aristotle and referred to by him in various ways as *noéma, logos, eidos, pathémata tés psuchés,* and *hupolépsis,* each latinized by Aquinas, who also adds *intentio, ratio, conceptus,* and *conceptio.* As a mental entity, the concept exists formally in the mind but objectively in the things themselves, although this distinction, implicit in Aquinas, receives its articulation by Cajetan:

> The formal concept is a certain image which the possible intellect forms in itself as objectively representative of the thing known: it is called an intention or concept by philosophers and a word by theologians. But the objective

concept is the thing represented by the formal concept as terminating the act of understanding. For example, the formal concept of a lion is that image of a lion which the possible intellect forms of the quiddity of a lion when it wishes to understand it; the objective concept is the very leonine nature represented and understood (Cajetan *In de ente* 1. 14).

Peifer adds that only the formal concept is properly a concept: 'It alone is a real entity, and entitative modification of the intellect.' Gilson, too, applauds the empirical base of concepts in Aquinas:

We can form no concept unless first we have received a sense impression, nor even return later on to this concept without turning to the images that sense has left behind in the imagination.[11]

In his masterly study, *The Christian Philosophy of St. Thomas Aquinas*, Gilson writes:

The name 'concept' is given to what the intellect conceives in itself and expresses by a word. The sensible species and then the intelligible species, by which we know but which we do not know, is still the form itself of the object. The concept is the similitude of the object which the intellect brings forth under the action of the species.[12]

The concept is distinct from the thing known;

but the intellect, which conceives the concept, is truly the thing of which it forms itself a concept. The intellect which produces the concept of book only does so because it has first become the form of a book, thanks to a species which is but such a form. Hence the concept necessarily resembles its object... The concept of an object resembles it because the intellect must be fecundated by the species of the object itself in order to be capable of engendering the concept.[13]

Forming concepts is a natural operation of the human intellect. Because forming concepts is expressing the intelligibles as they are impressed on the intellect, the intellect, Gilson concludes, 'conceives essences as infallibly as hearing perceives sounds and sight colours.'[14]

Finally, P. Geach, in *Mental Acts*, argues that Aquinas rejects the (incorrect) theory, traditionally attributed to him, that concepts are abstract mental entities and affirms the (correct) doctrine that concepts are mental capacities exercised in judgments. Geach supports this stunning double thesis by both refuting abstractionism and defending his theory with arguments he claims derive from Aquinas.

Abstractionism is the view 'that a concept is acquired by a process of singling out in attention some one feature given in direct experience – *abstracting* it – and ignoring the other features simultaneously given – *abstracting from* them.'[15] Geach demolishes this theory of concepts. That his demolition not only spares Aquinas but is aided by him, Geach supports by interpreting two passages in the *Summa Theologiae*:

> In accepting the comparison whereby the *intellectus agens*, the mind's concept-forming power, is likened to a light that enables the mind's eye to see the intelligible features of things, as the bodily eye sees colours, Aquinas is careful to add that the comparison goes on all fours only if we suppose that colours are generated by kindling the light – that the light is not just revealing colours that already existed in the dark (I*a* q. 79 art. 3 *ad* 2 um). Furthermore he says that when we frame a judgment expressed in words, our use of concepts is to be compared, not to seeing something, but rather to forming a visual image of something we are not now seeing, or even never have seen (I*a* q. 85 art. 2 *ad* 3 um). So he expresses anti-abstractionist views both on the formation and on the exercise of concepts.[16]

Geach also points out that abstractionism cannot allow concepts of material substances; yet it is one of Aquinas' main theses that our understanding grasps the nature of these material substances, of which we have no sense perception. It follows, according to Geach, that Aquinas could not have held that the concept of a material substance is an abstraction, hence that he is anti-abstractionist in his theory. Geach does not suggest another possibility that Aquinas' theory of concepts – abstractionist or not – may not be able to accommodate some of the actual concepts he employs, including that of a material substance.

That concepts are mental capacities to Aquinas, Geach supports by citing the passage in which Aquinas compares our use of concepts to the forming of a visual image of something we are not now seeing or never have seen rather than to seeing something (I*a*, 85, 2, *ad* 3); and by citing a crucial passage in which Aquinas talks of understanding simple things in their complexity without understanding them to be complex (I*a*, 13, 12, *ad* 3). Here, Geach suggests, Aquinas sees clearly that the mind makes concepts; it does not abstract them by discovering similarities.

What, then, in all this primary and secondary material, is Aquinas' theory of concepts? About all that seems clear is that any reduction of his theory to concepts as abstractions, universals, intelligibles, words, mental entities, or mental capacities oversimplifies his theory, even as he states it.

Further, any hypothesis about his theory has to accommodate the many different kinds of concepts Aquinas employs: including the concepts of God, the Trinity, angels, the soul, good, evil, genus and species, man, matter, truth, will, act, potency, substance, accident, essence, existence, cause, effect, end, love, law, grace, and faith, to mention only some of those dealt with in the *Summa Theologiae* alone. All of these are concepts in Aquinas' philosophy. Does each of them arise in and depend on sense-experience? It is most unlikely. Is each an abstraction? Then what about the concept of abstraction? Is each a mental entity? Then what about the concept of the active intellect without which we cannot even begin to explain concept formation and, therefore, is a condition of concepts as mental entities but not itself a mental entity like a concept?

My hypothesis is this: that no theory of concepts in Aquinas, whether stated by him or by others, can be adequate unless it goes beyond the so-called Aristotelian restriction upon knowledge as founded on sense-perception. The diversionary tactic of introducing indirect knowledge may cover the retreat of the unsuccessful attempt to know God but this move, applied to the concept of God, can end only in incoherence and defeat. We can have neither direct nor indirect knowledge of God without first having the concept of God. But we cannot have anything resembling a direct or indirect concept of God. Either we have the concept of God and then come to know Him directly or indirectly or we do not have the concept at all.

It seems to me that all the textual evidence, including that cited by Geach, points to the concept as a mental entity in Aquinas. As an offspring of the intelligible, as a representation or likeness of objects, even though the representation is of the species of objects, as a word, intention, or *ratio*, as interior meaning, as an object or instrument of thought, as an expressed species, and as an abstraction, the concept is an entity that exists in the mind, including God's mind when Aquinas talks of the Word in God. Thus for Aquinas every concept is a conception.

Concepts – at least human ones – are formed by abstraction in Aquinas' sense of considering or apprehending that which can be abstracted from something without contradiction, such as the colour of an apple as against the colour of a body. Since the colour of an apple can be abstracted from an apple to produce the concept of colour, Geach is correct in denying that Aquinas is an abstractionist: all Aquinas needs is one apple in order to abstract, not two or more apples, required by those who abstract similarities!

As complicated as Aquinas' account of abstraction and concept-formation is, I find no conflicting evidence to challenge the orthodox interpretation that this formation is grounded in initial sense-experience and ultimately returns to it. Sensation impresses on our bodies, gives rise to images that in turn give rise to the species impressa, impressed on the passive intellect by the active intellect, which species impressa are then illumined by the active intellect to create the species expressa or concept.

Having formed a concept, the intellect of course can employ it. It is in this sense that the concept is a mental capacity as Geach understands it, but only because this capacity rests on the mental entity. This dependence of capacity on entity is in strict conformity with Aquinas' fundamental principle that actuality is prior to potentiality – a principle that Geach violates in his interpretation.

If concepts are mental entities, dependent in their origin and application on sensation and images (phantasms), as I believe with the tradition that they are for Aquinas, we must now ask whether all of the concepts in Aquinas meet his definition?

God of course is the radiating centre of Aquinas' world and thought; hence his concept of God is basic. God he takes to be the Supreme Being Whose essence is His existence. God is and is demonstrably simple, one, perfect, omniscient, omnipotent, infinite, eternal, good, truth, immutable, and both immanent and transcendent. He is also but not demonstrably known to be by faith three Persons in one essence. We also know that although we understand God under these different conceptions of His nature, the intellect '...yet knows that absolutely one and the same reality corresponds to its conceptions' (*S. T.*, I*a*, 13, 12). We know too that although God's essence is His existence, we do not know His essence. Therefore, even though God's existence is necessary and 'God exists' is self-evident, it is not self-evident to us because we do not know His essence. But we can know that He exists by arguments from undeniable empirical facts and inferences based upon them.

Just here I wish to challenge none of these attributions to God or any of the claims about our knowledge of Him. All I wish to insist on is that none of these attributions or claims is possible without possessing the concept of God. If as Aquinas says, our knowledge of God is indirect, an inference from His effects, however much the possessive pronoun begs the question, and our attributions to God are primarily analogical, what about the concept of God? Is it formed by reflecting on lesser concepts as dependent on the concepts of God or is it formed by some sort of analogy? To be a concept according to Aquinas, the concept of God must be a mental entity, formed and sustained in part as he claims it is by the empirical sense materials and images. Even if I could come to know God from knowing His effects and in this manner satisfy the criterion of the empirical origin of all knowledge, insisted on by Aquinas, I could not even form the concept of His effects unless I already had the concept of Him. Aquinas' empirically based theory of knowledge of God works only if he begins with a less than empirically based theory of the concept of God. The concept of God may yet remain a mental entity but it can hardly maintain itself as originating in sensation and imagery. My knowledge of God may come from my knowledge of nature provided I assume that nature is God's creation (His effects); but my concept of God cannot come from my concept of nature unless I presuppose the concept of God in interpreting nature as effects of God's agency.

Aquinas cannot, nor can anyone else, derive the concept of God from empirically given materials unless, in the fashion of Locke or Hume, he forms the concept by augmenting some of these materials into a composite image. Obviously this way out, whether it leads anywhere or not, is not open to Aquinas.

Perhaps he does not need a way out of this impasse that he creates because of his insistence on the empirical grounding of all concepts, since he already has a way into the concept of God – his notion of the active intellect as the concept-forming power. In its capacity of illuminating the species impressa in the phantasm, the active intellect has the power of creating concepts. The active intellect is not, of course, Augustine's divine illumination, that serves as a test for necessary conceptual truths, but it is a divine gift, different from grace, that enables us to form certain concepts, one of which is the concept of God. The concept of God, on this reading, would not be innate, as Aquinas denies that it is, but it would be independent of any fatal empirical origins. Thus on this view, I do not know God through my active intellect, I conceive Him through it. Only then can I go on to ask whether any being answers to this concept and whether I can know this being?

Of course Aquinas would reject this option. But it seems to me that he cannot reject what is basic in this option: that no theory of concepts can explain the formation of concepts out of empirical materials without presupposing the presence of certain concepts that are not so formed. If this is one aspect of platonism, then this aspect of platonism is true. And both Aristotle and Aquinas, in spite of all their attack on Plato, recognize the need of the presence of a concept in order to render even an individual perception of an object intelligible. For Aristotle, we recall, I cannot perceive the man, Callias, without having the concept of a man. For Aquinas, I cannot see a stone or abstract the colour from an apple if I do not already possess the concept ('species') of a stone or colour. Thus, both abstractionism and Aquinas' abstraction presuppose non-abstracted concepts: I can neither find similarities among coloured objects nor consider the colour of an apple apart from considering the apple without first already having the concept of colour.

Aquinas asks throughout the *Summa Theologiae* (as well as in some of his other works), How can the human intellect know immaterial beings that transcend our sense-experience, having satisfied himself that he has successfully shown that we can and do know material beings – the human intellect's proper object? I have been arguing that this question implies a more basic one: How can we form concepts of anything, material or immaterial? To which the answer cannot be: From pre-conceptualized empirical materials, such as sensations and images, because these materials themselves are conceptualized.

If my argument is at all correct, it follows that Aquinas' theory of concepts covers not only his concept of God but any of his concepts, including the material ones. Concepts as mental entities, originating in sensations and phantasms, giving rise to species impressa and illuminated by the active intellect, thereby producing the concepts, cannot accommodate the concepts of God, the soul, substance, evil, analogy, matter, or colour, among others. Concepts as mental entities, without the fixation regarding their empirical origin and sustenance, recast with a different emphasis on the active intellect as independent from the passive intellect, remains as a possible theory of concepts. However, since such an alternative requires a conversion to Augustine, it is not possible for Aquinas. In the end, Aquinas' philosophy and natural theology are too rich for his Aristotelian-inspired theory of concepts.

CHAPTER 5

Descartes

To go from Aquinas to Descartes is to commit a great injustice on the important late medieval philosophers, William of Ockham and Duns Scotus. My apology for omitting them is that both their explicit theories of concepts are in basic agreement with the major tradition from Aristotle to Aquinas that concepts are mental entities, however differently each interprets these. As original and profound as they are in their philosophy, their views on the nature of concepts are similar to those of Augustine and Aquinas, hence add nothing substantial to our historical survey. Whether their stated theories coincide with their implicit theories as exemplified in their use of the particular concepts in their work is a subject well worth exploring but which I must forego here.

That Descartes has a theory of concepts follows from the fact that he does philosophy at all. That this theory is made explicit by Descartes rather than intimated by some of his statements about concepts is problematic. But that Descartes has a vocabulary of conceptions that distinguishes conceiving, conception and concept; and that he employs this vocabulary to mark certain crucial differences between concepts and his fundamental entities of mind, matter and God is absolutely certain, confirmed by both his Latin and French texts. It is therefore all the more remarkable that within the vast literature on Descartes, there is not a single essay – at least that I have been able to find – on Descartes' theory of concepts. There are of course essays on his theory of ideas in which the ambiguity of 'idea' as act and as object of understanding – already noted by Descartes – is resolved into a number of species, one of which is 'concept,' with the implication that for Descartes a concept is a variant of an idea. Whether this is Descartes' understanding of concepts is best assessed after an examination of the textual evidence to which I now turn.

In the *Rules for the Direction of the Mind (Regulae ad Directionem Ingenii*, 1628), Descartes' earliest philosophical work, his main objective of course is to formulate and defend a method for the discovery of truth and knowledge. In the course of presenting certain rules or principles that are to be followed if such knowledge is to be obtained, Descartes introduces a number of concepts: the concept of knowledge, the concept of method, the concepts of intuition and deduction, the concepts of understanding, sense, memory, and imagination; as well as concepts which *he* refers to as concepts, such as that of the relative, of figure, of a simple, among others. He also talks a great deal about conception (*conceptus*) and conceiving (*concipere*), distinguishing these from thought and understanding and from thinking (*cogitare*) and understanding (*intelligere*). Since he does not include conception along with sense, imagination and memory as aids or hindrances to the understanding, it is not clear what roles conception and conceiving play in Descartes' rules for directing the mind. Nor is it clear what status he assigns to the concepts he calls 'concepts.' Are they abstractions, objects of the understanding, simple natures, meanings of words, or what? If he thinks that concepts are not mental abstractions or simple natures – as he seems to in his discussion of the concept of figure as distinct from certain expressions about it or certain conceptions of it or figure as a simple nature relative to our knowledge of it – what, then, are we to make of his concepts of method, knowledge, etc., which he does not discuss as concepts?

Basic to the *Rules* is the concept of method in achieving truth and knowledge; the concept of figure serves merely as illustrative of the method. If the concept of method is basic, then it is as important to determine what Descartes takes a concept to be as it is to ascertain what he considers the proper method.

What do the rules say about some of these problems concerning Descartes' theory of concepts? In Rule III, Descartes distinguishes between intuition and deduction, the only two mental operations that attain knowledge of things. Intuition he characterizes as 'the undoubting conception (*conceptum*) of an unclouded and attentive mind, and springs from the light of reason alone' (Charles Adam and Paul Tannery eds., *Oeuvres de Descartes* – hereinafter *AT* – X, 368; Elizabeth Haldane and G.R.T. Ross eds., *The Philosophical Works of*

Descartes – hereinafter *HR* – I, 7). Examples of these conceptions are the intuitions each of us can have that he exists, that he thinks, or that the triangle is bounded by three lines only. There is no suggestion that such conceptions involve concepts rather than things. Deduction also is conception in which we infer from our intuitions. It differs from intuition in that it includes memory; but it is like intuition in that every inference drawn by deduction is itself an intuition. One way to put together what Descartes says here is that *all* knowledge is conception.

In Rule VI, Descartes introduces a distinction between the absolute and the relative which he restricts to deductive knowledge. By the first, Descartes means our knowledge of what is simple; and by the second, our knowledge, derived from the intuition of the simple, that is complex and is to be analyzed into the simple. The distinction itself, Descartes says, is relative to our search for truth, though the distinction upon which it rests, namely, that between the ontologically simple and complex, is not. As unclear as this distinction between absolute and relative is, since Descartes, in spite of his disavowal, does affirm the ontologically absolute – the pure and simple essence, it is clear (textually) that he recognizes the concepts of the absolute and relative: 'But the relative is that which... involves in addition something else in its concept (*sed insuper alia quaedam in suo conceptu involvit*) which I call relativity' (*AT* X, 382; *HR* I, 16). Here the concept of the relative and, in its context, the concept of the absolute are whatever they may be, neither words nor things.

In Rule XII, which serves mainly as a summary of the preceding rules, Descartes discusses the roles of sense, imagination and memory in understanding. Conception is not included but it plays as large a role in explicating these other roles as they do in understanding. For example, Descartes asks us to conceive (*concipere*) the senses as passive, modified by their objects, as the surface of wax is altered by the applied seal. He also tells us (without asking us) that '... we conceive the diversity existing between white, blue, and red, etc., as being like the difference between the... similar figures' (which he illustrates, *AT* X, 413; *HR* I, 37). Not only is anything coloured extended and, as extended, figure; but both figure and colour can be abstracted provided, Descartes adds, that we do not admit any new entity (universal?), which is abstracted. Here Descartes seems to imply that we can conceive figure and colour, can form concepts of them, by abstracting from particulars; however, abstracting is not creating or apprehending abstract entities.

He also relates conceiving to the simple and complex that he earlier calls 'absolute' and 'relative.' We know by intuition the simples: figure, extension, motion, etc. 'All others [things other than the simples] we conceive (*concipimus*) to be in some way compounded out of these' (*AT* X, 418; *HR* I, 41).

Simples are either material, spiritual or common, such as existence, unity, or duration; or common notions, e.g., things that are the same as a third thing are the same as one another; and privative simples, such as nothing, rest and instant. '... All the simple natures,' Descartes says, 'are known *per se* and are wholly free from falsity' (*AT* X, 420; *HR* I, 42). Are simples or only compounds conceived? Descartes does not say.

Simple natures, Descartes goes on, can unite either necessarily or contingently. This union is

> necessary when one is so implied in the concept of another (*in alterius conceptu*) in a confused sort of way that we cannot conceive either distinctly, if our thought assigns to them separateness from each other ... Thus ... if I say 'four and three are seven,' this union is necessary. For we do not conceive the number seven distinctly unless we include in it the numbers three and four in some confused way (*AT* X, 421; *HR* I, 42–43).

Descartes adds: 'if Socrates says he doubts everything, it follows necessarily that he knows this at least – that he doubts.' To which we may perhaps add that for Descartes, at least here, the concept of, not only the act of proclaiming, universal doubt entails, however confusedly, the existence of the proclaimer in exactly the same way that the concept of seven entails four and three. Descartes distinguishes also in this important passage 'I exist, therefore, God exists' as necessary from 'God exists, therefore, I exist' as contingent. Given his definition of 'necessary union of simple natures,' can we say that for Descartes the concept of myself entails that God exists but that the concept of God does not entail my existence? It seems to me that we can: I can no more form the concept of myself without bringing into the concept God's existence than I can exist without God; or than I can understand seven without understanding four and three; or than I can 'conceive of a figure that has no extension nor of a motion that has no duration' (*AT* X, 421; *HR* I, 42).

Rule XII, thus, is a singularly important document for Descartes' theory of concepts. Concepts in this rule are distinct from simple natures; they are present in deduction as conception, but not in intuition as conception; they contain conceptual entailments which are based upon but not identical with necessary connections, since these connections Descartes attributes only to the relations among natures.

Rule XII also distinguishes between meaningful words and concepts, meaningless words and concepts, and words that inadequately express certain correct conceptions. Examples of meaningless, vacuous concepts are to be found in the pronouncements by some philosophers about certain truths which are nothing more than visions 'which seem to present themselves through a cloud. These they have no hesitation in propounding, attaching to their concepts (*conceptus suos*) certain words by means of which they are wont to carry on long and reasoned out discussions, but which in reality neither they nor their audience understand' (*AT* X, 428; *HR* I, 47). Later, in Rule XIII, he is more generous to those who misuse words or who use wrong words, provided that they have the right concept:

> Thus when people call *place* the *surface of the surrounding body*, there is no real error in their conception; they merely employ wrongly the word *place*, which by common use signifies that simple and self-evident nature in virtue of which a thing is said to be here or there (*AT* X, 433; *HR* I, 51).

Rule XIV has a final reference to concepts: the concept of body – *corporis conceptum*. Descartes is again considering the relation between our conceptions and our expressions for them, using extension as his example. Various expressions regarding extension, e.g., 'extension occupies place,' 'that which is extended occupies space,' 'body is extended,' lead to no difficulties. But 'extension is not body' does. For it leads us to form an image of what is a pure abstraction. 'Now such an idea necessarily involves the concept of body, and if they say that extension so conceived is not body, their heedlessness involves them in the contradiction of saying that *the same thing is at the same time body and not body'* (*AT* X, 444–45; *HR* I, 59).

Descartes' *Discours de la Méthode* (1637), as important as it is to an understanding of Descartes' philosophy, has little to say about conception and conceiving and nothing about concepts. Of course, much is implied by Descartes' use of the concepts he discusses in the *Discours* – about method, doubt, God, the self, and matter – concepts that are more fully developed in the *Meditations*. Just here, however, I am interested only in what he says about conception and conceiving in the *Discours*.

In Part II, having stated the four precepts of his Method for arriving at the truth, Descartes writes: 'And besides this, I felt in making use of it that my mind (*esprit*) gradually accustomed itself to conceive (*concevoir*) of its objects more accurately and distinctly...' (*AT* VI, 21; *HR* I, 94).

This use of 'conceiving' as 'seeing clearly' (*que je vois clairement*) Descartes formulates into a general rule: 'that the things which we conceive very clearly and distinctly are all true' (*que les choses que nous concevons fort clairement et fort distinctement, sont toutes vraies*). To conceive is to see something clearly and distinctly. The certainty attributed to geometrical demonstrations, Descartes says, 'is founded solely on the fact that they are conceived of with clearness' (*on les conçoit évidemment*).

Is conceiving seeing clearly and distinctly or is seeing clearly and distinctly a form of conceiving? Descartes seems to waver on this, since he also talks about conceiving the object of the geometricians to be a continuous body, or a space indefinitely extended, and so on, which conceptions are neither clear nor distinct.

Descartes also says that there are ideas (*idées*) or notions (*notions*) that are clear and distinct, hence true. Since the truth of these ideas or notions as consisting in their clarity and distinctness follows from Descartes' principle of true conceptions, it is not immediately obvious that true ideas or true notions are one and the same as true conceptions.

Descartes also uses the verb *feindre*, which some translate as 'conceive.' If this is adequate, then Descartes sometimes means by conceiving something to feign it or pretend that it is the case. Here conceiving slides into imagining in a conjectural, hypothetical way. This is certainly a normal use of 'conceive' and one that does no injustice to any of Descartes' methodological doubts. For example, 'I could feign I had no body' and 'I could conceive I had no body' seem to express the same state of mind.

The *Meditations* (1641), published in Latin and with the second edition (1642), that included the *Objections* and *Replies*, again in Latin, which edition was translated into French with Descartes' revisions, is, especially in Descartes' *Replies*, a great source for Descartes' theory of concepts.

Just as the concept of method is basic in the *Rules*, the concepts of God, mind and matter are central in the *Meditations*. Yet Descartes nowhere in the *Meditations* refers to *these* as concepts, only as ideas. But as surely as anything is a concept, these three are concepts; and ultimately Descartes' theory of concepts turns on them more than on what he explicitly calls 'concepts.'

There is much talk about conceiving in the *Meditations*, from the Synopsis through the sixth *Meditation*. In the French, the verb is *concevoir* throughout; but in the Latin – make of it what we will – there is a shift from *concipere*, used in the early *Meditations*, to *cogitare* and *intelligere*, used in the later *Meditations*. *Percipere* also serves as a synonym of *concipere, cogitare*, and *intelligere*, more than it does elsewhere in Descartes. There is also the familiar difficulty, already in the *Rules*, about the exact nature and role of conceiving in Descartes' theory of knowledge or of the mental faculties. Conceiving does not occur in the Latin, only in the French, as a mode of a thing that thinks (*Meditation* II, *AT* VII, 28; *AT* IX, 22); and it disappears even in the French when Descartes reiterates what is included in a *res cogitans* (*Meditation* III, *AT* IX, 27). Nevertheless, Descartes talks throughout of the importance of conceiving (perceiving) clearly and distinctly if we are to secure a criterion of truth. Is, therefore, conceiving, thinking, intuiting, imagining, a mental operation, or the forming of an idea in the *Meditations*? I do not see that Descartes gives any univocal answer.

The first provocative use of 'conceive' (*concipere, concevoir*) occurs in Descartes' proof of his own existence: 'I am, I exist, is necessarily true each time I pronounce it, or that I mentally conceive it' (*vel mente concipitur; conçoit en mon esprit*). Much has been written on the pronouncement as well as on the related *cogito*, so perhaps a few words can be added to discuss Descartes' alternative. What does it mean to say: 'I am, I exist, is necessarily true each time I mentally conceive it?' First, because of Descartes' views on the relation between words and thoughts, no pronouncements or, more cautiously, not this one, can precede the conception that is prior to it and which it expresses. Second, in the sense that the utterance, 'I exist,' though odd or unusual, is self-verifying or always self-confirming, so that its denial, 'I do not exist,' is self-defeating or self-contradictory, my conception of my existence does not appear to be self-verifying, nor does its opposite – my conception that I do not exist – seem to be a contradiction. Even Descartes can conceive he does not exist without contradiction as he cannot utter 'I do not exist' without contradiction. 'I exist' is necessarily true every time I say it but 'I exist' is never necessarily true every time I conceive it, unless Descartes legislates a use for 'conceive' that is synonymous with 'intuit' so that he sees clearly and distinctly every time he forms the concept of himself that he exists. In which case 'I exist' is invariably true every time I conceive it – not necessarily true as it is every time I pronounce it. If 'I exist' is necessarily true each time I mentally conceive it, it follows that the concept of myself entails the existence of myself – and we have an ontological proof of the self as well as of God. This entailment is missing from the necessary truth of the utterance: my existence does not follow from my utterance 'I exist;' it is confirmed, not deduced.

Having established his existence as a thinking thing whenever he thinks, Descartes considers in turn the existence of his body, external material objects, God, the objects of mathematics, and matter. There is much talk about doubt, belief and knowledge, but little about conception and conceiving, at least in the Latin. Descartes speaks of imagining, doubting, or of the mind perceiving the piece of wax; he talks of the innate idea of God, of understanding and comprehending Him, but he does not ask us to conceive (*concipere*) God as he does of oneself. In his discourse in the third *Meditation* about whether God exists, Descartes' main verb is *intelligere*, not *concipere*. In the fifth *Meditation*, Descartes uses *cogitare* as his verb of conceiving God. God exists because I cannot conceive God without His existence, no more than I can conceive a mountain without a valley. If we allow *cogitare, intelligere* and *concipere* as equally translatable into 'conceiving,' as they are in the French edition's *concevoir*, then we may scratch my statement that Descartes does not ask us to conceive (*concipere*) God for the statement that he does ask us to conceive (*cogitare, intelligere*) God and that in doing so he affirms that conceiving God is thinking of – seeing clearly and distinctly – His attributes, including His existence. The activity, but not the verb, of conceiving, then, remains what it is in conceiving 'I exist:' intuiting, knowing something in all its simplicity or complexity with a clarity and distinctness that provide certainty and truth.

This sense of 'conceiving,' expressed indifferently by the Latin *concipere, cogitare* and *intelligere*, and by the French *concevoir*, Descartes also employs in his discussion of mathematical objects and of material substance. Conceiving a triangle, thus, differs from imagining it; I can conceive (*intelligo*) but not imagine a chiliagon. I can conceive myself without imagination and feeling but I cannot conceive the latter two without me or some other spiritual substance in which they reside. Finally, Descartes allows in the sixth *Meditation* that we can conceive corporeal objects as distinct from our ideas of them.

Conceptus, too, occurs often enough in the *Meditations*. Mostly it serves as a noun of conception, brought out in the French *conception*. Only once does it mean 'concept,' in the sixth *Meditation* where Descartes borrows the scholastic tag *formali conceptu* (*concept formel*) to talk about imagination and feeling considered as formal concepts rather than as modes of intelligent substances.

Let us next look at some of the relevant textual materials in Descartes' *Replies* to the *Objections*. In Descartes' *Reply* to the first set of *Objections*, he writes: '... We must distinguish between possible and necessary existence, and note that in the concept (*conceptu, concept*) or idea of everything that is clearly and distinctly conceived (*intelliguntur*), possible existence is contained, but necessary existence never, except in the idea of God alone' (*AT* VII, 116; *HR* II, 20).

Here we conceive concepts or ideas of things, not things. If I have the concept of God, I see clearly and distinctly that it includes His existence, as does no other concept. Such is Descartes' answer to Caterus, who allows only that the concept of existence (not existence) is inseparably united with the concept of highest being. Caterus, Descartes implies, has the concept of God all right, but his conception or interpretation of that concept is wrong. They do not disagree about 'God' or God but over the content of the concept of God. To go from words, things and conceptions to concepts seems exactly right – as Sextus Empiricus saw long before – when replies to objections or two opposing conceptions are at stake.

In his *Reply* to *Objections* II (by Mersenne), there is talk of the concepts of the divine nature, an indefinitely great number, the mind, and the body; of the obscurity of some concepts (those that are not clear and distinct); and there are these stunning statements in the Appendix (*HR* II, 52–9), in which Descartes lays out his system *more geometrico*:

> When we say that any attribute is contained in the nature or concept of anything (*Cum quid dicimus in alicujus rei natura, sive conceptu, contineri*), that is precisely the same as saying that it is true of that thing or can be affirmed of it (Definition IX).
>
> Existence is contained in the idea or concept of everything, because we can conceive nothing except as existent, with this difference, that possible or contingent existence is contained in the concept of a limited thing, but necessary and perfect existence in the concept of a supremely perfect being –
>
> In omnis rei idea sive conceptu continetur existentia, quia nihil possumus concipere nisi sub ratione existentis; nempe continetur existentia possibilis sive contingens in conceptu rei limitatae, sed necessaria & perfecta in conceptu entis summe perfecti (Axiom X).
>
> To say that something is contained in the nature or concept of anything is the same as to say that it is true of that thing (Def. IX). But necessary existence is contained in the concept of God (Ax. X). Hence it is true to affirm of God that necessary existence exists in Him, or that God Himself exists (Proposition I).

In these quotations from the Appendix, Descartes distinguishes between the idea, the concept and the nature of anything. In the fifth *Meditation*, Descartes says that many ideas that may not exist outside his mind but at any rate are not framed by him, though they can be thought or not as he wills, 'possess natures which are true and immutable' (*habent veras & immutabiles naturas*) (*AT* VII, 64; *HR* I, 180).

These four quotations raise the absolutely crucial question in Descartes' theory of concepts: Are concepts ideas or natures or both or something else? If the image of a triangle contains an immutable, eternal nature, form, or essence, that does not depend on its being conceived, the idea, nature or concept of a triangle becomes as fundamental in Descartes as God, mind, or matter.

That Descartes does distinguish between conception and concept, especially when there is a dispute over contending conceptions, is manifest in one of his replies to Hobbes' objections to Descartes' distinction between mind and body. Hobbes challenges Descartes on the alleged proof of the mind as distinct from the body as presented in the second *Meditation*. Descartes argues that the proof is in the sixth, not the second, *Meditation*. Nevertheless, rather than talking about conceiving mind apart from body, Descartes talks instead of two distinct concepts – *duos distinctos conceptus*. Having formed the concept of the mind and of the body, it is easy, he says, to determine that they are distinct. Once more Descartes shifts from psychological talk of conceiving to logical talk of conceptual content when he moves from meditation to reply.

In his *Reply* to Arnauld (*Objections* IV), Descartes talks of the concept of the triangle – *conceptus trianguli* – not the idea, conception or nature of the triangle; of the concept of body – *corporis conceptu*: '... There is nothing included in the concept of body that belongs to the mind; and nothing in that of mind that belongs to the body' (*AT* VII, 225; *HR* II, 101); of the notion of substance: 'No one who perceives two substances by means of two diverse concepts (*per duos diversos conceptus*) ever doubts that they are really distinct' (*AT* VII, 226; *HR* II, 101); of the concept of a superficies or of a line; and of the concept of efficient cause – *causae efficientis conceptus*.

In *Objections* V, Gassendi raises questions about what he calls 'the concept of wax,' 'the concept of substance,' and 'the concept of their accidents,' thereby distinguishing between Descartes' conceptions of these which he challenges and the concepts which he does not. Descartes replies in kind, challenging Gassendi's (incorrect) conceptions of Descartes' (correct) conceptions regarding the concept of wax – not the wax!

> For, neither have I abstracted the concept of wax from that
> of its accidents; rather have I tried to show how its
> substance was manifested by means of accidents, and how
> the reflective and distinct perception of it, one such as you,
> O flesh, seem never to have had, differs from the vulgar
> and confused idea (*AT* VII, 359; *HR* II, 212).

In *The Principles of Philosophy* (*Principia Philosophiae*, 1644), Descartes again talks of conceiving, conceptions and concepts; much of this talk presupposes or implies relevant concepts. Thus, we can doubt everything, Descartes says,

but we cannot in the same way conceive (*cogitamus*) that
we who doubt these things are not; for there is a
contradiction in conceiving that what thinks does not at the
same time as it thinks, exist. And hence this conclusion *I
think, therefore I am*, is the first and most certain of all
that occurs to one who philosophises in an orderly way
(VII, *HR* I, 221).

Here conceiving presupposes a concept – of that which thinks – and
consists in seeing clearly and distinctly what is entailed by the
concept: that that which thinks exists.

Second, the mind has the ideas of a triangle and of God. It
perceives that the three angles of a triangle are equal to two right
angles. 'In the same way from the fact that it perceives that necessary
and eternal existence is comprised in the idea which it has of an
absolutely perfect Being, it has clearly to conclude that this
absolutely perfect Being exists' (XIV, *HR* I, 225). Here, too, conceiving (perceiving) presupposes concepts – of a triangle, of God; and
consists in articulating their entailments.

Third, Descartes divides all objects of knowledge into things or
their affections and eternal truths that exist only in our thoughts. In
the *Meditations*, Descartes allows that these eternal truths might exist
independently of thought; here they are in the mind, as innate, along
with innate ideas. Since concepts are objects of knowledge and
presumably neither things nor their attributes, the concepts involved
in our apprehension of eternal truths must be construed as mental
and innate.

Fourth, we have the concept of substance. 'Created substances, however, whether corporeal or thinking, may be conceived under this common concept (*sub hoc communi conceptu intelligi*)' (LII, *HR* I, 240).

Finally, in listing the causes of error, Descartes gives as one of
them, 'that we attach our concepts to words which do not accurately
answer to the reality' (LXXIV, *HR* I, 252).

Notes against a Programme (*Notae in Programma*, 1647, *HR* I,
431–50), written against Regius' manifesto on the nature of the human
mind, quoted by Descartes, also contains talk of concepts: of mind, of
extension, and of God. Regius calls into question Descartes'
conceptions of these concepts; Descartes answers, as he does in the
Replies, by reverting to the concepts and what is contained in them.
For example, he says:

> I have shown that we have a notion or idea (*notitiam, sive ideam*) of God such that, when we sufficiently attend to it and ponder the matter in the manner I have expounded, we realise from this contemplation alone, that it cannot be but that God exists, since existence, not merely possible or contingent as in the ideas of all other things, but altogether necessary and actual, is contained in this concept (*in ejus conceptu continetur*) (*AT* VIII, 361; *HR* I, 444–45).

Descartes concludes against his opponent: 'I myself . . . have founded my argument [for God's existence] entirely on this preponderance of perfections, in which our concept of God (*quo noster de Deo conceptus*) transcends other concepts' (*AT* VIII, 363; *HR* I, 445).

I hope I have covered the main textual sources of Descartes' uses of 'conceiving,' 'conception,' and 'concept.' As far as 'concept' is concerned, his employment of this term does not seem to add up to a coherent explicit theory of concepts. Two conflicting theories emerge from the texts: that concepts are among the innate ideas in the human mind; and that concepts are among the simple natures that exist independently of the human and divine mind and, although not substances, are entities as fundamental and irreducible as God, mind and matter.

If we turn now, as we must, from what he says about concepts to what he implies they are in what he says about his major ones, what then can we say about his theory of concepts? Descartes' philosophy revolves around three fundamental entities: God, mind and matter. Descartes demonstrates their existence and articulates their nature. Corresponding to each of these entities is an idea of it, implanted in the human mind. And for each of these entities there is a concept of it that is not the same as the conception of it, or any thought of it, including our idea of it. God, for example, exists and has a nature that can be articulated if not fully comprehended; He exists and has a nature whether we think of Him or not. Our idea of God exists when we think of Him or, on one version of his theory of innate ideas as potentialities (*Notes against a Programme, AT* VIII, 366; *HR* I, 448), when we are capable of thinking of Him. But the concept of God is not the nature of God; and the concept of God exists whether we think of God or not, whether our innate idea of Him is activated or not. The concept of God exists but not as God exists or as our idea of Him exists. This concept also has a nature that is true, universal, eternal, immutable, capable of being known clearly and distinctly. However, this concept's nature is not God's nature. The concept of God is an entity but it is not a spiritual or corporeal entity or substance; nor is it a mode of spiritual substance, as our idea of God is. Descartes sees, especially in the *Replies*, that he cannot talk about or argue about the idea of God – lodged in all human minds – without the concept of God. Indeed, it seems to me, he sees as clearly as he sees anything that basic in our philosophical discourse and argument about God's existence and nature or about our idea of God is the concept of God which, as he says of the imagine triangle in the fifth *Meditation*, has '...a certain nature, form, or essence, which is ummutable and eternal, which I have not invented, and which in no wise depends on my mind...' (*AT* VII, 64; *HR* I, 180). There is God. There is the idea of God. This much is clearly in Descartes. That there is also the concept of God, as an entity which is not like God or our idea of God, is implied by there being the idea of God and by talk about God.

Are concepts for Descartes non-spiritual, non-corporeal entities, neither substances nor modes, but ontological realities nonetheless? That they are, consequently that concepts are not ideas or variants of them but are rather implied by ideas, I think, best explains Descartes' theory of concepts as they function in his philosophy. Concepts for Descartes, thus on this hypothesis, are like Plato's *noéta* but not like Plato's *eidé*; they are supersensible entities, not forms as universals. Nor are concepts among the ontological or epistemological simple natures or the composites for Descartes. Nor are they identical with common simples, common notions, simple privatives, or eternal truths. An eternal truth, for example, Descartes says (*Principles*, XLVIII, *HR* I, 238), exists only in the mind (as do his common notions). But the concept of an eternal truth exists nowhere, even though that concept (as well as the concept of a contingent truth) has a nature that is as real and inviolable for Descartes as the nature of God. Concepts, thus, are not variants of ideas; rather, some ideas are variants of concepts.

One cannot have the concept of God without having the idea of God, just as one cannot have the idea of God without possessing the concept of God. But there can be the concept of God without there being the idea of God as there could not be the idea of God without there being the concept of God. This asymmetry of the existence of the concept and the idea Descartes affirms in the fifth *Meditation*: the nature of the triangle exists whether there are triangles or not, whether there are ideas of triangles or not. It is this nature of the triangle that serves as the concept of the triangle in Descartes, as he makes abundantly clear in his *Replies*, especially to Arnauld, where he shifts from the idea of the triangle to its concept.

Concepts, thus for Descartes, are the natures of things, whether these things exist or not, are thought of or not. All concepts contain existence; but all concepts except the concept of God contain only possible existence. God's existence is necessary since 'necessary and perfect existence [is contained] in the concept of a supremely perfect being (*Reply* II, Appendix, Axiom X).

Concepts in Descartes, I submit, are fundamental, irreducible, ontological entities, distinct from simple or composite natures, spiritual or corporeal substances, or their attributes or modes, hence distinct from ideas, innate or not. Does this hypothesis elucidate Descartes' major concepts: of God, mind, matter; of truth; of method; of mathematical objects? Is there a concept of each of these in Descartes? Is this concept distinct from its corresponding idea? Is this concept a supersensible nature, form or essence?

God is central in the world as the principle of order – of creation and re-creation – according to Descartes. Therefore, God is Descartes' fundamental entity or being. This entails that the concept of God is the fundamental one in Descartes' philosophy. This concept is not the word 'God,' the thing God, or the idea of God. The word 'God' expresses the concept or idea of God; the thing God is not the word or idea or concept; the idea of God exists dependently on the mind; the concept of God, expressed by the word 'God' and present in the idea of God, does not depend upon the mind, no more than the properties of being a triangle do. Without the concept of God, our idea of God remains confused and obscure; our word 'God,' without a meaning; and God without any adequate vehicle of talking about Him. God is central in Descartes' world; but the concept of God is central in his philosophy.

What, then, is this concept of God? It is the independently existing object of understanding, thought, contemplation that includes in its nature, form, or essence all the attributes of the supreme, perfect or highest being: omnipotence, omniscience, infinity, eternality, and necessary existence. Each is contained in the concept as it is in the innate idea and in God as an entity. Each is a defining property of God and a necessary feature of the concept of God. God, like mind and

74

body, is ontologically a simple nature, although relative to our understanding of Him, He is a composite of His simple natures, including His necessary existence. Thus, the concept of God is a complex concept of a simple nature or substance. Although God is not fully comprehensible, the concept of God is fully comprehensible. Indeed, it is closed in the logical sense that it has a definitive set of necessary and sufficient properties that corresponds to the definitive attributes of God and which properties determine the criteria for the correct use of the word 'God' in any language. All correct talk of God and all correct conceptions of God derive from the concept of God as it is perceived clearly and distinctly by the human mind. That God exists can be proved by certain facts: that I have the idea of God as Perfection and that I who have this idea am re-created or conserved with this idea from moment to moment. But that the concept of God has application – is not empty – can be proved without any facts from the nature of the concept itself. That God exists and that I have the idea of God show that the concept of God has an application; but these do not prove or demonstrate that it does. For it does not follow from the existence of God or from my idea of God that He necessarily exists, that is, that the concept of God as containing necessary existence is instantiated.

The concept of God is central in Descartes' philosophy. That it is closed in the sense I have specified, that this closure is the supreme governing condition of the intelligibility of thought and talk about God, and that his closure functions as the paradigm of all concepts in Descartes, determining their logical character, illustrate further my overall thesis that basic in a philosophy is the individual philosopher's theory of concepts. In Descartes' case, that concepts as supersensible entities contain definitive sets of necessary and sufficient properties which reflect the essences of the things they apply to and that legislate the definitive sets of criteria of the correctness of the language which expresses these concepts – all of this adds up to the theory that concepts are closed, a theory that is basic in Descartes' philosophy. Thus, his theories of God, mind and matter – his metaphysics – embody the concepts of God, mind and matter; and these, in turn, his presupposition or assumption that all concepts are closed. He does not go as far as Frege in holding that 'a concept that is not sharply defined is wrongly termed a concept' (*Grundgesetze der Arithmetik*, vol. ii, 56), but his recognition of the difference between clear and confused concepts does not deny,

75

indeed, it rests on, closed concepts whose definitive constituents are either clearly discerned or not (see *Reply* to *Objections* II, *AT* VII, 147–48; *HR* II, 43).

The concept of mind also is a closed concept: it is the concept of a thing that thinks and all that that includes. Here, too, as with the concept of God – I may be improvising and, no doubt, for scholars of Descartes, far worse than that – Descartes distinguishes between the concept of a thinking thing, which has a determinate nature and exists as a supersensible entity, independently of our human mental apprehension of it, and our having that concept, which does depend on our minds, indeed, which is an innate idea. That there is the concept of mind as distinct from a conception of it follows from the fact that it is contingent, not necessary, that there are minds in the world whereas it is necessary, not contingent, that being a mind implies being a thinking thing. This is why Descartes can argue from the concept of mind and not from his mind, that the mind is distinct from the body. To claim otherwise – that the mind is not distinct from the body – is for Descartes to violate the concept of mind, to invest it with a self-contradictory set of attributes.

That Descartes construes the concept of mind as a closed supersensible entity also can be seen in the *Cogito* of the *Discours* and the *Principles*. 'I doubt, therefore I exist,' however we interpret this – as argument, intuition or performative – presupposes the concept of mind as that which thinks (including that which doubts). The *Cogito* may prove that Descartes exists whenever he doubts (thinks); but it just as certainly shows that the concept of a thinking thing is being instantiated. Descartes does not prove that the concept of mind is not empty since that concept, unlike the concept of God, does not contain necessary existence. All he can prove regarding the concept of mind is that it contains as a constituent a that which thinks and can exist. His proof that he exists whenever he doubts, hence thinks, proves (provided the argument is sound) that he exists; but that he exists does not prove that the concept of mind is not empty. What it does is to provide evidence that it is not.

The concept of body or matter also is for Descartes an entity distinct from matter, our varying conceptions or ideas of it, or the word expressing the concept or used to talk about matter. It, too, is a complex concept about an ontologically simple nature but relative to our understanding of it a composite nature. The concept is the nature, form or essence of that which is extended and the figure, place, quantity, and motion which are implied by the extended. Here, too, one must distinguish in Descartes between this concept, the having of it, the employment of it, and the instantiation of it. In the first and second *Meditations*, Descartes states and formulates the concept; in the second *Meditation*, he employs the concept to show that he knows it more clearly than he does its application, in this case, to what he assumes to be a piece of wax; that he has the concept of that which is extended is more certain than that the concept is instantiated in a piece of matter. It is only in the sixth *Meditation* that he proves that the concept is not empty. The proof does not derive from the concept as it does in the case of the concept of God; rather the proof is based on his demonstration that God is no deceiver and that his passive sense experiences, presented to his God-given faculty of sense-perception, incline him to believe in the external corporeal objects which he senses. That there is matter, that the concept is not empty, that his employment of this concept is not illusory – none of these is proved from the concept; but the demonstration that there is matter and not just the concept of it, requires that concept as much as it does the existence of God. In the sixth *Meditation*, Descartes not only proves that his employment of the concept of matter is not illusory but that the concept of matter is instantiated: there really is that which is extended in the world.

Finally, the concept of matter also is closed, governed by a definitive set of predicates or properties. Descartes restricts this set to the quantitative, thereby ruling out, as neither necessary nor sufficient, in the concept all the qualitative properties having to do with colour, taste, etc.

Descartes' meditations on God, mind and matter, I have suggested, best disclose his theory of concepts: that they are supersensible entities, distinct from spiritual and corporeal substances or their modes, and exist independently of our awareness or employment of them and of their instantiation in God, minds and material things. Each of these concepts, I also claim, in its determinate nature, essence or form, is closed: that is, contains a definitive set of predicates, attributes or properties. This set is the ultimate arbiter in talk, thought and argument about God, mind and matter. It can be known – discovered, not invented – by the human mind through clear and distinct perceptions of the members and unity of the set. Inspired by his passion for mathematics, especially geometry and the concept of the triangle – the key concept in

Descartes – his theory of closed concepts is the generating force of his philosophy, determining his specific doctrines about God, mind and matter; about causality, truth and error; about method, induction and deduction. Some of his concepts, for example, of the relative, may not fit the pattern of a supersensible entity; however, even in their stipulative character as invented concepts (like his 'formed ideas'), they are legislated as closed just as surely as his other concepts. As for the simple concepts, whether of simple natures or not, those of existence, knowledge and certainty (*Principles*, X, *HR* I, 222) and of nothing, rest and instant (*Rules*, XII, *HR* I, 35–49, especially 40–42), these, too, are supersensible entities, intuitable by the mind but independent of it. They are also closed, not of course in the sense of containing definitive sets of properties, but in the sense that their unanalyzable natures preclude the definability of their corresponding terms. Their simplicity determines and legislates the necessary and sufficient criteria that govern our correct employment of these concepts and of the words we use to express them.

CHAPTER 6

Spinoza

Spinoza leaves no place in his philosophy for concepts that exist independently of conception and conceiving. Both his vocabulary and ontology ensure this. In the *Ethics*, for example, there is much talk of conceiving and conception, rendered by *concipere* and *conceptus*; and there is a meticulous employment of the distinction between conceiving (*concipere*), understanding (*intelligere*), and knowing (*cogitare*). Spinoza also distinguishes between imagining, conceiving and intuiting; and his second level or stage of knowledge – *ratio* – assigns an important, though perhaps not central, role to conceiving and conception in the pursuit and attainment of truth.

Conceiving and conception are modes of thought in Spinoza's ontology. Ultimately, they can be understood, that is, conceived, and intuited, as finite modes of God as substance in His infinite attribute of thought. But even regarded as a mode of human thought, every conception is identical ontologically with a conceiving:

> For to say that A must involve the conception B, is the same as saying that A cannot be conceived without B (II, xlix) –
> Idem enim est, si dicam, quod A conceptum B debeat involvere, ac quod A sine B non possit concipere.

Of course God, substance, attribute, mode, or the cause of itself cannot be reduced to conceptions of them. But these conceptions are identical with finite conceivings – modes of thought. In keeping with his rejection of all abstract entities, Spinoza thus not only dismisses concepts as independent of conceptions, but also conceptions as distinct from individual conceivings.

Does Spinoza, then, have no theory of concepts? If he does not, that he does not would be devastating to my overall thesis that a theory of concepts is basic in an individual philosophy, since this generalization would not cover Spinoza's philosophy.

Let me, then, propose an answer immediately. Spinoza, in spite of his implied disclaimer, has a theory of concepts; this theory is basic to his philosophy; it is to be elicited from what he says about the particular concepts he deals with in his philosophy and not from what he says about conception; and this implied theory is that all concepts are closed in the sense that they are governed by necessary and sufficient criteria, which criteria correspond to the necessary and sufficient properties or essences of the things they apply to, which criteria determine the correct use of the words that express them, and which criteria can be formulated into a real, true definition of the concept.

Thus, on the view I am proposing, Spinoza not only has a theory of concepts, but a theory that historically is the culmination of the doctrine that concepts are closed, a doctrine held with varying degrees of generality from Plato to Spinoza and beyond. In Spinoza, this doctrine is total: all concepts are closed; these concepts both reflect and are part of the closed universe; and their closure legislates the criteria for correct thought and talk about the world. What remains in doubt is the metaphysical status of the concept. That concepts are not abstract entities is certain; that they are entities is also certain; but that they are finite modes, like conceiving and conception – modes of thought – is problematic, although no other status is available to concepts since they are neither attributes nor substances. So I suggest that a concept for Spinoza is the same as a conception or a conceiving, with the rather unexpected modern consequence that Spinoza identifies having a concept with the concept itself!

That Spinoza recognizes and has the concepts of God, substance, cause, the infinite, attribute, mode, and nature; of extension and thought; of freedom, emotion, truth, and error; of good and evil; and of the different emotions, as they derive from desire, joy, and sorrow, follow from the fact that he talks about these things in his persistent attempt to define them by stating their essences. He also has the clear and distinct concept of the imagination as an obscure and confused merging of images that though useful in practical affairs is deficient in providing causal knowledge of things. He also has the concept of intuition as the highest kind of direct knowledge or vision of the world as derived from the essence of God, although Spinoza seems to regard intuitive knowledge (as Plato does) as being non-conceptual. But whether this intuitive apprehension of the world as God in all His attributes and modes is any more or less conceptual than Spinoza's *ratio* in which we see any one thing under the aspect of Eternity, the concept of intuition remains intact as much as the concept of reason or, for that matter, as imagination.

Spinoza also talks about universals and common notions, both of which bear on his theory of concepts. The concept of a universal is a clear and distinct concept of a general idea that, because it is dependent on sense-perception, is a confused composite image, hence unserviceable in the pursuit of knowledge. These confused ideas include not only those of natural species, such as horse, dog, man, but even the ideas of being and thing (II, xl, Schol. 1). Spinoza calls the latter 'terms' and the former, 'notions,' but neither 'conceptions.' That either is a concept to Spinoza is dubious since concepts, as against ideas, must be clear and distinct.

A common notion is an idea, known by all men, that cannot but be clearly and adequately perceived by all (II, xxxviii, Corol.). That our bodies are modes of extension and that our minds are ideas of bodies are Spinoza's examples.These are necessary, self-evident truths that all humans share in virtue of their having a mind and a body. Presumably, there are many more examples of these common notions which Spinoza does not give but suggests in his claim that these notions are the foundations of reason, hence of knowledge of the second level (II, xliv, Corol. 2). Are these common notions propositions about ideas or notions (as they are for Descartes) or are they clear and distinct ideas shared by all? Spinoza does not say. In either case, a common notion involves a concept.

It is an understatement to say that God is central in Spinoza's ontology, for He is everything:

> By God, I understand Being absolutely infinite, that is to say, substance consisting of infinite attributes, each one of which expresses eternal and infinite essence (I, Def. vi).

In the First Part of the *Ethics* – 'Of God' – Spinoza states (real) definitions of cause of itself, substance ('that which is in itself and is conceived – *concipitur* – through itself'), attribute, mode, and eternity; a number of self-evident, necessary axioms (common notions?); and a series of propositions that he derives from the definitions and axioms. Among other things, he proves that there is substance, that there cannot be more than one substance, that substance is infinite, that substance has infinite attributes and finite modes; that God is substance, that He necessarily exists, that He is unique, that 'Whatever is, is in God, and nothing can either be or be conceived without God') (Prop. xv), that God is free in the true sense that He acts from the perfection and necessity of His nature, that He is omnipotent, that He is immanent, not transcendent, that He is eternal; that everything other than God is a mode of God's attributes; that all is necessary, not contingent; and that God is neither benevolent nor a final cause.

Spinoza's doctrine and arguments, cogent or not, are subjects of great debate. I shall not enter into it here except as his doctrines touch on concepts. And what is of singular interest in this regard is the stunning dilemma Spinoza poses but does not explicitly state: that either God exists (and He does) and we do not, or we exist and God cannot. For it seems to me that Spinoza is the only philosopher in the Jewish-Christian tradition who fully probes the reality and nature of God as an infinite, all-inclusive being and who draws the valid conclusion that if God exists nothing else exists except as an aspect of Him. In effect, then – to relate what he implies about God to the concept of God – Spinoza is the first philosopher to conceive clearly and distinctly what is contained in and implied by the concept of God as a closed concept.

Whether or not I am right in attributing this dilemma to Spinoza, it is as clear as anything is in Spinoza that his concept of God is closed: that the concept of God is governed by a definitive set of criteria that corresponds to the essence of God. Aquinas' problem of how one can know God in this life without knowing and partaking of His essence vanishes as a pseudo-problem for Spinoza. I (as a mode of God) can know God and know that I partake of His essence by my reason or intuition: by my seeing anything or everything under the aspect of Eternity. To be sure, I cannot know all of His attributes since they are infinite but I can know that this infinity of attributes is part of His essence.

For Spinoza, there is God, the idea of God, the conception of God, and the conceiving of God. What I claim is that conceiving God which is forming an adequate idea of Him cannot occur without the concept of God, even though this concept must be assigned the same status as the conceiving or conception, namely, as a mode of thought, ultimately in God. For Spinoza, the concept of God is identical with the having of that concept; and the having of that concept is the same as the mental mode of conceiving God. This does not mean that there is no concept of God in Spinoza; rather, it implies that there is such a concept and that it is fully present in the adequate conceiving of God.

Thus, the concept of God for Spinoza is an entity, in particular, a mental entity. Although he differs from Aristotle on concepts as definitional entities – *logoi* – and from Descartes on concepts as non-corporeal, non-mental, supersensible entities, Spinoza nevertheless is solidly in the tradition that stems from Aristotle that a concept is an entity.

That this entity or mode of thought – the concept – is closed, governed by a definitive, precise set of properties which in turn legislates correct thought and talk of God, also establishes Spinoza in the major tradition of concepts as closed. That the concept of God is closed – absolutely and rigorously governed by the necessary and sufficient criteria of infinity, all-inclusiveness, uniqueness, omnipotence, eternality, necessity, immanence, and existence – and that these criteria fix the correct idea of God and the correct use of 'God,' is fundamental in Spinoza's philosophy. This concept not only generates his doctrine of God; it also serves as his logical model for all his related doctrines, from substance to the particular emotions, and the relevant concepts he employs to express them: in short, for the whole of his philosophy.

CHAPTER 7

Leibniz

> Now, what is it to say that the predicate is in the subject if not that the concept of the predicate is in some manner involved in the concept of the subject?

This is Leibniz remarking on Arnauld's objection to Leibniz' doctrine that the individual notion of each person includes once and for all everything that will ever happen to him;[1] it is not, as one might expect, Wittgenstein remarking on the objection that he is talking about words, not things. Since the containment of predicates in their subjects is no small matter in Leibniz, we may attribute to him the first explicit statement in the history of philosophy that talk about things entails talk about concepts of things. Leibniz thus not only employs certain concepts in his philosophy; he also probes what he applauds in Aristotle's investigations of 'the innermost nature of concepts.'[2] What he does not do, unfortunately, is to develop the implications for philosophy already present in our first quotation. The transformation of ontology into conceptual elucidation, though hinted at by Leibniz, is nowhere carried out by him. Thus, what we find in Leibniz' work is a use of concepts, including that of concept, and a recognition of the importance of getting clear about their nature. Whether Leibniz succeeds in achieving clarity about their nature or role is best answered after an examination of his theory of concepts, to which I now turn.

Leibniz does not draw a sharp distinction between conceiving and conception and the other mental activities and their objects. Although he does employ the vocabulary of conceiving and conception, he does not systematically contrast these with sensing, imagining, thinking, and understanding. What is striking about his vocabulary of conception is his persistent, extensive use of 'concept.' Thus, he refers to the concepts of substance, predicate, body, God, and so on. Sometimes 'idea,' but mostly 'notion,' serves as a synonym for 'concept' in his writings. He also refers to 'simple concepts,' 'individual concepts,' 'full concepts,' and 'complete concepts.' Each of these, whether expressed as 'concepts' or 'notions' (e.g., *notio completa*) or 'ideas,' is of great importance in his philosophy. I have not, of course, done a word count – it is not even possible, if feasible, until all his papers have been published – but my general impression is that 'concept' (*conceptus*) or 'notion' (*notio, notion*) occurs as frequently as 'conceiving' (*concipere, concevoir*) and 'conception' (*conceptus, conception*) in Leibniz. (I have not found *Begriff* in his German writings nor *concept* in his French.) What all this particular use of vocabulary adds up to is that Leibniz, more than either Descartes or Spinoza, transforms philosophical concerns from the psychological to the logical: from conceiving to the concept.

What, then, is a concept to Leibniz? In the sense in which he asks and answers, 'What is an innate idea?' Leibniz nowhere asks and answers, 'What is a concept?' That is, he has no explicit theory of concepts. What we find instead is an explicit recognition and use of certain kinds of concepts that Leibniz sharply distinguishes from the mental conceptions or verbal expressions of them. His theory of concepts – of their nature and logical character – must be elicited from his particular discussions of the specific concepts he explicitly recognizes and employs in his philosophy.

Like Descartes and Spinoza (as well as Francis Bacon), Leibniz seeks and formulates a method for the discovery and certitude of truth and knowledge. From one of his very first writings, *De Arte Combinatoria* (1666) on, Leibniz promotes his *ars characteristica* as the proper philosophical method:

> the art of so forming and arranging characters, in so far as
> they refer to thoughts, that they have among them those
> relations which the thoughts have among themselves; so
> that out of the ideas composing the idea expressing things,
> an expression of the things is composed out of characters
> of those things.[3]

This universal characteristic or ideal language, as we call it today, Leibniz describes as 'a kind of alphabet of human thoughts, and through the connection of its letters and the analysis of words which are composed out of them, everything else can be discovered and judged.'[4] That the universal characteristic as Leibniz conceives it involves an alphabet of primitive characters that stand for irreducibly simple concepts rather than a mathematical symbolization and axiomization of our thoughts is not all that clear in Leibniz, or at any rate not as clear as his claims that this method can bring together 'diverse concepts and things' in an appropriate order; and that his method of symbolizing 'most concepts' by numbers will enhance the mind as the telescope enhances the eye. Indeed, it seems to me, that what is of singular importance to concepts in Leibniz' universal characteristic is not his affirmation of ultimate simple concepts but his presupposition that all concepts as they are present in knowledge and disputation are alike in that they can be modelled on mathematical concepts. This presupposition yields his utopian vision that all disputes that rest on different reasons can be resolved by calculation.[5] Disputes converge on relevant concepts; concepts are governed by necessary and sufficient criteria; good reasons refer to these criteria; every rational disagreement involves a conflict over the definitive criteria of the relevant concept; appeal to these settles the issue. Behind such a view is the assumption that concepts are logically homogeneous, that there is no logical difference between the scientific and humanistic disciplines, that all knowledge is one: all concepts are closed. 'Is x good?' 'Is x beautiful?' 'Is x just?' 'Is x a triangle?' are questions of the same logical type, to be answered by calculation of the presence or absence of definitive characteristics.

Another life-long interest of Leibniz' is the law. In one of his essays, '*Juris et aequi elementa*' (1669–70),[6] Leibniz says that the theory of the law rests on definition and demonstration. Basic is the concept of justice whose definition as harmony and proportion constitutes an eternal truth that he here regards as a hypothetical proposition about 'what follows under the hypothesis of a defined existence.' Like arithmetical or aesthetic judgments, judgments about justice and its derivatives converge on clear and distinct intuitions of platonic ideas. The concept of justice, or as Leibniz calls it here, 'the meaning of justice,' presumably is construed as a supersensible entity that the mind apprehends. However, unlike Plato, Leibniz suggests that the best way to arrive at these intuitions of concepts and conceptual truths is by collecting 'the most significant and best examples of the usage of words, and then think of what is common to these and all other instances as well.' The search for definitions and precise concepts begins with language and induction; but it ends in pure intuitions that arise in yet do not depend on sense-experience. Leibniz thus starts with Plato but ends with G. E. Moore in his examination of the relation between concepts and the use of language.

Let us next look at Leibniz' most provocative use of the concept of concept, his concept of an individual. In the *Discourse on Metaphysics* (*Discours de Métaphysique*, 1686), Leibniz first establishes God as an absolutely perfect being Who in His perfection creates individual substances. What then, Leibniz asks, is an individual substance? To answer that it is the subject of its attributes is merely to provide a nominal definition. Leibniz demands a real definition. 'We must therefore inquire what it is to be an attribute in reality of a certain subject' (VIII). To be such an attribute is to be a predicate contained in the subject.

> Thus the content of the subject must always include that of
> the predicate in such a way that if one understands
> perfectly the concept (*notion*) of the subject, he will know
> that the predicate appertains to it also. This being so, we
> are able to say that this is the nature of an individual
> substance or of a complete being, namely to afford a
> conception (*notion*) so complete that the concept (*notion*)
> shall be sufficient for the understanding of it and for the
> deduction of all the predicates of which the substance is or
> may become the subject (VIII; trs. Montgomery and
> Chandler).

Being a king, thus, does not determine being Alexander the Great. But the concept of Alexander the Great contains everything that can be truly asserted of him. The concept of him is complete: it contains all his predicates. To be Alexander the Great is to be a subject containing all his attributes; and, according to the quotation at the beginning of this chapter, this is the same as saying that the concept of the subject contains the concepts of the predicates.

In a letter to Hessen-Rheinfels (May, 1686),[7] in which he comments on Arnauld's objection to the doctrine that the individual notion of each person includes once and for all everything that will ever happen to him, Leibniz repeats his doctrine, buttressing its truth by what he calls an apriori reason for personal identity. Of course introspection, he says, convinces me that I am the same person now in Germany as I was in Paris. But this is aposteriori. For an apriori reason, without which there is no certainty of personal identity, we must return to the doctrine Arnauld rejects. 'The complete concept of me which constitutes the so-called ego and is the basis of the interconnection of all my different states' contains all that has happened, is happening, and will happen to me.

In the *Discourse*, XIII, Leibniz raises a central difficulty about his notion of a complete concept of an individual: Does it destroy contingency, hence human freedom? No, says Leibniz: What will happen to me is as certain as what has happened to me. However, since both depend on God's will, consequently, could have been or could be otherwise, they are contingent: their contrary is possible, not self-contradictory as is the contrary of that which is necessary. Thus, the concepts of a triangle or of Julius Caesar are both complete. Only the first involves necessary truths. The second involves truths that, though certain like those about the triangle, are contingent; that is, they could be otherwise.

In another manuscript, '*Specimen inventorum de admirandis naturae Generalis arcanis*' (1686), Leibniz distinguishes, as he does elsewhere, between the principle of contradiction and the principle that a reason must be given for every truth – what he calls the 'Principle of Sufficient Reason' in other essays. These two principles are primary in all reasoning. Here, he adds: '... a reason can be given for every truth (which is not identical or immediate), that is, the notion of the predicate is always expressly or implicitly contained in the notion of its subject...'.[8] Does Leibniz equate the principle of sufficient reason with the complete concept of an individual, as this quotation suggests? If he does not, what is the relation? On the face of it, these two principles do not even imply each other: one can be true without implying the truth of the other. Yet Leibniz seems to equate them.

Whatever the difficulties are with Leibniz' concept of an individual, the claim that there is such a concept is a striking innovation in the history of theories of concepts. What does Leibniz think the status of this concept is? Only one answer seems possible: since the complete concept of any individual is possessed only by God, and the concept consists of all the predicates in that subject, the concept must be an idea in God's mind. However, even though Leibniz, unlike God, does not possess a complete concept of any individual, he does possess the concept of a complete concept; otherwise he could not attribute its possession to God. Leibniz' concept of a complete concept, grasped by him or not, cannot be an idea only in God's mind.

A related, important concept is that of substance. Leibniz defines substance as 'a being capable of action' (*Principles of Nature and of Grace, Based on Reason; Principes de la Nature et de la Grâce, fondés en raison*, 1714, 1). It is simple, perdures, has attributes but no spatial parts. It includes God as well as other substances that depend on God's existence. In the *Monadology (La Monadologie*, 1714), substance becomes *monad* and as an active principle of unity is fundamental in Leibniz' ontology.

More relevant here is that Leibniz refers to the concept of substance as well as to substance. In a series of letters to De Volder, he shifts the argument about substance to its concept. It is a concept of a real thing, not of a thing of reason. 'Substance,' Leibniz says, 'must be a real, in fact the most real thing' (June 23, 1699).[9] He objects to Spinoza's conception of substance, arguing that such a conception makes the concept inoperative: if God alone is substance, 'I fail to see how it is a suitable concept (*notionem*) for the remainder of things or agrees with that of the general manner of speaking according to which all persons including yourself or myself are called substances' (Dec. 27, 1701).[10] As for the cartesian notion that some substances are extended, Leibniz again appeals to the concept, not the thing: 'But if they would go into an analysis of this concept (*sed si analysin hujus notionis instituerent*), they would see that mere extension does not furnish extended things any more than number yields things counted' (April, 1702).[11]

It is clear from these examples that Leibniz recognizes all sorts of concepts. Rather than multiply these examples, let us ask instead, What does he think a concept is – simple or complex, complete or incomplete, of God or of anything else? It is not a word; it is not a thing or real, like God or you or me; it is not a platonic idea existing independently of mind in a realm of its own; it is not exclusively an idea in God's mind; and it is not the meaning of a word if that meaning is some sort of existent.

The best candidate for the nature of a concept in Leibniz is that it is an innate idea in his sense of an innate idea as one the mind derives from itself, and not from sense-experience. In Locke's terminology, which Leibniz borrows, a concept is an idea of reflection. In reflection, however, the mind not only makes ideas or concepts, it finds them. Concepts, thus, remain mental entities for Leibniz.

What is the evidence for this hypothesis? Consider, first, the *Discourse on Metaphysics*. XXVI reads: 'Ideas are all stored up within us. Plato's doctrine of reminiscence.' What is an idea? Leibniz asks. It is neither an act of thinking nor an immediate object of thought or a permanent form that can exist when we no longer contemplate it. An idea is an activity of the soul, not of thinking:

> ...Our soul has the power of representing to itself any form or nature whenever the occasion comes for thinking about it, and I think that this activity of our soul is, so far as it expresses some nature, form or essence, properly the idea of the thing. This is in us, and is always in us, whether we are thinking of it or no.

An idea, Leibniz continues, cannot enter from outside the mind. Minds have no doors or windows:

> We have in our minds all those forms for all periods of time because the mind at every moment expresses all its future thoughts and already thinks confusedly of all that of which it will ever think distinctly. Nothing can be taught us of which we have not already in our minds the idea.

Leibniz compares his doctrine to Plato's theory of reminiscence, which he accepts but without Plato's pre-existence of the soul and its thoughts; what he does not state but implies is that an innate idea not only *is* not derived from the senses but *cannot* be so derived; nor can it be derived from anything else. It is innate in that it arises and remains in me.

In XXVII, Leibniz affirms that *concepts* or *notions* are in the soul whether they are conceived or not. Those 'I have of myself and of my thoughts, and consequently of being, of substance, of action, of identity, and of many others come from an inner experience.' Conception, thus, is a relation between an innate idea or concept and a mind that is thinking. But concepts – either articulated here in the language of the object of conception or in any case implied by his doctrine that talk of being, substance, and the like, entails or is the same as talk of their concepts – exist in the mind but are not dependent on their being thought of.

In his *New Essays on the Human Understanding (Nouveaux Essais sur l'Entendement Humain*, 1704), Leibniz contrasts Locke's (and Aristotle's) notion of the soul as a *tabula rasa* with his (and Plato's) notion according to which 'the soul contains originally the principles of several notions and doctrines which external objects and doctrines merely awaken on occasions...' (Preface). The senses are necessary conditions for knowledge of truths and their ideas but not sufficient. Some ideas, Leibniz grants, arise in sense-experience. But 'being, unity, substance, duration, change, action, perception, pleasure, and a thousand other objects of our intellectual ideas' cannot come from the senses. They are innate. And what else can this mean if it does not mean that they are concepts in our minds?

These ideas or concepts, Leibniz adds in a telling comparison, worthy of Michelangelo at Carrara, are like blocks of marble, to be worked on by sculptors. Some of these blocks possess veins which determine the course of the sculpted figure. As a particular figure or rendition is already marked out by the kind of marble it is, so too 'ideas and truths are innate in us, as inclinations, dispositions, habits, or natural capacities, and not as actions; although these capacities are always accompanied by some actions, often insensible, which corresponds to them' (Preface). Innate ideas as virtual in us should not suggest, as it might, that for Leibniz an innate idea is a potentiality in the soul, for it is not. It is something actual, real, in the soul, and potential only to its employment by the mind in a particular act of thought.

In Book I, Leibniz says that the idea of God is innate. Indeed, he goes further: '... I even believe that all the thoughts and actions of our soul come from its own depths and cannot be given to it by the senses...' (I, i, 1). He attributes this doctrine to the Cartesians: 'In addition to this new analysis of things, I have better understood that of notions or ideas and of truths' (I, i).

In Book II, Leibniz sums up his position on knowledge, sense-experience and innate ideas. There is nothing in the soul which does not come from the senses – except the soul: *Nihil est in intellectu, quod non fuerit in sensu, excipe: nisi ipse intellectus.* 'Now the soul comprises being, substance, unity, identity, cause, perception, reason, and many other notions which the senses cannot give' (II, i, 2).

These notions, if I am right, are Leibnizian concepts. They are innate ideas in the soul – there to be discovered, clarified, and rendered adequate by those agile minds who are able and who freely choose to recognize and work on them. They are not uniquely implanted in us by God to be intuited in their transparent natures by the mind; rather they are created by God as part of His total creation, hence as part of us, not too unlike our limbs or even our liver, which we must also understand if we are to master them. In Leibnizian terms, concepts as innate ideas are aspects of God's perfection and the principle of plenitude. In historical terms, his concepts are platonic ideas, as he thinks they are, but Leibniz removes them from their non-mental, supersensible realm to fix them in either God or us. In effect, he transplants Plato's *eidé* in Aristotle's *nous*.

It also follows from my hypothesis that Leibniz distinguishes sharply between a concept and the having of that concept. Of course, since concepts are innate ideas, we cannot but have them in the sense of their being in us. But we can have them in this sense and still not have the concept in the sense of understanding or knowing it. For example, I possess the concept of an individual; with sufficient probing, I can even find in me the concept of the complete concept of an individual. When I come to see that this concept involves the concept of an individual in which everything that happens to him is a consequence of its concept, I may be said to have – to understand – the complete concept of an individual. But even here I do not have this concept as God has it, since He knows all the consequences, which I do not. In less complicated examples, the same difference between the concept and its being in us as against our understanding it – seeing whether it is simple or not, complete or not, and its conceptual content and entailments – occurs. There are concepts and all of us have them because they are in us. But only a few understand them and can be said to have them in that crucial-to-Leibniz sense. For it is with this possession of the concept that philosophy begins and ends.

Let us now turn to that philosophy which according to Leibniz consists in conceptual analysis. For Leibniz, as it is for Descartes and Spinoza, as well as for all preceding Christian philosophers, God is absolutely fundamental and central in the world, hence in his philosophy. From which it follows that the concept of God is basic in his (and their) philosophy. Leibniz, however, is the first to make this entailment explicit in his maxim that to talk about God is to talk about the concept of God.

This concept as an innate idea is that of a perfect being:

The conception (*notion*) of God which is the most common and the most full of meaning is expressed well enough in the words: God is an absolutely perfect being. The implications, however, of these words fail to receive sufficient consideration. For instance, there are many different kinds of perfection, all of which God possesses, and each one of them pertains to him in the highest degree (*Discourse on Metaphysics*, I).

Analysis of this complex concept reveals that among its constituents are ominiscience, omnipotence and omnibenevolence. God as a perfect being knows everything: the eternal truths and the contingent truths about the past, present and future; God has the power to create anything, except the self-contradictory which would violate the eternal truths; and God creates the best possible world. From these constituents and their corresponding characteristics in God that depend on the demonstration that the concept is uniquely instanced – that God exists – Leibniz deduces further consequences about God and the world.

First, then, the proof that God exists – that the concept is not empty. Leibniz offers a number of proofs; his basic one is what he regards as an improvement on the traditional ontological argument that he attributes to Anselm and Descartes. It can be validly inferred that God exists from the concept of God as that than which nothing greater or more perfect can be conceived provided, Leibniz adds, it can be proved first that the concept of a necessary being – a being whose essence contains existence – is possible. The ontological argument, thus, is correct,

> but it is an imperfect demonstration which supposes something which has still to be proved in order to render it mathematically evident. This is, that it is tacitly supposed that this idea of the all-great or all-perfect being is possible, and implies no contradiction (*New Essays on the Human Understanding*, Book IV, x, 7).

In 'Reflections on Knowledge, Truth, and Ideas' ('*Meditationes de Cognitione, Veritate et Ideis*,' 1684), he says:

> In truth, however, this argument [the ontological, here called 'the famous scholastic argument'] permits us only to conclude that God's existence follows if his *possibility* is

already proven. For we cannot use a definition in an argument without first making sure that it is a *real* definition, or that it contains no contradiction.[12]

The authors of the second set of *Objections* had already made a similar criticism of Descartes' ontological argument: that Descartes assumes that God's existence is not a contradiction. Descartes replies that he does not assume this but rather shows that the concept of God contains constituents the denial of which would contradict the concept. In effect, God is possible because the concept of God is clear and distinct and involves nothing contradictory. Thus, it is not correct to say that Descartes proves that God is possible by denying that the concept of God is contradictory; he proves – not presupposes – that God is possible by proving that His nature follows from His concept.

Leibniz offers a different answer. He tries to prove that the idea of God – of the all-great or all-perfect being – is possible. In his paper, 'That the Most Perfect Being Exists' ('*Quod Ens Perfectissimum existit*,' 1676), he begins with the notion of a perfection: 'I call every simple quality which is positive and absolute or expresses whatever it expresses without any limits, a *perfection*.'[13] Such a quality, because it is simple, is irresolvable or indefinable. That two or more perfections are incompatible cannot be demonstrated, since such demonstration depends on the resolution of the terms. That two or more perfections are incompatible is not self-evident either. Thus, the incompatibility of perfections being neither demonstrable nor self-evident, it follows that there can be a subject of all perfections. 'It is granted, therefore, that either a subject of all perfections or the most perfect being can be known. Whence it is evident that it also exists, since existence is contained in the number of the perfections.'[14] God as the subject of all perfections is possible, therefore, because such a subject is not impossible.

Does Leibniz improve on – salvage – the ontological argument by proving its presupposition that God is possible; or does he weaken it by emasculating Descartes' conception of God as a possible being, which includes both the positive constituents involved in the concept of God, clearly and distinctly perceivable, and the negative lack of contradiction among the constituents?

It seems to me – we cannot speak for Descartes – that Leibniz weakens the argument since he does not prove that it presupposes rather than implies, as I believe Descartes suggested, the possibility of God. Nor does he prove this presupposition; all he establishes is that it is not impossible.

Besides the revised ontological argument, Leibniz employs the traditional arguments from Design, Eternal Truths, and Pre-established Harmony to prove God's existence. Recently Rescher has attributed a further argument to Leibniz which he dubs the 'Modal Argument.'[15] Like the ontological, it starts with the real definition of God, this time not as a Perfect Being but as the Necessary Being; God's existence follows from this definition provided that the concept of a necessary being – a being whose essence contains existence – is possible. Leibniz then shows that it is possible by a *reductio ad absurdum*:

> ...If the Necessary Being or *Ens a se* is impossible, then all of the things which owe their existence to others will be impossible, since they must ultimately stem from the *Ens a se*. Thus no existence at all will be possible.

Here Leibniz demonstrates that a necessary being is possible not because it contains no contradictory predicates but because its denial forecloses on anything existing. However, without the additional premise that something does exist, the foreclosure does not prove the possibility of a necessary being; and with the additional premise, the argument is no longer apriori. Why it is a new modal argument and not merely a variant on the old aposteriori argument from the contingency of created existence is hard to see. In any case, in spite of the textual evidence, Leibniz cannot define God as the Perfect Being and then as the Necessary Being. For this would be to imply that there are two concepts or two real definitions of God, one of which includes His necessary existence provided He is possible; the other of which does not include His necessary existence unless He is possible and something other than God exists.

If God as a perfect being is possible then He is necessary; He is possible, therefore, He is necessary. This argument which links the perfect with the necessary rather than separates them, is Leibniz' proof that the concept of God is not empty – that God exists. From it he derives all his subsidiary concepts and doctrines. These, presented in many letters and papers, some still being collected and edited, are given systematic exposition in the *Discourse on Metaphysics* and the *Monadology*.

The *Discourse* opens with the conception of God as an absolutely perfect being which all understand but whose implications few see. Power and knowledge, but not number or figure, admit of perfection; the first two are not contradictory as are the greatest number or figure. Without limits, then, power and knowledge pertain to God. It further follows that God as perfect acts in the most perfect manner metaphysically and morally (I).

It further follows from the existence of God, hence from the concept of God, that there are principles of goodness or perfection in the nature of things. The world is good and beautiful not only because God made it but because He made it according to standards of goodness and beauty, acting in His wisdom and justice as aspects of His perfection (II).

Since God is perfect, it also follows that the world He created could not have been better. To think otherwise is to detract from God, to violate the concept, one might say (III).

'The general knowledge of this great truth that God acts always in the most perfect and most desirable manner possible, is in my opinion the basis of the love which we owe to God in all things' (IV).

It further follows from the concept of God as Perfection that in creating the world, He chose and created the most perfect,' that is to say the one which is at the same time the simplest in hypotheses and the richest in phenomena...' (V-VI).

God creates individual substances. It is part of His perfection that He does. That He does, since He could have done otherwise, makes His creation contingent, not necessary as is His creation of the three sides of a triangle. But even as contingent, every individual substance contains all its predicates in the sense that every true statement about it is analytic (VIII).

Certain paradoxes follow from the nature, hence the concept of God:

> among others that it is not true that two substances may be exactly alike and differ only numerically...; that a substance will be able to commence only through creation and perish only through annihilation; that a substance cannot be divided into two nor can one be made out of two...; [that] every substance is like an entire world and like a mirror of God, or indeed of the whole world which it portrays, each one in its own fashion...; [that each

substance] expresses, although confusedly, all that happens in the universe, past, present and future ... (IX).

It further follows from the nature of substance (which derives from the nature and concept of God) that substance is in no manner extension. Bodies, too, are substantial forms (XII).

Since each substance expresses the whole of creation, which follows from the concept of God, it follows that the complete concept of an individual contains all that can happen to him. What happens to him is certain but nevertheless contingent because of God's free choice in His creation. We are therefore free, not compelled, creatures (XIII).

'... Each substance is a world by itself, independent of everything else excepting God; therefore, all our phenomena, that is all things which are ever able to happen to us, are only consequences of our belief.' We correspond to each other as substances; we do not act upon one another (XIV–XV).

God as Perfection includes God as Final Cause. No explanation of scientific phenomena is adequate without employment of the concept of a Final Cause (XVII–XXIII).

Ideas are not sufficient for knowledge. My idea of God as a perfect being may be like my idea of the greatest degree of swiftness – impossible. For me to have an idea of God which constitutes knowledge, God as possible must first be proved (XXIII).

Knowledge is confused when we can recognize and discriminate among things without being able to list the characteristics of the thing; it is distant when we can list them. But knowledge is adequate only when we can give a real definition of the thing. It becomes intuitive knowledge when we understand 'at once and distinctly all the primitive ingredients of a conception (*notion*).' A definition is nominal '... when there is doubt whether an exact conception of it is possible.' A definition is real when a distinguishing property of a thing 'brings us to see the possibility of a thing...'. The best kind of real definition is an apriori proof of the possibility of a thing. When this definition 'carries the analysis clear to the primitive conception (*notions primitives*), the definition is perfect or essential' (XXIX). (Leibniz does not say so but his sustained analysis and definition of the concept of God serves as the paradigm of a perfect and essential real definition.)

There are innate ideas, created by God in us, which exist in us independently of our actually thinking of them (XXVI-XXVII).

God alone acts upon individual substances. 'We have in our souls ideas of everything, only because of the continual action of God upon us . . .' (XXVIII). Nevertheless, our ideas are in us. 'It is indeed inconceivable that the soul should think using the ideas of something else' (XXIX).

God, in His perfection, foresees that there will be sinners as well as saints and good men. He knows, for example, in His complete concept of Judas that he will betray Christ because Judas freely chooses to do so. And it is part of God's perfection that Judas should so choose (XXX).

These principles 'and particularly the great principle of the perfection of God's operations and the concept of substance' (i.e., 'that everything which happens to a soul or to any substance is a consequence of its concept,' XXXIII) are of great usefulness to religion (as well as to science), not a threat to piety (XXXII).

'God is the monarch of the most perfect republic composed of all the spirits, and the happiness of this city of God in His principal purpose' (XXXVI).

Such in the barest outline is Leibniz' system. It begins and ends with God as the perfect being (with a final reference to the role of Jesus and Christianity). From the concept of God – as the outline discloses, even without my sparse interpolations – Leibniz derives all his concepts, doctrines and principles: ontological, epistemological, religious, and moral. Without mentioning them by name, he deduces from the concept of God as the perfect being his concepts and principles of plenitude, continuity, pre-established harmony, contingent and necessary truth, contradiction, identity, identity of indiscernibles, and sufficient reason as well as those of a substance as the centre of activity, of a complete concept of an individual, and of perfect and essential knowledge.

That philosophy as Leibniz construes it is conceptual analysis which starts and finishes with the concept of God can also be seen in his *Principles of Nature and Grace, Based on Reason*:

> It follows from the supreme perfection of God, that in
> creating the universe he has chosen the best possible plan,
> in which there is the greatest variety together with the
> greatest order; the best arranged ground, place, time; the
> most results produced in the most simple ways; the most of

power, knowledge, happiness and goodness in the creatures that the universe could permit. For since all the possibles in the understanding of God laid claim to existence in proportion to their perfections, the result of all these claims must be the most perfect actual world that is possible. And without this it would not be possible to give a reason why things have turned out so rather than otherwise (10).

The *Monadology* begins with substance rather than with God. The mode of argument is from the individual to God, not by way of derivations from the concept of the individual. Instead the argument proceeds as an exposition of the necessary and sufficient conditions for there being substances or monads. Thus, the exposition is more or less an inversion of the exposition in the *Discourse*. And there are important details regarding the attributes of the monads. But the argument is the same as that of the *Discourse*: From God as the Perfect Being to His creation as a logical sequence of derivations from Him.

Leibniz' philosophy centres on a number of related doctrines, principles or concepts. The great exegetical problem is to bring these into some sort of deductive order. Russell and Couturat argue that logical doctrines are basic to Leibniz' ontology. Couturat emphasizes the fundamental role of the assumption that all true propositions, whether necessary or contingent, are analytic: their predicates are contained in their subjects. Russell makes the further claim that Leibniz' assumption that every proposition has a subject and a predicate is inconsistent with his pluralism of substances. Although Russell's interpretation is the subject of much criticism, his major claim of inconsistency seems to me correct. Leibniz, unlike Spinoza, simply does not draw the inferences he must from his analysis and concept of God. One of these, I believe, is fatal. God in His perfection creates a plurality of substances, each with its set of attributes. For them to exist as subjects of their predicates, they must relate asymmetrically to God – as created to Creator. Creation is a relation that cannot be resolved into a shared predicate, as equality or inequality can. Now, if creation is an asymmetrical, hence a non-reducible, non-ideal, non-fictional relation, which it must be for Leibniz, it follows that not all attributes are predicates of subjects and not all predicates are predicates of God. What He creates is not a predicate of Him. Therefore, God does not include everything; He is consequently finite, hence, self-contradictory, since He must be infinite or all-inclusive. If, on the other hand, creation is a predicate of God, not an asymmetrical relation between God and the world, then all substances or monads are predicates of God. In the end, it seems to me, Leibniz cannot escape from Spinoza's dilemma: Either God exists and we do not; or we exist and He cannot. Recent attempts to deny that Leibniz rejects relations or to show that he affirms them or that he holds that only relations among substances (not among numbers) are reducible to shared predicates are of no avail whatever since they cannot help him avoid his dilemma. If God is possible, He is necessary. In the same way, if God is the Creator, He must include as a predicate of Himself His creation. Like Spinoza, Leibniz invests everything in the analysis of the concept of God. But, unlike Spinoza, he balks at the full cost. Whether his refusal bankrupts his system, I leave for the reader to decide. For myself, I am unable to criticize a man who is able to describe his God of Pure Perfection as 'the most just and the most debonnaire of monarchs' (*Discourse on Metaphysics*, XXXVI).

CHAPTER 8

Hobbes

Before we turn to Locke, Berkeley and Hume and their theories of concepts, we must consider Hobbes and his place in the history of philosphical theories of concepts. Unfortunately, this is an especially difficult task not only because he has no explicit theory but also because the concepts he presents in his works seem as logically varied as the extant interpretations of them.

Hobbes never uses 'concept,' only 'conception' or *conceptus*, translated invariably, presumably with his approval, as 'conception.' He talks a great deal about conceiving and conception. Indeed, conception plays a major role in his philosophy. But his materialism that reduces everything to body (or matter) and his empiricism that locates the source and origin of all knowledge in phantasms (or sense-experiences) that yield his definition of 'conception' as 'nothing but motion in the head' (*Human Nature*, ch. 7, section 1); and his classification of conception as a form of 'decaying sensation' along with images (*Leviathan*, Part I, ch. ii) rule out any non-material, non-empirical status of concepts. Thus, if there are concepts in Hobbes – and there must be since he does philosophy – these concepts, in order to leave Hobbes consistent, must be construed as matter in motion or at rest.

There are three major sets of concepts in Hobbes' writings: metaphysical, linguistic and political. Among the metaphysical are the concepts of phantasm, body, space, time, accident, motion, cause, effect, sense, imagination, and thought. Among the linguistic are the concepts of name, sign, signification, speech, science, and philosophy. Among the political are the concepts of the state of nature, law of nature, natural right, covenant, sovereignty, and commonwealth.

All of these are concepts. All are definable for Hobbes, with the possible exception of accident which he elucidates by examples rather than defines, although he offers a definition to those who demand it (see *De Corpore*, Part First, ch. 8, sec. 2).

Hobbes distinguishes among these three sets of concepts but he always regards them as a consistent, systematic set that can accommodate everything from body to man and society. The great problem, therefore, is not the unity of Hobbes' philosophy but the logical homogeneity of his concepts. Is, for example, his concept of the state like his concept of the state of nature? Is his concept of speech like his concept of the geometer without language or the sole philosopher in a world that has just been annihilated except for himself? Negative answers to these three questions include claims that Hobbes introduces the state of nature and the alinguistic geometer or sole philosopher as fictions, best construed along the Paduan, Galilean model as counter-factual conditionals rather than as true-false, empirical categories. On interpretations such as these, meticulously argued recently by Watkins and by Hungerland and Vick,[1] it follows that Hobbes' concepts of the state of nature or of an alinguistic geometer or a sole philosopher are at least logically different from other concepts in Hobbes in that their roles and governing sets of criteria are unlike the roles and criteria of the concepts, say, of body or speech or the state. But does it also follow from such an interpretation of Hobbes that those concepts that apply only to fictitious entities or states are themselves fictions, hence non-entities? If it does follow, then indeed Hobbes makes an original contribution to the history of philosophical theories of concepts; for fictional concepts of fictional states, unlike words for fictional states that express no concept for Hobbes (e.g., 'spiritual substance'), are recognized as legitimate without there being corresponding legitimate entities of some sort. The concept of the state of nature, then, is like a centaur, not like the concept or conception (as image) of a centaur: a fiction. And as a fiction, the concept of the state of nature is not like God – inconceivable; nor like a non-corporeal substance – a fraud.

That there are things and words – little things in their own right – and concepts, that are not things yet not dispensable either, therefore retaining their rightful place in any philosophy of the world even if they are not in the world, is a plausible doctrine about concepts. It is the theory, I think, of Sextus Empiricus; it is voiced again only to be abandoned by Ockham; and it has been revived by many recent philosophers for whom concepts are requisite but harmless non-ontological intermediaries between words and things. But is it Hobbes' doctrine, even with regard to some of his concepts?

Let us begin with the concept of the state of nature. In his famous Chapter xiii of the *Leviathan*, where he introduces the concept, he neither refers to this state by way of a concept or a conception nor does he call it 'the state of nature.' Rather he talks about 'the natural condition of mankind, as concerning their felicity, and misery.' Men, Hobbes begins, are naturally more or less equal in their bodily and mental strengths and weaknesses. Some of our physical weaknesses are cancelled or balanced by other bodily strengths or mental cunning. This equality of ability engenders equality of hope in achieving our ends. Inevitably this creates enmity, with its concomitant fear of being destroyed and desire to destroy or subdue those who compete for the same ends. 'So that in the nature of man, we find three principal causes of quarrel. First, Competition; Secondly, Diffidence [Mistrust]; Thirdly, Glory.' These make men invade, in turn, for gain, safety, or reputation.

Hobbes begins, then, with a large-scale empirical generalization about human nature. From which he draws his first inference: 'Hereby it is manifest, that during the time men live without a common Power to keep them all in awe, they are in that condition which is called Warre; and such a warre, as is of every man, against every man.' He then follows this inference with his description of such a state of war and the role and destiny of man in it.

Now – to keep things as clear as possible – what is manifest, hence inferable, from the generalization about human nature that Hobbes offers, is only that the condition of war (as he expands this condition) prevails, not that it prevails without a common power. To validate the latter inference more is required than a statement about the sources of man's quarrels, in particular, a true premise about the only way to quell them. (Hobbes, of course, provides this premise subsequently.)

Hobbes calls this picture of man as destructive an 'Inference, made from the Passions,' as indeed it is, as Hobbes enumerates these passions. However, lest this inferential argument is unacceptable, Hobbes appeals to a variety of precautionary procedures in a commonwealth which, as he says, 'accuse mankind by [their] actions, as I do by my words.'

Hobbes then asks whether there was ever this condition of war? Not everywhere but perhaps in some places, among the savages in America, for example. Moreover, this condition exists and can be perceived in a commonwealth degenerated into a civil war. So there is some empirical evidence independently of the inference from the passions that the condition of man without a common power to hold them in awe is a state of war. Further, even within commonwealths and among them there are in the preparations for war and for peace indications of this natural condition of man. The great difference, of course, between the presence of this condition in a commonwealth and the absence of a commonwealth is that in the one but not the other, the 'misery, which accompanies the Liberty of particular men,' is also absent.

Hobbes ends this crucial chapter by enlarging on the passions, which include man's desire for peace, his fear of death, his desire for a decent life, and his hopes for achieving it. Reason, working with all the passions, suggests the way to peace and 'The Lawes of Nature' – the first antidote to the destructive passions of man.

I have laboured the argument in Chapter xiii because certain extravagant claims are made for it that must be tested against the details of Hobbes' presentation. For example, it is said that Hobbes conceives the state of war – the natural state of human nature – as a fiction or postulate or abstraction rather than as an historical, empirical generalization about the genesis of commonwealths. Some commentators add that the concept of the natural state of war among men is best construed as a counter-factual conditional of the form: 'If there were no common power, then man's natural state would be war.' This addition is especially attractive since it relates Hobbes' concept of the state of war to Galileo's concepts of a frictionless body and an indefinitely moving body which are also fictions that correspond to purely theoretical entities or states and whose value consists in the inferences to be drawn from them and their accompanying experimental confirmations.

Now, whatever the historical evidence may be regarding the influence of Galileo on Hobbes, it does not appear to me that Hobbes construes his concept of the natural condition of man – the state of nature or war – as a purely theoretical term, whether as a fiction, postulate or abstraction. For what he says is that this condition is universal, from the most savage societies to the most healthy commonwealths. It simply does not follow from this empirical claim about human psychology that Hobbes also makes an empirical claim about the historical genesis of the state. Consequently, to maintain the empirical character of the concept of man's natural state of war does not imply any historical claim. Commentators infer from the fact that Hobbes does not offer a history of the genesis of the state that his claim and concept of man's natural state are not empirical, therefore apriori in a manner that would fit into Hobbes' system. But his claim, whether an inference from the passions or from human behaviour, is an empirical generalization about man and, in the total context of Hobbes' study of man, a generalization about one – the destructive – aspect of human nature. His concept of the state of nature or war, thus, is no less empirical, no more a fiction, postulate, abstraction, or theoretical term than his concepts of man's other passions of the fear of death, desire and peace, security and a commodious life, and his hopes for reaching his goals. Neither the state of nature nor its concept is a fiction for Hobbes. It is an empirical concept employed in an empirical generalization about one aspect of man that is as true as it is platitudinous, especially when it is put into its proper 'contexture' of the whole of man's powers (*Leviathan*, I, x).

In *De Corpore*, Part First, Hobbes introduces his alinguistic geometer, the concept of which it is claimed by some is hypothetical, on a par with man in a state of nature: a fiction for a fictitious entity that serves in the Paduan style that Hobbes employs as a necessary step in the resolution and recomposition of the concept, in this case, of speech. Here is the passage:

> For example, if anyone contemplating a triangle set before his eyes, should find that all its angles taken together are equal to two right angles, and do this by thinking silently without any use of words either conceived or expressed; and if it should happen later that another triangle unlike the first, or even the same but in a different spot should be offered to his sight, he could not know whether in it were the same property or not. Accordingly, for each new triangle brought before him – of which there are an infinite multitude – his contemplation would be begun anew. But this is rendered unnecessary through the use of vocables (Ch. 6, sec. 11; trs. Hungerland and Vick, from Hobbes, *Op. Lat.*, vol. I, p. 70).[2]

Does this example of a man without language doing geometry function as a hypothetical entity in order to show that speech is impossible in such a state and thereby to reveal 'the definitional connection between signifying and the intention to communicate?'[3]

In this example, Hobbes distinguishes between a man doing geometry without language, a man doing geometry with language, and a man propounding geometrical theorems to his fellows. Now, in order to bring out the distinction between naming and signifying and to reveal their relation as well as the entailment of signifying and intending to communicate, the first hypothesis must at least be coherent. A man could certainly recognize a triangle and some of its properties without the word 'triangle' or any other word. But then he would be alinguistic, not aconceptual, for he could not satisfy Hobbes' example without having and applying the concept of a triangle. He has that concept in that he can recognize a triangle though he cannot name it or define it. If he has the concept then he can go from one triangle to another without beginning his contemplation anew. He needs the ability to recognize triangles, not to name them, to remain an alinguistic geometer. Thus, Hobbes' example is either incoherent in giving his alinguistic geometer a concept and then taking it away from him or it involves more than a fictional entity, namely a man who can recognize triangles and some of their properties but cannot name or define them. If Hobbes' alinguistic geometer is bereft of concepts as well as of language, Hobbes introduces no such concept or hypothetical entity, for there can be none; if his alinguistic geometer has concepts but no language – no easy thing to imagine – Hobbes' concept of such a geometer is not a fiction of a fictitious entity but some sort of constructed concept of a remarkable person who may or may not exist. What is hypothetical is not the concept or the geometer but the supposition that such a person does exist, and consequently that the concept is exemplified.

Neither the concepts of the state of nature nor of the alinguistic geometer is a fictional concept that requires special consideration in Hobbes' theory of concepts. The state of nature and alinguistic geometry seem more like Wittgenstein's primitive language games than they do like Galileo's frictionless bodies: simplified, not fictitious, forms of life, introduced to throw contrasting light upon more sophisticated human activities, such as being a citizen of a commonwealth or the teaching of geometry.

What, now, about the third contending example of a fictional concept in Hobbes, that of the sole philosopher? Here is the passage:

> Things that have no existence, may nevertheless be understood and computed. In the teaching of natural philosophy, I cannot begin better... than from *privation*; that is, from feigning the world to be annihilated. But, if such annihilation of all things be supposed, it may perhaps be asked, what would remain for any man (whom only I expect from this universal annihilation of things) to consider as the subject of philosophy, or at all to reason upon; or what to give names unto for ratiocination's sake.
>
> I say, therefore, there would remain to that man ideas of the world, and of all such bodies as he had, before their annihilation, seen with his eyes, or perceived by any other sense; that is to say, the memory and imagination of magnitudes, motions, sounds, colours, &c. as also of their order and parts. All which things, though they be nothing but ideas and phantasms, happening internally to him that imagineth; yet they will appear as if they were external, and not at all depending upon any power of the mind. And these are the things to which he would give names, and subtract them from, and compound them with one another (*De Corpore*, Part First, 7, 1; *English Works*, vol. 1, pp. 91–92).

Hobbes joins a number of separate doctrines here: that there are sense-experiences whose constituents are phantasms; that philosophy begins with these phantasms which are given as external, with the consequence that solipsism but not idealism – *esse est percipi* – is the natural starting point of philosophy; and that an annihilated world with or without a sole philosopher is a fictitious entity. But, although he feigns the annihilation of the world with the sole exception of his philosopher, his feigning or assumption or hypothesis of such a minimal world does not render his concept of the sole philosopher in such a world a fiction. It, too, is a concept derived by subtraction from his empirical concept of a philosopher, with phantasms but no world to work on. Indeed, his concept of the sole philosopher is less radical than Descartes' universal doubter at the end of the first *Meditation*. For both, the philosopher or the doubter is a real entity without which the fictions about the world and, in the case of

Descartes', of mathematics as well, they feign are unintelligible. Their concepts of the sole philosopher or universal doubter are not fictions; what are fictions are what the instances of these concepts feign or hypothesize. Whether these concepts are ultimately coherent in that they both presuppose what they deny, I leave in abeyance. My only concern here is to point out that if they are coherent, they cannot be fictions.

What, then, is Hobbes' theory of concepts? I have tried to show that concepts for Hobbes are not fictions by exposing the three most plausible contenders of such concepts. It is also clear and hardly worth arguing that concepts for Hobbes are not marks, names, words, signs, or the signification of words; nor can they be on his materialism non-corporeal or supersensible entities. It thus seems to me that a remaining possibility, strongly suggested by what he says about the role of definition in philosophical method, is that a concept for Hobbes is a definition in his sense of 'the explication of a compounded name by resolution' (*De Corpore*, I, 6, 15; *E.W.*, 1, p. 85). A concept, thus, is a linguistic entity of a definitional sort. On this interpretation, a concept is identical with neither a conception nor the having of that concept. Conceptions are motions of matter in the head. Presumably, having a concept is having certain motions of matter in the head and in other parts of the body as one applies that concept. However, the concept is an entity – matter at rest? – in its own right. As fantastic as this sounds, it is consistent with Hobbes' materialism and nominalism; and it renders his theory of concepts no more implausible than his ontology. For Hobbes then, on my hypothesis, one conceives, say, a triangle. When one engages in that activity, one has a conception of a triangle. Further, one can recognize, name and communicate about triangles: these activities, as well as conceiving a triangle, involve one's conception of a triangle. But one cannot conceive or have the conception of a triangle unless there is the concept of a triangle. And that concept is not an actual triangle; nor can it be a particular conception of it since any particular conception must be assessed as correct or not by the concept.

What, now, is the evidence that concepts are definitional, linguistic entities in Hobbes' philosophy? I rest my case on Hobbes' brilliant chapter on Method in *De Corpore*: Part First, Chapter 6.

First, Hobbes reaffirms his definition of philosophy as knowledge acquired by ratiocination from causes to effects or from effects to causes. Method in philosophy '... *is the shortest way of finding out effects by their known causes, or of causes by their known effects*' (*E.W.*, 1, p. 66). While all knowledge begins in sense, it consists entirely in ratiocination, since the latter provides the *why*, the former, only the *what* of things.

Ratiocination is both division or resolution and composition: either analytical or synthetical. Take, for example, our conception of gold. This is a compound conception of something singular. By resolving this conception into its constituents we arrive at certain universals that are the causes of gold and our conception of it. These include:

> the ideas of *solid, visible, heavy...* and these [a man] may resolve again, till he come to such things as are most universal. And in this manner, by resolving continually, we may come to know what those things are, whose causes being first known severally, and afterwards compounded, bring us to the knowledge of singular things. I conclude, therefore, that the method of attaining to the universal knowledge of things, is purely *analytical* (*E. W.*, 1, p. 68).

To know what something is (its *dioti*), not that it is (its *hoti*), is to know the nature of that thing in Hobbes' sense of its universal accidents that cause it to be what it is. This knowledge of what or why a thing is involves giving the definition of that thing, and the definition is nothing but the explication of our simple conception of the thing.

> For example, he that has a true conception of *place*, cannot be ignorant of this definition, *place is that space which is possessed or filled adequately by some body*; and so, he that conceives *motion* aright, cannot but know that *motion is the privation of one place, and the acquisition of another* (*E.W.*1, p. 70).

What can this assignment of definitions in knowledge mean if it does not mean that when I know what or why a thing is I know its definition which is a concept? If I know, for example, what motion is, I can by analysis define 'motion.' My definition (as Hobbes gives it) is the concept of motion which I have if I have a 'true conception' of motion. Though Hobbes does not identify the definition with the concept, it is clear that they are identical; and that defining, explicating simple conceptions or compound names, and analyzing concepts are all one and the same to Hobbes.

Concepts, thus, are central in the method of analysis or resolution. What is their role in composition? Composition or synthesis is that use of ratiocination or reasoning or computing that begins with causes and derives effects or consequences from them. What, for example, does motion beget? It generates many things: different lines, different sense-experiences, and so on. '...We are to observe what proceeds from the addition, multiplication, subtraction, and division, of these motions, and what effects, what figures, and what properties, they produce; from which kind ot contemplation sprung that part of philosophy that is called *geometry*' (*E.W.*, 1, p. 71).

In the same manner of derivation of effects from motion (its definition or concept), we create further divisions of the multiple effects of motion, including physics and moral philosophy, the latter of which is the study of 'the motions of the mind' – the causes of the passions and their further effects – all of which studies, because they are demonstrative, rest on geometry. In connection with moral philosophy or civil philosophy, Hobbes says, it is synthetical not only in that it derives from motion but also in that it begins with principles. (When it starts from sense and proceeds to principles, it too may be considered as analytical.) Synthesis or composition begins with primary principles. These principles are ultimately definitions and, if I am correct, concepts. This gives us the answer to our question about the role of concepts in composition: composition is in its derivation of effects from causes a demonstration consisting of the entailments contained in the definition or concept that we have already ascertained by analysis.

Hobbes further supports the view of concepts I am ascribing to him by affirming that the primary principles of philosophy – the goal of analysis and the starting point of synthesis – are 'nothing but definitions, whereof there are two sorts; one of names, that signify such things as have some conceivable cause, and another of such names as signify things of which we can conceive no cause at all' (*E.W.*, p. 81). Examples of the first are the names 'body,' 'matter,' 'quantity,' and 'extension;' of the second, 'such a body,' 'such and so great motion,' 'so great magnitude,' and 'such figure.'

> And names of the former kind [e.g., 'motion'] are well
> enough defined, when, by speech as short as may be, we

raise in the mind of the hearer perfect and clear ideas or conceptions of the things named, as when we define motion to be *the leaving of one place, and the acquiring of another continually*; for though no thing moved, nor any cause of motion be in that definition, yet, at the hearing of that speech, there will come into the mind of the hearer an *idea* of motion clear enough (*E.W.*, 1, 81).

Here, according to Hobbes, I can teach someone what motion is by defining 'motion' with no reference to any actual thing moving. That is, I can raise in someone's mind a perfect and clear idea or conception of motion. This idea or conception cannot be an image since no image is present or necessary in the example. It therefore must be the concept of motion, which is the same as the definition of 'motion.'

Hobbes reinforces further the definition as a concept in his discussion of the nature and definition of definition (section 14). Definitions are principles, primary propositions, i.e., necessarily true hypotheticals.

...They are therefore speeches; and seeing they are used for the raising of an *idea* of some thing in the mind of the learner, whensoever that thing has a name, the definition of it can be nothing but the explication of that name by speech; and if that name be given it for some compounded conception, the definition is nothing but a resolution of that name into its most universal parts. As when we define man, saying *man is a body animated, sentient, rational*, those names, *body animated, &c.* are parts of that whole name *man* (*E.W.*, 1, 83).

Names for Hobbes are sensuous entities. They serve as marks to recall one's own ideas and as signs to communicate to others. Although Hobbes says clearly enough that names 'serve for marks before they may be used as signs' (*De Corpore*, I, ch. 2, sec. 3; *E.W.*, 1, p. 15), other interpretations that make naming dependent on speech are possible, as Hungerland and Vick have shown.[4] However, whatever the status of names may be in Hobbes, it is clear from the above quotation (*De Corpore*, ch. 6, sec. 14) that a definition is an explication of a name for purposes of communication. Explicating a name is explicating a sensible moniment. If concepts are definitions concepts are these names explicated. And this is exactly what Hobbes implies in his 'definition is the explication of a compounded name by resolution.'

Thus, that a concept for Hobbes is a definition follows from his notion of a definition as exhibiting a clear idea of the thing defined. That a concept is a linguistic entity follows directly from Hobbes' notion of a name as a sensible, hence physical, moniment.

Philosophy, Hobbes says again and again, is definition and demonstration. Demonstration, he claims, is syllogistic argument comprising two definitions and a conclusion. That most of Hobbes' philosophy consists in definition and demonstration requires no argument: it is obvious from his beginning definition of 'philosophy' to his final definition of 'a commonwealth.' Consequently, if a concept in Hobbes is a definition as a linguistic entity that is ultimately matter in motion or at rest, which I believe it is for him, then the centrality of definitions affirmed by Hobbes establishes at the same time the absolutely fundamental nature and role of the concept in his philosophy. And because of this identity of definition and concept, Hobbes also subscribes to the doctrine that all concepts are closed. Whether definitions are arbitrary, as he says; or are real, as he implies, they are, as concepts, governed by definitive sets of criteria that are as binding on the speakers who employ these concepts as is the covenant of the commonwealth on its citizens. As radical as his arguments for political authoritarianism may be, he remains a staunch conservative in the Aristotelian tradition of concepts as entities. His achievement, if it is one, was to reduce Aristotle's concepts as definitional entities – *logoi* – to purely linguistic ones.

CHAPTER 9

Locke

In his masterpiece, *An Essay Concerning Human Understanding*, Locke states as his aim 'to inquire into the original, certainty, and extent of human knowledge, together with the grounds and degrees of belief, opinion, and assent' (I, i, 2; all references are to Book, chapter and section of the Everyman Edition, 1961). His is to be a genetic account, using the 'historical, plain method' of the understanding, rather than a physical, physiological explanation or metaphysical search for its essence. This genetic account encompasses all the contents of the mind. Central to this investigation is a survey of our ideas; and Locke introduces his key definition of idea: Since words stand for ideas, the word 'idea' stands for 'whatsoever is the object of the understanding when a man thinks...' (I, i, 8). Ideas include phantasms, notions, species, 'or whatever it is which the mind can be employed about in thinking' (I, i, 8).

Though Locke does not say so, either here at the beginning or anywhere else in the *Essay*, his basic term 'idea' must be what he calls 'a general word affixed to a general abstract idea,' whose definition legislates a nominal essence of ideas. That 'idea' is a general word that stands for a general idea obtained by abstraction is a matter of fundamental importance because it undercuts any subsequent criticism of Locke that his term 'idea' is ambiguous or inconsistent with ordinary usage; and it forecloses on Locke's persistent implication that 'idea' is a basic empirical term that names an object with which we are immediately acquainted or which can be constructed from such objects. Thus, Locke's idea of idea is more like his idea of man or of gold than it is like his idea of the shape or colour of an object. And the word 'idea' is a term of art that marks the nominal essence of the natural objects of the understanding; it cannot be on Locke's own demolition of real essences a term that names the real nature of the objects of understanding.

Locke includes notions in his nominal definition of 'ideas.' Are these concepts? Locke nowhere talks about concepts. To be sure, he employs, throughout the *Essay*, a vocabulary of conceiving and conception. But 'notions' cover both some ideas as well as some principles or propositions; and sometimes Locke uses 'notions' to distinguish those ideas that are purely mental from those that may also apply to the world (III, v, 12).

Locke's survey of the objects of the understanding is more than an inventory of ideas for it includes and centres on the analysis of ideas:

> It [the mind] requires pains and assiduity to examine its
> *ideas*, till it resolves them into those clear and distinct
> simple ones, out of which they are compounded; and to see
> which, amongst its simple ones, have or have not a
> necessary connexion and dependence one upon another. Till
> a man doth this in the primary and original notions of
> things, he builds upon floating and uncertain principles,
> and will often find himself at a loss (II, xiii, 28).

Here analysis – resolution – of ideas is not the same as analysis of concepts. Nevertheless, this analysis cannot be carried out without concepts. For example, Locke's analysis of the complex idea of substances is not a resolution of the concept of substances; it is a resolution of the ideas of substances. But without the concept or notion, as Locke sometimes refers to it, of substance, his resolution of his idea of substances as well as his denial that there is an idea of substance remain incomplete. He needs the concept of substance in order to distinguish as he so powerfully does between the idea, however 'inadequate,' of substances and the non-existent idea of substance.

Thus it seems to me, Locke's is an implicit theory of concepts, not an explicit one that identifies concepts with a variant of idea, unless that variant is non-propositional notions; in which case, according to Locke's omnibus definition of 'idea,' concepts are a species of idea, to be distinguished from the other ideas of sensation and reflection. However, if this is Locke's theory, it is open to the fatal objection that one can have the idea of, say, red, without having the concept of red. To be sure, for Locke, one can experience red without calling it 'red;' without, or before one has, the word. But can one experience red – have a simple idea of red – without the concept of red? Locke concedes '... that the *ideas we receive by sensation are often* in grown people *altered by the judgment*, without our taking notice of it' (II, ix, 8). However, it is not enough to admit '... that our mind should often change the *idea* of its sensation into that of its judgment...' (II, ix, 10). What is at stake is that more is involved in the idea of a sensation than the bare sensation. Concepts, thus, must play a role in all of Locke's ideas, not simply in some of them, designated as a kind of idea.

What I submit, then, is that Locke cannot pursue or achieve his 'purpose' in the *Essay* without the recognition of the fundamental role of concepts in his inquiry. Whether he calls them 'notions' and not 'concepts' is not important. What is important is that without notions (or concepts), his entire programme, as it revolves around his inventory and analysis of ideas, is unintelligible. Locke cannot 'inquire into the original, certainty, and extent of human knowledge, together with the grounds and degrees of belief, opinion, and assent' with words, ideas and things alone. His inquiry, as empirical as it may be, is a conceptual account of the notion of knowledge. One result of this inquiry is certain: that Locke offers his conceptual account as a real definition of the real essence of knowledge, not as a legislated nominal definition of its nominal essence. Thus, his concept of knowledge differs radically from his concept of idea: the latter must be an abstract idea for Locke; the former cannot be. Locke may have demolished the quest for the real essences of things. But his demolition rests on his seeking and finding the real essence of some basic concepts, including those of knowledge and certainty.

Locke divides ideas into simple and complex; the simple into those of modes, substances, and relations. The complex arise from the simple and the simple rest on ideas of sensation and reflection. Sensation and reflection are claimed to be the only two sources of all our ideas, the materials of all knowledge. Locke wavers on whether ideas of reflection have an independent source or arise from sensation; but his claims, that '*ideas* in the understanding are coeval with *sensation*' (II, i, 23) and 'In time, the mind comes to reflect on its own *operations* about the *ideas* got by *sensation* and thereby stores itself with a new set of *ideas*, which I call *ideas* of *reflection*' (II, i, 24), seem to clinch his view that sensation is the only original of ideas and knowledge.

Among the specific ideas Locke describes or analyses are those of solidity, existence, unity, power, primary and secondary qualities, perception, space, time, substances, duration, infinity, number, pleasure and pain, liberty, cause and effect, and identity and diversity. In the later editions of the *Essay* and included in the fifth edition, Locke reduces these primary and original ideas to eight: extension, solidity, mobility, perceptivity, motivity, existence, duration, and number. These are 'perhaps, all the original *ideas* on which the rest depend' (II, xxi, 73).

Each of the ideas Locke describes or analyses is simple or complex. With all of them, Locke follows his plain, historical method and traces them to their origins, either in sense or reflection and their simple ideas. This genetic account yields him a theory of the formation of ideas and the words or terms affixed to them. But because each of these ideas, simple and complex, involves a concept, his genetic account yields both a theory of the formation and nature of concepts: that they are mental entities – objects of and in the understanding – rooted in and dependent on our sense-experiences. Innate ideas or concepts or notions, either in the sense that Locke gives them or in Leibniz' sense (which Locke of course does not discuss) of ideas that though suggested by sense-experience are neither derived from them nor dependent on them, is rejected.

That concepts are mental entities for Locke is implied not only by all the ideas he enumerates, describes or analyses but, as important, also by his other concepts – what else can we call them? – of knowledge, certainty, probability; sensation, reflection, understanding, reason, faith; naming, abstraction, meaning, truth; and essence, among others.

These along with what is involved in the ideas Locke offers are concepts. As concepts, they are mental entities and, because of their range, cannot be identified with abstract ideas, composite reflection, formed by neither combination, comparison nor abstraction, must name a concept as distant from an idea. Thus, his sustained arguments against the idea of substance and ideas of specific substances rest not only on the lack of empirical evidence but also and, I think, more basically, on the disparity he finds between the concept of substance and our experiences – our ideas of sensation and reflection. For Locke, the concept of substance is the clear and distinct supposition of the support or substratum of co-existing attributes. However, although the concept supposes a something we know not what, and is not a verifiable idea derived from and confirmed by experience, the concept is not empty, as is the *idea* of substances; the concept is simply not known to be and cannot be known to be instantiated. The word 'substance' may not, in Locke's terms, stand for or signify anything; but it does express a concept and, at least in that sense, has a meaning.

Locke's implicit distinction between the concept and the non-existent idea of substance leads naturally to Locke's contrast between real and nominal essence, the consequences of which are of central importance to his theory of concepts. The tie is this: all ideas of particular substances, such as man, gold or horse, are of sorts of things. These sorts (or kinds or species) have essences by virtue of which they are a sort and in virtue of which each of its members is of that sort. But these sorts or species are not unknown and unknowable internal constitutions – real essences. Rather they are abstract ideas, fabrications of the mind, hence essences that depend on us, not nature – nominal essences.

> ...To be a *man* or of the same species *man* and have the
> essence of a *man* is the same thing. Now, since nothing can
> be a *man* or have a right to the name *man* but what has a
> conformity to the abstract *idea* the name *man* stands for,
> nor anything be a man or have a right to the species *man*
> but what has the essence of that species, it follows that the
> abstract *ideas* for which the name stands for and the
> essence of the species is one and the same. From whence it
> is easy to observe that the essences of the sorts of things
> and, consequently, the sorting of things is the workmanship
> of the understanding that abstracts and makes those general
> *ideas* (III, iii, 12).

Locke's demolition of the doctrine of real essence and his elucidation of nominal essences are among the jugular moments in the history of philosophy, giving the lie to the assessment of his philosophy as one of moderation and common sense. For his attack is lethal and his substitute far from common sensical.

How does the problem of essences arise? It arises because we must generalize if we are to facilitate our private thought and to expedite our public communication. We cannot attain or share knowledge with particular words for particular things. For this we need general words which indeed we already have or invent. These general words are affixed to general ideas, and general ideas are formed by abstraction from similar particular ideas. It is these general words and their general ideas that serve as the principles of classification or 'sorting,' as Locke calls it. Thus we need general words in order to make the transition, for example, from 'This is Peter' to 'This is a man' or 'Peter is a man.' 'Man' is a general word. Without it and multiple other words, we cannot classify or sort. However suspect Locke's theory that general words name general ideas gotten by abstraction may be, that general words and general ideas are requisites of classification – sorting and ranking – is undeniable. Locke sees here that without concepts, whether as general ideas or abstract ideas, we cannot classify.

Locke asks as his central question concerning sorting and the consequent use of general words, whether such sorting rests on real essences. Is it a necessary condition of intelligible classificatory utterance and thought that there are real essences and that these essences determine the criteria and standards of classification? He does not so much deny real essences as he denies them as a necessary condition of the cogency of classification. Thus his discussion of real essences in Book II, chapter xxi, section 6, and throughout Book III, it seems to me, is closer to Wittgenstein's *Philosophical Investigations* than it is, for example, to Popper's attack on real essences in *The Open Society and Its Enemies*, in Locke's stunning exercise in logical grammar.

To be sure, Locke asks both the ontological question, Are there real essences? and the logical question, Do we need them in order to sort? or Must we assume their existence in order to render classification intelligible? However, Locke never conflates the ontological with the logical questions.

So far as the ontological question is concerned, Locke wavers between denying and affirming real essences. Sometimes he concedes that things and persons have internal constitutions or essences, from which their powers flow, some of which engender our ideas (II, xxxi, 6; III, iii, 15). At other times, he argues that there are no and indeed cannot be any real essences since the doctrine of real essences entails that our complex ideas of particular substances consist of mutually entailing simple ideas, which is false:

> It is usual for men to make the names of substances stand
> for things as supposed to have certain real essences,

whereby they are of this or that species; and names standing for nothing but the *ideas* that are in men's minds, they must consequently refer their *ideas* to such real essences, as to their archtypes... And thus they ordinarily apply the specific names they rank particular substances under to things as distinguished by such specific real essences... The complex *ideas* we have of substances are... certain collections of simple *ideas* that have been observed or supposed constantly to exist together. But such a complex *idea* cannot be the real essence of any substance; for then the properties we discover in that body would depend on that complex *idea* and be deducible from it, and their necessary connexion with it be known... But it is plain that in our complex *ideas* of substances are not contained such *ideas*, on which all the other qualities that are to be found in them do depend. The common *idea* men have of *iron* is a body of a certain colour, weight, and hardness; and a property that they look on as belonging to it is malleableness. But yet this property has no necessary connexion with that complex *idea*, or any part of it; and there is no more reason to think that malleableness depends on that colour, weight, and hardness than that that colour or that weight depends on its malleableness (II, xxxi, 6).

Though Locke wavers on the ontology of real essences, there is no vacillation on the logical issue of real essences as a prerequisite of classification. It is simply not true, Locke says, that real essences or their assumption is a necessary condition of sorting or ranking. If it were, then because they cannot be known, classification would be impossible (III, vi, 9). Further, they could not serve in sorting not only ordinary cases but marginal ones as well; any theory of classification must provide criteria for sorting and answering '*Why* is x P?' and '*Is* x P?' But the appeal to real essences can no more resolve, for example, 'Why is Socrates a man?' and 'Is a changeling a man?' than it can 'What is a man?' (III, vi, 22).

What, then, does sorting rest on? On abstract ideas or nominal essences. Again, in a remarkable anticipation of the later Wittgenstein, Locke suggests that if we look and see instead of impose a theory, we shall find that our general words are sortal terms, affixed to general ideas, obtained by abstraction, which ideas

119

are sets of simple ideas, bundled together as the criteria of the terms and employed as the standards of classification:

> But since...we have need of general words, though we
> know not the real essences of things, all we can do is to
> collect such a number of simple *ideas* as, by examination,
> we find to be united together in things existing, and thereof
> to make one complex *idea*. Which, though it be not the
> real essence of any substance that exists, is yet *the specific
> essence* to which our name belongs, and is convertible with
> it; by which we may at least try the truth of these nominal
> essences (III, vi, 21).

Locke of course does not predate Wittgenstein's wholly original rejection of real essences as a necessary condition of intelligible discourse in favour of family resemblances – disjunctive sets of non-necessary, non-sufficient conditions – as the overall contingent condition of classificatory discourse. Nevertheless, Locke's rejection of the traditionally accepted necessary condition along with his substitution of nominal essences as abstract general ideas, however adequate this substitute may be, is the first articulate challenge in the history of philosophy to the platonic-aristotelian tradition that real essences determine and govern the conceptual life.

For Locke, then, sorting presupposes nominal, not real, essences. To classify, to determine species and genera, their 'measure and boundaries,' and to give criteria or reasons for something being of one sort rather than another turn on these nominal essences, encapsulated in abstract ideas. Indeed, Locke suggests, behind every real definition of a real essence lies a nominal definition of a nominal essence (III, vi, 7). (Compare: '*Essence* is expressed by grammar,' *Phil. Inv.*, I, 371.) Gold or man or any natural object may or may not have a real essence in the sense of an internal constitution from which its powers to engender ideas in us flow. But definitions of their terms and answers to '*Why* is this gold (or a man, a horse)?' or '*Is* this gold (a man, a horse)?' cannot be determined by the unknown and unknowable essences or constitutions of these things. Instead definitions, sorting, and giving reasons converge on complex, general ideas, abstracted from multiple possibilities of collections of simple ideas. It is the specific abstraction from these collections that serves as the nominal essence: 'the *nominal essence* of *gold* is that complex *idea* the word *gold* stands for, let it be for instance a body yellow, of a certain weight, malleable, fusible, and fixed' (III, vi, 2). To sort gold is to employ these attributes as criteria; but none of these is essential. How diverse are these sets of criteria?

> A child having taken notice of nothing in the metal he hears called gold but the bright shining yellow colour, he applies the words gold only to his own *idea* of that colour and nothing else, and therefore calls the same colour in a peacock's tail gold. Another that hath better observed adds to shining yellow great weight, and then the sound gold, when he uses it, stands for a complex *idea* of a shining yellow and very weighty substance. Another adds to those qualities fusibility, and then the word gold to him signifies a body, bright, yellow, fusible, and very heavy. Another adds malleability. Each of these uses equally the word gold, when they have occasion to express the *idea* which they have applied it to; but it is evident that each can apply it only to his own *idea*, nor can he make it stand as a sign of such a complex *idea* as he has not (III, ii, 3).

Here Locke suggests that there are many different nominal essences of gold, hence many different sets of criteria for the correct use of the word 'gold,' each as good as the next since it is founded on a distinct abstract idea. He reinforces this suggestion later in the claim 'that *every distinct abstract* idea *is a distinct essence*, and the names that stand for such distinct *ideas* are the names of things essentially different' (III, iii, 14); and, speaking of the various qualities children and adults invest in their ideas of gold,

> one has as good a right to be put into the complex *idea* of that substance, wherein they are all joined, as another. And therefore *different* men, leaving out or putting in several simple *ideas* which others do not, according to their various examination, skill, or observation of that subject, *have different essences of gold*, which must therefore be of their own and not of nature's making (III, vi, 31).

Nominal essences, abstract ideas, sets of qualities or attributes or simple ideas of a natural substance, such as gold, *vary* with individual complex ideas of it. Is one set of attributes or criteria as good as another to Locke? Consider Locke on what Waismann later was to call 'open texture':

> Should there be a body found having all the other qualities of gold except malleableness, it would, no doubt, be made a question whether it were gold or no, i.e. whether it were of that *species*. This could be determined only by that abstract *idea* to which everyone annexed the name *gold*; so that it would be true gold to him and belong to that *species*, who included not malleableness in his nominal essence, signified by the sound *gold*; and on the other side, it would not be true gold or of that *species* to him who included malleableness in his specific *idea* (III, vi, 35).

In the sense that Locke does not waver on the variability of the nominal essences of natural substances, it seems to me that he is of two minds on the status of these varying nominal essences. At times, he speaks as if one nominal essence, one idea, hence one set of criteria, is as good as another. But at other times, he suggests that the best available set of criteria is that garnered by experiment and skill, so that those who sort gold by the nominal essence of its colour, weight, fusibility, malleability, etc., have not simply a different idea of gold from a child's but also a better, therefore, a better set of criteria.

In any case, the central problem occasioned by nominal essences and of direct concern to Locke's theory of concepts is this: Suppose there are a competing number of nominal essences, say, of gold. For one, 'gold' or his abstract idea of gold includes in its collection of simple ideas *a, b* and *c*; for another, only *a*; for a third, *a, c* and *d*; for a fourth, *b, c, d,* and *e*; and so on. Without identifying the individual abstract ideas with the concept or concepts of gold, we may still ask, whether these sets of ideas serve as necessary and sufficient criteria for the correct use of 'gold'? There is one word 'gold' but many distinct abstract ideas. Does it follow for Locke that there is one word expressing one concept of gold but with varying, competing sets of criteria? Or, if we take account of Adam's 'zahab' (III, vi, 46) or all the different words for gold, does Locke contend that there are many different words for each of the abstract ideas formed of gold? I think Locke's position is that there are many words for gold and many more different abstract ideas or nominal essences of gold, and consequently many different sets of criteria for the correct use of 'gold.' Each of these sets is a closed set of definitive criteria for the specific use of the word for gold and of the specific abstract idea of gold. Instead of arguing that these different, competing nominal essences – sets of criteria – reflect on the ambiguity, vagueness or openness of the concept of gold, Locke opts for the thesis that different nominal essences reflect different abstract ideas or concepts. Thus, for Locke, we may share the same word and the same abstract idea. However, if my idea and affixed word for it is a collection of *a, b* and *c* and yours a collection of *b, c* and *d*, we may have the same word but we have a different idea of gold, each governed by a definite, closed set of criteria embodied in the nominal essence. This implies, even if it is not identical with, the doctrine that there are as many different concepts of gold as there are nominal essences of it, each of them closed. In the end, Locke's substitution of nominal essences for real as the condition of sorting and classificatory procedures and utterances leaves untouched the traditional view that all concepts are closed: all abstract ideas are nominal essences – sets of necessary and sufficient, if not really essential, attributes and criteria. Locke comes as close as anyone since Sextus Empiricus to the discovery of open concepts, as these are implied by varying and competing sets of criteria concepts, but chooses instead to multiply concepts (abstract ideas) in order to keep them closed. However difficult it is to pin down Locke's conception of a concept as a mental entity that may be involved in but is not the same as an idea, a notion, or a nominal essence, that concepts are closed, governed by definitive sets of criteria, is as clear as anything is in Locke, since it follows directly from his theory of nominal essences. Berkeley is correct in claiming that Locke's theory of abstract ideas is a disaster. But not only, as Berkeley shows, because it entails impossible entities; for it also compels Locke to multiply concepts (abstract ideas) to cover multiple sets of criteria (nominal essences), thus making it impossible for him to multiply instead the logical varieties of concepts: that is, that some but not all abstract ideas are governed by competing sets of criteria, yet may remain the same abstract ideas.

CHAPTER 10

Berkeley

Berkeley, like Locke, never uses 'concept'; and conceiving for him reduces to imagining. His nearest equivalent of 'concept' is 'notion' as a mental entity that is neither a proposition nor (unlike Locke) an idea. Moreover, as initially plausible a case can be made for Berkeley's rejection of concepts, therefore of a theory of concepts, as can be for any theory of concepts implicit in his work. On the view that concepts are abstract general ideas or are implied, perhaps even tainted, by them, Berkeley's attack on these ideas may be construed as a denial of concepts as well. Since I have been maintaining throughout that philosophy without concepts and an explicit or implicit theory of them is impossible, this reading of Berkeley according to which his rejection of abstract general ideas entails his rejection of concepts must be examined and refuted.

I shall argue that his negative account of abstract general ideas, his positive account of general ideas, and his inventory of particular ideas and notions presuppose or imply that there are concepts – which are none of these – and that these concepts are the only thing they can be in a world of percepts and perceivers: mental entities. Thus, to attribute to Berkeley a dispositional theory according to which having a concept is being able to employ a particular idea as a sample of similar ideas is to conflate that which must be kept distinct in order to identify and discriminate among particular ideas, namely: possessing concepts and being able to apply them. Without concepts and an implicit theory of their status and role in human knowledge, he cannot render intelligible his account of particular or general ideas. According to Berkeley, there are, for example, particular triangles that are the particular ideas of triangles and there is the general idea of a triangle which is a particular idea of a triangle that is assigned a representative status as a sign of all triangles. What there is not is an abstract general triangle – a triangle without particular qualities. None of this, I submit, can be made clear without the concept of a triangle and the possession of that concept.

Berkeley's animadversions on abstract general ideas pervade his philosophical works, from his early notebooks to the *Alciphron*. It is universally accepted, however, that his most powerful attack is in the Introduction to *The Principles of Human Knowledge*, to which I now turn.

There are, Berkeley begins, true principles and false ones of human knowledge. One of these false principles – the major obstruction to human knowledge – is that there are abstract ideas; and that these ideas constitute the fundamental objects of logic and metaphysics, objects with which the mind is supposedly immediately acquainted. We perceive things as compounds or blends of particular, concrete qualities. Just as we can distinguish, for example, the colour from the length of an object so, according to the doctrine of abstraction, we can distinguish colour from its particular colour. We perceive a number of particulars, discern a common factor in them, abstract it, name it, secure an object which it means or stands for, and in this manner frame an abstract general idea: of colour without any particular hue; of extension without any particular length; of a triangle without any particular sides and angles; or of motion without extension.

Berkeley begins his attack by construing the framing of these abstract ideas as the imagining them. He can, he says, imagine all sorts of abstractions of concrete qualities or features from their compounds – even a nose from its head. But he cannot, and doubts that anyone else can, abstract noseness from all noses, or motion from extension. He lays down as a principle of legitimate abstraction that things which can exist separately from each other even though they invariably go together can be abstracted. But not things that cannot exist so separated, such as noseness from particular noses or motion without a body. It is therefore not simply difficult to conceive abstract ideas, it is logically impossible. Thus, all abstract ideas are self-contradictions, hence cannot be.

Berkeley attributes this doctrine of abstract ideas, as he states it, to Locke who, Berkeley quotes, affirms the absurd view that the mind can form the idea of a triangle 'which is neither oblique nor rectangle, neither equilateral, equicrural, nor scalenon, but *all and none* of these at once' (sec. 13).

Whether Locke thought that such an idea could be *imagined* is extremely doubtful. But that Berkeley does less than justice to the complexities and subtleties of Locke's theory of abstract general ideas, especially as nominal essences fabricated by the mind for purposes of sorting, is certain. What Berkeley (in his notebooks, now called *Philosophical Commentaries* by his recent editors, Luce and Jessop) referred to as his 'killing blow' against Locke's abstract idea of a triangle rests on Berkeley's conception of Locke's abstract idea as an image, not on Locke's insight that the nominal essence – or what I have called the stipulated set of criteria of the concept – of a triangle includes neither the oblique, nor rectangle, neither equilateral, equicrural, nor scalene. I have already argued that Locke's abstract idea of a triangle is or implies the concept of a triangle. More relevant here, however, is that Berkeley cannot argue that there is no abstract image of a triangle unless he too recognizes the concept of a triangle and utilizes it to contrast the concept with the image of a triangle. And indeed he does acknowledge the concept, although he calls it a definition, which is exactly what the abstract general idea as a nominal essence is to Locke:

> For example, a triangle is defined to be 'a plain surface comprehended by three right lines,' by which that name is limited to denote one certain idea and no other. To which I answer, that in the definition it is not said whether the surface be great or small, black or white, nor whether the sides are long or short, equal or unequal, nor with what angles they are inclined to each other; in all which there may be great variety, and consequently there is no one settled idea which limits the signification of the word triangle. It is one thing for to keep a name constantly to the same definition, and another to make it stand everywhere for the same idea; the one is necessary, the other useless and impracticable (sec. 18).

With minor adjustments, this is more a summary of Locke's theory of the abstract idea of a triangle in Book III of Locke's *Essay* than it is a criticism of Locke. And for both philosophers the concept (as abstract idea or as definition) contains none of the concrete properties of particular triangles, ideas of triangles, or images of triangles. In Berkeley's case, his whole argument against the non-existent, inconsistent general image of a triangle rests on rather than dismisses the abstract idea or concept of a triangle. For without his definition of a triangle, he cannot claim he cannot imagine an abstract one.

That there are concepts for Berkeley as distinct from ideas and notions can also be seen in his positive account of general ideas and their formation. Each idea, he says, is particular. It can become general 'by being made to represent or stand for all other particular ideas of the same sort' (sec. 12). For example, all lines are particular ones of determinate length. But any of these can be picked out and made to serve as a sign or representative of all lines that 'it indifferently denotes.' The idea of a line is a general idea, then, not because it is a bare line – an abstract image – but because it is an individual line that is employed as an example of all lines. The word 'line' becomes a general word not by being affixed as a name to an abstract general idea but by being employed in a general way.

As original as Berkeley's shift from 'What does "line" mean or stand for or name?' to 'How does "line" function in the language of mathematics?' may be, his positive account of the formation of general ideas and their general words creates difficulties as great as Locke's account. What exactly is it that the mathematician does when he singles out a particular line and uses it to denote all lines indifferently?

> ...Suppose a geometrician is demonstrating the method of cutting a line in two equal parts. He draws, for instance, a black line of an inch in length: this, which in itself is a particular line, is nevertheless with regard to its signification general, since, as it is there used, it represents all particular lines whatsoever; so that what is demonstrated of it is demonstrated of all lines, or, in other words, of a line in general (sec. 12).

The geometrician cannot use a one inch black line as a vehicle for abstraction. Nor can he, by disregarding its length and colour, use it as a vehicle for subtraction, since that too would yield an illegitimate abstraction of a line with no particular colour or length. Does he, then, in using it as a sample, employ the one inch black line as an instance of the concept of a line? It seems to me that he does and that Berkeley's example implies that he does. The geometrician is able to use the particular line as a general line because he has the concept of a line (which is not the same as a general image). However, his concept of a line differs from his having that concept, in the dispositional sense of being able to do certain things, such as to use a line as a sample for all lines. For Berkeley, I know what a line (a triangle, a man, a tree) is when I have a particular idea of a line; I do not have to be able to use that line as a sample in order to know what a line is. If knowing what a line is or implies is having the concept of a line, I can have that concept without being able to use a line as a sign or representative of all lines. The latter presupposes but is not identical with having the concept – knowing what a line is. Berkeley's concept of a line is neither the immediate possession of that concept in the experience or particular idea of a line nor the capacity or ability to use a particular line in a general way. Being able to denote lines indifferently derives from having a particular idea of a line; having a particular idea of a line already involves the concept of a line that is had in the experiencing of a line (as a line). Which brings us back to the primary use of concepts in Berkeley: his inventory of particular ideas and notions – his metaphysics of perceivers and their percepts.

Berkeley divides all objects of human knowledge into ideas and notions. That there can be no such ideas or notions without concepts Berkeley neither denies nor affirms; nevertheless, his inventory presupposes a corresponding list of concepts. For every particular idea or notion, there is a relevant concept; otherwise Berkeley's ideas become mere indiscriminate and undiscriminated sensations, not particular ideas. Why Berkeley does not recognize what he must and affirm what he should in all his talk about particular ideas, that these particular ideas or experiences are of a certain specific sort, hence involve Locke's sortal terms, it is difficult to understand. His wish to dispense with language in order to concentrate on phenomena is as futile as his hope of ridding philosophy of language altogether is fatuous. His appeal to sensations and introspection is no substitute for a philosophy of sensationalism and its implicates. And a philosophy of percepts and their perceivers cannot dispense with concepts. If Locke falls on the rocks of abstract ideas, Berkeley is crushed by his denial of them as they include concepts. Fortunately, however, these *are* mere metaphors since Locke happily only slips and Berkeley reluctantly stumbles into an acceptance of abstract general ideas as concepts that are present in every particular idea or notion inventoried by them in their various writings.

Thus – to return to Berkeley – in *A New Theory of Vision*, for example, he designs 'to shew the manner wherein we perceive by Sight the Distance, Magnitude, and Situation of objects: also to consider the difference there is betwixt the ideas of Sight and Touch, and whether there be any idea common to both senses' (1). In this early work, Berkeley raises many questions about distance, magnitude, situation, sight, and touch; and he proffers answers to them. As original as his inquiry is, just here all I wish to point out is that none of his new theory of vision, none of the acute analyses of the phenomena he discusses, is possible without the relevant concepts of distance, etc. These concepts are not words or meanings or things.

Berkeley defines none of these concepts. Instead he takes for granted, as well he might, with the exception of situation, that we understand what distance, magnitude, sight, touch, and situation are – that we have these concepts. His main concern here is with neither the definition nor the application of these concepts but with the analysis of the phenomena these concepts sort. That we do not perceive distance but rather infer or judge it is one of his major claims. True or false, my point is that without the concept of distance, Berkeley could not make the claim or carry through his analysis or argument. Berkeley recognizes distance (the phenomenon) and 'distance' (the word). He further recognizes that distance is not magnitude and that 'distance' differs from 'magnitude.' He can do neither without the concepts of distance and magnitude. These concepts are not abstract ideas, particular ideas, general ideas, words or things. What, then, are they? The only thing they can be for Berkeley: mental entities.

Berkeley's central doctrine, expressed in his major writings, *The Principles of Human Knowledge* and *Three Dialogues between Hylas and Philonous*, is that there are only ideas and notions which exist in their spiritual perceivers, including God. To be is to be perceived or a perceiver. That all our ideas and notions involve concepts (as well as experiences) follows from the fact that Berkeley sorts these into distinct ideas of sense or imagination and distinct notions of oneself, other selves, and God. He can no more identify an idea of red or distinguish that idea from an idea of hardness or sort them as ideas of sight and touch without the relevant concepts than he can talk about distance and magnitude without their concepts in the *New Theory of Vision*.

That there are concepts in Berkeley's philosophy and that their primary use is in his inventory of ideas and notions need no further elaboration. However, his inventory raises a question that does require further consideration if we are to elucidate Berkeley's implicit theory of concepts and to show that it is basic in his philosophy: Is the range of concepts in Berkeley's philosophy coincident with the range of concepts in his inventory? I have already argued that it is not since concepts play a role in his denial of abstract ideas and in his account of general ideas, neither of which ideas are among the particular ideas or notions of Berkeley's inventory of percepts and perceivers. Nevertheless, we are still left with the crucial, perhaps central, question: Does Berkeley, in spite of his thorough, devastating attack on matter as an entity, idea, or notion, have the concept of matter? Or does it follow from his conclusion that the idea of matter is a self-contradictory abstract idea that there is and can be no concept of matter?

It is well to remind ourselves just how extensive his attack on matter is. Berkeley affirms that there are things – ordinary objects. These are composite ideas of congeries of sensed qualities. He then denies that there is anything which is not mental, matter being one of those. He also denies that if there were matter, it could be known, either by sense or reason. He further considers the possibilities that matter is an instrument, occasion, or archtype of our experiences of things, dismissing each as a superfluity. He ends by claiming that 'matter' names nothing, unless it serves as a synonym for 'sensible object,' in which case 'matter' is a name for mind-dependent percepts. He can assign no use to the word, explain nothing by it, 'or even conceive what is meant by that word' (*Principles*, sec. 79). Philonous sums up this side of the attack in the second *Dialogue*:

> Either you perceive the being of Matter immediately, or
> mediately. If immediately, pray inform me by which of the
> senses you perceive it. If mediately, let me know by what
> reasoning it is inferred from those things which you
> perceive immediately. So much for the perception. Then for
> the Matter itself, I ask whether it is object, *substratum*,
> cause, instrument, or occasion? You have already pleaded
> for each of these, shifting your notions, and making Matter
> to appear sometimes in one shape, then in another. And
> what you have offered hath been disapproved and rejected
> by yourself. If you have anything new to advance I would
> gladly hear it.

Hylas responds with a last, desperate (Lockean): Matter is a 'Something entirely unknown.' Philonous retorts with his killing pun: 'which being interpreted proves *nothing*.'

All these skirmishes against matter, however, are aposteriori window dressing, Berkeley suggests. 'Matter exists' is a simple contradiction, like '2+2=7.' It is therefore apriori that matter does not exist; consequently, the notion of matter is necessarily false, not merely empirically false or unverifiable. Again, Philonous sums up this side of the attack, this time in the third *Dialogue*:

> ... I do not deny the existence of material substance, merely
> because I have no notion of it, but because the notion of it
> is inconsistent; or, in other words, because it is repugnant
> that there should be a notion of it. Many things, for aught
> I know, may exist, whereof neither I nor any other man
> hath or can have any idea or notion whatsoever. But then
> those things must be possible, that is, nothing inconsistent
> must be included in their definition... In the very notion or
> definition of *material Substance*, there is included a manifest
> repugnance and inconsistency. But this cannot be said of
> the notion of Spirit. That ideas should exist in what doth
> not perceive, or be produced by what doth not act, is
> repugnant.

The notion of matter is an illegitimate abstraction – a separation of ideas or sensibles from their perceivers which cannot exist apart from their perceivers: to be a sensible is to be perceived. For Berkeley, this is a necessary truth. The notion of matter is the notion of ideas, sensations, sensibles, necessarily dependent on minds, existing apart from minds; it is therefore self-contradictory and for Berkeley no notion at all.

Does it follow from there being no notion of matter that there is no concept of matter? It seems to me that it does; and because it does, the notion of matter for Berkeley cannot be an abstract idea since the repugnancy of the latter rests on the inability to imagine it. Berkeley, we remember, cannot conceive Locke's abstract triangle because he cannot imagine it. But he cannot conceive Locke's matter not because he cannot imagine it (which of course he cannot) but because it embodies a self-contradiction. Consequently, I cannot argue that Berkeley's denial of the notion of matter presupposes the concept of matter as I argued that his denial of the abstract idea of a triangle presupposes the concept of a triangle. For Berkeley 'matter' is not only a word without a meaning – an empty name; it is a word that names a self-contradiction: unsensed sensibles. Thus, it is no word at all, only a noise.

Berkeley's argument against the notion (and concept) of matter rests initially on his ontological-logical doctrine of *esse est percipi*. This means that any revitilization of the concept of matter requires a refutation of his doctrine. That it has been refuted by denying its analytic character – in Moore and Russell – I think needs no further comment here. Rather than argue that there is a non-self-contradictory concept of matter and that Berkeley's premise of *esse est percipi* is neither logically nor empirically true, I want to emphasize a different point, one related to his implicit theory of concepts, namely, that even if his denial of the concept of matter rests on his metaphysics, it does not follow that his implicit theory of concepts also derives from his metaphysics. Indeed, I claim the opposite: that Berkeley's implicit theory of concepts – of their nature and role – is basic in his metaphysics. Berkeley's theory of concepts, I have already said, is to be elicited from the concepts involved in his inventory of ideas and notions, his account of certain general ideas, and his rejection of some abstract general ideas, such as a bare triangle or extension without motion, but not matter. Among these concepts are those of distance, magnitude, situation, sight, and touch; of an abstract idea, a general idea, line, triangle, language, notion, object, thing; of spirit, quality, substance, unity, being, causality, image, idea, sign; of colour, taste, figure, motion, extension, sound, time, space, number, heat, sensation; of red, blue, orange; of sweet, sour, bitter; and of God. These divide fairly neatly into concepts of ideas and notions, various particular ideas and notions, general ideas, and abstract general ideas. That every one of these is a concept it seems to me cannot be denied; the fact that Berkeley talks about these at all and regards this talk as consistent talk about consistent things implies that he employs concepts of as well as words about them.

I take it as established that Berkeley does not identify the concepts he employs in his philosophy with words, ideas, notions or even with general ideas and certainly not with abstract general ideas. Given his metaphysics – but this does not mean that his metaphysics legislates his theory of concepts – there is only one answer: that his concepts are mental entities other than ideas, notions, or spirits; that they are dependent on spirits, present in ideas and notions, yet not dissolved into them. Thus, to be a concept is to be conceived. Nevertheless, concepts are perceived or imagined no more than notions. As unorthodox as it sounds, what I submit is that Berkeley cannot explain his uses of the concepts he does employ without giving them a separate entry on his list of the furniture of the world.

There are then on my reading of Berkeley concepts in his philosophy. They are mental entities, along with ideas and notions. They are constituents of ideas and notions, and wholly dependent on their conceivers. That they are mental entities does not by itself explain his metaphysics of minds and their dependent entities, since other philosophers also subscribe to concepts as mental entities without maintaining an immaterialistic universe. It is rather that Berkeley builds into his concepts the principle that all their criteria must be not only empirical and verifiable but verified by sense or inner experience: by particular ideas or notions. This principle is his overall criterion for the intelligibility and acceptability of a concept. Therefore, for him, no concept whose criteria of use transcend the bounds of actual sensing or introspection is legitimate. It is this stringent empirical principle that is fundamental in his metaphysics of minds and their mental events; and that establishes the priority of his implicit theory of concepts in his philosophy. Only concepts that turn on the mental are acceptable. This doctrine rules out the concept of matter as a concept and at the same time reduces the concepts of mathematics and physics to concepts dependent on ideas of sensation, so that even the concept of a triangle is intelligible only in relation to actual triangles. *Esse est percipi* or *percipere*, thus, rests ultimately on Berkeley's theory of concepts as mental entities. These concepts are governed solely by criteria derived from sense and inner experience. That there is no matter or no notion of matter, thus, ultimately is an inference from his theory of concepts, not from his ontology. The latter also derives from his theory of concepts.

CHAPTER 11

Hume

Hume is as fond of paradoxes and dilemmas as he is wary of them. Some he formulates and demolishes; others he clarifies and embraces; one he neither states nor resolves. The latter is a set of contrary theses implicit in his philosophy: that there are no concepts, only ideas as copies of their antecedent impressions; that there are concepts, only one of which is that of an idea as a copy of an impression. Like Hume, who cannot renounce or reconcile his two contrary principles: *that all our distinct perceptions are distinct existences*, and *that the mind never perceives any real connexion among distinct existences*' (*A Treatise of Human Nature*, hereinafter *THN*, Appendix, p. 636 of Selby-Bigge one-volume edition; all references are to his edition of *THN* and of Hume's *Enquiry Concerning the Human Understanding*, hereinafter *E*), I find it difficult to deny either and impossible to render consistent both his implicit denial and implicit affirmation of concepts as independent of ideas. Hume begins his *Treatise* with the thesis that 'All the perceptions of the human mind resolve themselves into two distinct kinds, which I shall call IMPRESSIONS and IDEAS.' That impressions and ideas exhaust not only perceptions but the whole content of the human mind he states in Book I, Part II, section vi: '... nothing is ever really present with the mind but its perceptions or impressions and ideas...;' and in I, IV, ii: 'We never can conceive any thing but perceptions, and therefore must make every thing resemble them' (*THN*, pp. 67, 216).

Now, if we add to this Hume's revealing note in his section on belief (I, III, vi) that the traditional trichotomy of conception, judgment and reasoning as distinct acts of the understanding must be resolved into the one act of conception, to be contrasted not with

134

judgment and understanding but with belief, conception (if not concepts) takes on a major role in Hume's theory of the understanding:

> What we may in general affirm concerning these three acts of the understanding is, that taking them in a proper light, they all resolve themselves into the first, and are nothing but particular ways of conceiving our objects. Whether we consider a single object, or several; whether we dwell on these objects, or run from them to others; and in whatever form or order we survey them, the act of the mind exceeds not a simple conception; and the only remarkable difference, which occurs on this occasion is, when we join belief to the conception, and are persuaded of the truth of what we conceive (*THN*, p. 97).

Belief, Hume adds here, 'is only a strong and steady conception of any idea, and such as approaches in some measure to an immediate impression.'

These remarks add up to Hume's identification of thought with conception and conception with the having of ideas, where each conception originates in and is a copy of its impression. Concepts and the possession of them by the mind are simply not present or needed to explain knowledge or belief.

At the same time, it seems difficult to see how conception or varying conceptions can be identified and discriminated or, to borrow Hume's terminology, distinguished, differentiated and separated, without concepts. How can Hume distinguish between, say, a particular idea of x and a particular impression of x, without employing at least the concepts of idea and impression? He needs both concepts to sort perceptions and to proclaim ideas and impressions as the entire content of the mind. The concept of a perception, or of an idea, conception or impression cannot be a copy of an impression. My idea of red may be a copy of my impression of red; but my idea of my idea as distinct from my impression of red can scarcely be a copy of anything, let alone of an impression. 'There are only impressions and ideas in the human mind' may be a metaphysical truth of the highest order and not merely a conceptual or verbal truth. However, even if it is either, it must involve concepts that are not conceptions, perceptions, ideas, or impressions. Hume's implicit denial that there are concepts as distinct from conceptions, therefore, affirms as well that there are conceptions without concepts. The denial may be true, the affirmation must be false. This being so, the first cannot be true: there must be concepts distinct from conceptions.

Hume's theory of concepts or his denial of them, consequently his anti-theory, cannot be univocally elicited from his general theory of the understanding. It is as plausible to argue that he has an implicit theory of concepts as it is that he rejects concepts entirely and would castigate them as obfuscations of conceptions.

We must therefore turn elsewhere in Hume for his implicit theory or denial of concepts. A strong possibility is his theory of general ideas (I, I, vii). Hume follows Berkeley in his account, although he conflates general with abstract ideas and he proffers original theses of his own.

Hume's account turns on one dilemma, which he analyzes and demolishes; and on one paradox, which he clarifies and defends. The first yields the proposition that there are no concepts, the second, that there are. The dilemma Hume states concerns two contrary views of the nature of abstract ideas. Hume begins by affirming that there are abstract ideas: 'The abstract idea of a man represents men of all sizes and all qualities.' How this is done constitutes his own theory of abstract or general ideas. That it is done, as some philosophers hold, 'by representing at once all possible sizes and all possible qualities' or, as other philosophers claim, 'by representing no particular one at all' provides the dilemma. Both conceptions of abstract ideas, Hume argues, are absurd. The first implies an infinite capacity in the mind, which is an impossibility. The second implies that quantity and quality differ and are distinct from their particular degrees of quantity and quality, which they are not.

> ...*The mind cannot form any notion of quantity or quality without forming a precise notion of degrees of each*...The precise length of a line is not different nor distinguishable from the line itself, nor the precise degree of any quality from the quality. These ideas, therefore, admit no more of separation than they do of distinction and difference (*THN*, pp. 18–19).

Every idea or every idea of an object – which, Hume forever reminds us, is the same thing – is a particular. It is therefore absurd in fact, in reality, and in idea, he concludes, that we can form abstract ideas of no particularity.

Hume's attack on the traditional notions of an abstract idea includes more than a denial that there are generic or bare images. His central argument against the separability of that which cannot be conceived as distinct applies to concepts too. That there are concepts without their particular conceptions is on a par with there being lines without determinate degrees of quantity and quality. For Hume, I can have an idea of a line (or whatever). My idea, whether particular or general, is tied to my particular idea of a line. If my idea of a line is a particular conception of a line – as Hume says it is – I cannot claim that in having the conception I have the concept unless I mean them to be the same. My concept of a line (or whatever) is my idea or conception of a line with some degree of particularity or it is nothing.

Hume's paradox – '*that some ideas are particular in their nature, but general in their representation*' (*THN*, p. 22) – which he clarifies and defends, suggests a different approach to concepts: that there are concepts which consist in our abilities to conjure up particular images under appropriate verbal stimulation.

Every idea of an object, that is, every idea, Hume says, is a particular. Some particulars resemble each other in certain observable ways. We have a name or can name any of the particulars. Because of their ostensible similarities with other particulars, we 'apply the same name to all of them,' whatever their differences may be. This general application of a word that names a particular to its resembling particulars, Hume calls a custom. It serves to conjoin the hearing of a word with the imagining of a particular idea. 'The word raises up an individual idea, along with a certain custom; and that custom produces any other individual one, for which we may have occasion.' A particular idea, thus, becomes general not by separation and abstraction but 'by being annex'd to a general term; that is, to a term, which from a customary conjunction has a relation to many particular ideas, and readily recalls them in the imagination.'

Customs or established habits of joining names with particulars cannot serve as concepts in Hume. To have the general idea of a line or a man is not to have a habit of joining 'line' or 'man' to similar particulars; it is rather to be able to apply the word to any resembling particular we conjure up, which we could not do without custom. Custom, thus, is a necessary condition for having a general term; it is not identical with it. If for 'general term' we substitute 'concept,' Hume's theory of general ideas yields the view that a concept is the having of that concept which consists in being able, because of certain customs of joining certain words to certain things, to 'raise up an individual idea.' Thus, I have the concept of man when, having the habit of joining 'man' to particular men, I can, whenever I hear 'man,' imagine a particular man. My concept of man (or whatever) is an ability to create particular images when the corresponding word (or words) are uttered. Hume's is a dispositional theory of concepts; but concepts are abilities, not capacities. They are abilities to conceive or to have conceptions, not simply conceptions.

Even if we can attribute this dispositional theory of concepts to Hume, it still leaves us with particular ideas, both individual and resembling, with the sorting of ideas, and with customs or habits as lacking concepts. If I have a concept of man, why cannot I be said to have the concept of man when I see a man, recognize him, distinguish him from other animals, and so on? If concepts are abilities, they ought to accommodate particular as well as general ideas.

Hume employs many concepts in his philosophy, whether he calls them ideas or not. How does his implicit dispositional theory square with his use of these concepts? Are all of them abilities to respond to words by raising ideas? Is, for example, his concept of causation such an ability?

Hume's analysis of cause and effect or the relation of causation is as brilliant a piece of philosophical writing as any in the history of philosophy. Throughout his discussion, both in *A Treatise of Human Nature* (Book I, Part III) and *An Enquiry Concerning Human Understanding* (Sections iv–vii), Hume talks about the idea of causality and its corresponding impression or rather, because it is a complex idea, its corresponding impressions. Though he never mentions the concept of causality, our central question is whether it is nevertheless implicit, required in his analysis?

In the *Enquiry*, Hume divides all objects of human reason into relations among ideas and matters of fact. 'All reasonings concerning matter of fact seem to be founded on the relation of *Cause and Effect*' (*E*, p. 26). It is therefore fundamental in the natural and human sciences as well as in ordinary life.

In the *Treatise*, Hume first enumerates seven philosophical relations, divides them into those that depend on ideas alone and those that do not, and sets the stage by singling out the relation of causation as 'the only one, that can be trac'd beyond our senses, and informs us of existences and objects which we do not see or feel' (I, III, ii; *THN*, p. 74).

What, Hume begins, is the origin of the idea of causation? It is not in the qualities of objects 'since, which-ever of these qualities I pitch on, I find some object, that is not possessed of it, and yet falls under the denomination of cause or effect.' If not in qualities, then the idea 'must be deriv'd from some *relation* among objects.' Hume then lists contiguity and priority as two relations he finds 'essential to causes and effects.' He follows this with a crucial paragraph:

> Shall we then rest contented with these two relations of contiguity and succession, as affording a compleat idea of causation? By no means. An object may be contiguous and prior to another without being consider'd as its cause. There is a NECESSARY CONNEXION to be taken into consideration; and that relation is of much greater importance, than any of the other two above-mention'd.

Hume then says:

> Here again I turn the object on all sides, in order to discover the nature of this necessary connexion, and find the impression, or impressions, from which its idea may be deriv'd. When I cast my eye on the *known qualities* of objects, I immediately discover that the relation of cause and effect depends not in the least on *them*. When I consider their *relations*, I can find none but those of contiguity and succession...(*THN*, p. 77).

Hume then asks whether his idea of necessary connection has an antecedent impression, which he proposes to answer by first answering why we think it necessary that everything that begins has a cause and why we infer from certain causes to certain effects. In section iii, he demolishes the traditional assumption that 'Every event must have a cause' by showing that its denial cannot be self-contradictory. In section vi, he introduces a new relation, that of constant conjunction, which he finds also essential to cause and effect; it is this relation that explains why we infer certain causes from certain effects:

> We have no other notion of cause and effect, but that of
> certain objects, which have been *always conjoin'd* together,
> and which in all past instances have been found
> inseparable. We cannot penetrate into the reason of the
> conjunction. We only observe the thing itself, and always
> find that from the constant conjunction the objects acquire
> an union in the imagination (*THN*, p. 93).

In section xiv, Hume returns to the idea of necessity. What, then, is
its antecedent impression? It is nothing external; rather it is an
internal determination in the mind, produced by constant
conjunction:

> For after a frequent repetition, I find, that upon the
> appearance of one of the objects, the mind is *determin'd* by
> custom to consider its usual attendant, and to consider it in
> a stronger light upon account of its relation to the first
> object. 'Tis this impression, then, or *determination*, which
> affords me the idea of necessity (*THN*, p. 156).

If necessity or necessary connection is not this determination in the
mind, Hume says, there is no idea of it. Hume concludes his
discussion with two definitions of the relation of cause and effect,
one of which will suffice here: 'A CAUSE is an object precedent and
contiguous to another, and so united with it, that the idea of the one
determines the mind to form the idea of the other, and the impression
of the one to form a more lively idea of the other' (*THN*, p. 170).

Hume's analysis of causation is infinitely richer than my bald
summary and quotations suggest. But since I am not concerned with
the details of his analysis or even with the adequacy of his analysis,
the latter of which has been a major concern of philosophy since
Hume, I hope I have included enough detail to deal with the
questions that prompted this summary: Does Hume employ the
concept of causality as well as the idea of causality in his analysis
and, if he does, does it square with his implicit theory of concepts as
abilities to conjure up images under appropriate verbal stimulation?

For Hume, causality or the idea of causality (which, we recall, are
the same according to him) is a complex consisting of a number of
constituents: two or more objects or events; spatial contiguity among
these; temporal priority among them; constant conjunction; and
necessary connection. These, I believe, are necessary and sufficient

(for Hume), therefore, a definitive set of constituents of causality. Hume says his is an inquiry into the origins of the idea of causality. However, 'origins' covers more than the antecedent impressions from which the idea derives; it applies as well to the constituent ideas of the complex idea of causation. His search for the origins of the idea of causality is primarily a probing of the correct analysis of the complex idea of causality, without which he cannot go on to ask whether there are antecedent impression for *all* the constituent ideas of the complex idea of causality.

Hume says he 'finds' the constituent ideas of two or more objects or events, contiguity and priority, and constant conjunction; and that he 'discovers' their impressions in experience. It is interesting and, more important, important, that he does not say he finds the idea of necessary connection and he does say that he does 'not find' its impression. He does ask, in the case of each of the constituent ideas of causation, what is its corresponding impression? But it is only of the idea of necessary connection that he asks, Does it have a corresponding impression? Does not this addition or shift imply that Hume presupposes the idea of necessary connection as he does not the other constituent ideas which he finds and for which he discovers a corresponding impression?

Hume's insistence on necessary connection or its idea as a constituent, indeed, the most important constituent, of the idea of causality, strongly suggests that he does assume before he affirms and tries to verify this idea. His whole analysis of causation, as his equivocation on 'origins' reveals, is as much (if not primarily) conceptual as it is empirical. His crucial insistence on the necessity of necessary connection – 'There is a NECESSARY CONNEXION to be taken into consideration' (*THN*, p. 77) – clinches that Hume begins with the concept of causation and not simply with a complex idea of causation.

In inquiring into the origins of the idea of causation, Hume begins with the concept of causation. He states its components: two or more objects or events, contiguity and priority among them, and necessary connection. No idea – no conception – is adequate that adds to or subtracts from these components. He then tries to find impressions from which these are derived. On the way, he also rejects other putative constituents, such as external necessity or power, and refutes certain competing conceptions, such as that every event must have a cause. Hume does not therefore disagree with Descartes or Locke or

Aristotle on the concept of causality which is the concept of a necessary connection between two events or objects that are spatially contiguous and temporally asymmetrical. He disagrees with their conceptions of causality – that the necessity is logical or objective or that causality includes purpose (final cause). His idea – conception – which does justice to the concept as well as to his principle that every conception derives from and is traceable to sense-impressions, Hume implies throughout, is the only adequate one. Without the concept of causality, Hume can neither proclaim his idea of causality nor declaim the conceptions of others. His concept of causality, from which he derives the idea of necessary connection that he then tries to fix in an impression, is closer to Plato's *eidos* or Descartes' *conceptus* than it is to his *idea*. Hume denies that he or anyone else intuits that every event must have a cause; but I cannot see that he can both affirm the relation of necessary connection as an essential constituent of causality and deny that he intuits this since he does not find it in experience.

Well, now, if the concept of causality includes the concept of necessary connection, neither can be said to be an ability to generate images under the verbal stimulants 'causation' or 'necessary connection.' 'Causation' and 'necessary connection' may be general terms; but unlike 'line' or 'man,' any attempt to render these general abstract ideas, founded on resembling particulars, linguistic customs, and abilities to conjure up particular causal situations under the appropriate utterances, abandons both Hume and sense. Whatever Hume's concept and idea of causality may be, it cannot be a general idea which itself depends on the idea of causality as custom; nor does Hume ever hint that it is.

For Hume, at least as I understand his analysis of causality, he not only has the concept of causality as an entity of some non-perceptual kind, but that concept is closed: governed by necessary and sufficient criteria or properties. Causality is a hard-edged concept. On this point, Hume the empiricist is at one with Descartes the rationalist.

Hume's discussions of substance and mode, mind and matter, body and soul, self and person (in Book I of the *Treatise*) reveal the same ambivalence about there being and there not being ideas of them: there are no impressions of these, so there can be no ideas; there are ideas of them but these ideas must be construed as complex ones of collections of impressions.

This explicit ambivalence about these as ideas reflects a similar ambivalence about there being concepts of them: there are no ideas of them, so there are no concepts of them; their complex ideas as collections of impressions leave out something essential – 'the principle of union being regarded as the chief part of the complex idea' (I, I, vi; *THN*, p. 16) – which principle, though without an impression, is not meaningless as the principles of inhesion or substratum, also without buttressing impressions, are meaningless; so there is a concept, in the case of substance as a unity rather than as an assemblage of qualities. This 'uniting principle,' Hume says, is fundamental to substances but not to modes, though both are collections of impressions. Like necessary connection as fundamental to causation, the principle of unity points to a concept as distinct from an idea or conception; and to such a concept that can serve as the standard in the construction of an idea which can be derived from its antecedent impressions.

Hume hedges on the principle of unity in the idea of substance as a collection of impressions. That it is essential to that idea he affirms; but that it is other than a fiction he leaves unclear. This hedging disappears when he turns from substance in general to personal identity in particular, where Hume expresses his own dissatisfaction at his reconstruction of the idea of the self. Nowhere in Hume is it more apparent that his failure to distinguish between concept and conception plagues him. His reconstructed idea of the self, he acknowledges, does not do justice to the unity of the collections of perceptions we call 'myself,' even though, he is convinced, it does full justice to the attributed but false simplicity of the self. In the Appendix to the *Treatise*, Hume offers as bald a summary of his rich analysis of personal identity, especially in I, IV, vi, as I have given of his discussion of causality. His summary and confession of failure can suffice here to substantiate my thesis: that Hume needs and presupposes the concept of the self as a unity of perceptions in order both to reject the putative idea of a simple self and to reconstruct the idea of a complex self founded on impressions. (I do not claim that he presupposes the unity of the self in order to render intelligible the concept of the self; all I claim is that he presupposes the concept of the unity of the self in order to render intelligible the idea of the self. Whether he succeeds or not is not at issue; what it is is that Hume is no Kantian on this principle.)

Hume begins his summary and statement of impasse:

> When we talk of *self* or *substance*, we must have an idea annex'd to these terms, otherwise they are altogether unintelligible. Every idea is deriv'd from preceding impressions; and we have no impression of self or substance, as something simple and individual. We have, therefore, no idea of them in that sense (*THN*, p. 633).

He then turns to introspection:

> When I turn my reflexion on *myself*, I never can perceive this *self* without some one or more perceptions; nor can I ever perceive any thing but the perceptions. 'Tis the composition of these, therefore, which forms the self.

To reinforce this idea of the self, Hume asks us to consider the mind reduced to a minimum:

> Suppose the mind to be reduc'd even below the life of an oyster. Suppose it to have only one perception, as of thirst or hunger. Consider it in that situation. Do you conceive any thing but merely that perception? Have you any notion of *self* or *substance*? If not, the addition of other perceptions can never give you that notion.

The mind or self is a collection of perceptions; the notion of the mind or self is of these perceptions: '*we have no notion of it* [the mind], *distinct from the particular perceptions.*'

What, now, Hume asks, is 'the principle of connexion, which binds them together, and makes us attribute to them a real simplicity and identity'? We do not perceive connections; yet without them there can be no idea of the mind, the self, personal identity. Since we do not perceive connections and we need them as part of our idea of the mind, Hume, turning to inner determination that also serves in his account of necessary connection, offers his only alternative:

> It follows, therefore, that the thought alone finds personal identity, when reflecting on the train of past perceptions, that compose a mind, the ideas of them are felt to be connected together, and naturally introduce each other.

So far, so good, Hume says: '...Personal identity *arises* from consciousness; and consciousness is nothing but a reflected thought or perception.' Then, the shattering conclusion:

> The present philosophy, therefore, has so far a promising aspect. But all my hopes vanish, when I come to explain the principles, that unite our successive perceptions in our thought or consciousness. I cannot discover any theory, which gives me satisfaction on this head.

To discover such a theory, that would explain the unity of the mind, would be to find something simple and individual in which our perceptions inhere or to perceive real connections among our perceptions. For Hume, neither is forthcoming or possible. So, though he does not say it, he has no idea or notion of the mind: either of something simple or of something complex. All he has is an idea or a notion of an assemblage that is joined by an inclination to unite its members.

As his summary shows, Hume struggles with a dilemma he cannot resolve: that no theory of the self (or mind, personal identity, oneself) can be adequate without a principle of unity; and that no such theory can be adequate with such a principle. However – and this is my point – he cannot even state this dilemma without the concept of the self as a unity of perceptions. So the concept of the self cannot be the idea or notion of the self, but something distinct, meaningful, and a criterion of any adequate idea of the self: a criterion that Hume ensures cannot be satisfied since it conflicts with his other criterion of an antecedent impression for any adequate idea.

There are, then, at least two irreducible concepts in Hume – that of necessary connection and that of unity of perceptions – that are not conceptions or abstract general ideas in Hume's dispositional sense of them. That these concepts are entities follows from Hume's principle that what is distinct, hence separate, exists. That they are not entities, however, follows from Hume's other principle that only perceptions exist or, in its more modest version, that 'nothing is ever really present with the mind but its perceptions or impressions and ideas.' This dilemma perhaps can be resolved but only by returning to one of Hume's sources, the scepticism of Sextus Empiricus, according to which concepts are entities in the minimal sense of metaphysically neutral, irreducible intermediaries between words, thoughts and things; and, applied to Hume, indispensable and irreducible principles that are non-perceptual. On this view, that there are concepts, that concepts are entities amounts to no more but also no less that this: Concepts are not conceptions.

There are other concepts in Hume which also are not ideas or reducible to ideas, space and time, for instance: 'The ideas of space and time are therefore no separate or distinct ideas, but merely those of the manner or order, in which objects exist' (I, II, iv; *THN*, pp. 39–40). However legitimate or illegitimate Hume's 'manner or order' may be, given his theory of ideas, that Hume employs the concepts of space and time as distinct from either their non-existent ideas or existent manner, is plain enough from his discussion in Part II of Book I: 'Of the Ideas of Space and Time.'

There are also the many moral, religious and emotional concepts Hume employs in his various writings. Each of these, as well as his concepts of belief, imagination, existence, and human nature, deserved detailed consideration. However, perhaps I have said enough to substantiate my claim that Hume has a theory of concepts, to be elicited from the concepts he employs, and that this theory – ambivalent and diversified as it is – is basic in Hume's philosophy. Or, because I remain uneasy about the initial dilemma I posed in Hume that either there are only ideas, so there are no concepts or there are concepts, so they are not ideas, perhaps I should claim rather that Hume's theory of ideas is basic in his philosophy, a claim universally accepted. However, if that claim stands, as I have tried to show, it implies there are no concepts in Hume, which is false; or it is not true because ideas rest on concepts as much as they do on impressions. Again, in either case, Hume's implicit theory of concepts is basic.

CHAPTER 12

Kant

Kant's theory of concepts is as remarkable a piece of work as any of his great philosophical achievements. Whatever the details of the influences upon him may be, which include the ancients as well as his immediate predecessors, he articulates an explicit theory of concepts – of their nature and role – that, like Leibniz, makes it central in his philosophy but without rendering concepts ontologically basic. Kant, unlike Locke, Berkeley and Hume, reveals concepts to be a class of their ideas or anyhow implied by them without his reducing them to mental entities. In this connection, how apt and refreshing it is that Kant unabashedly refers to Hume's concept (*Begriff*), not his idea (*Idee*) of causality, in order to show that Hume seeks the origin of that concept in the wrong place (Introduction to the *Prolegomena*). Thus, it does not bother Kant – as it bothered me in my account – that Hume never talks of the concept of causality (or of any other concept). Whether Hume does or not, Kant rightly insists, Hume's problem concerns the origins of that *concept*. Here Kant's shift from talk about an idea to talk about a concept and his earlier rejection of 'idea' as a term for sensation resolve the traditional ambiguities invested in 'ideas' by destroying the whole theory of ideas as expressed by Locke, Berkeley and Hume, and even in part by Descartes and Leibniz. In a crucial terminological passage in *The Critique of Pure Reason* (A 320/B 377), Kant sums up the relations among 'ideas,' 'sensation,' and 'concept,' among other terms:

> The genus is *representation* in general (*repraesentatio*)
> [*Vorstellung überhaupt*]. Subordinate to it stands
> representation with consciousness (*perceptio*). A *perception*
> which relates solely to the subject as the modification of its

state is *sensation* (*sensatio*), an objective perception is *knowledge* (*cognitio*). This is either *intuition* or *concept* (*intuitus vel conceptus*). The former relates immediately to the object and is single, the latter refers to it mediately by means of a feature which several things may have in common. The concept is either an *empirical* or a *pure concept*. The pure concept, in so far as it has its origin in the understanding alone (not in the pure image of sensibility) is called a *notion*. A concept formed from notions and transcending the possibility of experience is an *idea* or concept of reason. Anyone who has familiarised himself with these distinctions must find it intolerable to hear the representation of the colour, red, called an idea. It ought not even to be called a concept of understanding, a notion (tr. N. Kemp Smith; all English references are to his edition and translation of the *Kritik der Reinen Vernunft*).

Kant is not simply legislating meanings of terms here; he is also tying distinct terms with their putatively original meanings to real distinctions among representations. For him, it is the distinctions that matter, not their names, though their names must not blur these distinctions nor evoke distinctions where there are none.

A related linguistic fact is that Kant uses '*Begriff*' consistently for concept throughout. '*Begriff*' names concept and nothing else: neither conception nor thought. This stringency regarding the reference of the word '*Begriff*', however, Kant couples with a bounty of uses of the word. For example, there is scarcely a page of his most important work, *The Critique of Pure Reason*, which does not contain the word. '*Begriff*' is one of his key words. But, more important, *Begriffe* are among his avowed important and key philosophical (transcendental) elements. Kant recognizes the concept of a concept and concepts of much, perhaps everything, else. Whatever their nature may be, they are as populous as anything else in his world. Moreover, Kant enumerates and distinguishes among various kinds of concepts: empirical, *a priori*, synthetic *a priori*, discursive, and problematic as well as forms of intuition, ideas and ideals. Each of these is a concept according to Kant, though of course, as he stresses, space and time – the forms of intuition – or the thing-in-itself or God are not concepts like the concepts, say, of substance or cause. Further, Kant extends the role of concepts by establishing their omnipresence in perception or sense-experience: 'intuitions without concepts are blind' (B 75/A 51).

Kant distinguishes between knowledge and thought and within knowledge between sensibility and understanding. All involve concepts. In sensibility, the matter of sensation is ordered by the forms of intuition, space and time, which are non-discursive concepts. In understanding, the intuitions yielded by sensibility are organized by categories that are *a priori* concepts, with the concept (but not the category) of the I or the transcendental unity of apperception being basic. In pure thought, there are concepts that are consistent but with no intuitions or possible intuitions to render them experiential. They are therefore empty, transcendent concepts, serviceable as regulative but not as constitutive principles of experience.

Kant states as his major problem in *The Critique of Pure Reason*: How much can reason and understanding know apart from experience (A xiv, xvii)? His answer, roughly, is: Nothing. However, since experience is sensibility or intuition and understanding, and reason is none of these, knowledge as experience – as sensibility and understanding – is possible. How, Kant asks, is it possible? Most of the *Critique*, especially the 'Transcendental Aesthetic' and the 'Transcendental Analytic,' supplies the answer. Part of that answer – of direct concern to Kant's theory of concepts – is that knowledge or experience is possible because it contains as 'the objects of pure understanding' *a priori* concepts.

That concepts are objects (*Gegenstände*) of the understanding is further enforced in the Preface to the Second Edition. The first man to demonstrate the properties of the isosceles triangle, Kant says, did more than inspect a figure or its concept; rather than 'read off' the properties from the concept, he brought out

> what was necessarily implied in the concepts that he had
> himself formed *a priori*, and had put into the figure in the
> construction by which he presented it to himself. If he is to
> know anything with *a priori* certainty he must not ascribe
> to the figure anything save what necessarily follows from
> what he has himself set into it in accordance with his
> concept (B xii).

That concepts are not objects but rules also is expressed in this Preface:

For experience is itself a species of knowledge which
involves understanding; and understanding has rules which I
must presuppose as being in me prior to objects being
given to me, and therefore as being *a priori*. They find
expression in *a priori* concepts to which all objects of
experience necessarily conform, and with which they must
agree (B xvii–xviii).

Kant also states his principle of intelligibility for concepts of the
understanding: 'We have no concepts of understanding, and
consequently no elements for the knowledge of things, save in so far
as intuition can be given corresponding to these concepts' (B xxvi).
Strawson construes this as a principle of significance for all concepts
in Kant: '... There can be no legitimate, or even meaningful,
employment of ideas or concepts which does not relate them to
empirical or experiential conditions of their application.'[1]

Although Strawson supports this reading by quotations as well as
by sustained analysis, it conflicts with Kant's distinction between
knowledge and thought since in thought we may think concepts
without intuitions so long as they are consistent. Kant's principle of
significance, primarily a criterion of the concepts of the
understanding, thus, is Kant's effort at establishing the grounds (*die
Gründe*), not the bounds, of sense.

Kant distinguishes between pure, *a priori* knowledge and
empirical, *a posteriori* knowledge. All knowledge begins with
experience but some arises from the understanding alone. This latter
is *a priori* and is 'knowledge absolutely independent of all experience'
(B 3). Such knowledge is both necessary and universal. Both
judgments, such as 'every alteration must have a cause,' and
concepts, such as that of substance, are *a priori*. Judgments but not
concepts can be analytic when their predicates explicate their
subjects; they are synthetic when the relation of the predicates to
their subjects is ampliative. Among the synthetic judgments are those
that are *a priori* as well. 'Everything which happens has its cause'
contains two concepts that are related synthetically yet necessarily
and universally. 'Upon such synthetic, that is, ampliative principles,
all our *a priori* speculative knowledge must ultimately rest' (A 10/B
13).

All mathematical judgments are synthetic and *a priori*. For
example, '7+5=12' presents us with the concept of the sum of 7+5

and the concept of 12. The first does not contain the second: 'The concept of 12 is by no means already thought in merely thinking this union of 7 and 5; and I may analyse my concept of such a possible sum as long as I please, still I shall never find the 12 in it' (B 15). To determine the sum we must needs secure an intuition.

That Kant wavers between logical and psychological criteria of the synthetic *a priori* in establishing '7+5=12' as synthetic *a priori* – a criticism often made – is true enough; but this criticism does not detract from the fact that for Kant, at least here, concepts, such as the sum of 7 and 5, are inspectable entities, hardly rules or dispositions manifestable in abilities.

Geometry, too, consists of synthetic *a priori* judgments that relate concepts as entities. 'The straight line between two points is the shortest' is Kant's example. 'For my concept of *straight* contains nothing of quantity, but only of quality. The concept of the shortest is wholly an addition, and cannot be derived, through any process of analysis, from the concept of the straight line' (B 16).

Physics, too, contains synthetic *a priori* judgments. Kant cites two: the quantity of matter remains unchanged in all material change; and action and reaction must always be equal in all communication of motion. These are synthetic *a priori*:

> For in the concept of matter I do not think its
> permanence, but only its presence in the space which it
> occupies. I go outside and beyond the concept of matter,
> joining to it *a priori* in thought something which I have not
> thought *in* it (B 18).

Metaphysics also rests on synthetic *a priori* judgments, both in intention and in deed, if it is to become knowledge. Whether its results match its intention and obligation is one of Kant's central concerns in the *Critique*.

Kant thus transforms his query, How is knowledge possible? into How are synthetic *a priori* judgments possible? Central in the last question is the nature and role of *a priori* concepts, concepts that anticipate and do not derive from experience.

Kant's whole programme in *The Critique of Pure Reason* is to validate knowledge or science and, by the principles involved in this validation, to invalidate metaphysics. The details and structure of this programme, fortunately expounded and commented on by a voluminous literature, we must forego discussing here, in order to keep within bounds Kant's contributions to the history of philosophical theories of concepts. That his programme rests on a theory of concepts no one makes clearer than he does. And there is no reason to debate this. That concepts play diverse roles in Kant's *Critique* also is not subject to interesting debate. What is of concern (and what Kant does not make clear) is the nature of the concept as he employs the term and as he employs the concepts that he does in his work. Are concepts entities or are they, as one aspect of Kant's revolution in philosophy, dispositions or rules and abilities? There is conflicting textual and doctrinal evidence.

In the 'Transcendental Aesthetic,' Kant analyzes intuition or, if we may impose on him as he does on Hume, he analyzes the concept of intuition. Whether this concept is *a priori* or not, Kant does not say. What he does say – and that not too clearly – is that intuition is a mode of knowledge whose object is immediately given. Intuition involves sensation, through sensibility, which corresponds to the matter of an appearance; and concepts that arise in understanding, that correspond to the form of appearance. These concepts Kant calls 'the forms of intuition:' space and time. By 'transcendental aesthetic' he means 'the science of all principles of *a priori* sensibility' (A 21/B 35), when these principles are abstracted from a sensibility isolated from the understanding.

He proceeds to show that a metaphysical exposition of these concepts reveals them to be non-empirical, non-abstractive and non-discursive, albeit *a priori*, forms without which the temporal and spatial cannot be experienced. Perhaps space and time are not concepts at all, he suggests, and even makes explicit with regard to space:

> Now every concept must be thought as a representation which is contained in an infinite number of different possible representations (as their common character), and which therefore contains these *under* itself; but no concept, as such, can be thought as containing an infinite number of representations *within* itself. It is in this latter way, however, that space is thought; for all the parts of space coexist *ad infinitum*. Consequently, the original representation of space is an *a priori* intuition, not a concept (B 40).

The great difference between space and time is that the first is the *a priori* condition of outer intuition, while the second, the condition of all appearance, outer and inner. Both space and time are forms of our sensible knowledge (*sinnlichen Erkenntnis*), with sensation as its matter; they are not relations among objects, either as appearance or things in themselves. That sensibility or appearance is but confused representation – a view Kant attributes to Leibniz – is itself a false conception of the concepts of sensibility and appearance. Hence, space and time are not the only concepts introduced in the 'Transcendental Aesthetic.' He also refers to the concepts of sensibility and appearance (A 43/B 61) as well, of course, by implication, to the concept of intuition. All five must come into any adequate account of Kant's theory of concepts. Kant concludes the 'Transcendental Aesthetic:'

> When in *a priori* judgment we seek to go out beyond the given concept, we come in the *a priori* intuitions upon that which cannot be discovered in the concept but is certainly found *a priori* in the intuition corresponding to the concept, and can be connected with it synthetically (B 73).

In the 'Transcendental Logic,' Kant distinguishes between sensibility as the mind's power of receiving representations and understanding as the mind's power of producing representations. Without sensibility, no object would be given; without understanding, no object would be thought. But without both, thought is empty and intuition blind; concepts must be made sensible, intuitions, intelligible. Nevertheless, Kant allows, concepts can be non-sensible, whereas intuitions cannot be non-conceptual. Thus, although knowledge depends on the union of intuition and concept, these latter two do not entail each other.

Logic deals with the understanding as Aesthetic deals with sensibility. Transcendental logic, as against general logic, either applied or pure, concerned with both empirical and pure knowledge of reason, deals 'with the laws of understanding and of reason solely in so far as they relate *a priori* to objects' (B 82). It includes transcendental analytic, which sets forth and proves 'the principles without which no object can be thought' (A 62); and transcendental dialectic, which clarifies and exposes transcendental illusion (A 295/B 352).

Knowledge is a union of intelligible intuitions. Both intuition and understanding, however, are modes of knowledge. Intuitions rest on affections, concepts, on functions. 'By "function" I mean the unity of the act of bringing various representations under one common representation...Now the only use which the understanding can make of these concepts is to judge by means of them' (B 93). Here Kant ties concepts to their use; but he neither affirms nor implies that there is no difference between a concept and the use of a concept or that having a concept is the ability to use it to make judgments. Rather the intimation is that there is a distinction between a concept and its use – its 'function' – and between the having of that concept and being able to make a judgment by means of it. Judgment may be an ability to Kant, the ability to represent objects mediately; but the concepts it employs to do so need not be abilities or rules. Kant's example in this passage does not support any identification of concept with the having of it or of its possession with an ability to use it to judge:

> Thus in the judgment, 'all bodies are divisible', the
> concept of the divisible applies to various other concepts,
> but is here applied in particular to the concept of body,
> and this concept again to certain appearances that present
> themselves to us. These objects, therefore, are mediately
> represented through the concept of divisibility (B 93).

In his 'Table of Categories,' that he derives from but fortunately does not prove by his 'Table of Judgments,' Kant lists a dozen 'original pure concepts of synthesis that the understanding contains within itself *a priori*' (B 106). Without these there can be no understanding of the manifold of intuition, no thinking an object of intuition. That they are purely *a priori* in their employment, like the concepts of rights and claims, requires a deduction since they relate to objects without being induced from them. 'The explanation of the manner in which concepts can thus relate *a priori* to objects I entitle their transcendental deduction' (A 85).

How do these categories differ from the concepts of space and time which also relate to objects in an *a priori* manner? Unlike space and time which as forms of intuition contain *a priori* the condition of the possibility of objects as appearances, the categories 'do not represent the conditions under which objects are given in intuition' (B 122).

How then, Kant asks, can subjective conditions of thought have objective validity? Only through concepts:

> Concepts of objects in general thus underlie all empirical knowledge as its *a priori* conditions. The objective validity of the categories as *a priori* concepts rests, therefore, on the fact that, so far as the form of thought is concerned, through them alone does experience become possible (B 126).

The categories, thus, are necessary conditions not only of experience in general but of our knowledge of any object of experience whatever.

Kant distinguishes between the unfolding of these categories in experience and their deduction. Their unfolding may reveal their universal presence in experience but does not prove their *a priori* necessity, without which there is no objective validity of concepts. Kant offers two versions of the deduction: in the first edition of the *Critique* and in the second. In the first, he examines the subjective sources of this *a priori* foundation of experience. Knowledge, he begins, is a whole in which representations are compared and connected. This whole or synopsis, grounded in the spontaneity of the mind rather than in its receptivity, constitutes a threefold synthesis of knowledge, necessary to it: 'namely, the *apprehension* of representations as modifications of the mind in intuition, their *reproduction* in imagination, and their *recognition* in a concept' (A 97). All representations, being modifications of the mind, belong to inner sense, consequently, are subject to time, the formal condition of inner sense. Intuitions as representations are not only subject to time but are unified in time; otherwise we have a manifold of succession, not unity. The manifold 'must be run through and held together.' This act Kant calls 'the *synthesis of apprehension*.' Without it and its corresponding *a priori* concept, there could be representations and intuitions but no unified representations and intuitions, hence no manifold.

Experience also presupposes reproducibility of appearances. If, for example, I draw a line in thought, I must apprehend the first part when I draw the second, and so on, if I am to complete the line. I reproduce the preceding representations by imagination; and because this act of reproduction is not derived from experience but rather anticipates experience, the concept of the reproductive synthesis of

155

the imagination (inseparably bound with the concept of the synthesis of apprehension), involved as it is in a transcendental act, must be *a priori*.

Reproduction of representations without consciousness that what we think is the same as what we reproduce also forecloses on any unity of the manifold. The concept of an object rests on this unity of consciousness that Kant declares to be the fundamental condition of experience:

> There can be in us no modes of knowledge, no connection or unity of one mode of knowledge with another, without that unity of consciousness which precedes all data of intuitions, and by relation to which representation of objects is alone possible. This pure original unchangeable consciousness I shall name *transcendental apperception*. That it deserves this name is clear from the fact that even the purest objective unity, namely, that of the *a priori* concepts (space and time), is only possible through relation of the intuitions to such unity of consciousness. The numerical unity of this apperception is thus the *a priori* ground of all concepts, just as the manifoldness of space and time is the *a priori* ground of the intuitions of sensibility (A 108).

The categories Kant moves in are the *a priori* conditions of thought. 'They are fundamental concepts by which we think objects in general for appearances, and have therefore *a priori* validity' (A 111). These concepts are not empirical and they have no application to things in themselves. They apply only to appearances to which they bring a necessary unity that makes them knowledge of objects.

In the second edition, Kant begins with the act of synthesis, the combining of representations:

> But the concept of combination includes, besides the concept of the manifold and of its synthesis, also the concept of the unity of the manifold. Combination is representation of the *synthetic* unity of the manifold. The representation of this unity cannot, therefore, arise out of the combination. On the contrary, it is what, by adding itself to the representation of the manifold, first makes possible the concept of the combination. This unity, which precedes *a priori* all concepts of combination, is not the

category of unity...; for all categories are grounded in
logical functions of judgment, and in these functions
combination, and therefore unity of given concepts, is
already thought. Thus the category already presupposes
combination. We must therefore look yet higher for this
unity, namely in that which itself contains the ground of
the unity of diverse concepts in judgment, and therefore of
the possibility of the understanding, even as regards its
logical employment (B 130–131).

This, surely, is one of the most important passages in the *Critique*.
Its relevance to Kant's theory of concepts – their nature as well as
their role – is as profound as its relevance to his transcendental
philosophy. That some concepts entail each other; that they are
necessary conditions, presuppositions, of experience and knowledge;
that they constitute a hierarchy in which some presuppose rather
than entail others – each of these is declared. But that concepts are
rules rather than that rules derived from them govern their
application, for example, that the concept of combination is itself a
rule or ability in the way that combining is, is not affirmed, implied,
or even intimated. The possibility that the concept, for example, of
combination as an object of thought, remains.

Unity presupposes combination. What does combination
presuppose if not a synthetic unity of self-consciousness: the
transcendental – not transcendent or empirical – I that Kant calls 'the
original synthesis of apperception'? It generates the representation 'I
think' that can accompany all other representations and which
makes these *my* representations. Thus, the identity of self-
consciousness – 'the analytic unity of apperception' – presupposes its
synthetic unity which is prior and from which it is derived. Because it
is basic to all representations, that is, all intuitions and all thoughts,
'the principle of apperception is the highest principle in the whole
sphere of human knowledge' (B 135). From which it follows that the
concept of self-consciousness is supreme in Kant's philosophy.

The categories, Kant also says, 'are merely rules (*nur Regeln*) for an
understanding whose whole power consists in thought, consists, that
is, in the act whereby it brings the synthesis of a manifold, given to it
from elsewhere in intuition, to the unity of apperception' (B 145).
They are therefore concepts that function in knowledge of objects
and do not, as other concepts, function only in thoughts of objects.

Consequently, they have application only to that which may be objects of possible experience. *'There can be no* a priori *knowledge, except of objects of possible experience'* (B 166).

The categories are rules. They rest on the principle of self-consciousness, therefore, on the concept of the transcendental I or self. Are all concepts rules, if the categories (which are also concepts) are rules? Kant says that the categories 'prescribe laws *a priori* to appearances' (B 163). Are they then laws, not mere rules? If the principle and the concept of the synthetic unity of apperception underwrite the categories, concepts and intuitions, are they also rules? Or are the categories and concepts objects that can serve in thought and understanding and intuition as universal rules which because they are necessary to any and all experience are *a priori* laws that govern knowledge of objects as appearances? Each of these questions is as difficult to answer as the others in Kant. Only one thing seems clear from Kant's discussion and deduction of the categories: that they affirm or imply that concepts are rules, and the having of them involves a set of abilities not unequivocal. That they are concepts whose conditions of significance depend on their application to intuitions is not yet inconsistent with concepts being entities as objects of understanding.

Kant next deals with the schematism of the pure concepts of understanding. Does the schematism throw additional light on the nature and role of concepts in Kant? The problem of the schematism is this: concepts must be homogeneous with the objects they subsume. But pure concepts or categories do not meet this criterion. Causality, for example, cannot be intuited nor can it be an object of appearance. 'How, then, is the *subsumption* of intuitions under pure concepts, the *application* of a category to appearances, possible' (B 177/A 138)? Only through a transcendental schema: a mediating representation that has no empirical content, yet is homogeneous with the category and with the appearance.

Time, because it is a necessary condition of the synthetic unity of both concepts of the understanding and manifolds of intuition, serves in its homogeneity to mediate the subsumption of appearances under the categories. Thus, both intuitions and concepts contain formal conditions of sensibility. 'This formal and pure condition of sensibility to which the employment of the concept of understanding is restricted, we shall entitle the *schema* of the concept' (A 140).

Schemas, though produced by imagination, are not images: I can have an image of the number five but not of one thousand. Here I have a thought representing a method whereby the multiplicity of a thousand may be represented in an image in conformity with my concept of one thousand. We have schemata, not images, that underlie our pure sensible concepts. I have the concept of a triangle. It applies universally to all triangles. There is no image of all triangles, only the schema, as 'a rule of synthesis of the imagination, in respect to pure figures in space' (A 141). Even our empirical concepts relate to schemas, not images:

> The concept 'dog' signifies a rule according to which my imagination can delineate the figure of a four-footed animal in a general manner, without limitation to any single determinate figure such as experience, or any possible image that I can represent *in concreto*, actually presents (A 141).

Here Kant distinguishes pure sensible concepts, such as that of a triangle, and empirical concepts, such as that of a dog, among all concepts. Both involve schemata – rules of synthesis and of delineation. These schemas, let us grant, are rules. Does it follow that the concepts for which they are schemas, are rules? Kant says the concept dog signifies (*bedeutet*) a rule, not that it is a rule. Nor does he say or imply that having the empirical concept of a dog is the same as being able to delineate the figure of a four-footed animal in a general manner. Having this ability is required if the concept of a dog is to have application to dogs; if the concept is to be mediated and rendered homogeneous with its objects. What is striking, therefore, is not that Kant construes at least these concepts as rules but that he allows that there can be such empirical and purely sensible concepts at all, that is, concepts that are not *a priori*, as these are not for him.[2]

'The schemata are thus nothing but *a priori* determinations of time in accordance with rules' (A 145). Are schemata concepts as well as exercises of rules? Kant says 'the schema is, properly, only the phenomenon, or sensible concept, of an object in agreement with a category' (B 186). But he does not identify schemas with all concepts, certainly not with the pure concepts of understanding, which require schemas for their significance. The pure concepts of the understanding, Kant concludes, remain concepts with their meanings without corresponding schemas or application. What they lack is a use, not a nature. Kant's schematism, thus, furthers our understanding of the role of concepts in his philosophy; but it adds nothing to the synthesis of manifold uncertainty regarding the nature of the concept.

Having argued for the deduction of the categories and their mediating schemas, Kant turns to the actual judgments the understanding achieves *a priori*. The Table of Categories, derived from his Table of Judgments, serves as his guide in the construction of these judgments that he calls principles and which are rules for the objective employment of the categories. These principles are: the axioms of intuition, anticipations of perception, analogies of experience, and postulates of empirical thought in general.

Kant has already shown that intuitions are ordered by space and time and that consciousness of their synthetic unity is a condition of intuitions as representations of objects. In the Axioms of Intuition, he adds that these intuitions are all extensive magnitudes, made possible by the *a priori* concept of a magnitude. With this concept I can represent extensive magnitudes, that is, wholes whose parts precede them. 'All intuitions are extensive magnitudes' is thus synthetic *a priori* and, as such, can validate the application of pure mathematics to objects of experience, in the same *a priori* manner in which the transcendental aesthetic validates pure mathematics.

The principle of the Anticipations of Perception, 'in all appearances, the real that is an object of sensation has intensive magnitude, that is, a degree' (B 208), enables us to go beyond the empirical assertions about our sense impressions by anticipating further impressions that may or may not occur but whose anticipation renders the principle that every object of sensation has a certain degree synthetic and *a priori*.

The principle of the Analogies of Experience is: 'Experience is possible only through the representation of a necessary connection of perceptions' (B 218). Kant offers a proof of this principle: Duration, succession and coexistence are the three modes of time. These are possible because all relations of appearances in time are ordered by three corresponding rules which are prior to experience. The rules, as he has already showed, rest on the necessary synthetic unity of apperception in time. By an analogy of experience Kant means 'a rule according to which a unity of experience may arise from perception' (A 180). There are three such analogies. The first is the synthetic *a priori* rule that substance is permanent in all change of appearances. Time as the permanent form of inner intuition is thus a substratum; only through it can co-existence or succession be represented. But time cannot be perceived; hence, if time is to be represented, only objects of perception can do this. 'But the substratum of all that is real, that is, of all that belongs to existence of things is *substance*' (B 225). Substance, therefore, is a necessary condition of our experience of all time-relations: coexistence, succession and duration. And because our experiences of these time-relations also presuppose the principle of synthetic unity of apperceptions, substance is the condition of all experience. 'All existence and all change in time have thus to be viewed as simply a mode of the existence of that which remains and persists' (B 227). 'In all change substance is permanent, accidents are not' is synthetic, Kant says, but it is where 'it is very seldom placed, where it truly belongs, at the head of those laws of nature which are pure and completely *a priori*' (A 184).

The first analogy argues that substance is permanent in all change (alteration). Kant calls it a rule. Does it follows that the concept of substance or of alteration is also a rule? It does not seem to me that it follows; all that follows is that the concept of substance and its derivative, alteration, are employed in rules which, because they legislate for possible experiences, are *a priori* and which, because they are found in experience, are synthetic. That the category of substance is a rule simply does not follow from its being employed in the formulation and practice of rules, however binding.

The second analogy argues: 'All alterations take place in conformity with the law of the connection of cause and effect' (B 234). What does this important analogy reveal about the concept of causation, that Hume calls an idea and Kant a category? Like Hume, Kant begins with the manifold of appearances – their objects, not things in themselves. All we apprehend is succession. I apprehend a house (the appearance). Its manifold as I apprehend it is successive; but its manifold is not. How, then, can the manifold contain a connection, which it must contain if it is to be an object of appearance? Only by distinguishing successive apprehension as representation from appearance (though no more than the sum of representations) as an object. But to do this, the appearance must stand 'under a rule which distinguishes it from every other apprehension and necessitates some one particular mode of connection of the manifold. The object is *that* in the appearance which contains the condition of this necessary rule of apprehension' (A 191).

My perception of a house, like my perception of a ship moving down stream, is a synthesis of apprehensions. Both involve a necessary rule of apprehension. But the perception of the ship at sea involves more, for here there are events that precede and succeed each other. This order of the perceptions is determined. Thus, 'in the perception of an event there is always a rule that makes the order in which the perceptions (in the apprehension of this appearance) follow upon one another a *necessary* order' (A 193). Subjective succession of apprehension, therefore, must derive from objective succession of appearances. And this 'objective succession will therefore consist in that order of the manifold of appearance according to which, *in conformity with a rule*, the apprehension of that which happens follows upon the apprehension of that which precedes' (A 193). This rule entails that 'there must lie in that which precedes an event the condition of a rule according to which this event invariably and necessarily follows' (B 239).

I am not concerned with whether Kant proves 'all changes take place in conformity with the law of the connection of cause and effect' (B 232) or 'Everything which happens (begins to happen) presupposes something which it follows in accordance with a rule' (A 189); or with whether Kant refutes Hume, as he thinks he does. My concern is only whether his principle of causality, as he articulates it in this analogy, and which is an *a priori* rule about necessary order, entails that the concept or category of causality is a rule as well? Of course, the concept of causality is a concept of a rule (better, a law) among events: that they are necessarily connected. But the concept of causality need not be itself a rule, any more than the concept of a rule need be a rule. The view that the category of causality *is* a rule, rather than that it is *of* a rule, is not warranted. Indeed, all the categories, rather than being rules, are rules of combination under the presupposition of self-consciousness and its concept of self-consciousness which is not itself a rule. These categories yield rules; but this does not foreclose on the categories being objects, therefore entities, of the understanding.

The third analogy argues: 'All substances, in so far as they can be perceived to coexist in space, are in thoroughgoing reciprocity' (B 257). Coexistence of appearances of substances presupposes more than their mere existences. For A and B to coexist, there must be something causally determining in each that gives it its position in time: 'the substances must stand, immediately or mediately, in dynamical community, if their coexistence is to be known in any possible experience' (A 213). This, too, yields a synthetic *a priori* truth about a category.

Nature is the connection of appearances according to necessary laws that are *a priori*. 'Taken together, the analogies thus declare that all appearances lie, and must lie, in *one* nature, because without this *a priori* unity no unity of experience, and therefore no determination of objects in it, would be possible' (A 216/B 263).

'The Postulates of Empirical Thought' explicates the concepts of the possible, actual and necessary. Kant distinguishes between an empirical concept – one derived from experience; a pure concept – one on which experience in general in its formal aspect rests; and a synthetic *a priori* concept – one that is presupposed by empirical knowledge of objects. The possible, Kant says, must be non-contradictory and intuitable: 'That which agrees with the formal conditions of experience, that is, with the conditions of intuition and of concepts, is *possible*' (B 266). Fictitious concepts, such as the concept of a special ultimate mental power of intuitively anticipating the future, though not self-contradictory, are not possible since they are groundless.

Kant distinguishes sharply between the concept of a thing and its existence: the possible and the actual. 'For that the concept precedes the perception signifies the concept's mere possibility; the perception which supplies the content to the concept is the sole mark of actuality' (B 273). When we know the existence of a thing prior to perceiving it, what we know of it is bound up with actual perceptions connected by the analysis of experience: we have *a priori*, not empirical, knowledge.

Necessity, the third postulate, concerns material, not formal necessity: 'The necessity of existence can never be known from concepts, but always only from connection with that which is perceived, in accordance with universal laws of experience' (A 227). Necessity depends on causality; consequently only states of substances can be necessary. 'We thus know the necessity only of those *effects* in nature the causes of which are given to us' (B 280). Since necessity applies only to effects that are not yet given, necessity pertains only to possible experience. However, according to the second analogy, all that is actual is necessary; so Kant's third postulate must be only a partial account of the concept of necessity, as it pertains to inferences from given causes and effects and as it pertains to a present cause to a future effect as necessary. For Kant's final thesis is that everything that happens – causes and effects – are actual and necessary and, as such, possible.

The postulates, thus, deal with modal concepts. Kant shows how these postulates relate to knowledge. They may be rules, though Kant does not say they are. But that the concepts involved in the postulates – of the possible, the actual and the necessary – are rules or that the having of these concepts are abilities rather than objects of the understanding seems more suspect than the attribution of a dispositional theory of concepts does elsewhere. At the end of his discussion of the third postulate Kant seems to clinch the distinction between a concept and a rule in his remarks on the concept of absolute possibility:

> But as a matter of fact absolute possibility, that which is in all respects valid, is no mere concept of understanding, and can never be employed empirically. It belongs exclusively to reason, which transcends all possible empirical employment of the understanding (B 285).

The concept of absolute possibility leads naturally to the Transcendental Dialectic. However, Kant adds an intervening discussion of the distinction between phenomena and noumena which, while summative of his theory of the understanding, enlarges his theory of concepts to include the problematic or limiting concept of the noumenon. The problem that introduces this concept is this: The concepts and principles of the understanding can be employed only in an empirical manner. Without an object to which it applies, a concept lacks content, indeed 'it has no meaning (*keinen Sinn*).' This is true of all concepts and all principles that embody them; they must relate to intuitions if they are to be more than mere logical forms of concepts. The most, then, 'the understanding can achieve *a priori* is to anticipate the form of a possible experience in general' (B 303). The categories, however, unlike the forms of intuition, are not grounded in sensibility. This gives rise to the illusion that they can be extended beyond intuitions. Now, if we call the sensible objects of the intuition *cum* understanding 'phenomena,' thus distinguishing

> the mode in which we intuit them from the nature that belongs to them in themselves, it is implied in this distinction that we place the latter... in opposition to the former, and that in so doing we entitle them intelligible

entities (noumena). The question then arises, whether the pure concepts of understanding have meaning (*Bedeutung*) in respect of these latter, and so can be a way of knowing them (B 306).

The concept of noumenon is not a concept of the understanding: it is an indeterminate concept of an intelligible entity, not a determinate concept of a knowable entity. Kant further distinguishes between the negative sense of the term – 'not an object of our sensible intuition' and the positive sense – 'an object of non-sensible intuition.' He of course opts for its negative sense. But this still leaves him with the concept of the noumenon. This concept is not self-contradictory; its objective reality cannot be known; it is indispensable in order to prevent intuition from being extended to things in themselves; and it connects with acceptable concepts, for example, that of phenomenon. So Kant, rather than dismissing it as a concept because it is not a concept of the understanding, calls it 'problematic' or 'limiting;' its function is to 'curb the pretensions of sensibility' (B 311).

Objects cannot be divided into phenomena and noumena; the world cannot be divided into a world of the senses and a world of the understanding; but concepts, Kant concedes, can be distinguished as sensible and intellectual.

In the Transcendental Dialectic, Kant exposes the inevitable proclivity of reason to extend the employment of the categories beyond the limits of intuition and understanding. Kant raises what for his (and my) purpose is a fundamental question: 'Can we isolate reason, and is it, so regarded, an independent source of concepts and judgments which spring from it alone, and by means of which it relates to objects...' (A 305/B 362)? Kant's answer is negative. Does this negative answer imply that because reason is no independent source of concepts applicable to objects, there are no concepts of reason which differ from those of the understanding, therefore, no additional kinds of concepts that must be considered in any elucidation of Kant's theory of concepts?

It seems to me that the answer to this question is also negative: that Kant does recognize and accept as concepts certain ones that do not and cannot relate to intuition and understanding. The concepts of reason differ from the concepts of understanding. They even give rise to metaphysical illusion. However, they are concepts nevertheless, and they must be accommodated in any overall view of Kant's theory of the role and nature of concepts.

There are, Kant begins, pure concepts of reason: Such concepts '. . . can in general be explained by the concept of the unconditioned, conceived as containing a ground of the synthesis of the conditioned' (B 379). Or, in the wide sense of the term 'absolute,' a pure concept of reason aims 'towards absolute totality in the synthesis of conditions, and never terminates save in what is absolutely, that is, in all relations, unconditioned' (A 326). In effect, reason employs the concepts of the understanding and tries to render their synthetic unity unconditioned. In prescribing to the understanding the quest for a unity that the understanding cannot conceive, reason transcends the employment of the concepts of the understanding.

An idea Kant defines as 'a necessary concept of reason to which no corresponding object can be given in sense-experience' (A 327). He calls such concepts 'transcendental ideas.' As illusory as they are in the quest for knowledge, they are indispensable in the practical employment of the reason. The transcendental idea of a necessary unity of all possible ends is a standard of the moral life. (Later, in A 641/B 669, he says that these transcendental ideas are indispensable for the theoretical employment of reason as well, in reason's inevitable search for total unity, as the absolute ground of knowledge and experience.)

There are three classes of trancendental ideas: those containing the absolute unity of (1) the thinking subject; (2) the series of conditions of appearances; and (3) the condition of all objects of thought in general. The arguments for these unities rest respectively on the forms of the categorical, hypothetical and disjunctive syllogisms.

In 'The Paralogisms of Pure Reason,' Kant begins with the transcendental concept or judgment, 'I think,' which, he reminds us, is the vehicle of all concepts serving, as it does, to introduce rather than to designate our thought as belonging to consciousness. This concept enables us to represent two kinds of object: the thinking I of the inner sense, called 'soul;' and the object of the outer sense, called 'body.' Accordingly, the expression 'I' is taken to signify the object that psychology refers to in its rational doctrine of the soul. '"I think" is, therefore, the sole text of rational psychology . . .' (A 343). Rational psychology construes this 'I' as designating a thinking being, thus subsumes its designatum under the category of substance. In this way, the text of rational psychology provides its topics: that the soul is substance; it is simple; it is a unity; and it relates to possible objects in space. These topics and their derivative doctrines of the immateriality, incorruptibility, personality, spirituality, and immortality of the soul as substance turn on an erroneous interpretation of the simple, empty representation 'I' which, Kant says, is not even a concept but only 'a bare consciousness that accompanies all concepts' (B 404/A 346). The I that thinks represents at most a transcendental subject of thoughts, not a substance; consciousness is not a representation of an object, but a form of representation in general.

As he does with the 'Transcendental Deduction of the Categories,' Kant offers a first and second edition version of the paralogisms. For our immediate purpose – to catalogue Kant's views regarding concepts – an examination of his second edition version will suffice, especially since he omits the first in the second.

The 'I' in 'I think' is the subject in judgments. That it is a subject and never a predicate is analytic. 'I, as object, am for myself a substance' neither is equivalent to nor implied by '"I" in "I think" is a subject.' There is no and can be no proof of myself as a substance. The 'I' of every act of thought as one is already contained in the concept of thought; so '"I" is a logically simple subject' is also analytic. It also is neither equivalent to nor implies 'The thinking I is a simple substance,' which is not analytic and, because it relates the concept of substances to thought rather than to the only thing it can relate to – intuitions, cannot be synthetic either. 'In the manifold of which I am conscious I am identical with myself' is also analytic. But the identity of the subject provides no intuition of the subject as object, therefore cannot signify the identity of the person, that is, 'the consciousness of the identity of one's own substance, as a thinking being, in all change of its states' (B 408). 'I as thinking being am distinct from other things outside me, including my body' also is analytic; it implies that I am other than my body but not that I might exist apart from outside things. Analysis of consciousness of myself – of 'I think' – provides therefore no knowledge of myself as object. 'The logical exposition of thought in general has been mistaken for a metaphysical determination of the object' (B 409). Indeed, if it were otherwise, that if it could be proved *a priori* that thinking beings are simple substances with inseparable personalities, conscious of their separate existence distinct from matter, Kant acknowledges, the whole *Critique* would collapse. 'Every thinking being is a simple substance' is therefore synthetic *a priori*. However, unlike synthetic *a priori* propositions in mathematics and physics, its predicate cannot be given in experience; consequently, it is not possible, hence it is not admissible.

The metaphysics of rational psychology, not its critique, thus, collapses. Its argument that the subject of thought is substance is a paralogism in which 'subject' means that which can be given in intuition in its major premise, 'That which cannot be thought otherwise than as subject does not exist otherwise than as subject, and is therefore substance;' and means only that which thinks, the logical subject, not the object of thought, in its minor premise, 'A thinking being, considered merely as such, cannot be thought otherwise than as subject.' The paralogism is a fallacy: *per sophisma figurae dictionis*. The only valid conclusion Kant allows is from the minor premise: 'In thinking my existence, I cannot employ myself, save as subject of the judgment (therein involved).' But this conclusion, he adds, 'is an identical proposition and casts no light whatsoever upon the mode of my existence' (B 411).

'I think,' then, yields only the unity of consciousness as a mere form of knowledge. This unity is basic to all the categories, to all knowledge. It is itself not a category or a concept. Nor is the consciousness of unity a category. It is a transcendental idea. The synthetic unity of apperception, we remember from the Metaphysical Deduction of the Categories, is not a category either but a presupposition of all the categories. All three – unity of consciousness, consciousness of unity, synthetic unity of apperception – raise a fundamental question: If they are not concepts, and they are not Kant insists, how can we talk about them at all without concepts of them? Kant's universe of transcendental idealism revolves around its centre of the unity of self-consciousness; it would be incoherent, not a lapse, if it were not amenable to conceptualization, even though its concept is totally dissimilar to all the others. Indeed, its non-conceptualizability would render his Copernican revolution unintelligible: an ineffable revelation, not an articulated discovery.

The 'Paralogisms' adds to Kant's list of concepts those of substance, simple nature and person. It also reinforces the difficulty surrounding the concept of the I, self, ego, self-consciousness, or subject of thought as a concept but not like a category. In 'The Antinomy of Pure Reason,' Kant introduces further complexities into his theory of concepts. The concept or transcendental idea is, once again, that of unconditioned unity, in particular, of the objective conditions in appearances. This concept, unlike that of unconditioned unity of the soul, which generates paralogisms, yields contradictions, hence antinomies that in this case follow the pattern of hypothetical syllogisms. Reason argues that 'if *the conditioned is given, the entire sum of conditions, and consequently the absolutely unconditioned ... is also given*' (B 436). It is only of an ascending series of conditions, not of a descending series of consequences, that reason demands absolute totality. Four categories lead to four (and only four) cosmological ideas regarding absolute completeness: (1) of the composition of the given whole of all appearances; (2) in the division of a given whole in the field of appearance; (3) in the origination of an appearance; and (4) as regards dependence of the existence of the changeable in the field of appearance.

The antinomy of pure reason is the conflict of two dogmas, each of which is not self-contradictory, but rather contradicts the other. The critique of pure reason reveals the source of the conflict to be the extension of the principles of the understanding beyond the limits of experience. It recognizes the inevitability of these dogmas at the same time as it exposes them. The first of these antinomies is that the world has a beginning in time and is limited as regards space versus the world has no beginning in time, no limits in space, and is therefore infinite. The second is that every substance is composed of simples and that everything is simple or composed of simples versus no composite is made of simples and there are no simples. The third is that freedom is a kind of causality which differs from causality in accordance with laws of nature versus there is no freedom, only natural causality. The fourth is that there is an absolutely necessary being that belongs to the world as its part or cause versus there is no such being.

Kant's procedure is to present side-by-side the dialectical arguments for each of these pairs of conflicting doctrines and to show that each separate doctrine is consistent and true, assuming that its premise is true. Whether Kant has correctly interpreted the traditional doctrines regarding the infinity of space and time, the relation between the simple and the complex, causality and freedom, and necessary being; and whether his version of the argument is adequate, I need not consider here. All that is of concern are the concepts or transcendental ideas brought into the arguments and

169

antinomies. The two concepts new to our list are freedom and necessary being; the others we have met with before in the *Critique*.

After some preliminary skirmishing, in which Kant charmingly engages the theses and antitheses of the antinomies with the perennial conflict between Epicureanism and Platonism, he suggests that the unconditioned is both too large and too small to be accommodated by the concepts of the understanding. And he reminds us of the transcendental idealism implied by the transcendental aesthetic and then settles down to resolve the cosmological conflicts.

The argument of the antinomies, patterned after the hypothetical syllogism, is this: 'If the conditioned is given, the entire series of all its conditions is likewise given; objects of the senses are given as conditioned; therefore, [the entire series of conditions of objects of the senses also must be given]' (A 497). This argument, Kant contends, commits the same fallacy as the paralogisms, namely, that of using a word in one sense in the major and in a different sense in the minor premise: in the major, 'conditioned' expresses a pure category whereas in the minor, a concept of the understanding, applicable to appearances. Hence, 'I cannot say, in the same sense of the terms, that if the conditioned is given, all its conditions (as appearances) are likewise given, and therefore cannot in any way infer the absolute totality of the series of its conditions' (A 499). Kant makes the further point that though these premises contain the same word, their different senses show there are two different concepts, the concept of the conditioned without succession, as employed in the major premiss; and the concept of the conditioned as necessarily successive, in the minor. 'In the major premiss all the members of the series are given in themselves, without any condition of time, but in this minor premiss they are possible only through the successive regress, which is given only in the process in which it is actually carried out' (B 529/A 501).

The fallacy and the illusion it spawns in exponents of either side of the cosmological antinomies rest on this confusion of extending the idea of absolute totality, which can be only a condition of things in themselves, to the concept of a regressively successive series, which is a condition of appearances.

As empty and fallaciously based as the idea of absolute totality is, Kant allows it and its principle, as expressed in the major premise of the argument of the antinomy, a regulative role in reason: to enjoin reason to search for the conditions of conditions. What the principle cannot do is to serve as a constitutive principle, either of appearances or of things in themselves.

Kant concludes this section with his solutions of the antinomies. The first, that space and time are and are not finite, rests on the assumption that the world, the complete series of appearances, is a thing in itself. Kant rejects this assumption as a transcendental illusion. Instead, the world exists in the regressive series of empirical representations. In this world, the magnitude of space and time is a regress that proceeds indefinitely but not to infinity. That it is such a regress, Kant adds, provides a further proof of transcendental idealism, 'that appearances in general are nothing outside our representations' (B 535/A 507).

The second, that compounds are made of indivisible simples (thesis) and that compounds are composed of compounds, not simples, of which there are none (antithesis), Kant also rejects. Nothing in experience is absolutely simple. And no compound, though divisible to infinity, is infinity divided. Both the thesis and its antithesis are transcendental illusions. So far as intuition is concerned, it is a compound of parts; these parts are regressively, not actually, infinite.

The third, that freedom is and is not natural causality, Kant transforms from an antinomy into two propositions, both of which can be true; hence, they are neither contradictories nor contraries. So far as the natural order – our intuitions – is concerned, causality is a categorial condition of it; consequently, there can be no freedom, that is, a spontaneous first cause within the natural order. Can causality, within the natural order, arise from freedom? Freedom is 'the power of beginning a state *spontaneously*' (A 533/B 561). The concept of it is a transcendental idea, borrowing nothing from experience and referring to no object of experience. Its intelligibility rests in part on the absence of a totality of conditions determining causal relations and in part on the distinction between appearances and things in themselves, according to which at least appearances require grounds that are not appearances. Freedom, thus, can be a cause and an intelligible ground of appearances. Instead of two concepts of causality, 'we should therefore have to form both an empirical and an intellectual concept of the causality of the faculty of such a subject, and to regard both as referring to one and the same effect' (A 538/B 566). Such a subject, in its intelligible character, would be exempt from the sensible, therefore from time and, most important, from the natural law of causality. As noumenon, nothing happens in the subject; but it is not impossible that something happens because of him: he is the cause of a sensible effect. 'Man's freedom causes event x' is not a contradiction of 'Everything that happens must have its cause in the appearances that precede it' since they are at least compatible and both may be true. Even event x – one and the same event – can be regarded in one aspect as an effect of nature and in another aspect as an effect of freedom. Kant then adds a third ground of the intelligibility of freedom as non-natural cause, drawn from morality. 'Ought' implies 'can;' but 'ought' presupposes 'freedom.' We can know only what is in nature; nature does not contain what ought to be.

> This *'ought'* expresses a possible action the ground of which
> cannot be anything but a mere concept;... The action to
> which the *'ought'* applies must indeed be possible under
> natural conditions. These conditions, however, do not play
> any part in determining the will itself, but only in
> determining the effect and its consequences in ... appearance
> (A 548/B 576).

Freedom, thus, is not only compatible with natural causality, but is the foundation of the moral life, and therefore of practical reason. Kant does not prove there is freedom or even that it is possible since that would be to make the concept transcendental. All he shows and tries to show is that it is a transcendental idea which is not incompatible with the transcendental concept of causality.

The fourth antinomy, that there is and that there is not a necessary being, Kant resolves in the same manner as the third. That there is no such being holds for the empirical world, whereas that there is does not. Nevertheless, the empirical world may be contingent, 'while yet there may be a non-empirical condition of the whole series' (A 560/B 588). This intelligible condition would be necessary being and, as such, a ground of appearance. Unlike causality which, as intelligible ground, belongs to the series of conditions of appearance, necessary being 'must be thought as entirely outside the series of the sensible world (as *ens extramundanum*), and as purely intelligible' (A 561/B 589). The regulative principle of reason that enjoins us to seek conditions for conditions does not justify the existence of an unconditioned, necessary being; but neither does it disbar the possibility. Kant does not go on to show that it is possible (and of course does not prove that it is actual). What he shows is that there is no incompatibility between thoroughgoing contingency of nature and 'the optional assumption of a necessary, though purely intelligible, condition' (A 562/B 590). Kant adds that such a being may be impossible; but its impossibility does not follow from the contingency of the world or from the regulative principle of reason. Whether it is possible and whether it exists Kant saves for his next section, 'The ideal of Pure Reason.' In raising these questions, we shift from the cosmological, transcendental idea of necessary being, which is concerned with the ground of the totality of conditions in the sensible world, to the transcendent idea of necessary being, which is concerned with the unconditioned, outside all possible experience. We go from objective reality based on completion of the empirical series to objective reality based on pure *a priori* concepts.

In 'The Ideal of Pure Reason,' Kant distinguishes between concepts of experience, idea and ideal. The first is a concept of understanding *in concreto*; the second cannot be represented *in concreto*; and the third is the idea *in concreto* and *in individuo*: it is 'an individual thing, determinable or even determined by the idea alone' (A 568/B 596). The ideal, thus, is a transcendent object that is completely determinable, formulated by reason in accordance with *a priori* rules. Kant introduces the arguments, here patterned on the disjunctive syllogism, and the illusion they sponsor and generate, with a consideration of the concept of an *ens realissimum*. Every concept is subject to the principle of determinability, according to which of every pair of contradictory predicates, only one can belong to a concept. Likewise, everything is subject to the principle of complete determination, according to which '*if all the possible* predicates of *things* be taken together with their contradictory opposites, then one of each pair of contradictory opposites must belong to it' (A 572/B 600). This principle, because it goes beyond the analyticity of the first to consider everything in relation to the sum of all possibilities, is synthetic *a priori*: 'the principle of the synthesis of all predicates which are intended to constitute the complete concept of a thing...' (A 572/B 600). From this principle it follows that everything which exists is completely determined which, Kant claims, is equivalent to: 'that to know a thing completely, we must know every possible [predicate], and must determine it thereby... The complete determination is thus a concept ...' (A 573/B 601).

Thus, the concept or idea of the sum of all possibility becomes the concept of a completely determined individual object: *ens realissimum*. This is the concept of an individual being, of a thing in itself as completely determined, therefore of that which possesses all reality. This idea 'is also the only true ideal of which human reason is capable. For only in this one case is the concept of a thing – a concept which is in itself universal – completely determined in and through itself, and known as a representation of an individual' (A 576/B 604). Since the idea, ideal or concept of such a being is the concept of God, can we, Kant asks, prove His existence through the concept of the highest being?

First, Kant claims that this argument, notwithstanding the fact that it is not fundamental for religious people or, more important, that it is taken as independent of other arguments, is basic. For Kant's great thesis is that all arguments for God's existence reduce to the argument from the concept of God – the ontological argument. To show that this argument is invalid is sufficient to dispel the illusion of transcendental theology, that there is an object whose existence as *ens realissimum* is necessary.

We can give a verbal definition of the concept of an absolutely necessary being: 'it is something the non-existence of which is impossible.' However, this does not guarantee the conditions that necessitate the non-existence of a thing as absolutely unthinkable. Without these, Kant says, we cannot know if in employing this concept we are thinking anything at all. We cannot infer from the unconditioned necessity of judgments, including the verbal definition, to the absolute necessity of things. The premise is at most only a necessary condition for the conclusion. I cannot posit God without positing His omnipotence. But I can deny 'God exists' without contradiction; I reject both subject and predicate. The attempt to rescue the concept of the *ens realissimum* as the one concept for which this rejection of subject and predicate is self-contradictory, Kant demolishes further, thinking it necessary to do so because of its strong hold on reason. The argument is this: '"all reality" includes existence; existence is therefore contained in the concept of a thing that is possible. If, then, this thing is rejected, the internal possibility of the thing is rejected – which is self-contradictory' (A 597/B 625). Kant's reply is lethal: (1) To introduce the concept of existence into the concept of a thing that is construed as possible is already a contradiction; (2) the proposition that all-reality includes existence, like any existential proposition, must be synthetic; therefore, the denial of the predicate of existence cannot be contradictory; (3) the argument confuses real predicates with the purely logical predicate of existence or being. 'The proposition, "God is omnipotent", contains two concepts, each of which has its object (*Objekte*) – God and omnipotence. The small word "is" adds no new predicate, but only serves to posit the predicate *in its relation* to the subject' (A 598–99/B 626–27). 'God is' or 'There is a God' adds nothing to the concept of God; rather it posits the subject with all its predicates. If 'existence' were a real predicate, Kant adds, no concept could apply to anything, since the thing would have one more predicate than the concept applied to it; and 'non-existence' would also be a real predicate, so that 'God does not exist' would both deny and affirm His existence.

Though the argument and all arguments dependent on it fail, Kant regards the concept of God as legitimate, provided it is taken as a regulative idea, to be employed in the regulative principle of reason, 'which directs us to look upon all connection in the world *as if* it originated from an all-sufficient necessary cause' (A 619/B 647). The concept also is of the greatest importance to the practical reason. But even without its implications for morality – for reason itself – the concept, while only an ideal, is 'yet *an ideal without a flaw*, a concept which completes and crowns the whole of human knowledge' (A 641/B 669).

There are, of course, other important concepts in Kant's work. Any complete statement of his theory must include, for example, his ethical and aesthetic concepts. Whether Kant's theory of these concepts – of their nature and role – differs radically from that in *The Critique of Pure Reason* is doubtful; but I must forego any consideration of this possibility here in a chapter that is already inordinately, perhaps devouringly, long. Instead, I shall simply assume, whether correctly or not, that an adequate (if not complete) statement of Kant's theory of concepts can be elicited from his major and basic book, *The Critique of Pure Reason*.

What, then, by way of summary, is Kant's theory of concepts? First, it is well to reiterate his concepts: intuition, space, time, sensibility, appearance, manifold, understanding, synthetic unity, unity, magnitude, substance, causality, coexistence, possibility, actuality, necessity, noumenon, phenomenon, unconditioned,

conditioned, subject, I, self-consciousness, soul, person, simple, cosmos, God, freedom, necessary being, existence, among many others, including transcendental logic, analytic, and dialectic. Each of these is said or implied by Kant to be a concept. Some are more, such as the unconditioned; some are sometimes less, such as space and time; some are rejected as concepts, such as self-consciousness; some are forms, others, categories; many are ideas, and one is the ideal. Some – not on the above list – are empirical, such as dog; some are sensible, such as triangle; others – on our list – are *a priori* or synthetic *a priori*. Each of these concepts entails others; some mutually entail each other; some presuppose others, such as that of unity which presupposes combination; many – the categories – presuppose the synthetic unity of apperception, which Kant disclaims is a concept.

These concepts also differ in their specific roles. Space and time serve as forms of intuition. The categories organize our intuitions, enable us to make judgments and, because they are *a priori* forms of understanding, to transform the subjective conditions of thought into objectively valid knowledge. The limiting concept of the noumenon serves to curb the pretensions of sensibility; and ideas and the ideal function as regulative injunctions to reason. Each makes a distinctive contribution to the conceptual life according to Kant. Central of course are the categories that render experience and knowledge possible. That concepts play crucial roles in *The Critique of Pure Reason* has its best statement by Kant himself. Indeed, one might not unjustly characterize the whole of the *Critique* as Kant's persistent attempt to elucidate the various roles of concepts in sense-experience, science and metaphysics. Kant says that basic to knowledge and experience are intuitions and concepts. This is a thesis which implies that concepts, in particular, those of intuition and concept, are basic in philosophy: Give me these two concepts and I will build you a world, which Kant proceeds to do. He labels it the world of Transcendental Idealism.

All the certainty regarding the place and centrality of concepts in Kant's philosophy vanishes as we turn to Kant's theory of the nature of concepts. Kant is not as explicit about their nature as he is about their roles; and his statements about concepts retain an ambivalence about their nature throughout the *Critique*. The textual and doctrinal evidence – at times the same piece of evidence – yields both that concepts are entities and that they are rules. Precisely which they are has become a focal problem in exegesis of and commentary on the Kantian philosophy, especially since concepts are so clearly central in Kant. Much of this commentary claims that concepts to Kant are rules, consequently that the having of them are abilities, thus rendering Kant as one of the forerunners of the modern dispositional theory of concepts which, some add, is the true theory, thereby attributing an extra dimension to the Kantian revolution.

The reader will note that I have not been sympathetic to such an interpretation of concepts in Kant. Whatever the evidence may be in favour of an entity reading, the reasons proffered for a dispositional theory are far from overwhelming.

Kant says we create concepts, we form things in accordance with concepts; that concepts have certain roles, which are governed by rules; that the understanding is the faculty of rules; that recognition in a concept is one aspect of synthesizing the manifold of intuition; that the schemata of concepts are rules; that the only use the understanding can make of concepts is to make judgments by means of them; that the significance of concepts rests on their application to objects; that the analogies of experience consist of rules; and, most important, perhaps, that the categories 'are merely rules' and that concepts rest on functions, with the implication that functions, that is, the unity of the acts of bringing various representations under one common representation, do not rest on concepts. Kant also implies throughout that there can be no real difference between a concept and the having of it, any more than there can be a difference between an object, an intuition, an appearance and the having of them. Concepts simply cannot be things in themselves without violating the intrinsically phenomenological character of them. Consequently, even if concepts are entities, not rules, in Kant, they must satisfy this criterion of being part of the phenomenal world, and must not be noumena that subsist independently of space and time in some supersensible realm.

In spite of the fact that there is no analysis of rules in the *Critique* and there is an intimate relation between laws and rules that Kant affirms, a consequence of which is that rules are binding, therefore presuppose a grounding of them that can hardly be a further rule, all of these claims and intimations that concepts are rules are impressive. However, as I have already suggested in this chapter, they do not add up to any convincing dispositional theory of concepts and the having of them. Most of the arguments rest on a conflation of concepts with their employment, a conflation shared by Kant and his commentators. Moreover, there is something radically amiss in attributing to Kant the theory that having a concept is having an ability, in its dispositional sense, since concepts – at least those that are *a priori* – are not acquired and enhanced by their employment, as skills are, but for Kant are had, whether we choose to have them or not. Indeed, in the sense that we can choose our intuitions, though not their forms, simply by shifting our senses, we cannot choose our categories. Thus, we cannot but have the basic concepts we have; this being the case, it sounds odd, if not incoherent, to speak of having concepts as abilities or dispositions rather than as innate, categorical powers, which they seem to be for Kant, very much like the space and time of intuition. Kant's theory of the understanding, thus, seems to preclude a dispositional theory of concepts according to which the possession of them is a set of skills or abilities.

However correct, therefore devastating, this consideration may be to the dispositional theory attributed to Kant, the thesis that concepts are rules rather than that some of them involve rules as constituents or that all of them yield rules, is suspect by itself. Even the concept of causality – the leading contender of a concept as a rule – as Kant analyzes it, both in the Metaphysical Deduction and in the Second Analogy, is no more 'merely a rule' for him than it is for Hume or Descartes. For all three, it is a concept that consists of four constituent concepts: of two or more events and the relations of priority, contiguity and necessary connection between them. Kant does not disagree at least with Hume on the content of the concept of causality; he disagrees with Hume on its origins: that it is wholly empirical. And he disagrees with Descartes (as Hume does) primarily on its status: that it is analytic *a priori*; as well as on some of its content: that the cause has more reality than or as much reality as the effect. It is also true that Kant regards necessary connection as binding regularity among preceding and succeeding events. It is also possible to construe his conceptions of the concepts of events, priority, and contiguity as rules of synthesis, although I think these concepts are rather governed by these rules of synthesis according to Kant. But let us grant that the concept of causality for Kant is a rule consisting of four constituent rules. What, then, are we to say of the relation of entailment which obtains among the rules? Two or more events, priority, contiguity do not entail necessary connection;

necessary connection, however, entails two or more events, priority and contiguity. That there is this asymmetrical relation of entailment as another constituent of the concept of causality is no rule; and to insist that it is is to destroy Kant's own distinction between General and Transcendental Logic. Even if we grant that event, priority, contiguity, and necessary connection are synthetic *a priori* concepts (i.e., concepts presupposed by empirical knowledge of objects) and judgments about them are synthetic *a priori*, Kant would be the first to reject the doctrine that asymmetrical entailment is synthetic *a priori*; it is a pure *a priori* concept of General Logic. Causality without this asymmetrical entailment of necessary connection to the other constituents is unthinkable to Kant. The concept of causality, therefore, cannot be a mere rule.

Another compelling reason for rejecting the thesis that concepts are rules in Kant is that even if it holds for some concepts, it does not for all. There are some concepts in the *Critique* – which are not debatable as space and time or the self or God are – for example, possibility, actuality, and necessity, or sensibility, appearance, or existence, for which the claim that they are rules does not make sense.

I do not think the doctrine that concepts are rules, that concepts are the having of them, and that the having of them are abilities in Kant's philosophy can be definitively refuted. Nor do I think the hypothesis that concepts to Kant are entities – objects of the understanding and thought – or that the having of them may yield abilities but are not the same as abilities can be confirmed. All I feel comfortable with is that the latter is more plausible than the former, and then only in the sense that it is more in keeping with the architectonic of Kant's Transcendental Idealism than perhaps it is with any convincing theory of concepts in general.

Kant defines 'concept' as a species of representation: it is a kind of *Vorstellung*. He also refers to concepts as objects: *Gegenstände*; and in one passage on 'God is omnipotent,' he says the two concepts of God and omnipotence have objects: *Objekte*. In rejecting space as a concept, he distinguishes between a representation that contains an infinite number of representations within itself (space) and a representation which is contained in an infinite number of different possible representations as their common character but which contains them not within, rather under, itself. He talks about the concept of the sum of 7 and 5, the concept of 12; how the thought of one concept does not contain the concept of the other. He distinguishes between the concept of straight and the concept of shortest. He remarks that the concept of matter implies something in space but does not imply that which is permanent. He speaks of the concepts of sensibility and appearances and, by implication, the concept of intuition. All the categories, though they serve as rules of the understanding, are *a priori* conditions of knowledge. In giving a metaphysical deduction of the categories, he distinguishes (in the first edition) between the act of combining apprehensions and the concept of combination and what that concept presupposes. He defines the concepts of the possible, actual and necessary, for example, 'The possible is that which is both non-self-contradictory and intuitable;' and he characterizes the concept of existence as a logical, not an ontological, predicate. Finally, he denies that any of the concepts of reason can yield rules, though they can be employed to formulate rules as injunctions, not laws; and at the same time he articulates the entailments within and among these concepts.

Of course, all this talk is variously interpretable. However, it seems to me that it tends toward the direction of talking about certain kinds of objects, not those of appearances, but objects of the understanding and reason: of the mind. Kant says we 'create' concepts. But in the *Critique* he finds them all, with the exception of the technical ones, such as Transcendental Analytic or Dialectic. And he finds them in the language of past philosophers and in the sciences of his day as well of course as in the language of ordinary speech about the world. He concentrates on the language of the sciences, especially their propositions or judgments which he then declares to be synthetic *a priori* or founded on, grounded in fundamental synthetic *a priori* judgments and concepts, all secured by a non-conceptual unity of self-consciousness. The concepts he finds employed in the sciences or presupposed by them become focal as he proceeds in his great endeavour to show how scientific knowledge is possible. These concepts must anticipate and connect with the empirical if the justification of science is to be achieved. These criteria become basic in determining the roles of concepts. But the establishment of these criteria involves Kant in the investigation of the concepts that will satisfy these criteria. And it is in this investigation that he inspects the nature of concepts: what they contain, what they entail, what they presuppose. These concepts can only be objects of such inspection – of the understanding or reason, by the mind in its quest for a certain kind of *a priori* grounding and empirical connection that will validate knowledge. Of course he does not find causality or substance in experience. But he does find in his mind that objective necessary connection, without which there can be no difference between succession and causality, between regularities and laws in nature, is an essential feature of any adequate concept of causality. He examines the concept of causality, expressed by science and required by science, and finds in the concept, not in the language of science, its constituents, including the all-important asymmetrical relation of necessary connection. He examines the concept as an object of his understanding. That his analysis of this concept is suggested by the language of science or even by ordinary language and provides the buttress of this language support the analysis but in no way supplant it. Kant is not a pre-Wittgensteinian; he is a post-cartesian in his conception of concepts: concepts are entities, objects of some sort that can be perceived by the mind and, when complex, analyzed by the intellect.

Suppose, then, concepts are entities, not dispositions in Kant: What kind of entities are they in the Kantian universe? They cannot be things in themselves. They must be either intuitions or concepts. But they are not intuitions; and to say that the entities or objects of the mind which are concepts *are* concepts is to say nothing or to pervert Kant's distinction between a concept and an object. Concepts must find their place in the phenomenal world. If they are objects, concepts cannot be objects in this – the only world. And to remind ourselves that for Kant there can be no real difference between a concept and the having it does not help locate concepts for now we must ask, Where in Kant's Transcendental Idealism is there room for the act of having a concept? a question to which there is no answer as there is to, for example, Where is the act of judging that every triangle has three sides? Answer: in the understanding and the intuition together. Further, to dismiss the question, What is the nature of a concept? as legitimately askable of Kant does not help either, since 'nature' here is phenomenal, not noumenal. Therefore the question cannot be ruled out as a transgression of the bounds of sense. Lastly, to castigate the question: What is the nature of a concept in Kant? as a barbarism on What is a concept in Kant? – which he does answer – is to up-date Kant and in such a manner as to render all his other What is the nature of x? questions otiose as well. I end by confessing that I find no answer in Kant to my question:

What kind of object or entity is a concept, granted that it is an entity or object of the mind? Only two, equally unattractive, inferences from this impasse seem possible: either my question about Kant is illegitimate or Kant has no answer and, within his system, can give none. If the latter is correct, Kant's Copernican Revolution in philosophy is what it always was, a utopian dream.

CHAPTER 13

Some nineteenth and twentieth century theories: Frege, Russell and Moore

A salient feature of nineteenth and twentieth century philosophy is its persistent formulation of theories of concepts. Speaking in general terms, 'concept' replaces 'conception' as the object of conceiving, though Thomas Reid, a little before, in spite of his recognition of the traditional ambiguity of 'conception' as act and as object, insists that things, whether they exist or not, are the objects of conception;[1] and explicit theories of the nature and role of concepts become integral doctrines of individual philosophies. This use of 'concept' and this concern with a theory of concepts no doubt reflect the continuing influence of Kant on the language as well as the problems of philosophy.

The prevalence of theories of concepts in these two centuries creates a problem for our survey. To do full justice to the explicit theories of concepts in the nineteenth and twentieth centuries would be (almost) to rewrite the entire history of philosophy during this period. This I cannot do here; nor is it necessary for our aim, which is to survey the major historical theories. Consequently, whether rightly or wrongly, I shall deal only with the theories of Frege, Russell and Moore and, with an eye on the sources of the rejection of traditional theories, of Ryle and Geach. This leaves out of major consideration Reid, Hamilton, and especially J. S. Mill, among the British; Hegel, Brentano, and Husserl, among other German or Austrian giants; and Peirce, James, and Dewey, the Americans; as well as H. H. Price and C. D. Broad, among the recent English philosophers. Should the reader violently object to my list of omissions, I beg him to make the necssary amends by offering elucidations of those theories of concepts he regards as more important historically than the ones I have chosen. I also ask him to share my pleasure in the refreshing fact that mine is at least one survey of problems in philosophy in which the modern period is not acclaimed as the great culmination and solution of the problem under discussion and, consequently, given inordinate space. Indeed it seems to me that even the theories of the philosophers I shall deal with before we turn to the critique of traditional theories of concepts are only versions, perhaps more incisive, of earlier theories or misreadings of them, as in the case of Plato's theory.

Before I come to Frege, let me try to justify or at least explain the omissions. I leave out Reid because he has no explicit theory of concepts and, notwithstanding the excessive space he occupies in (mostly Encyclopedia) articles on concepts or their philosophical history – a place that reflects more the deficiency of these articles than it does the originality of Reid – he has no striking implicit theory either. His main concern is with conception as an act of the understanding. That he has an implicit theory of concepts, namely, that concepts are the meanings of general words, is, I think, pretty clear in his Fourth Essay, 'Of Conception.' However, he seems to reject even this doctrine in his denial that the act of conception has for its object an image, an idea, or a thing; rather its object are certain attributes collected together by the mind into a Lockean nominal essence. He does, then, make a singular contribution to the psychology and logic of perceiving and to the related topics of abstraction, generalization and language. This, however, adds little, if anything, to the history of theories of concepts.

John Stuart Mill is a different story. The concepts he employs in his writings and his discussion of the nature of concepts are eminently worth detailed examination. Probably his best analysis of concepts is contained in Chapter XVII, 'The Doctrine of Concepts, or General Notions,' in his book, *An Examination of Sir William Hamilton's Philosophy* (1865). Much of that chapter is a criticism of Hamilton's uneasy amalgam of nominalism and conceptualism that Mill rejects. Unfortunately, however, Mill also conflates the problem of the nature and role of concepts with the traditional problem of universals. Nevertheless, in the middle of the chapter (pp. 331ff.), Mill offers these observations on Hamilton's theory that are among the first – if not *the* first – rejections of concepts: the first 'antitheory,' one might call it (unless, of course, we include the implication regarding the non-existence of concepts in Hume's doctrine that there are only impressions and ideas):

> To say, therefore, that we think by means of concepts, is
> only a circuitous and obscure way of saying that we think
> by means of general or class names.
> ... I consider it nothing less than a misfortune, that the
> words Concept, General Notion, or any other phrase to
> express the supposed mental modification corresponding to
> a class name, should ever have been invented. Above all, I
> hold that nothing but confusion ever results from
> introducing the term Concept into Logic, and that instead
> of the Concept of a class, we should always speak of the
> signification of a class name.

Here Mill anticipates Ryle in Ryle's castigation of traditional philosophers' talk about concepts as 'only a gaseous way of saying that they are trying to discover what is meant by the general terms contained in the sentences whch they pronounce or write.'[2]

What about Hegel? How can one survey major theories of concepts without a thorough examination of his explicit theory, especially in his *Science of Logic* and its revision in the *Encyclopedia*, where Hegel divides Logic into the Doctrine of Being, Essence and Concept; and, as important, his implicit theory, as it is embodied in his work? Perhaps one cannot leave out Hegel in such a survey. But at least it seems to me that as important and profound as Hegel's philosophy is or is claimed to be, his theory of concepts is inextricably tied to his metaphysics in which concepts are ontological entities *in* the world. Though the details of such a theory are an inviting challenge to critical examination, the main thrust of the theory is traditional, stemming from Plotinus and culminating in Spinoza, thus, a recapitulation, to be sure in a new dialectical dress, of one version of neo-platonism, but not of Plato.

Brentano is generally regarded as having reintroduced the platonic doctrine that concepts are supersensible entities. That this is Plato's theory of concepts rather than of forms is questionable; but the theory persists through Meinong and Husserl and is varied or echoed in Frege, Russell and Moore, whom we shall discuss.

The Americans, Peirce, James and Dewey, as well as C. I. Lewis, who reconciles Kant's *a priori* with the conventionalism of pragmatism, are also worth intensive consideration in regard to their theories of concepts. Each in his own way transforms concepts from mental entities into objective instruments that serve as directives in inquiry. A dispositional theory is hinted at but never fully developed. In Peirce and Dewey, the having of concepts is related to habits; and in Peirce, to signs and their nature and use. Peirce, perhaps the greatest of these pragmatists, comes close to a dispositional theory of concepts in his essay, 'How To Make Our Ideas Clear:'

> Consider what effects, which might conceivably have practical bearings, we conceive the object of our conception to have. Then, our conception of these effects is the whole of our conception of the object.[3]

That this is a criterion of the intelligibility of concepts is as impeccable as Kant's principle of significance. But that it is a theory of the nature of concepts and a dispositional one at that, though intimated, is neither implied nor the only possible reading. Peirce's may be an operational definition of a concept. However, as it stands, it only identifies the meaning of an idea or conception with its verifiability.

C. D. Bread, especially in the *Examination of McTaggart's Philosophy*, volume I, pp. 29–53, and H. H. Price, in *Thinking and Experience*, especially Chapter XI, also offer important views about concepts and their own theories, certainly as finely wrought as those of Ryle or Geach. But, here again, their theories are versions, brilliant as they are, of traditional theories and can therefore be safely left to themselves to compete for the ultimate truth about concepts, so that we can expeditiously conclude our survey of the major theories and the very recent criticism and rejection of them.

Frege

Frege's theory of concepts is inextricably tied to his philosophy of arithmetic and the derivation of arithmetic from logic. His theory covers not only concepts in and of arithmetic and mathematics but all scientific and ordinary concepts as well. The assignment of numbers to concepts and the definitions of the concepts of numbers, whether cardinal, ordinal, rational, irrational, complex, or infinite; and of arithmetical operations, such as addition, establish the nature, criteria and role of all concepts. A concept, thus, is governed by a definitive set of necessary and sufficient criteria that determines whether or not an object falls under that concept or, indeed, whether it is a concept at all. Ambiguity, vagueness and indeterminacy are ruled out. Concepts are necessarily closed; their sense and the intelligibility of the questions and assertions in which they are expressed rest on absolutely determinate criteria. Nowhere does Frege make clearer his theory that all concepts – to be concepts – must be closed than in his *Grundgesetze der Arithmetik* (vol. ii, section 56):

> A definition of a concept (of a possible predicate) must be complete; it must unambiguously determine, as regards any object, whether or not it falls under the concept (whether or not the predicate is truly assertible of it). Thus there must not be any object as regards which the definition leaves in doubt whether it falls under the concept; though for us men, with our defective knowledge, the question may not always be decidable. We may express this metaphorically as follows: the concept must have a sharp boundary. If we represent concepts in extension by areas on a plane, this is admittedly a picture that may be used only with caution, but here it can do us good service. To a concept without sharp boundary there would correspond an area that had not a sharp boundary-line all round, but in places just vaguely faded away into the background. This would not really be an area at all; and likewise a concept that is not sharply defined is wrongly termed a concept. Such quasi-conceptual constructions cannot be recognized as concepts by logic; it is impossible to lay down precise laws for them. The law of excluded middle is really just another form of the requirement that the concept should have a sharp boundary. Any object Δ that you choose to take either falls under the concept *ø* or does not fall under it; *tertium non datur*. E.g. would the sentence 'any square root of 9 is odd' have a comprehensible sense at all if *square root of* 9 were not a concept with a sharp boundary? Has the question 'Are we still Christians?' really got a sense, if it is indeterminate whom the predicate 'Christian' can truly be asserted of, and who must be refused it? (trs. Black and Geach).

As original and foundational as his philosophy of arithmetic may be, Frege's theory of concepts – which is an essential part of his philosophy of arithmetic – is as old as Plato and as up-to-date as the ensuing *Tractatus Logico-Philosophicus*, inspired in great measure by Frege, at least in its demand (confused with discovery) that all concepts be closed.

What, now, in its particulars, is Frege's theory of concepts? In *Die Grundlagen der Arithmetik* (1884), Frege defines the concept of number which is fundamental to arithmetic. First, however, he considers individual numbers and certain theories about them. No theory other than the one he proposes – that numbers are assigned to concepts, not to objects – can explain numbers and the concept of number. He lays down three principles of his inquiry: to separate the logical from the psychological; to determine the meaning of a word only in the context of a proposition; and to distinguish concept from object. In arithmetic, rigour of proof and precise limitation of extent of validity rest on sharp definition of concepts.

Numerical formulae, such as '2 + 3 = 5,' deal with particular numbers. Arithmetic, however, includes also general laws that obtain among all whole numbers. Both are provable; it is a mistake to regard the first as immediately evident. Nor are numerical formulae provable by intuition. '135664 + 37863 = 173527' is neither self-evident nor an intuition. If Kant is wrong to regard numerical formulae as intuitions, J. S. Mill is equally at fault in reducing them to empirical generalizations, since he cannot explain large numbers or even 0 by observation, or why the symbol of the latter has a sense. Frege, however, distinguishes between arithmetic and geometry and agrees with Kant that the axioms of geometry are synthetic even though the laws of arithmetic are not.

Numbers are not properties of physical objects, like weight or colour. I can point to the colour of an object, I can ask how much it weighs; but I cannot point to its number or ask how many without specifying what it is that is to be counted. Further, all kinds of things that are not physical can be counted. Again, neither 0 nor 1 can be a property of things; and number cannot be a set or plurality, vague as these are, without leaving out of its account 0 and 1. That numbers are not objective properties of things, however, does not yield that numbers are subjective creations or Kantian intuitions. For numbers are objective in the same sense that the axis of the earth or the centre of gravity of the solar system is objective. Numbers are independent of our thinking of them; and they are not abstracted from the sensible: 'It is in this way that I understand objective to mean what is independent of our sensation, intuition and imagination, and of all construction of mental pictures out of memories of earlier sensation, but not of what is independent of the reason' (no. 26; tr. J. Austin, *The Foundations of Arithmetic*).

Although Frege rejects numbers or number as abstractions from the sensible or from units, he does not reject abstractions altogether as a mode of concept formation. The concept of cat can be derived from a white and a black cat by disregarding their distinguishing properties. 'The concept "cat", no doubt, which we have arrived at by abstraction, no longer includes the special characteristics of either, but that is the very reason why it is only a concept' (no. 34). Elsewhere, he adds: 'What is it, in fact, that we are supposed to abstract from, in order to get, for example, from the moon to the number 1? By abstraction we get, indeed, certain concepts, namely the following: satellite of the Earth, satellite of a planet, non-self-luminous heavenly body, body, object' (no. 44). 'We now see also why there is a temptation to suggest that we get number by abstraction from things. What we do actually get by such means is the concept, and in this we then discover the number. Thus abstraction does genuinely often precede the formation of a judgement of number' (no. 48). So much, then, for the reading of Frege's theory of concepts as a total rejection of abstractionism. All he rejects is that 0 and 1, therefore, that all numbers can be formed by abstraction: 'What will not work with 0 and 1 cannot be essential to the concept of number' (no. 44).

If number is not abstracted from things in the way that colour, weight and hardness are, and is not a property of things, as they are, what then do we talk about when we make a statement of number? A concept – not an object, an idea, an abstraction, or a thing: '...A statement of number contains an assertion about a concept' (no. 46). Consider the assertions, 'Venus has 0 moons' and 'The King's carriage is drawn by four horses.' In the first, a property, namely, that of including nothing under it, is assigned to the concept moon of Venus; in the second, the number four is assigned to the concept horse that draws the King's carriage. Some concepts, such as that of inhabitant of Germany, have a time reference as one of their variables. And because this concept is mathematically a function of the time, the concept is fluid; nevertheless, the addition of a time reference renders the concept – in this case, of the inhabitant of Germany, January 1, 1883, Berlin time – fixed. Thus, that a concept may be fluid contravenes nothing of its essentially determinate character.

Frege also distinguishes between a proper name and a general term. The name of a thing is a proper name. General terms, however, do not name things; they signify concepts. They become proper names, hence cease to be general terms, only when they are joined to definite articles or demonstrative pronouns. With a proper name, but not with a concept, the question whether anything and, if so, what, falls under it, makes no sense. Concepts are composed of characteristics (*Merkmale*) that are the properties of the things that fall under them. These characteristics or marks are different from the properties that are asserted of concepts. The concept rectangular triangle, for example, does not have the characteristics rectangular; the statement, 'There is no rectangular equilateral rectilinear triangle,' assigns the number 0 to the relevant concept.

Frege can now define the numbers: 'The number 0 belongs to a concept, if the proposition that a does not fall under that concept is true universally, whatever a may be' (no. 55). 'The number 1 belongs to a concept F, if the proposition that a does not fall under F is not true universally, whatever a may be, and if from the propositions "a falls under F" and "b falls under F" it follows universally that a and b are the same' (no. 55). 'The number $(n\text{-}1)$ belongs to a concept F, if there is an object a falling under F and such that the number n belongs to the concept "falling under F, but not a"' (no. 55). An individual number, Frege concludes, is a self-subsistent object. 'In the proposition "the number 0 belongs to the concept F", 0 is only an element in the predicate (taking the concept F to be the real subject)' (no. 57).

Number words have no meaning in isolation, only in their propositional contexts. To define a number is to define the sense of a proposition in which a number word occurs. Number words stand for self-subsistent objects. 'And that is enough to give us a class of propositions which must have a sense, namely those which express our recognition of a number as the same again' (no. 62). Number is to be defined in terms of numerical identity, not vice versa. In particular, what is to be defined is the sense of the proposition. 'The number which belongs to the concept F is the same as that which belongs to the concept G' without using the expression 'the number which belongs to the concept F.' Frege's definition, then, is this: 'The Number which belongs to the concept F is the extension of the concept "equal to the concept F"' (no. 68). Number derives from the relation of similarity; similarity, from many-one correlation which is a purely logical concept. This reduction establishes Frege's logistic thesis of arithmetic.

In 'Function and Concept' (1891), Frege elucidates function and concept in mathematics. The thesis that functions are expressions, for example, that '$2x^3 + x$' is a function of 'x' and that '$2.2^3 + 2$' is a function of '2', does not distinguish sign from thing signified. 'What is expressed in the equation "$2.2^3 + 2 = 18$" is that the right-hand complex of signs has the same reference as the left-hand one. I must here combat the view that, e.g., $2 + 5$ and $3 + 4$ are equal but not the same. This view is grounded in the same confusion of form and content, sign and thing signified' (*Translations from the Philosophical Writings of Gottlob Frege*, eds., P. Geach and M. Black, hereinafter *GB*, p. 22). Numerals, thus, must be distinguished from what they stand for: many expressions, such as '2,' '$1 + 1$,' '3–1,' '6:3,' stand for the same thing.

Frege distinguishes between function, argument and value. Consider '$2.1^3 + 1$,' '$2.4^3 + 4$' and '$2.5^3 + 5$.' These expressions, he says, have the same function but different arguments – '1,' '4,' '5' – and different values – 3, 132, 255. 'It is the common element of these expressions that contains the essential pecularity of a function; i.e. what is present in "$2.x^3 + x$" over and above the letter "x." We could write this somewhat as follows: "2. ( )^3 + ( )"' (*GB*, p. 24).

The argument is not part of the function; it and the function make up a whole. But the function is incomplete, 'unsaturated.' In this it differs fundamentally from a number. '$2.1^3 + 1$' and '$2.2^3 + 2$' are different expressions; they stand for different numbers, but they have the same function. '$2.1^3 + 1$' and '4–1' have equal numerical values but they do not have the same function. Besides the ordinary signs of functions, such as '+,' '-,' etc., Frege adds '=,' ' > ,' ' < ,' as signs for constructing functional expressions: '$x^2 = 1$' is a functional expression; 'x' takes the place of the argument. Suppose now we replace 'x' successively by '-1,' '0,' '1,' and '2.' Then we get: $(-1)^2 = 1$; $0^2 = 1$; $1^2 = 1$; and $2^2 = 1$. The first and third equations are true, the second and fourth, false. 'I now say "the value of our function is a truth-value" and distinguish between the truth-values of what is true and what is false' *GB*, p. 28). '$2^2 = 4$' stands for the True as '2^2' stands for 4. From which it follows that '$2^2 = 4$,' '$2 > 1$,' and '$2^4 = 4^2$' stand for the same thing – the True. From which it further follows that $(2^2 = 4) = (2 > 1)$ is a correct equation.

To the objection that '$2^2 = 4$' and '$2 > 1$' are different assertions, express different thoughts, as do '$2^4 = 4^2$' and '$4.4 = 4^2$,' yet because '2^4' can be replaced by '4.4,' '$2^4 = 4^2$' and '$4.4 = 4^2$' have the same reference, Frege concludes that from identity of reference there does not follow identity of the thought expressed. 'The Evening Star is a planet with a shorter period of revolution than the Earth' expresses a different thought from 'The Morning Star is a planet with a shorter period of revolution than the Earth.' Nevertheless, they have the same reference. 'The Evening Star' and 'The Morning Star' are proper names of the same heavenly body. Hence we must distinguish between sense and reference. So, too, with '2^4' and '4^2;' they are proper names of the same number; they differ in their sense but have the same reference. Thus, since $2^4 = 4.4$, $(2^4 = 4^2) = (4.4 = 4^2)$; and $(2^2 = 4) = (2 > 1)$.

Consider next the functional expression '$x^2 = 1$.' The value of this function is either the True or the False. If for a different argument, for example, '–1,' the value of this function is the True, we can say: '"The number –1 has the property that its square is 1"; or, more briefly, "–1 is a square root of 1"; or, "–1 falls under the concept: square root of 1"' (*GB*, p. 30). If, on the other hand, the value of this function for an argument 2 is the False, we can say: "2 does not fall under the concept: square root of 1." We thus see how closely that which is called a concept in logic is connected with what we call a function. Indeed, we may say at once: a concept is a function whose value is always a truth-value' (*GB*, p. 30).

In addition to equations and inequalities, statements can be split into two parts, one complete, the other unsaturated. 'Caesar conquered Gaul,' for example, can be split into 'Caesar' and 'conquered Gaul.' The latter contains an empty place; it must be filled in by a proper name or an expression that replaces a proper name in order to get a sense. As it is, 'conquered Gaul' stands for a function or concept whose argument here is Caesar.

As far as arguments are concerned, not only numbers but objects in general, including persons, can occur as arguments of functions. Objects – without restriction – can be values of functions. 'The capital of the German Empire' is an expression that takes the place of a proper name and stands for an object. Split it up into 'the capital of' and 'the German Empire.' The first is unsaturated, incomplete; the second is complete. 'The capital of x,' then, is the expression of a function. If the German Empire is the argument, Berlin is the value of the function. An object, thus, which can be an argument or a value of a function, Frege says, 'is anything that is not a function, so that an expression for it does not contain any empty place' (*GB*, p. 32).

A statement contains no empty place. So what it stands for – a truth-value – is an object. Thus, the True and the False are objects. Value-ranges of functions, but not functions, are objects. And because value-ranges, e.g., $\epsilon^2(\epsilon^2 - 1)$, are extensions of concepts, their extensions, but not their concepts, are objects.

Scientific rigour requires that expressions have a reference: 'We must see to it that we never perform calculations with empty signs in the belief that we are dealing with objects' (*GB*, p. 32). It is essential, for example, that '$a + b$' have a reference, whatever signs for definite objects we put in place of 'a' and 'b.'

> This involves the requirement as regards concepts, that, for any argument, they shall have a truth-value as their value; that it shall be determinate, for any object, whether it falls under the concept or not. In other words: as regards concepts we have a requirement of sharp delimitation; if this were not satisfied it would be impossible to set forth logical laws about them (*GB*, p. 33).

In 'On Concept and Object' (1892), Frege distinguishes between the logical and the psychological senses of 'concept.' In its logical sense, a concept, he repeats, is predicative and, as such, it differs radically from a proper name, which is never employed as a grammatical predicate. Examples that seem to contradict this non-predicative character of proper names, such as 'This is Alexander the Great' or 'It is the number four' or 'It is the planet Venus,' do not contradict Frege's dictum since they express equations, not predications. 'This is green' or 'This is a mammal,' however, says that something falls under a concept. Further, equations are reversible; an object's falling under a concept is not.

Suppose now I say, 'The morning star is Venus.' Is 'Venus' a proper name as a predicate? Frege says it is not: 'What is predicated here is ... *no other than Venus*' (*GB*, p. 44). These words stand for a concept that must be distinguished from the object that 'Venus' names. 'Venus,' thus, can never be a predicate, only part of a predicate. Hence, the reference of 'Venus' is an object, not a concept.

Although concepts are predicative, they can be represented by an object – by prefixing the words, 'the concept;' 'The concept man is not empty' is about the object designated by its proper name, 'the concept man.' 'The concept *square root of 4* is realized' is also about an object of which something is asserted. 'There is at least one square root of 4,' however, is not about an object, neither the numbers 2 or –2, but about a concept, square root of 2, which asserts that the concept is not empty. In the sentence, 'There is at least one square root of 4,' 'square root of 4' cannot be replaced by 'the concept square root of 4.' As Frege says, 'the assertion that suits the concept does not suit the object' (*GB*, p. 49).

The words, 'the concept square root of 4,' behave differently from the words, 'square root of 4,' as their possible substitutions show. Consequently their references are essentially different. Furthermore, an object falls under a concept; a concept falls within another concept. The latter, Frege calls 'a second-level concept.'

In 'On Sense and Reference' (1893), Frege begins with equality. Whether he begins with the concept or the word, he does not say. By 'equality' he means '"$a = b$" has the sense of "a is the same as b" or "a and b coincide".' Is equality a relation? Between objects, names, or signs of objects? Frege says equality is a relation between signs of objects: The assertion '$a = b$' says that the signs or names 'a' and 'b' designate the same thing. If equality were a relation between objects, '$a = b$' would be the same as '$a = a$', provided of course that '$a = b$' is true.

A sign or name is a designation representing a proper name that has as its reference a definite object. A sign generally has a sense and a reference. A reference may have many different signs. However, not all signs have a sense to which a reference corresponds: 'The words "the celestial body most distant from the Earth" have a sense, but it is very doubtful if they also have a reference' (*GB*, p. 58).

We ordinarily use words to speak of their reference. Sometimes, however, we wish to talk only of the words or of their sense as, for example, in quoting another's words. Here words are enclosed in quotation marks, which take away their ordinary reference. But in direct speech, a proper name, which can be a word, a sign, a combination of signs, or an expression, expresses its sense and stands for or designates its reference. With declarative sentences, their senses and references differ from proper names. A declarative sentence contains a thought. If it has a reference it remains the same when we replace one word of the sentence with another having the same reference but a different sense. Yet the thought changes, as in the exchange of 'the morning star' for 'the evening star' in 'The morning star is a body illuminated by the Sun,' since someone who does not know the one is the other might consider one true, the other false. 'The thought, accordingly, cannot be the reference of the sentence, but must rather be considered as the sense' (*GB*, p. 62). Sentences have references as well as senses, as is shown by our seeking references of their components. But the references of sentences are not the references of their components. Instead, they are their truth values: we may consider the whole sentence as a proper name and its reference, if it has one, as the True or the False.

The relation of the thought expressed by a sentence and the True is one of sense to reference, not of subject to predicate. The latter gives only a thought. By combining subject and predicate, one reaches only a thought; one never passes from sense to reference, or from a thought to its truth value.

All true sentences have the same reference, as do all false sentences, since the reference of a sentence is its truth value. The truth value of a sentence remains unchanged when an expression is replaced by another having the same reference. What, now, if the expression to be replaced is itself a sentence? Do these subordinate sentences or clauses, at least in direct speech, have for their reference truth values? Frege then argues, by examples, that a subordinate clause has for its sense a part of a thought, therefore, no truth value as reference. Frege concludes:

> When we found '$a = a$' and '$a = b$' to have different
> cognitive values, the explanation is that for the purpose of
> knowledge, the sense of the sentence, viz., the thought
> expressed by it, is no less relevant than its reference, i.e. its
> truth value. If now '$a = b$', then indeed the reference of 'b'
> is the same as that of 'a,' and hence the truth value of '$a =
> b$' is the same as that of '$a = a$.' In spite of this, the sense
> of 'b' may differ from that of 'a,' and thereby the sense
> expressed in '$a = b$' differs from that of '$a = a$.' In that
> case the two sentences do not have the same cognitive
> value (*GB*, p. 78).

I hope I have covered Frege's main discussions of concepts. What they add up to is that concepts are functions in the mathematical sense, for example, $x^2 = 4$, as distinct from objects, arguments, proper names, truth values, and their linguistic correlates of general terms or predicates. Among the concepts Frege mentions are those of square root of 1, square root of 9, cat, satellite of the earth, body, moon of Venus, horse that draws the King's carriage, inhabitant of Germany, inhabitant of Germany, January 1, 1883, Berlin time, conqueror of Gaul, no other than Venus, rectangular triangle, and Christian. But of course there are thousands more, including the concepts of argument, object, proper name, truth value, general term, and predicate, that are concepts of items which items are no more concepts in themselves than is virtue for Frege. However, whether a concept is a concept of a concept or of something else, it is a mathematical function that occupies a predicative place in talk and thought about the world. As a function, it is unsaturated, i.e., contains an empty place which must be filled in with an argument to be completed and thereby to obtain a truth value. A concept, thus, is a function whose value is always a truth value.

The concept of x is an object, named by its proper name, 'the concept of x.' But a concept is not an object. What, then, is it? What is a function? Even if it is not an object, it is objective, that is, it is independent of our sensation, intuition and imagination, though it is dependent on reason. Numbers are objective and are objects. Functions are not objects but they are objective. Otherwise we are left with functions as mere signs without sense, a view Frege roundly rejects. $x^2 = 4$, though like number it exists nowhere, yet must have some reality; or, in Frege's terms, it must subsist even if it is not a subsistent object. It seems to me then that a function is an entity and, because it is, its concept as a function whose value is a truth value is also an entity. Square root of 1 and the concept of square root of 1 (but not the concept of *the* square root of 1) are both entities, the one expressed by a predicate, the other, by a proper name. However, if square root of 1 or any concept is an entity, that is expressed by a predicate, it seems arbitrary to rule out predicates, as names of entities, on a par with proper names, as names of objects. Frege, thus, it seems to me, faces this dilemma which I cannot find that he resolves: Either concepts as functions are entities named by predicates or concepts as functions are mere signs which while they may have sense do not signify anything. Not even the divine Frege can have his platonic *Noéta* and have them too.

Concepts, thus, are platonic ideas for Frege. (They are not platonic concepts for Frege, at least on my reading of Plato; but that concepts or the having of them are skills or abilities Frege, I think, would reject.) Frege says that not everything is definable; but he does not say there are ultimate simples. This allows us to ascribe to him the general thesis that all concepts are definable and definable in a complete way that precludes once and for all any indeterminacy about them. Every concept is composed of characteristics or marks (*Merkmale*) that are the properties which fall under it. In the *Grundgesetze*, to turn to a fresh example, Frege considers square, which is a concept, as against the concept square, which is an object:

> If we say: 'A square is a rectangle in which the adjacent sides are equal,' we define the concept *square* by specifying what properties something must have in order to fall under this concept. I call these properties 'marks' of the concept. But it must be carefully noted that these marks of the concept are not properties of the concept. The concept *square* is not a rectangle; only the objects which fall under this concept are rectangles... (*GB*, p. 145).

Squares, thus, have necessary and sufficient properties – real essences. These properties serve as the marks of being square: the defining characteristics of the concept square. And these characteristics serve as the definitive criteria for determining whether something is square or not. Being square, consequently, is a closed concept for Frege: a concept composed of a definitive set of necessary and sufficient characteristics. This set not only settles whether a particular object falls under the concept square but, as important, legislates the correct use of the word 'square' or its non-English equivalents. Thus, we may say that for Frege, a necessary condition for the intelligible correct use of 'square' is knowing the essence of square, having the definition of its concept. The criteria of the employment of the word 'square' are fixed by the characteristics of the concept square.

What holds for square obtains for all concepts, according to Frege. All concepts are real essences – mathematical functions as subsistent entities – that determine what, if anything, falls under them and, at the same time, the criteria of the use of the corresponding words. The precision, clarity and determinacy of the concepts of mathematics and formal logic govern the whole of conceptualization. What is required for square or square root of 9 or satellite of the earth is also a requisite for Christian, to use Frege's example; and, if for Christian, for all concepts in order for them to be concepts at all: 'The concept must have a sharp boundary... A concept that is not sharply defined is wrongly termed a concept.'

Central, then, in Frege's theory of concepts is not that concepts are functions whose values are always truth values – as important as this thesis is – but his universal claim that all concepts, to be concepts, must be closed: composed of definitive sets of characteristics that determine exact classification of objects and correct use of language. Rather than revolutionary or even original, his theory of concepts represents in its explicitness the consummation and culmination of the whole classical tradition, stemming from Plato and Aristotle, that concepts must be closed if the conceptual life is to be rendered intelligible.

Russell

Having argued some 30 years ago that the method of analysis as Russell conceived it is basic in his philosophical writings, giving them a unity often belied by his many ostensible changes of doctrines,[4] it may seem strange that I now wish to claim that it is – as it is with all philosophers – his theory of concepts or, more accurately in his case, two theories of concepts that are fundamental in his philosophy. I did not then see, as I think I do now, that his conception of analysis, as it revolves around real definition and contextual definition, is, whether ontological or linguistic, inquiry into concepts. From his early books on mathematics and logic to his middle and late works on metaphysics, theory of knowledge, and philosophy of science, Russell's great concern is with a number of fundamental and related concepts. His two theories of concepts, that concepts are ontological entities which subsist independently of the mind and that they are logical fictions constructed by the mind, both stated or implied by the concepts he employs and the doctrines he maintains or repudiates, are to be found especially here – in his specific analyses of the concepts in mathematics, logic and the sciences of physics and psychology.

Russell's first explicit statement of a theory of concepts is in *The Principles of Mathematics* (1903). The overall aim of that work of course is not to formulate such a theory but to establish the logistic thesis of mathematics. Arithmetic and geometry derive from logic: the principles of mathematics are deducible from the principles of logic; and the concepts of mathematics are definable in terms of the concepts of logic. In the *Principles*, there are not only concepts in mathematics and logic, concepts or 'notions,' as Russell calls them, such as number, one, addition, or proposition, variable, implication, and constant; there are also concepts of mathematics and logic and, indeed, of all intelligible discourse. The relation between the concepts in mathematics and logic and the concepts of these disciplines, without which neither mathematics nor logic can be rendered certain and independent of the mind, becomes crucial in Russell's philosophy of logic, however dispensable it may be for the logistic programme for mathematics generally.

This distinction between concepts as subjects and concepts as objects of discourse, including mathematics and logic, first occurs in Chapter IV, 'Proper Names, Adjectives, and Verbs.' Russell introduces philosophical grammar as *a* – not the – clue to what there is. The distinction between speech or linguistic expression and what these indicate, whether things, concepts or propositions, all as non-linguistic entities, is preserved throughout. The three most important parts of speech – substantives, adjectives and verbs – indicate (are about) entities, whatever their grammatical roles may be. Substantives that are only proper names and cannot be logically derived from adjectives or verbs denote things. Substantives that logically derive from adjectives or verbs (such as 'humanity' from 'human' or 'sequence' from 'follows') as well as adjectives and verbs denote concepts. Adjectives, Russell adds, name predicates and verbs name relations. Presumably, substantives, whether primary or derivative, name subjects.

That concepts are objects of discourse, to be distinguished from concepts in discourse, such as the concepts of number, formal implication, and the like, Russell makes as clear as he does anything else in this obscure chapter. First, he introduces his concept of a term:

> Whatever may be an object of thought, or may occur in any true or false proposition, or can be counted as *one*, I call a *term*. This, then, is the widest word in the philosophical vocabulary. I shall use as synonymous with it

the words unit, individual, and entity. The first two
emphasize the fact that every term is *one*, while the third is
derived from the fact that every term has being, i.e. *is* in
some sense. A man, a moment, a number, a class, a
relation, a chimaera, or anything else that can be
mentioned, is sure to be a term; and to deny that such and
such a thing is a term must always be false (p. 43).

Every term is a logical subject; and, like traditional substance, is
immutable and indestructible. And every constituent of every
proposition is a term; and every proposition contains at least two
constituents or terms. But, most important for our immediate purpose, terms are of two kinds, Russell claims: things and concepts.
Since concepts are denoted by, indicated by, or named by adjectives,
verbs, and some substantives, concepts are divisible into predicates
and relations. Discourse, thus, may be about things; but the concepts
in this discourse are always about predicates and relations, concepts
as terms; ontological entities in a supersensible, platonic realm.
Without such a realm, there could be no propositions since there
would be no constituents of them; and therefore there could be no
discourse, whether mathematical or not, about anything. That some
terms are things is a necessary condition of some discourse; that
other terms are concepts – predicates and relations – is a necessary
condition of any discourse, hence a ground of its very intelligibility.
In the next chapter, 'Denoting,' Russell further complicates his
theory of concepts in the *Principles*. 'Denoting concepts' name
certain concepts in discourse that inherently denote things, not
concepts, whether these things exist or not, are many or one. Denoting concepts, thus, differ from ordinary denoting by pointing or
describing or using words as symbols for concepts; and from the concepts of discourse: what the derivative substantives, adjectives and
verbs indicate.

But the fact that description is possible – that we are able,
by the employment of concepts, to designate a thing which
is not a concept – is due to a logical relation between
some concepts and some terms, in virtue of which such
concepts inherently and logically *denote* such terms (p. 53).

Thus, a concept is a denoting concept when the proposition in
which it occurs is about a term – a thing, however, not a concept. The

proposition, 'I met a man,' is about a thing, not the concept *a man*. The proposition, 'Any finite number is odd or even,' is about numbers, not about the concept *any finite number*, nor about the entity, any number, which is a non-entity. The proposition, 'Man is mortal,' is about men, not *man* as concept or man as thing; nor is it about *men* as a concept. The proposition, thus, is about what the concept *men* denotes. The concept of a denoting concept – of a concept that inherently denotes things, not concepts – Russell insists, is a fundamental concept of logic, required to explain definition, identity, classes, symbolism, and the variable, in any book on the principles of mathematics.

Every predicate generates allied concepts, some of which are denoting concepts:

> Starting, for example, with *human*, we have man, men, all men, every man, any man, the human race, of which all except the first are twofold, a denoting concept and an object denoted; we have also, less closely analogous, the notions 'a man' and 'some man,' which again denote objects other than themselves (p. 55; 'Object,' which covers both singular and plural as well as ambiguities, such as 'a man,' Russell adds in a note, is an even wider term than 'term;' from which it follows that terms are species of objects, just as concepts are species of terms).

Besides denoting concepts, there are denoting phrases: these are phrases that are prefixed by the words 'all,' 'every,' 'any,' 'a,' 'some,' and 'the.' Each of these words introduces a denoting phrase which contains a class-concept. Russell raises as a central problem regarding denoting phrases: Do denoting phrases denote different objects or are they merely different ways of denoting? After an examination of the roles of these denoting phrases, he concludes, as he puts it best in his next chapter on 'Classes': 'there are not different ways of denoting, but only different kinds of denoting concepts and correspondingly different kinds of denoted objects' (p. 72).

That Russell does distinguish between concepts in discourse and concepts of discourse can also be seen in his discussion of classes. The concept of a class is another fundamental concept in mathematics. Russell distinguishes this concept from both a class-concept and a class: 'Thus *man* is the class-concept, *men* (the concept) is the concept of the class, and men (the object denoted by the concept *men*) are the class' (p. 67). As prolix as Russell is on concepts and classes, what he seems to hold is that: the concept of the class of men is a concept but it is about the class of men, not about the concept of men or man; it is consequently not like the concept of humanity, which is about the (predicate-) concept, being human, and is not about any thing, as the concept of men is about things. Thus, class-concepts seem to reduce to concepts about predicates, themselves concepts; concepts of classes reduce to concepts of collections of terms; from which it further follows that discourse in which concepts of classes are present is not discourse about concepts at all. Or, to put it in Russell's terminology, the object of thought when we think about classes is a term but of a collection of things, not of a concept.

Classes, too, can be denoted by denoting concepts. The null-class – the class with no members – is denoted by the denoting concept *Nothing*. '*Nothing* is a denotings concept, which denotes nothing' (p. 75). That the null-class can be denoted, however, does not imply that the null-class is actual; all it allows are the null-class-concept and the null concept of a class. The null-class, Russell says, 'is a fiction' (p. 81); the null-class-concept is not. This, so far as I know, is Russell's first use of 'fiction'; here it is attributed to a class. Later it shall apply to all class-concepts, all concepts of classes, all concepts in and of discourse.

As difficult, perhaps incoherent, as much of Russell's theory of concepts is in the *Principles*, it is clear, I think, that at least he finds a legitimate place for concepts in language which he does not reduce to purely verbal equivalents and in the realm of terms whose super-sensible nature he does not challenge or reduce to things or the sensuous. Denoting concepts, like class-concepts, complicate his theory, as indeed does his theory of propositions and their constituents. However, since these complications neither add to concepts as entities nor subtract from concepts as embodied in uses of language, their presence does not compromise or alter his theory of concepts as ontological, platonic entities – in particular, pre-dicates and relations – that constitute a, perhaps the, necessary condition of order in the world and of intelligibility of our thought and talk about it, including mathematical and logical. That Russell ever abandons this condition as necessary, that is, that his later resolution of talk about the world as talk about the values of certain propositional functions repudiates or, oppositely, rests on the ontology of predicates and relations, is one of the great cruces in the exegesis of Russell as well as of contemporary philosophy of logic.

Two years after *The Principles of Mathematics*, Russell published 'On Denoting' (1905). This paper, justly universally acclaimed, is also universally acknowledged, and by Russell, too, to be a rejection of his ontology of terms and objects – things and concepts – in the *Principles*; and, more important, as the beginning of Russell's shift from real definition to contextual definition of concepts. Neither claim, it seems to me, is true: Russell does not reject his ontology; all he rejects is that denoting concepts inherently denote things, not concepts; and all he contextually defines are propositions containing denoting concepts. The things and concepts (predicates and relations) of the realm of terms remain intact; and there is not even a hint that concepts other than denoting must or should be defined away in their propositional contexts. Russell's later theory of descriptions is present in his theory of denoting phrases; but his claim that denoting phrases have no meaning in isolation is not yet the later claim that they are incomplete symbols, to be rendered complete in contexts in which they disappear, nor is it the accompanying claim that many, perhaps all, scientific concepts are, like denoting phrases, incomplete symbols to be logically constructed out of symbols that do have meaning in isolation.

The theory of denoting phrases was designed as a theory to deal systematically and homogeneously with all denoting phrases in such a manner that the propositions in whose verbal expressions they occurred would no longer be about things but instead about the variables of propositional functions. But the theory was logically motivated by the fact that Russell's theory in the *Principles* that every denoting concept inherently denotes things, not concepts, implies the existence not only of non-existent things but also of self-contradictory things, about both of which self-contradictory propositions could be made: 'The centaur (which is a non-existent term) does not exist;' 'The round square (which is a self-contradictory term) does not exist.' These existential disclaimers, especially the second – Russell seems not to have been troubled by the first – both presuppose and deny the existence of the things disclaimed. That denoting concepts denote things, thus, entails the intolerable consequence that existential disclaimers embody self-contradictions. A new, radical, solution of denoting concepts and of the phrases that express them was required. The main problem that generated the theory of denoting phrases was: How can we talk about anything without presupposing that it must exist in order to talk about it? It is the avoidance of contradiction, not the (later) preservation of 'a robust sense of reality' (*Introduction to Mathematical Philosophy*, 1919, p. 170), that prompts the theory.

Russell begins 'On Denoting' with a list rather than a definition of denoting phrases, which includes phrases with 'a,' 'some,' 'any,' 'every,' 'all,' and 'the.' '... A phrase is denoting solely in virtue of its *form*,' Russell says, without adding what *form* contrasts with here; presumably it contrasts with *what* the phrase denotes. Some of these phrases denote nothing, some, one definite object, others, ambiguously. What is needed is a theory that primarily will cover all three uniformly without falling into contradiction and, secondarily, can resolve certain traditional puzzles of identity, excluded middle and difference generated by denoting phrases.

The subject of denoting, he also points out, and which is of relevance to his ontological theory of concepts, is important in theory of knowledge as well as in mathematics and logic. The centre of mass of the solar system at a definite instant is some definite point. However, we have no immediate acquaintance with this point, known to us only by description. Russell thus distinguishes between acquaintance and knowledge about – not knowledge by acquaintance as against knowledge by description, a distinction developed later in *The Problems of Philosophy* (1912) and elsewhere. The distinction here is 'between the things we have presentations of, and the things we only reach by means of denoting phrases' ('On Denoting'; reprinted in R. C. Marsh, ed., *Bertrand Russell, Logic and Knowledge: Essays, 1901–1950*, hereinafter *Marsh*, p. 41). Of direct concern to Russell's theory of concepts is his related distinction between our acquaintance in perception with certain objects and our acquaintance in thought 'with objects of a more abstract logical character' (*Marsh*, p. 41). Are these objects of thought among the concept-terms of the *Principles*? It seems most likely; and, further, though Russell does not say so here, nor does he rule it out, some of these objects of thought can also be known by denoting phrases or, as he claims in the *Problems*, by description. It is also these objects, presented in or known by acquaintance or by description that Russell refers to as the objects of conception, both in the *Problems* and in his essay, 'On the Relations of Universals and Particulars' (1911).

Russell takes as fundamental to his theory of denoting phrases the notion of the variable. He then declares that 'x has C' means a propositional function in which 'x' is a constituent and, as a variable, is undetermined. With this minimum logical machinery of propositional function and variable, he can now interpret phrases containing 'everything,' 'something' and 'nothing,' which are, to him, the most primitive denoting phrases: 'everything has C' is to mean 'the propositional function "x has C is false" is always true;' 'nothing has C' is to mean 'the propositional function "x has C is false" is always true;' and 'something has C' is to mean 'it is false that the propositional function "x has C is false" is always true.' Because 'nothing' and 'something' are defined in terms of 'x has C is always true,' the latter is taken to be ultimate and indefinable. Further, 'everything,' 'nothing' and 'something' are said to have no meaning in isolation. A meaning is assigned to the propositions in which they occur: thus, 'nothing has C' is to mean 'the propositional function "x has C is false" is always true.' This, Russell says, is the basic thesis of the theory of denoting phrases: 'that denoting phrases never have any meaning in themselves, but that every proposition in whose verbal expression they occur has a meaning' (*Marsh*, p. 43).

In the *Principles*, 'I met a man,' Russell wrote, is about an actual man, a thing-term, not the concept *a man*. Now, in 'On Denoting,' because of the difficulties already noted about the self-contradictory character of existential disclaimers, Russell says 'I met a man' is neither about a thing nor a concept. Rather it affirms 'the propositional function "I met x and x is human" is not always false.' 'A man' disappears in its sentential, propositional context. If the utterance is about anything, it is about the variable of a compound propositional function. Thus, denoting concepts are reduced to denoting phrases and resolved into contexts that are given meanings. Whether the propositional functions remain ontological predicates, among the terms of the *Principles*, or are reducible to linguistic entities, is once again left in abeyance; although Russell's rejection of denoting concepts as a special class of concepts about things in favour of his acceptance of propositions containing denoting phrases in their verbal expressions as being affirmations about the (always, sometimes or never) satisfaction of predicates expressed by the propositional functions, strongly supports, even reinforces, the ontological status of concepts of the *Principles*. The resolution of denoting phrases, indeed, rests on the predicates-concepts-terms of the *Principles*. Thus, so far as I can see, 'On Denoting' repudiates only one kind of concept – the denoting; it leaves absolutely untouched the concepts present in discourse, e.g., 'the notion of the variable,' or the concepts of discourse, e.g., 'the predicate *human*.'

'On Denoting,' of course, offers analyses of all the denoting phrases, including 'the author of *Waverley*' and 'the present King of France,' both of which Russell was to make famous. 'The' in the singular, like 'a,' has no meaning by itself; but unlike 'a,' it involves uniqueness; and Russell's analysis proceeds in exactly the same way as it does with 'a,' except that it adds as part of the meaning of the proposition in whose verbal expression 'the' occurs, that one and only one value satisfies the propositional function in question, e.g., '*x* wrote *Waverley*.' The essay also contains some criticisms of Frege's theory of denoting, now fairly discredited as an accurate account of Frege's distinction between *Sinn* and *Bedeutung* in that it confuses sentence and proposition in Frege, for whom a sentence has a meaning, sometimes a denotation, and the proposition is the meaning of the sentence not, as Russell expounds it, that for Frege, a proposition has both meaning and denotation. The essay also presents Russell's own account of meaning and denotation, much muddled by his confusions over inverted commas, yet beautifully summarized in his next major essay, 'Mathematical Logic as Based on The Theory of Types' (1908):

> ... A denoting phrase is defined by means of the propositions in whose verbal expression it occurs. Hence it is impossible that these propositions should acquire their meaning through the denoting phrases; we must find an independent interpretation of the propositions containing such phrases, and must not use these phrases in explaining what such propositions mean. Hence we can not regard 'all men are mortal' as a statement about 'all men' (*Marsh*, p. 70).

Denoting phrases, thus, neither have meaning nor denote. The propositions in whose verbal expressions these phrases are contextually defined so that they disappear do have meaning but they do not denote either: they assert or deny values of certain propositional functions which functions, stressed in this essay, because of contradictions engendered by propositions about illegitimate totalities, must be restricted in their range of significance.

As revolutionary as this 1908 essay is in its formulation of the doctrine of the hierarchy of types, Russell still adhers to the ontology of the *Principles*. Basic in logic are elementary propositions; all generalized propositions presuppose them. And what is an elementary proposition?

> A proposition containing no apparent variable we will call an *elementary* proposition.... In an elementary proposition we can distinguish one or more *terms* from one or more *concepts*; the *terms* are whatever can be regarded as the *subject* of the proposition, while the concepts are the predicates or relations asserted of these terms. The terms of elementary propositions we will call *individuals*; these form the first or lowest type (*Marsh*, pp. 75–76).

Here, although concepts contrast with terms rather than things, as they do in the *Principles*, the ontological status of both remains the same as it is in the *Principles*, as Russell makes clear in his reference to section 48 of that work.

It is in the first volume of *Principia Mathematica* (1910), written in conjunction with Whitehead, not earlier, that Russell generalizes his theory of denoting phrases into a theory of incomplete symbols that encompasses descriptions, both definite and indefinite – the denoting phrases of 'On Denoting' – as well as symbols for classes and relations in extension. Certain concepts in discourse, such as denoting concepts, the concept of number, the concept of the class of men, or the concept of the relation between a father and a son, are treated as incomplete symbols, with no meanings in themselves but which are defined in use in such a manner that the symbol disappears in the whole sentential context. The only difference Russell allows between three symbols is that descriptions can be proved to be incomplete symbols whereas classes and relations cannot. Even so, Russell stipulates, all talk of classes and relations in extension, like all talk of described objects, can dispense not only with non-linguistic objects but also with concepts of them. All we require are symbols – 'linguistic conveniences' – that can be defined away.

The details of Russell's theory of descriptions are so well known and so easily accessible not only in *Principia Mathematica* but also in his sixth Lecture on 'The Philosophy of Logical Atomism' (1917–18) and his chapter 16 of *Introduction to Mathematical Philosophy* (1919) that I need not rehearse them here. Assuming, now, in accordance with the theory, that all talk of described objects, actual or not, and that all talk about classes and relations in extension can be reduced to talk about propositional functions or the values of propositional functions, so that we no longer require some concept-talk, except stylistically or as a linguistic convenience, what does the theory imply for Russell's theory of concepts? On the discourse side, we no longer need denoting concepts or concepts of number, of men, of relations. Whether we still need the concept, say, of an incomplete symbol, along with other concepts or notions, including those in physics and psychology, Russell does not say until 1914 and later, starting with *Our Knowledge of the External World*. But what about the concepts of discourse – the predicates and relations – of the *Principles*? Does the theory of descriptions dispense with these in its talk of propositional functions? There is no answer in *Principia Mathematica*: propositional functions serve as both linguistic expressions and as non-linguistic predicates and relations; and there is no suggestion that all talk about predicates and relations is reducible to talk about linguistic expressions, adjectives and verbs, and that the phrase, 'propositional function', replaces either its concept or the concepts it expresses. The ontology of the *Principles* hovers over the philosophy and formalism of *Principia*.

From 1914–1927, in *Our Knowledge of the External World* (1914), 'The Relation of Sense-Data to Physics' (1914), 'The Philosophy of Logical Atomism' (1918–19), *The Analysis of Mind* (1921), and *The Analysis of Matter* (1927), Russell extended his theory of descriptions from the entities and symbols of mathematical logic to the natural sciences and even to common sense. He variously referred to this extension as the substitution of logical fictions for the entities of science; the replacement of inferred, unempirical entities by logical constructions out of empirical entities, such as sense-data, or out of these data plus entities continuous with them, such as unsensed sensibilia; the principle that dispenses with abstractions; and the logico-analytic method. Each of these, he claims, is an equivalent outgrowth of his resolution of the incomplete symbols of denoted objects, classes, and relations in extension. Russell also variously tied these extensions with metaphysical dualism, neutral monism, and logical atomism; but never, I think, with the rejection or acceptance of the ontology of the *Principles*.

Instead of detailing the historical development of the extension of the theory of descriptions to the natural sciences, a task which I have already attempted, as have others,[5] I want to ask what bearing, if any, Russell's theory of logical constructionism, logical fictions, dispensing with abstractions, or resolution of the incomplete symbols of the natural sciences and of ordinary speech has on his theory of concepts, both in and of discourse? Russell says that atoms, minds, desks, persons, etc., are all logical fictions or constructions, to be contrasted with entities, actual, inferred, or assumed. What has this to do with language?

Consider these two propositions: 'X is a logical fiction (or construction)' and '"X" is a logical fiction (or construction).' Russell claims throughout this period of 1914–1927, and beyond, since he never abandoned his theory of descriptions and its extension, that X – for example, the atom or electron or quantum the physicist talks about, the mind or the person the psychologist or we talk about, and the desk or other physical object we say we see – is a logical fiction, a construction of other, more empirical, entities. He also says that the words all of us use to talk about these inferred, unempirical entities are not symbols that serve as names; rather they are incomplete symbols, that is, symbols with no meaning in isolation since they stand for nothing; hence they must be given a meaning in their sentential contexts that express propositions about collections or classes of empirical data which can be interpreted as the symbols for classes in *Principia Mathematica*: as the values of propositional functions. It is not clear, then, that Russell identifies or renders equivalent 'X is a logical fiction or construction' and '"X" is a logical fiction or construction.' What does seem clear, however, is that Russell thinks that the first of these propositions implies or entails the second: If X is a logical fiction or construction, then 'X' is an incomplete symbol, to be resolved propositionally into the requisite assertion about the values of a propositional function. It is perhaps because of this implication that Russell regards the various characterizations of his theory of descriptions and its extension as equivalent: each involves the resolution of an incomplete symbol, inherently defective, into symbolic contexts that eliminate the defect by affirming or denying values of certain propositional functions.

Now, if 'X is a fiction' does entail '"X" is a fiction,' as I think it does for Russell, then we are warranted in inferring that Russell also implies that all the concepts in discourse, like the denoting concepts of the *Principles*, are reducible to incomplete symbols to be defined away in propositional assertions about values of propositional functions. Thus, not only the denoting concepts but the concepts or notions in the *Principles* go, to be replaced by logical fictions; and not only these, but *all* concepts in discourse, since none of them are the only complete symbols there are, proper names. A concept in discourse, whether the concept of number, of one, of man, of mind, of desk, is like a denoting concept, reduced to a phrase and rendered as a logical fiction. Whether this reduction of concepts in discourse to logical fictions results in the thesis that there are no concepts in discourse, but rather logical fictions; or the more moderate thesis that the concepts (and notions) in discourse are logical fictions, I cannot answer. However, if we follow Russell's lead regarding logical fictions, that, with the exception of denoted objects, the inferred, unempirical entities we talk about may exist but we need neither affirm nor deny they do in construing them as logical fictions, perhaps we can offer a similar claim about concepts: there may be concepts in discourse; but we need not assume there are, and each can be replaced by a logical fiction.

This replacement in any case rests on the conversion of concept-talk to talk about propositional functions. What, then, about them? Do they remain as the predicates and relations – the concepts – of the *Principles*? Does Russell's displacement or rejection of concepts in discourse by logical fictions rest on or reject the ontology of the *Principles*? Russell's answer, equivocal in *Principia Mathematica* becomes, I think, self-contradictory in the 1914–1927 period, as can be seen in 'The Philosophy of Logical Atomism.' In his early lectures, Russell affirms that predicates and relations are among the ultimate entities of the world, along with the particulars that have them. This is the basic ontological thesis of Logical Atomism. He goes on to state as truisms about the world that there are facts and beliefs. Although propositions are no longer in the world but are now complex symbols, it is facts that make propositions true or false. Facts are not particulars; there are many kinds of fact, and the basic ones – the atomic – are composed of particulars and their predicates or relations. In the second Lecture, 'Particulars, Predicates, and Relations,' Russell articulates the ontological status of the concepts – the predicates and relations – of the *Principles* as clearly as he had done earlier:

> The things in the world have various properties, and stand
> in various relations to each other. That they have these
> properties and relations are *facts*, and the things and their

qualities or relations are quite clearly in some sense or
other components of the facts that have those qualities or
relations (*Marsh*, p. 192).

In the fifth Lecture, 'General Propositions and Existence,' Russell
inquires into the nature of the propositional function, which he has
used in interpreting general propositons: If 'All Greeks are men' is an
assertion about the truth of all values of a propositional function, as
Russell says it is, it becomes important to determine what a propositional function is. Is it an expression for a predicate or a relation
or is it a purely linguistic entity?

...A propositional function in itself is nothing: it is merely
a schema. Therefore in the inventory of the world, which is
what I am trying to get at, one comes to the question:
What is there really in the world that corresponds with
these things (*Marsh*, p. 234)?

However, instead of answering this last question, Russell says
there are general propositions in the same sense that there are atomic
ones. But neither of these are in the world in the sense that the facts
they correspond to are. Propositional functions do not correspond to
facts, only their true propositions do. And propositions for Russell
are propositional functions whose undetermined constituents are
determined. Facts, he insists, are composed of particulars, their
qualities and relations. Do not, then, the propositional functions
correspond to qualities and relations? How else can Russell hold that
propositions that affirm or deny values of propositional functions
can be about anything, including facts? The proposition, 'All men are
mortal,' is not about the entity, all men, which of course it is not, as
Russell teaches us, but is rather an assertion that 'The propositional
function "x is human and x is mortal" is true for all values of x' [(x:
H$x \supset$ Mx)]. Is, then, the proposition about nothing because it is not
about the entity, all men; or is it about the predicates human and
mortal? If propositonal functions are purely verbal – airy nothings –
propositions can be assertions about the values of these functions,
but not about the world, the facts in it or, at least in some cases,
about the individuals that satisfy the propositional function, with
which Russell is concerned.

That Russell wavers on propositional functions as purely verbal
schemas or as verbal expressions of ontological predicates and

relations can also be seen in his discussion of formally equivalent propositional functions. '*x* is a man' and '*x* is a featherless biped' are formally equivalent, Russell says; nevertheless, what can be said truly of the one need not always be true of the other. 'For instance, the propositional function "*x* is a man" is one which has to do with the concept of humanity. That will not be true of "*x* is a featherless biped"' (*Marsh*, p. 265). So here a propositional function 'has to do' with a concept; it is not a purely verbal schema, it is rather that as it expresses a concept.

In his final Lecture, 'Excursus into Metaphysics: What There Is,' Russell resolves the contradiction I attribute to him over the status of propositional functions to reiterate, once again, the ontological nature of the concepts of the *Principles*:

> There are particulars and qualities and relations of various orders, a whole hierarchy of different sorts of simples, but all of them, if we were right, have in their various ways some kind of reality that does not belong to anything else (*Marsh*, p. 270).

Without these simples, there could be no facts; and without the facts and the particulars among the simples, there could be no complete or incomplete symbols, no proper names or propositions. That the concepts in discourse, such as the concept of number, name entities in the realm of being – Russell's view about 'number' as a name of the thing-term in the *Principles* – is replaceable by logical fictions that name nothing, but are convertible into propositional assertions about classes of classes, thence, about values of propositional functions, rests on the ontology of simples, without which there could be no facts to be asserted by propositions. In effect, then, Russell's whole resolution of the concepts in discourse depends on the reaffirmation of the ontology of the *Principles*, with particulars, qualities and relations replacing things, predicates and relations. These ultimate simples, thus, constitute a necessary condition for there being facts and talk about them. The propositional functions must express ontological entities just as surely as the proper names name particulars. If propositional functions do not serve in this way, as the adjectives and verbs did in the *Principles*, to 'indicate' the ontological, Russell's shift from concepts in discourse as names to concepts in discourse as logical fictions renders everything – language, thought and the world – fictional. The ontology of the *Principles*, thus, remains intact. To be sure, talk of things is given up for talk of particulars or of values of propositional functions. But talk of propositional functions rests on, does not dispense with, the concept-terms of the *Principles*. Their names change, perhaps the assigned supersensible status of the predicates and relations, but the entities they name do not change.

Nor does Russell's distinction between perception and conception and the related distinction between their objects change. In the *Problems*, Russell articulates his view that 'awareness of universals is called *conceiving*, and a universal of which we are aware is called a concept' (p. 52). In 1927, at the end of the period, 1914–1927, Russell reaffirms his belief in concepts as the objects of conceiving: 'we "conceive" whenever we understand the meaning of an abstract word, or think of that which is in fact the meaning of the word ... If you think about whiteness, you have a concept ... The object of your thought, in such a case, is a *universal* or a Platonic idea' (*An Outline of Philosophy*, p. 203). Russell invariably tied these concepts to universals. However, at least if we can judge from his most important paper on the subject, 'On the Relations of Universals and Particulars' (1911), it is not clear that universals are identical with concepts or even which is a species of which. For that paper begins with 'If there is a distinction between particulars and universals (which he then proceeds to prove), percepts will be among particulars, while concepts will be among universals' (*Marsh*, p. 105); and it ends with the claim that 'we can make an absolute division between percepts and concepts. The universal whiteness is a concept, whereas a particular white patch is a percept' (*Marsh*, p. 122). Universals can occur as predicates or relations in complexes but do not exist in time; whether some of these universals are not concepts or whether there are concepts that are not universals, Russell does not say. In any case, although Russell expresses reservations about the reality of universals during the period 1914–27, especially in *The Analysis of Mind* (p. 196), he reaffirms his *Problems* view in *An Inquiry into Meaning & Truth* (1940, pp. 429–437), where he argues – this time from the causal theory of the meaning of words – to the reality of universals. However, so far as concepts are concerned, the same vacillation (or contradiction) over there being no concepts, only logical fictions and there being predicates and relations – concepts – without which no logical fictions are resolvable into their propositional contexts, prevails throughout his philosophical writings after 1927.

Russell, to conclude, formulates two different theories of concepts: . that they are ontological entities and that they are logical fictions. I have argued that though the second theory replaced the first (from 1914), the first is a necessary condition of the intelligibility of the second. That these two theories are basic in his philosophical doctrines and their changes follows from the fact that the method of analysis is the fundamental and unifying principle in Russell's philosophy; and that this method converges on a combination of real and contextual definition. (These theses are argued in my 'Analysis and the Unity of Russell's Philosophy,' 1944; Russell accepted them. Ayer, however, has recently challenged my interpretation on the wayward inference that I attribute to Russell a practice of analysis for its own sake.)[6]

That Russell's theory of concepts as ontological entities is his central doctrine follows from the fact (as I have argued here) that contextual definition – the resolution of incomplete symbols – presupposes as its very condition of coherence the predicates and relations – the ontological concepts of the *Principles* – which, along with the things of the *Principles* or the particulars of the later works, constitute the ultimate simples of real definition.

Moore

G. E. Moore is the dream of the historian of philosophical theories of concepts. Throughout his writings, he affirms certain doctrines that he later assesses as confused or that he retracts altogether. His belief in concepts, however, boldly asserted in his early work, Moore staunchly upholds to the end. That there are concepts, that they are the subjects of analysis and of philosophical definition, that they are objects of thought which, though not in space or time or dependent on mind, are real or have being rather than exist – that they are like Plato's *eide* – Moore declares at the very beginning, in 'The nature of Judgment' (1899), and never repudiates. To be sure, he employs different terms to talk about them: *ideas, notions, properties, universals, conceptions, abstract ideas, general ideas, objects of thought, meanings,* and *concepts.* Some of these name other things as well, such as propositions, but all are also used by him to refer to concepts.

Besides the concept of a concept, Moore deals with many other concepts, only some of which he acknowledges as concepts (or ideas, notions, etc.). These include the concepts of *esse, percipi*, qualities, such as blue, sensation, sense-datum, consciousness, knowledge, certainty, common sense, external world, time, space, analysis, meaning, and the basic ethical and aesthetic concepts of good and of beauty. One of the great problems, then, in the elucidation of Moore's theory of concepts is whether or not all the concepts he explores conform to his explicit claims about the nature of concepts. For example, the concept of good Moore characterizes in *Principia Ethica* as a platonic form. He distingushes sharply between good and the good. On his own principles of differentiating words, the concepts they express, and the things that fall under the concepts, this implies a distinction between the concept of good and the concept of the good. Is, then, the concept of the good – that has application to those things ('organic unities') that are good – also a platonic form? Or, to take another, less rarified, example: blue. Blue is a colour, a universal that has many instances. Idealists claim that being a blue thing is being perceived as blue. In 'The Refutation of Idealism' (1903), Moore rejects this *esse est percipi* doctrine. It assumes that being blue entails being perceived as blue. Moore counters that the concept of being blue carries with it no such entailment; indeed, if it does, the concept would be self-contradictory, affirming and denying that that which is blue is distinct from being perceived as blue. An instance of blue, of course, is not a concept. Blue is a universal. But what about the concept of an instance of blue, without which Moore's rejection of *esse est percipi* cannot proceed? Is that a concept like blue or good – an entity that has being as distinct from existence?

Moore first articulates his theory of concepts in 'The Nature of Judgment' and in *Principia Ethica* (1903; hereinafter *PE*). His fullest exposition of it, however, is in *Some Main Problems of Philosophy* (1953; based on lectures presented in 1910–11; hereinafter *SMP*), to which I now turn. It begins in Chapter XI, 'Is Time Real?' Moore first distinguishes between the claims that time is not real and that time is a mere appearance. Both contradict common sense. He rejects the first because it implies that all beliefs about the temporal are false, which implication itself is false. The second he also rejects because it implies that time both exists and is not real. But the second, which he ascribes to Bradley, puzzles him and provokes the question whether existence is a notion different from that of reality, in which case Bradley's doctrine that there is time but it is mere appearance rests on an intelligible (if not justifiable) distinction between what exists but is not real and what is real but does not exist.

What, then, Moore continues, do we mean by 'Time is real' or 'Time is not real?' We understand these and similar expressions of the form 'So and so is real,' 'So and so does not exist,' etc. Therefore, in one sense we do know what 'Time is real' means: we understand it. But in the sense that we are not able to give an analysis of *what* it means, we do not know what it means. However, it does not follow from the fact that we are not able to provide an analysis or a definition of the notion of real or existence that we lack understanding of the expressions employing their terms. Nor is the question of meaning in either sense logically relevant to what things are real or exist? 'What is meant by "real"?' is important in understanding the common property shared by all that is real. And it has a bearing on trying to understand what philosophers take reality to be. What, for example, does Bradley mean by 'Time is not real'? For Bradley, 'x is real' presumably does not follow from 'x exists.' Perhaps, Moore suggests, 'real' is ambiguous for Bradley and can best be elucidated by contrasting 'real' with 'imaginary.' Bears exist, centaurs do not and never have. What more natural than to say that bears are real, centaurs, imaginary? And to imagine a centaur is to imagine something – not nothing which, if it were nothing, would eliminate the difference between imagining a centaur and imagining a griffin. Imagining is a something imagined. A centaur, thus, could be said to exist but not be real. 'So that, in one respect, we should be maintaining about a centaur, exactly what Bradley seemed to maintain about Time: just as he seemed to say Time indubitably *is* and yet is not real; so we seem driven to say: Centaurs indubitably *are*, but yet they are certainly not real' (*SMP*, p. 213). This may clarify Bradley's use of 'real' and 'exist.' Its great drawback is that it forces us to attribute being to that which is not real – the imagined. Moore thus must look elsewhere.

In the next chapter, Moore asks, 'What is the meaning of "real"?' If we understand English, we know its meaning; and we have the notion or idea suggested by the word before our minds.

> So I am now supposing that the word 'real' has already
> called up to your mind the *object* or *objects* I wish to talk

about – namely the property or properties which you wish
to assert that a thing possesses when you say that it *is real*
– and unless the word has called up before your mind this
property or properties, everything that I say will be quite
unintelligible (p. 217).

Giving the meaning of the word 'real,' then, is giving an analysis or a
definition of the object, property, idea, notion, conception – concept
– already before the mind. To do this, one must know English. But
knowing English or using language at all, Moore says, is incidental.
Theoretically, to give the meaning – to state the nature – of real
requires only acquaintance with the notion before our minds.
Presumably, I need 'real' or a word in a language other than English
in order to state the meaning of 'real;' but I do not need the word to
unravel its meaning. Having the concept, then, is either having the
notion before your mind or being able to provide its analysis or
definition.

If real is a notion or concept, how do we know, Moore asks, if it is
the same notion or a different one called up when we use 'real' on
different occasions? How, for example, can I tell if the 'real' in 'This
is a real horse' stands for the same notion as the 'real' in 'Time is
real?' Suppose I say, 'Elephants are real animals but griffins are not.'
Then, Moore says, I assert that elephants have a property that
griffins do not. Nevertheless, griffins have being in our imagination;
therefore griffins are not real in the same sense that elephants are.

But, if so, it follows that we have here two different
properties before our minds, one of which may be
expressed by the word 'is' or 'has being', and the other by
the word 'real', one of them a property which is possessed
by griffins and all imaginary things and the other a
property which isn't possessed by them (pp. 224–5).

What, then, is the difference between these two properties? Moore
considers a number of explanations: that the imaginary is mind-
dependent, the real is not; that the real has certain connections with
predictable events, the imaginary has not; that the real has degrees,
the imaginary has none; and that the real is the highest possible
degree of reality. Moore rejects the first three possibilities, and uses
the last to explicate Bradley's distinction between the Absolute and
appearances, according to which the Absolute possesses the highest

degree of reality and appearances are unreal in the sense that they do not possess this highest degree. 'Real,' then, for Bradley, has two senses:

> In one sense of the word, 'real' certainly stands for a property which, according to him, has degrees, and this is the sense in which Time and all other Appearances, as well as the Absolute *are* 'real'. And in the other sense, 'real' may perhaps stand exclusively for the highest possible degree of this first property (p. 232).

The fourth explanation, Moore says, is a possible one of the true distinction between the real and the imaginary; its great difficulty is that 'it is nonsense to talk of one thing having *more* being than another' (p. 233). Moore, thus, fails to provide the criterion for distinguishing between the imaginary and the real; he also fails to answer his question: How do we know if 'real' stands for the same property on different occasions of its use? since he rests his answer on the distinction between the real and the imaginary.

Though Moore wavers in *SMP* on 'real' as the name of a property or concept that he can clearly define, he does not vacillate on the real as a property or concept he is acquainted with every time he calls it up before his mind. However, in 'The Conception of Reality' (1917–18), still haunted by Bradley, he goes over the same material and concludes that there is no concept of the real. Even so, he does not infer from this that there are no concepts or that concepts are not platonic forms; all he allows is that real is not a concept and that 'real' expresses or names no concept but instead performs a different role in assertions.

In this essay, he asks again what Bradley means by 'Time is unreal?' He must mean, Moore says, that there are no temporal facts. Thus, what he must or ought to mean by 'Time is unreal' can be defined in terms of one usage of the word 'real' or one conception for which 'reality' stands. The latter is an 'excusable' way of talking.

> But it would, I think, be more correct to say that we have pointed out one particular, and that the most important, usage of the terms 'real' and 'unreal,' and that one of the peculiarities of this usage is that it is such that the terms 'real' and 'unreal' cannot, when used in this way, be

properly said to stand for any conception whatever (*Philosophical Studies*, p. 212).

To illustrate this usage, Moore contrasts 'Lions are real' with 'Unicorns are not real.' The first attributes the property of being a lion – not the property of being real – to something; the second denies that the property of being a unicorn belongs to anything. Thus 'real' and 'unreal' do not stand for any conceptions. 'Lions are real' involves the conceptions of being a lion and of belonging to something. 'Real' stands for neither of these conceptions. 'Lions are real' is grammatically similar to 'Lions are mammalian.' But since 'mammalian' stands for a property and 'real' does not, they are different kinds of assertions.

Moore also repudiates the possibility that 'exists but is not real' has application to the imaginary. He contrasts 'I am imagining or thinking of a unicorn' with 'I am hunting a lion.' The first does not assert 'that the two properties of being a unicorn and of being thought of by me both belong to one and the same thing; whereas, in the latter case, I am asserting that the two properties of being a lion and of being hunted by me *do* belong to one and the same thing' (*Phil. Studies*, pp. 216–17). Though he confesses he does not know what the correct analysis is of 'I am thinking of a unicorn,' Moore affirms that its truth does not depend on the property of a unicorn belonging to anything whatever. The fallacy of inferring 'Unicorns exist' from 'Unicorns are imagined' is precisely Bradley's fallacy in inferring from 'We think of Time' to 'There is Time.' 'Exists but is not real' describes nothing. Nor are existence and reality properties or concepts of any kind.

Moore returns to concepts in Chapter XVI of *SMP*, 'Being, Fact and Existence.' There are, he says, two classes of things in the Universe of which we do not say that they exist; yet they are: facts and general or abstract ideas. The latter are what we apprehend, for example, the number two, not the act of apprehension. The act exists, the number two does not. Because of the traditional ambiguity of 'idea,' Moore substitutes 'universal' as the name of what is apprehended. He then argues that there are universals: common properties shared by particulars. These include relations and relational properties. Another name for these 'is "concepts" or "conceptions"' (*SMP*, p. 312; this is Moore's first use of 'concept' in the book). Besides universals or concepts of relations and of properties that consist in the having of a relation to something or other, Moore finds a third kind, though he is hesitant about it, in qualities, such as pure whiteness and, without hesitation, in numbers, such as the number two:

> The property in question does seem to consist in the fact that *the number two* belongs to every such collection and only to such a collection; and the number two itself does seem to be a universal of my third kind: something which is neither a relation, nor a property which consists in the having of a relation to something or other. And it seems to me that in this case we can perhaps distinguish the universal in question: that we can hold the number two before our minds, and see what it is, and *that* it is, in almost the same way as we can do this with any particular sense-datum that we are directly perceiving (p. 366).

All universals, Moore concludes, are abstractions; indeed, they are the same. But to identify them is not to subscribe to universals as a product of abstraction; '... the process of abstraction is a process by which we become aware of universals; it is our *awareness* of them which is a product of the process; not the universals themselves' (p. 371). Universals, thus, are not definable in terms of abstraction; rather, abstraction is definable only in terms of universals: 'what we mean by abstraction is just the process by which we first learn to distinguish universals, and there is no other way of defining it' (p. 371). Finally, abstractions or universals are not fictions. They are, along with particulars and truths or facts, ultimate constituents of the Universe. Whether we say that abstractions do not exist but are real or have being does not matter. What does matter is that we are not to conclude from the fact that they do not exist that they are only imaginary, for that would then rule them out of the Universe altogether and, by so doing, foreclose on the fundamental problem of philosophy, which is to explore what things there are, whether some exist or have being, whether others do not exist but are wholly imaginary. That universals are not fictions is a great discovery, Moore exclaims, than that they are distinct from particulars.

If we are to take Moore seriously – and how else are we to take him? – Moore affirms a platonic realm of forms in *SMP*. These forms he identifies with a number of things, including concepts. Concepts, thus, are entities that are real or having being independently of our apprehensions of them, and are neither particulars that exist nor imaginary objects that do not. His identification of universals with concepts not only perverts Plato's implicit distinction between a form and a concept but, even worse, forces Moore into the position that all concepts – from that of God or the good to those of consciousness and sensation – are entities we can hold before the mind but which do not depend for their reality on any mental act or other empirical fact. Concepts as platonic forms, whether they are called 'abstract ideas,' 'universals,' 'meanings,' or whatever, simply cannot do justice to Moore's own use of the varieties of concepts he employs in his writings.

This same tension between the concept as a platonic form and the concept as something less than that is already present in his first major work, *Principia Ethica*. That the notion or idea of good is the same as the concept of good, Moore makes explicit only in the Preface where he compares his view with Brentano's: 'Brentano appears to agree with me completely … in regarding all ethical propositions as defined by the fact that they predicate a single unique objective concept' (p. xi).

This remark serves not only to identify concept with notion or idea but also to introduce Moore's fundamental doctrine in *PE*: That good is a simple, therefore unanalyzable, indefinable concept, notion, idea, or property, without which there is no subject of Ethics.

Ethics is concerned, among other things, with good conduct. But it must begin with good as basic since many things are good and much conduct is not. Consequently, '"good" denotes some property, that is common to them and conduct' (p. 2). 'What is good?' means different things. Central, Moore says, is 'How "good" is to be defined?' because that which is meant by 'good' (or 'bad') is '…the *only* simple object of thought which is peculiar to Ethics' (p. 5). Moreover, it is real, not nominal, definition that is required: 'My business is solely with that object or idea … that the word is generally used to stand for. What I want to discover is the nature of that object or idea…' (p. 6). And the correct answer to this question, 'How is good (the property) to be defined?' is: that it cannot. Good is good, and that is the end of it. Or, to express it differently, all propositions about good (goodness) are synthetic, never analytic. Good is a simple notion, like yellow. Neither is definable because both are simple; only the complex is definable.

Good is indefinable; the good is definable. The good – things that are good – may have other properties besides good. But these properties are distinct from the property of good. All attempts to define good in terms of these other properties commit what Moore calls 'the naturalistic fallacy:' the fallacy of identifying (by definition) two distinct things. That it is a fallacy can be seen from the fact that if good is defined by anything P, then 'P is good' = 'P is P,' which renders 'P is good' – a synthetic, informative claim – analytic and uninformative; and from the fact that of anything having P, we can always ask, 'Is it good?' which would be senseless under the definition of good as P. 'Good,' thus, denotes this simple object good or nothing, in which case Ethics is not a proper subject at all. And everyone, Moore says, who asks himself, 'Is this good?' has before his mind this unique object or property (or concept) good.

The good – all things that are good – contains good and other properties as well. The various good things there are are complexes. These, Moore insists, are organic unities in the sense that the value of the individual wholes is not proportionate to the sum of its parts. Independently of the truth or falsity of what Moore says about the good as organic unities, it seems quite clear that Moore cannot set forth his doctrine without the words 'the good' and 'organic unity,' the things these words relate to, and the concepts the words express, as well as the things that fall under these concepts. What, one must ask, would Moore say about these concepts, notions, ideas of the good or of organic unity? Are they, too, abstract entities held before the mind?

Moore proceeds to demolish the history of ethics, comprised of various, opposing theories of good, each on the ground that it defines good as some natural or metaphysical property other than good. All identify the simple notion (concept) of good – what we mean by 'good' – with some other notion (concept). Of direct relevance to our theme is Moore's sympathy with the *metaphysics* of the metaphysical naturalistic fallacy. Metaphysics, he says, has always been concerned with objects and properties that do not exist in time or at all.

> To this class ... belongs what we mean by the adjective 'good.' It is not *goodness*, but only the things or qualities which are good, which can exist in time – can have duration, and begin and cease to exist – can be objects of *perception*. But the most prominent members of this class

are perhaps numbers...Two and two *are* four. But that does not mean that either two or four exists. Yet it certainly means *something*. Two *is* somehow, although it does not exist (pp. 110–11).

Moore accepts the metaphysical – non-natural – character of good and rejects the identification of it with some other metaphysical character, whatever that character may be.

In the final chapter, 'The Ideal,' Moore considers what things are good or ends in themselves. These are certain states of consciousness having to do with the pleasure of human intercourse and the enjoyment of beautiful objects. Of direct concern to his theory of concepts is his rejection of traditional definitions of beauty and a definition of his own. Beauty, unlike good, is a definable concept: It is that of which the admiring contemplation is good in itself. Beauty, thus, is subordinate to good; the concept of the beautiful entails the concept of good. Beautiful objects, like good objects or beauty, are complex, unlike good. As complex, they too are organic unities.

Principia Ethica raises many questions that Moore does not ask, but that his critics do or we can. One of these concerns Moore's notion of good: What is implied by this notion? It certainly follows from his understanding of a concept (as expressed in the Preface) that good is a concept as a supersensible entity. To have or to possess this concept is to be aware of this entity: to apprehend it as it is before the mind, but not as dependent on the mind. The apprehension of this concept functions as a necessary condition of any correct understanding of the nature or analysis of good. But is this apprehension of the concept also a necessary or a sufficient condition or both of the correct use of the word 'good?' Is correct understanding of its simple, non-analyzable nature necessary or sufficient or both of the correct use of 'good?'

It is, for Moore, a correct use of the word 'good' to proclaim 'Pleasure is good.' It is an incorrect use of the word 'good' to say 'Good is pleasure.' It seems to follow, then, that apprehending good as well as knowing its nature as simple are neither necessary nor sufficient for knowing how to use 'good' in making synthetic claims about what is good, such as pleasure; that is, I am speaking correctly and truly and I know how to use the word 'good' when I say 'Pleasure is good,' even though I have not grasped the nature of or even apprehended good. However, it also seems to follow from

223

Moore's doctrine that good is a supersensible concept, the apprehension of which is a necessary condition of understanding its nature, that this apprehension and understanding are necessary conditions for knowing how to use the word 'good' as a non-analytic predicate; that is, I am speaking correctly and truly and I know how to use the word 'good' when I say 'Good is not pleasure,' because I have apprehended and grasped the nature of good. But, since I must also know English, including the word 'good,' this apprehension and understanding of good is not a sufficient condition for knowing how to use 'good' as a non-analytic predicate. But now if having the concept for Moore includes both apprehending it and understanding it, then that one is able to use 'good' correctly, e.g., 'Pleasure is good,' 'Friendship is good,' 'Good is not pleasure,' 'Good is not the good,' etc., does seem to be a sufficient condition for having the concept of good. From which it directly follows that the having of the concept of good is a necessary condition for being able to use the word 'good' correctly. If this is Moore's position on the relation between having concepts and being able to use language, Moore would not tolerate the contemporary conflation: that having the concept of good (or any other concept) is the same thing as being able to use 'good' (or certain other expressions) correctly.

Good in *PE* is simple. It has no set of necessary and sufficient properties, as apparently beauty does on Moore's analysis of beauty. The concept of beauty is governed by definitive properties that determine the definitive criteria of the correct use of 'beautiful.' However, since good is simple, what governs the set of criteria for the correct use of 'good?' There certainly are these criteria on Moore's account: the fact that good is simple does not rule out criteria for the correct use of 'good.' At least one necessary criterion for the correct use of 'good' (or '*gut*,' or '*bon*') is knowing the language of which this word is a part of its vocabulary. What about apprehending the concept? Neither this nor the analysis of the concept, which rests on its apprehension, seems to be a necessary condition of the correct use of 'good' in the making of ordinary synthetic judgments about good things. But these two – the apprehension and the subsequent analysis of the concept good – do seem to function as necessary conditions for the correct use of 'good' to make certain statements in which we quash and reject putative definitions of good. And in this strong sense of knowing how to use the word 'good,' there are these three necessary criteria: of knowing part of a language, apprehending good, and intuiting its simple nature. These three together, I think, are both necessary and sufficient for the correct total use of 'good' according to Moore.

The concept good is a simple concept; it therefore has no constituent properties, hence no definitive set of properties. The word 'good,' which for Moore names the concept, is governed by a definitive set of criteria. Is good, then, a closed concept? Since it has no constituent properties, it cannot be closed. Nevertheless, it is the simplicity of the concept that determines the three definitive criteria of the full use of the word 'good.' The relation between good and 'good,' thus, differs from the relation between, say, beauty and 'beauty,' for Moore. For the concept of beauty is a complex concept whose constituents are a definitive set of necessary and sufficient properties; and whose properties determine the definitive set of criteria for the correct use of the word 'beautiful.' That beauty is a closed concept entails that 'beauty' and 'beautiful' have definitive criteria for their correct use. This entailment from properties to criteria vanishes with good.

This problem of how concepts that are simple can nonetheless govern the criteria of their corresponding words we have met before. It is present in Plato's concept of the good, in Descartes' concepts of simple natures, in Leibniz, and in others. As concepts, because they are simple, they are not closed in the sense of having or being governed by definitive sets of properties or criteria, depending on the ontological status accorded the concepts. But these concepts are not open either, in the sense that they are composed of sets of properties or criteria less than definitive sets of them. Certainly neither Plato's nor Moore's good is constituted by definitive or non-definitive sets of properties. Yet this platonic form and Moorean concept are as hard-edged, fixed and determinate as any closed concept and legislate the same fixed sets of criteria for the correct employment of the words that name them. The putative simplicity of a concept, thus, is not incompatible with the requirement that its corresponding word must be governed by a closed set of criteria if it is to be used correctly, both about the concept and the things that fall under it.

It is often said that Moore's theory of concepts, in particular, of good, rests on a naming theory of language or of the meaning of words: that good, for example, is a projected object of the word 'good' which has this object as its meaning. Moore's theory of concepts rests on a theory of the meaning of words, a theory, which once stated, is seen to be erroneous, since the meaning of a word is not the object for which it stands.

Now, it is true that Moore says that the concept of good is the only answer he can secure to: 'What does "good" mean?' It is also true, I think, that Moore never asks, 'What does "good" do?' or at least never suggests that the quest for the use of a word should supplant the quest for its meaning. Does this omission or dereliction permit us to say, as some of his critics do say, that Moore's theory of concepts is a misreading of the actual functioning of general words, such as 'good?' Does Moore arrive at the concept of good not by finding it before the mind, pure and simple, but by the circuitous route of asking what 'good' means or names? Or, to put it another way, Does Moore separate what cannot be separated: What is the concept of good? from How does 'good' function in discourse? Many of his critics hold that once we ask the last question – 'the right question' – the first about the meaning of 'good' becomes otiose. On this criticism, it is claimed, there is the word 'good' or '*bon*' or '*gut,*' among others. There are things that are said to be good. And there is the concept of good. But the concept, though neither the word nor a thing, is the ability to use 'good' (or an equivalent word in another language) to do something, whether to describe, ascribe, emote, or whatever. The concept of good is an ability, not an entity.

Does Moore's theory of good as a simple concept rest on a naming theory of meaning that is joined with a confusion of an ability with an entity? If it does, Moore does not first find a word, then the notion it stands for, then discover that that notion is simple, unanalyzable and non-natural: a meaning, universal, property, or concept. What he does is to fix on a word and ask the wrong question about it.

His critics, I think, are right that Moore's concept of good is a projection of a wrong answer to a wrong question: 'What does "good" mean or denote?' Further, it is true that he does distinguish the use of language from the possession of concepts; and he does make the possession of them – their apprehension and understanding – independent of the use of language, at least in *PE*. (Later, in his Reply, *The Philosophy of G. E. Moore*, 1942, p. 664, he says: 'But, of course, in order to *give* an analysis, you must *use* verbal expressions'.) However, I am not convinced by his critics that the possession of concepts, even though it is not independent of the employment of language and is certainly not the possession of meanings, is consequently the same as or reduces to the ability to use language; in which case all talk of concepts is simply talk of the roles of general terms. Moore may be disastrously wrong about the relations between words and their meanings, between the uses of language and the having of concepts; but I cannot see that he is mistaken in implying that the relation between having concepts and being able to use certain words correctly is not one of mutual entailment or, at any rate, that no one has demonstrated that there is such a relation which both undercuts Moore's entity theory of concepts and provides the true answer to the question, What is the concept of good?

There is, I think, a different kind of difficulty in Moore's theory of good. As plausible or not as it is that good is a property that 'good' predicates, to identify this property with a notion or a concept, as Moore does, is to leave nothing for the intermediary Moore needs in order to bridge the gap between words and things, whether natural or non-natural. It is not enough to say, as Moore does, that 'good,' '*gut*,' '*bon*,' etc., mean the same thing: the property of good. For these words express the same concept (or, it can be claimed, different concepts). And that concept is not the same as the property or object good, but something that the different words share: if good is a simple property or object, Moore needs a distinction between good and the concept of good in order to elucidate different words that supposedly name the same thing. Only the concept of good – not good as a concept – can serve to do this. Plato saw this; Moore, because he confuses Plato's theory of concepts with Plato's theory of forms or universals (as do Frege and Russell), does not. In the end, it seems to me, it wrecks his theory of concepts, for this conflation cannot do justice to the distinction between good as a property and the concept of good which is the concept of that property, different from it as well as from the words used to express that concept, even if they serve to name it. Nor can his theory of concepts do justice to all those concepts which are not forms, and without which much of Moore's philosophy is incoherent.

Concepts for Moore are intimately tied to his method of analysis. After almost 50 years of practising philosophical analysis, Moore in his 'Reply to My Critics' (*The Philosophy of G. E. Moore*) states what he persistently meant or intended to mean by 'analysis.' Analysis, he says, is a form of definition, not of words, but of concepts or propositions. One starts with a particular concept or proposition – the *analysandum* – and attempts to provide another set of concepts or propositions – the *analysans* – which is logically equivalent to or identical with the original concept or proposition. Although Moore confesses that he is unable to formulate the necessary and sufficient conditions of a correct analysis, consequently cannot give an analysis or definition of the concept of analysis, he does offer at least three necessary conditions for a correct analysis:

> If you are to 'give an analysis' of a given *concept*, which is the *analysandum*, you must mention, as your *analysans*, a *concept* such that (a) nobody can know that the *analysandum* applies to an object without knowing that the *analysans* applies to it, (b) nobody can verify that the *analysandum* applies without verifying that the *analysans* applies, (c) any expression which expresses the *analysandum* must be synonymous with any expression which expresses the *analysans* (p. 663).

According to (c) analysis, though not linguistic, involves the use of language. What, then, Moore asks, is the proper way of expressing an analysis? Employing as his example the concept of a brother, he suggests four such ways: 'The concept "being a brother" is identical with the concept "being a male sibling";' 'The propositional function "x is a brother" is identical with the propositional function "x is a male sibling";' 'To say that a person is a brother is the same thing as to say that that person is a male sibling;' or 'To be a brother is the same thing as to be a male sibling' (p. 664).

Each of these ways of expressing the analysis of the concept of brother satisfies the three requirements. But it also engenders 'the paradox of analysis.' Take, for example, 'To be a brother is the same thing as to be a male sibling.' If this statement is true, it seems identical with the statement 'To be a brother is to be a brother;' yet it is obvious that these are not the same and that the latter, unlike the former, is not an analysis of the concept of brother. Moore admits he cannot solve the problem. But he does insist that any purported solution must 'hold fast' to the facts that the *analysandum* and *analysans* of a correct analysis are the same concept and that the expression used for the *analysandum* must differ from that used for the *analysans* so that the latter expression must explicitly mention concepts not explicitly mentioned by the former and the way in which these concepts are combined.

As Moore formulates analysis in his 'Reply', then, analysis presupposes a distinction between words and concepts (and sentences and propositions). Analysis is confined to clarification and definition of concepts (or propositions). And the verbal expression of an analysis must follow a standard pattern of paraphrase in which what is analyzed is equivalent to a larger, more explicit, and synonymous expression. The central point of doing analysis is the clarification of concepts, not the discovery of facts about the world.

Is analysis, as Moore conceives it, identical with philosophy? Moore denies that it is. Analysis is but one task, among many, of philosophy: it is a, but not the, proper function of philosophy. As he says in *SMP*, philosophy has, as a legitimate goal, to 'give a general description of the *whole* of the Universe' (p. 1). And, more important, at least for Moore's own work, philosophy also includes the attempt to state certain undeniable truths about the universe, especially those denied by other philosophers, without in any way providing a general description of the whole of the universe. For example, in 'A Defence of Common Sense' (1925), Moore distinguishes sharply between philosophical statement of common sense truisms, which all of us understand and know to be true, and philosophical analysis of these truisms. Everyone knows, for example, that he has a body, was born a certain number of years ago, has lived on or near the surface of the earth, that the earth itself has existed for many years past, and that other human beings are living or have lived. Each of these propositions is true; none of them is either doubtful or obscure. It is only the analysis of them that is open to question.

So, too, in 'Proof of an External World' (1939), Moore distinguishes between giving a proof of a philosophical proposition and giving an analysis of the premises and conclusion of that proof. After clarifying the concept of an external world, which he equates with 'things outside us,' such as dogs, trees, planets, and hands, he offers a proof that there are things that exist outside us by holding up his hands and stating: 'Here is one hand,' 'Here is another,' 'Therefore, at least two things outside us exist.' The premises, he concludes, are true, and known to be true, and the conclusion follows from the premises, hence the proof is conclusive. The analyses of the premises and the conclusion, however, remain in doubt.

Thus, to Moore, philosophy can properly state undeniable truths about the world and proffer proofs of the existence of things, as well as provide analyses of concepts or propositions. But now we must ask, is analysis as Moore conceives it, compatible with his practice of it? It is true that many of his specific analyses of ethical and perceptual concepts and propositions are attempts at definitions of concepts that satisfy his criteria of a correct analysis. Although there is nothing in Moore's contributions to analysis that *he* would compare to the almost perfect analysis that he regards Russell's to be of propositions involving definite descriptions (see 'Russell's "Theory of Descriptions",' *The Philosophy of Bertrand Russell*, pp. 177–225), he does insist on the truth of his partial analysis, for example, of certain perceptual judgments, such as 'This is a hand.'

> Two things only seem to me to be quite certain about the analysis of such propositions... namely that whenever I know, or judge, such a proposition to be true, (1) there is always some *sense-datum* about which the proposition in question is a proposition – some sense-datum which is *a* subject (and, in a certain sense, the principle or ultimate subject) of the proposition in question, and (2) that, nevertheless, *what* I am knowing or judging to be true about this sense-datum is not (in general) that it is *itself* a hand, or a dog, or the sun, etc. etc., as the case may be ('A Defence of Common Sense,' *Contemporary British Philosophy*, Second Series, p. 217).

Moore's practice of analysis reveals another use of it that is not definition of concepts and does not result in linguistic paraphrase. This use is the same as Russell's conception of analysis as the discovery of the constituents of certain non-linguistic, non-conceptual complexes. An indisputable example of this use of analysis as real definition is his analysis of sensation in 'The Refutation of Idealism:'

> The true analysis of a sensation or idea is as follows. The element that is common to them all, and which I have called 'consciousness,' really *is* consciousness. A sensation is, in reality, a case of 'knowing' or 'being aware' or 'experiencing' something. When we know that the sensation of blue exists, the fact we know is that there exists an awareness of blue. And this awareness is not merely... utterly different from blue: it also has a perfectly distinct relation to blue... This relation is just that which we mean in every case by 'knowing.' To have in your mind

'knowledge' of blue... is to be aware of an awareness of
blue (*Philosophical Studies,* pp. 24–25).

Thus, for Moore, philosophy in its analysis, for example, of the
non-linguistic sensation of blue, discovers blue, awareness, and a
unique external relation of awareness and blue. Whatever we may
think of Moore's analysis of sensation, it is clear that Moore regards
it as true and philosophically important. Indeed, the conception of
analysis employed here is identical with his statement of analysis as
real definition in the opening chapter of *PE*. Much of Moore's
philosophy, especially his analysis of the good and of sense-data, and
even of relational properties, as he unfolds them in 'External and
Internal Relations' (1919), is intelligible only on this conception of
analysis as real definition. Analysis as real definition of concepts and
of ordinary and not so ordinary things, thus, occupies an important
place in Moore's philosophy. Perhaps it is not central as it is for
Russell and others. Perhaps it is not even his most important contribution to philosophy for, as recent admirers of Moore note, it is
his persistent concern for clarity of expression, his insistence on
linguistic propriety, his devotion to common sense and, above all, his
incipient recognition that analysis of concepts must ultimately give
way to their elucidation, that constitute his great achievement. His
great distinction between understanding the meaning of an
expression and knowing what it means in the sense of being able to
give a correct analysis of its meaning leads naturally to the distinction between knowing how to use an expression and being able to say
how we use it, where the latter is not defining the concept denoted by
the expression but describing the function or functions of an
expression and the conditions under which it functions.

His distinction, I say, leads to this latter distinction. But it is clear
that Moore does not accept the transformation. His extreme concern
for correct analysis, whether of concepts or things in the world,
though it yields a greater insight into the relation between language
and concepts, retains his early belief in concepts as non-linguistic
entities. Concepts remain: they are not words, uses of words, abilities
to use words or to elucidate their use. They retain their platonic
status. The difficulty of how one can render concepts such as brother,
consciousness, sense-datum, the good, among others – all platonic
eide – stands.

CHAPTER 14

Some nineteenth and twentieth century theories: Ryle and Geach

Ryle

I conclude this survey of philosophical theories of concepts with brief considerations of the views of Gilbert Ryle and Peter Geach, both of whom offer devastating accounts of traditional theories as well as provocative theories of their own which, in their emphasis on the roles of expressions rather than on the apprehension of concepts as entities, introduce us to the contemporary dispositional theories of concepts.

In 'Systematically Misleading Expressions' (1931–2),[1] Ryle states that the primary (perhaps the whole) task of philosophy is the analysis of certain expressions which systematically mislead philosophers into thinking that these expressions record one kind of fact when they actually record another; and whose logical form, as against grammatical form, can be elicited only by correct logical paraphrase of these original expressions. The major result of this analysis is that it reveals as the sources of traditional philosophical theories and disputes – including theories of concepts – the persistent confusions of grammatical with logical form. Employing Russell's theory of descriptions as a model of logical paraphrase of certain expressions, Ryle classifies and analyzes a number of expressions that mislead (of which 'the author of *Waverley*' is not an example since it does not mislead as 'the present King of France' does; thus, Ryle says, Russell is correct in his theory of descriptions, but not correct in thinking that all descriptions mislead).

Among systematically (i.e., classes of) misleading expressions are (1) quasi-ontological assertions, such as 'God exists,' 'Carnivorous cows do not exist,' 'Mr. Pickwick is a fiction;' (2) quasi-platonic statements, such as 'Virtue is its own reward,' 'Unpunctuality is reprehensible;' (3) certain descriptive statements, such as 'Whoever is Vice-Chancellor of Oxford University is overworked,' 'The present King of France is wise;' and (4) quasi-descriptive claims, such as 'I saw the top of the tree.' Each of these is misleading in that its grammatical form is improper to the fact recorded: each must be paraphrased so that the real logical form of the fact recorded is brought out. Thus, 'Carnivorous cows do not exist' is true, significant, and looks grammatically like an ordinary subject-predicate statement. But when compared to the fact recorded, 'carnivorous cows' does not denote and 'does not exist' does not predicate. So the grammatical clue of subject-predicate must be rejected, and the real logical form of the fact must dictate the restatement. The fact recorded by the original statement is better expressed by 'Nothing is both a cow and carnivorous,' since this latter statement does not imply that anything is either. To generalize from this one example, philosophical analysis, as Ryle conceives it, can then say that one expression means another and that that other is a better expression than the original because it exhibits better the logical form of the fact it records.

So far as concepts are concerned, Ryle says, 'X is a concept' and 'the concept of X' are systematically misleading, the one because it is quasi-ontological, the other because it is quasi-descriptive. But unlike other systematically misleading expressions, Ryle does not paraphrase them, he gets rid of them. There is no paraphrase of 'The number four is a concept' or 'the concept of number,' which brings out the real logical form of these expressions as 'Nothing is both a cow and carnivorous' does of 'Carnivorous cows do not exist.' Ryle describes the philosophers' attempts at clarifying or analyzing concepts employed by them or by others as 'a gaseous way of saying that they are trying to discover what is meant by the general terms contained in the sentences which they pronounce or write' (II, 39). 'What is meant by a (specified) general term?' presumably is all the cash value Ryle finds in 'What is a (specified) concept?' Talk about concepts is not paraphrasable or even reducible to talk about general terms: it is replaceable by it. Thus, it is more than misleading to talk about concepts; it is a mistake. If 'The number four is a concept' is systematically misleading, 'There are no concepts' is not; as Ryle says: '. . . it can be shown that it is not true in any natural sense that "there are concepts" . . .' (II, 41).

Ryle compares 'the thought or idea of x' to 'the concept of x.' But the first reduces to 'Whenever A thinks of x' whereas the second is replaced by 'Whenever we use "x".' 'X' – the expression – has a meaning. Philosophers who convert this meaning into a concept misdescribe 'the meaning of the expression "x".'

> I suspect that all the mistaken doctrines of concepts, ideas, terms, judgements, objective propositions, contents, objectives and the like derive from the same fallacy, namely, that there must be *something* referred to by such expressions as 'the meaning of the word (phrase or sentence) "X",' on all fours with the policeman who really is referred to by the descriptive phrase in 'our village policeman is fond of football'. And the way out of the confusion is to see that some 'the'-phrases are only similar in grammar and not similar in function to referentially-used descriptive phrases, e.g. in the case in point, 'the meaning of "X"' is like 'the King of France' in 'Poincaré is not the King of France', a predicative expression used non-referentially (II, 55).

'The meaning of the expression "x"' is systematically misleading and is quasi-descriptive, to be paraphrased as Ryle suggests. But 'the concept of x' is a mistaken doctrine – not a wrong paraphrase – about meanings. As Ryle says, 'the meaning of "x"' can be redrafted as 'what "x" means;' however, 'the concept of x' cannot be redrafted, only thrown out as unfit for service.

The beauty of this paper is, I think, that it does proclaim the view, first intimated by Hume, then articulated by Mill, that there are no concepts; that all talk and theories of concepts are mistaken doctrines about words and what they mean. There is language. There are theories about language. Among these theories are mistaken views about how general terms function. It is therefore a particular theorizing about language that generates concepts and a theory about them. Correcting the theorizing about language is in effect to undercut the need for concepts altogether. Ryle's paper, thus, is not a defence of his later doctrines that there are concepts and that these are the roles of certain expressions or that to have a concept is to be able to wield an expression of a certain sort. For this view is to admit concepts, not to reject them as misguided projections onto language. Ryle does not say in this paper 'The concept of x is the same as what "x" does in the language,' as he does say 'The meaning of "x" is the same as what "x" means.'

In 'Categories" (1938),[2] Ryle suggests that asking what type or category does so and so belong to? is equivalent to asking what sort of true or false propositions and in what positions in them can the expression 'x' for so and so occur? He introduces the term 'proposition-factor' to replace 'propositional function.' It names an abstractable item from families of similar propositions, not separate entities. Talk about concepts is talk about these abstracted proposition-factors, so that now Ryle allows 'What sort of concept is the concept of x?' This becomes equivalent to 'What sort or type or category of expression is "x"?' 'What position can it occupy in a sentence?' Clarifying and classifying concepts are no longer gaseous, but a legitimate and fruitful charting of what we can and cannot do with certain expressions.

Ryle's acceptance of the legitimacy and irreducibility of concepts along with his employment of them continues in *Philosophical Arguments* (1945).[3] Philosophy, he says, is neither inductive nor deductive argument. Instead, 'A pattern of argument which is proper and even proprietary to philosophy is the *reductio ad absurdum*' (II, 197). And it is a *reductio* in the strong sense of reducing a proposition to nonsense by showing that its implications lead to absurdities. The aim of such arguments is not a nihilistic one but rather to test the logical powers of certain philosophical ideas and doctrines. 'Every proposition has ... certain "logical powers"; that is to say, it is related to other propositions in various discoverable logical relationships' (II, 198). For the most part, all of us understand these logical powers of the ideas and propositions we employ; the difficulty is to state them, to test them against possible implications and absurdities.

It is a function of philosophy to chart these logical powers.

> When several different propositions are noticed having something in common (and when this common feature or factor is not itself a constituent proposition) it is convenient and idiomatic, though hazardous, to abstract this common factor and call it (with exceptions) an 'idea' or 'concept'. Thus men learn to fasten on the idea of mortality or the concept of price as that which is common to a range of propositions in which persons are affirmed or

denied to be mortal or in which commodities are said to cost so much or to be exchangeable at such and such rates. Later they learn to isolate in the same manner more abstract ideas like those of existence, implication, duty, species, mind, and science (II, 199).

Concepts are not terms in the historical sense of substantial parts of propositions. Rather they 'are absractions from the families of propositions of which they are common factors or features' (II, 199). Talk of a concept, thus, is talk about no entity, but of a family of propositions, that share a common feature. 'Statements about ideas [concepts] are general statements about families of propositions' (II, 199).

Concepts, like the propositions from which they are abstracted, differ in their types or categories. The concepts of three and large have different logical powers than the concepts of green and merry. Concepts of different types cannot be coerced into similar logical conduct without contradiction.

Philosophers ought to chart the logical powers of concepts. And like geographers, they cannot do this by concentrating on one item but instead must '... determine the cross-bearings of all of a galaxy of ideas belonging to the same or contiguous fields. The problem, that is, is not to anatomize the solitary concept, say, of liberty but to extract its logical powers as these bear on those of law, obedience, responsibility, loyalty, government and the rest' (II, 202). The search for the types and logical powers of concepts and the testing of these concepts by reducing to absurdity their being placed in types they do not belong to or their being given powers they do not have Ryle calls 'dialectical.' It is, he says, the true method of philosophy as the clarification and analysis of concepts and the search for definitions.

Ryle next amends 'proposition' to 'expression' in order to avoid having to assert that philosophy attempts to reduce propositions to absurdity, since such reduction would nullify the original as a proposition. 'The solution is that expressions and only expressions can be absurd' (II, 203). The reduction to absurdity operates only on expressions, disclosing 'that a given expression cannot be expressing a proposition of such and such a content with such and such a logical skeleton, since a proposition with certain of these properties would conflict with one with certain of the others' (II, 203). Thus, the pattern of the *reductio* is that of *ponendo tollens*.

Not all ideas or concepts generate puzzles, Ryle says, only abstract ones. A concrete idea or concept is one '... the original use of which is to serve as an element in propositions about what exists or occurs in the real world' (II, 207). 'Ideas like *spaniel, dog, ache, thunder* in their original use are instances of concrete concepts ... Such concepts are formed from noticing similarities in the real world' (II, 207). Abstract concepts, on the other hand, are not formed by noticing similarities and do not correspond to anything. 'To form abstract ideas it is necessary to notice not similarities between things in nature but similarities between propositions about things in nature or, later on, between propositions about propositions about things in nature...' (II, 208).

All this talk about propositions (and, by implication, about concepts) reduces to talk about expressions as they are employed by persons. With this safeguard, we can now say that certain propositions – things people say – share a common factor: 'Socrates is wise' and 'Plato *sapiens est*' share the common factor that can be expressed as 'so and so is wise.' Propositions about such factors are propositions about abstract ideas. And such ideas are always subject to the test of absurdity. But, Ryle concludes, these ideas, when they generate new theories or new questions in philosophy, are as important in their logical powers as any concepts.

Philosophical Arguments, thus, is as remarkable in its conservatism about the nature and role of concepts as 'Systematically Misleading Expressions' as in its radicalism. According to its main theses, there are concepts; and the claim that there are is neither systematically misleading nor mistaken, only hazardous. Though not entities, they are, when concrete, items extracted from the world and, when abstract, common factors found in language about the world. More-over, though there is original talk about the charting of concepts, there is nothing about this charting as the elucidation of the use of expressions and about concepts as the roles of expressions. Ryle's theory of concepts here is a form of traditional abstractionism, except that what is abstracted is not an entity, neither mental, physical, nor linguistic.

The Concept of Mind (1949) owes much to the *reductio* of *Philosophical Arguments*. One of its theses, that Cartesianism, in all its varieties, from Descartes to Russell, is fundamentally a logical mistake in that it reduces certain crucial statements about the mind which are not and cannot be categorical to categorical ones, stems from his Inaugural Lecture. Cartesianism or 'Descartes' Myth' (as he calls his first chapter) is a category-mistake, that is, a misplacing of one kind of concept or expression in a type whose logical powers yield implications that are absurd.

However, *The Concept of Mind* is much more than a *reductio* of Cartesianism. Its three other main theses, I think, are these: (1) the philosophy of mind is fundamentally the logical elucidation of mental concepts or expressions and the logical mapping of their cross-bearings; (2) statements about mental phenomena are, logically, at least irreducibly threefold: categorical, hypothetical and mongrel-categorical; and (3) the mind is not an extra, metaphysically hidden entity, affixed to the body – a 'Ghost in the Machine' – but a 'person's abilities, liabilities and inclinations to do and undergo certain sorts of things, and of the doing and undergoing of these things in the ordinary world' (p. 199). Even the title of the book indicates that Ryle's primary concern is with the concept, not the nature of mind. Philosophy as analysis shifts to philosophy as elucidaton of concepts. (Contrast, for example, Russell's title, *The Analysis of Mind*, with Ryle's.) The preoccupation is with the logical mapping of central mental concepts or expressions. Ryle's basic claim, which pervades the book, is that the description of the logical behaviour of mental concepts constitutes the whole philosophical story of the mind; and neither in plot nor in character is it the story narrated by the orthodox, classical amalgam of traditional theories, from Descartes to Russell, that Ryle calls 'Cartesianism.'

In this book, whether under the influence of the later Wittgenstein or not, Ryle comes to see that there are concepts, not just general words or abstractable features of language and things – though there is much expository identification of concepts with their conveying words, where the concept of x simply replaces x with inverted commas ('x') – and that these concepts are the same as certain abilities or capacities to move about in various ways in the world, one of which is the ability to use language. In this way, concepts are assimilated to the having of them and the having of them is being able to do certain sorts of things, only one of which, but a very important one, is employing expressions correctly. Talk of concepts is mostly tantamount to talk of the roles of corresponding linguistic expressions. It is not clear – nor is it, I think, in the whole of Ryle's work – that a necessary condition for being a concept or for having a concept is being able to use an expression correctly. However, it is clear that such a necessary condition is being able to perform a certain range of tasks; it is also clear that a sufficient condition for having a concept of a certain sort is being able to use its word correctly. That not all concepts are abstractions from families of propositions or things we say about the world follows from the fact the concept of volition is both a concept and yet has no legitimate role in any linguistic family of propositions.

In 'The Theory of Meaning' (1957),[4] Ryle's theory of concepts comes full circle: from a rejection of concepts in any form to their identification with the roles of expressions. Traditional theories of concepts, he claims, rest on a misdescription of the functioning of language; a correct theory rests on a correct description of the functioning of language. The decisive moment in the history of theories of concepts occurs when Wittgenstein exchanges 'What is the role of an expression?' for 'What is the meaning of an expression?' The latter question, Ryle points out, led philosophers to search for a realm of non-natural, non-metal objects which could serve as the denotata of meanings of expressions. That every word (with the exception of the syncategorematic) stands for an object that it denotes or means, from Plato to Mill, Russell and Moore, is the root of all traditional theories of concepts as entities. That this denotational theory of the meaning of words is an erroneous answer to 'What do words mean?' to be replaced by a different question, 'What do words do?' is the beginning of the correct approach to concepts. A realm of meanings as concepts is no longer needed. Having a concept is not being acquainted with a meaning but being able to wield expressions according to conventionally accepted rules. A concept is the role of similar expressions. Analysis, as practiced by Russell and Moore, no longer has a realm to analyze; philosophy now has as its great task the elucidation of the roles of expressions, not the analysis of meanings.

In the Introduction to his *Collected Papers*, Ryle writes: 'To elucidate the thoughts of a philosopher we need to find the answer not only to the question, "What were his intellectual worries?" but, before that question and after that question, the answer to the question, "What was his overriding Worry?"' (I, ix). So far as his own philosophy is concerned, Ryle confesses as his overriding worry, in a number of essays that span his career, to discover what, if anything, is proprietary to philosophy? His answer is that it is conceptual inquiry. Such inquiry, though not the same as analysis of concepts for Ryle, is equivalent to inquiry into concepts. This inquiry, I think, has taken two main preliminary directions: to determine whether there are concepts and to determine what they are. Though Ryle has wavered on his different answers to both questions, I do not find that he has ever denied the distinctness of these two questions. Whatever concepts are or are said to be by philosophers, 'There are concepts' and 'Concepts are ...' are different answers to different questions. There is hardly an essay of Ryle's as well as *The Concept of Mind* and *Dilemmas* (1954) that does not centre on or raise these two questions and provide answers to them. They may not add up to Ryle's overriding worry, but they are pretty close to it.

I have concentrated on those writings of Ryle's which, at least in my judgment, contain the major moves Ryle has made in the development of his theory of concepts. These writings show that Ryle went from There are no concepts, therefore, there is nothing that they are to There are concepts and they are abstractable common features of families of sentences or propositions, tied to language, not to things; they are these features, with all their logical powers, plus extracted similarities from things, not just language; and they are roles of expressions in one or more languages or certain abilities for performing tasks, including being able to wield certain expressions.

If we turn from these essays and their varying answers to others of Ryle's writings, especially those that explore different kinds or logical types of concepts, we find not only further clarifications of Ryle's views about whether there are concepts or what they are but, as important, perhaps more important, both statements and examples of the point of conceptual inquiry. And because no adequate answer to What is Ryle's theory of concepts – their nature and role? – can be forthcoming without consideration of these writings, I include them here. If they add to the difficulty of arriving at an univocal theory attributable to Ryle, they equally enhance the richness of the conceptual life that he so abundantly unfolds.

Ryle's early essay, 'Are There Propositions?' (1929–30)[5], examines arguments for and against an affirmative answer. He concludes that there are no propositions, only facts and symbols or sentences and statements made with sentences about facts. 'Proposition' denotes sentence or statement; and is a name for what one thinks with or talks in, not for what one thinks. Now, if propositions are not sentence-meanings, as the tradition assumes they are, are concepts word-meanings? Ryle raises this question, only to drop it, since after all his topic is Propositions. However, we can ask, in the spirit of this essay, whether concepts too can be resolved into symbols we think or talk with, not entities we think of? Because we are given nothing like *facts – things* seem to be the only possibility – it is difficult to project a Rylean answer to what a concept is about if it is a symbol, if 'concept' denotes symbol, and if 'concept' names what we think and talk with or in, not what we think. Nevertheless, that concepts remain legitimate word-meanings while propositions do not as sentence-meanings is not implied in this paper, and is rejected completely in his next, 'Systematically Misleading Expressions.'

In 'Plato's "Parmenides"' (1939),[6] Ryle proposes that the dialogue is primarily an early exploration into different logical types of concepts. Plato does not distinguish between generic and specific concepts, as he does elsewhere; but between 'formal' and 'proper' concepts. The formal, Ryle says, include the concepts of existence, negation, being an instance of; and the proper, concepts such as triangle, courage, piety, and so on. In the *Parmenides*, Ryle hypothesizes, Plato was feeling his way into this radical type difference. Ryle also proposes that Plato here introduces the *reductio* (that Ryle later in *Philosophical Arguments* makes central in philosophy) as the method of deducing absurdities from erroneous placing or identification of formal and proper or non-formal concepts. To treat existence, for example, like square is to sin against logical syntax: this is the major point of much of the argument in the *Parmenides*, according to Ryle. This distinction between formal and non-formal concepts as they differ in their logical type, demonstrated by anomalies deduced by denying their different logical types, Ryle attributes not only to Plato but to Aristotle as well. Ryle introduces a variety of names in his essays on Plato and Aristotle – 'common,' 'ubiquitous,' 'neutral,' 'topic-neutral' – to mark these concepts that run though all discourse and thought; and he differentiates these formal concepts from the non-formal which, throughout his work, include task, achievement, heed concepts, dispositional, process, activity concepts and even polymorphous concepts, each different from the others, but all to be distinguished from the formal ones in their lack of ubiquitousness. Ryle's essay on the *Parmenides*, because of its introduction of this division of concepts and independently of its validity of application to Plato, is as important as anything in Ryle's work, so fundamental has the search for types of concepts been to Ryle: it is perhaps the persistent theme that underwrites his inquiry into concepts.

In 'Ordinary Language' (1953),[7] Ryle distinguishes between the ordinary (or standard) use of expressions as against their non-standard use; the use of ordinary as against the use of technical (or uncommon) expressions; and a linguistic usage (or custom). The primary task of philosophy is to give logical accounts of the roles of ordinary and technical terms in their standard modes of employment. Talking about the uses of expressions replaced talk about concepts and talk about the meanings of expressions, since the former but not the two latter raises no questions about status or provenance. However, inquiry into concepts is, Ryle says, shorthand for the longwinded inquiry into uses of expressions; while inquiry into meanings of expressions is a perversion of the description of uses of expressions. Thus, concept talk remains in this article, meaning talk does not; the first, but not the second, is the same as talk about the ordinary use of both ordinary and technical expressions. Conceptual elucidation is an alternate for description of uses of expressions; whether concepts are alternates for uses of words, so that the concept of, say, cause, is the same as the role of 'cause,' '*Ursache*,' etc., and the having of that concept is the same as being able to use 'cause,' etc., Ryle does not say. But he leaves little doubt that they are the same. Four years later, in 'The Theory of Meaning,' he says as much.

In *Dilemmas*, Ryle contrasts competing theories that can be adjudicated by the theorists themselves with dilemmas that can be litigated only by philosophy. Litigation, thus, becomes, along with reformulation of systematically misleading expressions, the *reductio*, and the charting of logical powers or the mapping of concepts, one of the proprietary tasks of philosophy. Competing theories are most rival solutions to the same problem; dilemmas are apparent but not really rival solutions to the same problem. Competing theories differ over the truth or falsity of putative propositions; dilemmas arise because certain, mainly ordinary, concepts and their categories are misconstrued. Their resolution proceeds by detailing reminders of the category status of the various concepts involved in the seeming dispute; and with the overall reminder that, though the category status must be considered piecemeal since there is no table of categories, neither Aristotle's nor Kant's, to determine its status, the concepts cannot be taken one apart from others related to it. Thus, 'Whatever is was to be' seems to conflict with 'Some things which have happened could have been averted.' This dilemma, however, rests on a mistaken notion of anterior truths about happenings as causes of these happenings; and is to be litigated by the reminder that only truths necessitate truths, while events can be effects but not implications. The concepts of truth, cause, necessity, and the related ones of prevention and responsibility have been wrongly categorized: the necessitation of truth is not the necessitation of causality. Whatever the category or logical power of the concept of cause or truth may be, the philosophical truth that they are different in their types and cannot be assimilated without, in this case, generating the dilemma, also dissolves it.

Just here, I am not interested in pursuing the question of the adequacy or inadequacy of Ryle's statement and resolution of this dilemma or any of the others he presents; nor, more important, of the differences, if any, between a dilemma and a *reductio* as Ryle conceives them. My sole concern is the role of concepts in these dilemmas and their litigation. A dilemma, Ryle says, centres on the misconstrual of concepts. Both the concepts and their misconstruals do not merely rest on but are equivalent to what we say and what we cannot say, that is: to expressions, their use and misuse. The concepts of cause, truth and necessity; or of whole, part and sum; or of pleasure, pain and enjoyment, and so on for all the concepts involved in the dilemmas Ryle discusses, are shorthand for the employments of the words 'cause,' 'truth,' etc., that convey the concepts. If I have any of the concepts that may become enmeshed in dilemmas, Ryle seems to allow, I still know how to use certain words, even if I then go on to misuse them as I generate a horn of a dilemma. However, whether I use these words correctly or not, I still may not be able to state the criteria and the rules for the correct use of the word in question. Ryle distinguishes sharply between being able to use a word correctly and being able to state its criteria and rules of correct employment. But he does not say what is to count as having or understanding the concept: being able to use a word or being able to state its criteria and rules? If it is the former, concepts are equivalent to uses of expressions; if it is the latter, concepts are not, unless uses include their criteria and rules, which they do not. In any case, even if we grant that Ryle's distinction between employing a concept efficiently and describing its employment efficiently is equivalent to using an expression and describing that use, so that all talk about concepts is the same as talk about uses of expressions, what shall we say about the concepts of litigation, the *reductio*, and logical powers? Can these concepts be rendered equivalent to uses or roles of expressions? Is talk about the 'notion of litigation' (p. 6) the same as talk about 'litigation' or any other word or words, as talk about the concept of cause is talk about 'cause' or '*Ursache*,' or some other word? Of course the concept of litigation as Ryle describes it depends on language and especially on some of the snares we encounter when we depart from standard uses of certain terms; but does it depend on language as the concept of cause depends on 'cause' or of pleasure depends on 'enjoy' and 'being pleased?' The concepts of cause and pleasure reduce to or are equivalent to the roles of certain words, about which we need philosopical reminders when we lose our ways in handling them. But the concept of litigation, though it depends on language, indeed, lives off it, cannot be reduced to or rendered equivalent to any employment or description of that employment of expressions. The concept of litigation, as Ryle abundantly shows, is a concept of a skill, in particular, of being able to resolve dilemmas by amassing reminders about the logical types of the concepts or words conveying them whose boundaries have been transgressed. In the spirit, if not according to the letter of Ryle, one might say the concept of litigation is an elucidatory concept, not a concept to be elucidated. As such, it is a concept about the employment and the rules of employment of certain expressions, irreducible to expressions or their roles. And having or understanding this concept includes more than being able to use expressions and state their criteria and rules of correct use; it is being able to wield this knowledge in the detection of misuses that generate dilemmas and in the resolution of these dilemmas by nosing out and stating the type or category mistake.

In the Discussion of Ryle's paper, 'Thinking Thoughts and Having Concepts' (1962), which unfortunately is not included in the reprinting in *Collected Papers*, Professor J. N. Findlay asks Ryle 'why he thinks that his entirely acceptable view that having a concept entails being able to apply it in a certain way in various classificatory and argumentative contexts should justify the patently false view that there is no such thing as a particular recollectable experience of having a concept in mind, dwelling on it, soaking oneself in it, realizing what it involves, profoundly understanding it?'[8] Ryle's reply is not printed; however, it is safe to assume that Ryle would not countenance having a concept in mind as a particular recollectable experience. Nevertheless, Findlay's point that one sometimes dwells on a concept, soaks oneself in it, trying to understand what it includes and entails, whether we agree with him or not that these imply having a concept in mind or just having a concept of a certain sort, illumines Ryle's concept of litigation and the having of it better than Ryle's account of concepts as uses of expressions and the having of them as being able to wield these expressions. In effect, then, Ryle creates his own dilemma with the concept of litigation (and with the concepts of the *reductio* and logical powers as well): Concepts are the roles of expressions or those plus their rules versus the view that some concepts are about the roles or rules of expressions, their transgressions, and their logical types. The having of concepts is being able to use certain expressions and to state the rules of their correct employment versus some havings of concepts being able to assemble reminders of the categories or types to which they belong with the express purpose of exposing and resolving dilemmas. The way out of this dilemma (and similar ones could be constructed for the concepts of the *reductio* and of logical powers) is to remind Ryle and ourselves that it rests on a confusion perhaps not of categories or types but, since the term has a use, of orders. Concepts like that of cause reduce to the use of 'cause.' These are first order concepts, whatever their types or categories may be. Concepts such as litigation, the *reductio*, or logical powers, however, depend on but do not reduce to words or their uses or their rules of use. These, then, are second order concepts, about other concepts in their propositional contexts, dependent on but neither reducible nor equivalent to the first order. That their nature and role differ from the nature and role of the first order concepts, whether concrete, such as enjoyment or pain, or abstract, like pleasure; or whether topic neutral or proper, proposition-factors abstracted from families of propositions or extracted from similarities among things; or whether formally logical, like negation – whatever the order of these may be – is the philosophical truth that resolves Ryle's dilemma about concepts.

Ryle's 'Phenomenology Versus "The Concept of Mind"' (1962)[9] includes, among other things, Ryle's Retrospect on his various thoughts about concepts. Both Phenomenology and Cambridge Philosophy began with a fundamental doctrine that concepts are platonic essences. The great difference between them is that the first never repudiated this doctrine and the realm it affirmed while the second, at least as represented by Russell and Wittgenstein, rejected it, at first in part, then totally, in Wittgenstein's *Tractatus*.

Ryle offers this preliminary definition of a concept:

> By 'concept' we refer to that which is signified by a word
> or a phrase. If we talk of the concept of *Euclidean point* we
> are referring to what is conveyed by this English phrase, or
> by any other phrase, Greek, French, or English, that has
> the same meaning (I, 182).

'There are concepts' and 'Concepts are what certain words mean' are
neutral and only the second is potentially harmful since it may invite
status questions, both about concepts and meanings. But even
independently of this danger, there are some words, such as 'exists'
or 'not' or 'pleased,' which are meaningful yet do not convey
concepts as their abstract nouns, 'existence,' 'negation' and 'pleasure'
do; and there are also some concepts that do not get conveyed by
verbs or adjectives, such as the concept of pleasure that neither
'enjoys' nor 'pleases' signifies. The relationship between words, their
meanings and the concepts conveyed by words is thus at best an
uneasy one: Not all concepts are meanings of words; not all meanings
of words are concepts.

Ryle's greatest objection to the definition he offers is that it yields
too easily to identification of meanings with entities that exist in
isolation. Concepts are not meanings if meanings are entities of any
sort, platonic or not. Russell proved this even as early as the
Principles for the logical concepts *all, some, any, a, the* (in the
singular and plural), *not, exists*, among others, although his
commitment to Platonism, Ryle claims, prevented him from drawing
the consequence that the words for these logical concepts as well as
the verbs of action, such as 'assassinate,' convey no entities, hence no
platonic essences either. Russell recognized but disregarded the fact
that the logical words and the live verbs have meanings but only as
auxiliary to the senses of the whole sentences in which they occur. It
was left to Wittgenstein to invert the traditional ascent from separate
word meanings to sentence meanings, as he followed Frege in
starting with the sense of the complete sentence.

Ryle generalizes from this historical demolition of concepts and
meanings as separate items, an achievement of 'The Cambridge
Transformation of the Theory of Concepts' (I, 182), to formulate the
doctrine, first articulated by him in 'Categories' (1938) that concepts
are proposition-factors, now as the theory that:

> Concepts are not things that are crystallised in a splendid
> isolation; they are discriminable features, but not detachable
> atoms, of what is integrally said or integrally thought. They
> are not detachable parts of, but distinguishable
> contributions to, the unitary sense of completed sentences.
> To examine them is to examine the live force of things that
> we actually say. It is to examine them not in retirement,
> but doing their co-operative work (I, 185).

A concept, thus, is exactly what the meaning of a logical word or a verb was to Russell: 'an abstractible feature, not an extractible part of the unitary senses of the different sentences that incorporate it' (I, 184); and all concepts are what meanings of parts of sentences were to Wittgenstein: 'abstractible differences and similarities between the unitary sense of that sentence and the unitary senses of other sentences which have something but not everything in common with that given sentence' (I, 184).

Ryle's preliminary definition stands: There are concepts and they are the meanings of words in their complete sentential contexts. Conceptual inquiry turns from the 'Platonic dream of a descriptive science of Essences' (I, 188) to 'what can be significantly said but also ... what cannot be significantly said with the word or phrase conveying the concept under investigation' (I, 186). Since the meanings of words are their contributory roles in the sentences in which they occur, concepts remain the uses of expressions, to be abstracted as common features, not extracted as common separate items. Concepts, thus, are not entities. But they are not abilities either. Conceptual inquiry is a skill; but the having of concepts is an amalgam of knowing that certain words, in contributing as they do to the unitary sense of the sentences that incorporate them, do their jobs under certain conditions or rules; and of knowing how to wield words according to their rules, with or without being able to state them.

One final observation on Ryle on Plato: In his *Encyclopedia of Philosophy* article, 'Plato,' Ryle interprets Plato's Theory of Forms as Plato's ontology of concepts: 'A general idea or concept, according to this ... doctrine, is immutable, timeless, one over many, intellectually apprehensible and capable of precise definition at the end of a piece of pure ratiocination *because it is an independently existing real thing or entity*' (vol. 6, p. 322). He also argues that 'Plato did not deduce the Theory of Forms from the false premise that verbs and verb phrases function like extra nouns' (*ibid.*). Rather his arguments were based on epistemic considerations regarding the certainties attributed to the sciences, especially mathematics, and the objectivity of truth required in intelligible disputation. Elsewhere, from 'Systematically Misleading Expressions' on, Ryle hammers away at the idea that all traditional philosophical theories of concepts are mistaken theories of the meanings of words. If, therefore, Forms are super concepts for Plato, these form-concepts are also mistaken projections of the meanings of words. Ryle cannot have it both ways: Either some philosophical theories of concepts as entities do not derive from mistaken, on the whole, denotative theories of meanings of words, in which case, there is no wholesale formula for disposing of entity theories of concepts; or all entity theories of concepts – including Plato's – are badly mistaken doctrines about the meanings of words.

There is, I think, another, perhaps deeper, problem in Ryle's interpretation of Plato's theory of concepts. Like almost every one else, he identifies concepts in and for Plato with the forms. This identification, as I have tried to show, is untenable: Plato's forms are necessary conditions for some concepts, not all, and never identical with concepts in Plato. (How, one wants to ask Ryle, would Plato reconcile the concept of love with the lack of the form of love in the *Symposium*?) Ryle's real target is not Plato's theory of concepts which are neither entities nor forms but Aristotle; and it is Aristotle's direct concerns with what we say and cannot say that divert Ryle from seeing that these concerns were integral to, not substitutes for, Aristotle's persistent search for the real definitions of things that, once completed, offered up concepts as definitional *Logoi*.

To return, finally, to our original question: What is Ryle's theory of concepts? I hope it is now evident there can be only one answer: that he formulated a number of theories, as well as an anti-theory, soon abandoned. His most persistent theory, I think and have tried to show, is the one he first states in 'Categories,' that concepts are proposition-factors. To be sure, he refers to these by various names; and, more important, he explores their different facets – as logical powers or as logical types or as categories. What remains univocal, however, throughout his work, is not a theory of concepts, but the absolute centrality of conceptual inquiry, as it is tied inextricably to language or uses of expressions. This predominant concern, fixed on concepts in their linguistic employment, rather than fixated on concepts as inspectible entities of any sort, has led Ryle into conceptual terrains where he staked proprietarily philosophical discoveries of the highest order, especially about the different logical types of concepts, there to be discerned and abstracted from what we say and what we cannot say. My major criticism, if that is the right word, is not so much with his theory or theories of concepts as it is with the fact that these theories, so carefully formulated by him at different times, simply do not do justice to the multiplicity of the logical kinds of concepts that Ryle uncovered.

Geach

I finish this survey with Geach's theory of concepts in *Mental Acts* (1957). Whatever other merits this book may possess, it serves my historical purpose both by offering a summary statement of traditional abstractionist views, which Geach rejects, and by setting forth a dispositional theory that he finds in Wittgenstein, with hints in Aquinas, that he accepts. In this way, he thus brings us up to the present and, for some, to the great moment of truth in the history of philosophical theories of concepts. It is because his theory performs this role, not merely because of its intrinsic value, that I close with it.

Geach begins by affirming the existence of mental acts: what we see, hear, feel, think. These can be narrated, described, reported on. When they are, claims about them are categorical, not semi-categorical or hypothetical. These claims or reports employ certain expressions, such as 'pain' in 'I am in pain.' These expressions, Geach says, have a public sense and a private reference. They are not formed, nor are the concepts they express, by a process of abstraction from sets of similar experiences. Rather, they precede the reports themselves: it is because I have the concept of pain or the word 'pain' that I am able to recognize pain or similarities among pains. Thus, for Geach, my actually being in pain or having any other experience or mental act is not a necessary or a sufficient condition for my knowing what pain is, what 'pain' means, or how to use 'pain' correctly, or for having the concept of pain.

Among mental acts are acts of judgment. A statement of belief is such an act of judgment; 'I think it might rain,' for example, is a judgment – a species of the genus, mental act – that is of an episodic act, irreducible to hypothetical or semi-hypothetical statement. Concepts, Geach claims, are capacities exercised in such mental acts. Concepts are presupposed to judgments, not abstracted from them, as Ryle wrongly says in *Philosophical Arguments*. This seems to imply that for Geach concepts are not present in species of mental acts other than judgments, which contradicts what he says about the concept of pain in reports on mental acts that are not judgments. I think he must mean that concepts are capacities presupposed to *all* mental acts, not merely judgments. In any case, according to Geach, a necessary condition for the making of a judgment is the having of a concept as a mental capacity:

> The ability to express a judgment in words thus presupposes a number of capacities, previously acquired, for intelligently using the several words and phrases that make up the sentence. I shall apply the old term 'concepts' to these special capacities – an application which I think lies fairly close to the historic use of the term (p. 12).

It follows from his necessary condition that the ability to express a judgment in words is a sufficient condition for the having of a concept. It is not a necessary condition because one struck by aphasia and who can still play, say, chess, has concepts that are involved in playing the game. Nevertheless, the normal applications of 'having a concept' are those in which we are masters of bits of language. Indeed, with some concepts, for example, *the day after tomorrow*, being able to verbalize judgments about it is a necessary and sufficient condition of having the concept.

Concepts, thus, are skills, not learned responses. They are made by the mind, not conditioned in us by the environment. As mental capacities, concepts are subjective, not objective in Frege's or Russell's sense. Nor are concepts entities, either in the mind or in nature or in some supersensible realm. Nor is there simple apprehension of concepts; there is no mental act of intuiting concepts. Concepts exist only in their application – in their being exercised.

What sort of 'can' is involved in the capacities that are concepts? '... To say that a man has a certain concept is to say that he *can* perform, because he sometimes *does* perform, mental exercises of a specifiable sort. This way of using the modal word "can" is a minimal use... What is can be, what a man does he can do; that is clear if anything in modal logic is clear, and no more than this is involved in my talking of concepts' (p. 15).

Humans have concepts, animals only discriminative responses. For Geach, this is not linguistic stipulation but a recognition of the irreducible differences between the performances of human beings who possess concepts and animals who do not. Animals, like humans, have native responses to features of the environment or can be conditioned to respond to them in certain uniform ways. But such responses involve no mental exercises, consequently satisfy not even the sufficient condition for having concepts.

Concepts, thus, are mental capacities, skills or abilities, the best manifestation of which is in the use of language to make judgments. Having a concept is being able, on the basis of past performances, to express these capacities, skills or abilities. Concepts are dispositional powers, not dispositional hypotheticals.

By 'Abstractionism,' Geach does not mean the view that concepts are *entities* in the mind which are abstracted from things; rather it is the view that concepts are recognitional *capacities* that are 'acquired by a process of singling out in attention some one feature given in direct experience – *abstracting* it – and ignoring the other features simultaneously given –*abstracting from* them' (p. 18). According to this theory, judgments are exercises of concepts got from abstraction. But Geach also says (p. 11) that abstractionism is the view that judgments precede concepts, which are derived from similarities among judgments. In any case, Geach rejects the theory: '...no concept at all is acquired by the supposed process of abstraction' (p. 18). Indeed, he argues, '... the whole idea of abstraction – of discriminative attention to some feature given in experience – is thoroughly incoherent' (p. 19). For Geach, then, the concept of abstraction not only has no applicaton but is senseless, hence no concept at all. There is and can be no mental act or judgment in which the concept of abstraction is exercised. Perhaps Geach does countenance abstraction as a self-contradictory concept, yet (like Frege) nevertheless a concept. However, there is no evidence that he does; and his notion of a concept as a mental capacity to be exercised in acts of judgment seems to rule out incoherent concepts. How one can argue against the coherence of a concept or of there being instances of it without acknowledging it as a concept seems difficult to understand and impossible on the view that a concept is a mental capacity.

Geach apparently does not see or share this difficulty as he proceeds to demolish abstractionism in all its varieties. First, he shows that concepts of sensible things, if they are derived by abstraction, cannot include proper concepts of substances, such as water or gold, or the concept of substance which, on the abstractionist theory, ought not to be a proper concept at all. Then he shows that psychological concepts, supposedly derived from inner experience, rest on a fictitious inner sense that forms concepts such as desiring or judging by doing the requisite abstracting. Next come logical concepts – disjunction, negation, and the like. That these are abstractions from inner or outer experiences may do justice to the mental associations of these logical constants but hardly to their formal powers. Nor, in the case of the concept of the other of two – a concept close to that of negation – is there even a plausible candidate for a corresponding feeling. Arithmetical concepts fare no better. We do not form number concepts by abstraction; indeed, before we can apply a number concept, 'we must first apply the concept of some kind of things to the things that we count' (p. 28). Counting is itself a skill that involves the exercise of number concepts previously acquired, not simultaneously derived from the things counted. Relational concepts resist abstractionism altogether. For 'the concept of a relation and of its converse is one and the same indivisible mental capacity' (p. 33). To explain the concept of right-left ordering on abstractionist grounds would be to reduce the ability to tell right from left to a recognition of a recurrent characteristic. Finally, and most important, Geach argues that not even colour concepts are formed by abstraction. If these or other concepts of simple qualities cannot be accounted for by abstractionism, abstractionism is bankrupt right at the beginning. What, then, is it to have the concept, say, of red? For Geach, I can perform acts of judgment that are expressed by sentences containing the word 'red.' I cannot learn to do this by attending to red patches, no more than I can learn how to use 'red' by hearing the word in the presence of a red object. Ostensive definition of words is in the same untenable position as abstractive definition of concepts. Part of the employment of words and concepts is their application to absent objects; this use needs more than ostensive definition or abstraction. Further, some sense concepts and words can be deployed and understood by people bereft of the sense organs that supposedly are needed to grasp them. 'A man born blind can use the word "red" with a considerable measure of intelligence' (p. 35). Again, abstractionism has no explanation of the concept of chromatic colour, i.e., colour other than white, grey and black. It is a simple concept, like red. It is impossible to form this concept by discriminative attention: all I get is one sensation, not two from which I can abstract one: 'Failing to account for so simple a concept as *chromatic colour*, abstractionism must be pronounced finally bankrupt' (p. 38).

Is Geach's criticism of abstractionism lethal? Has he shown that no concept can be so formed, or only that not all of them are? It is often said that Wittgenstein shows that there are no ostensible definitions; yet all he shows and wishes to show is that ostensive definition is not primitive in the learning of language; that it rests on a mastery of certain techniques, such as naming and pointing. It is precisely this distinction between the primacy and the possibility of ostensive definition that Geach overlooks in his refutation of both ostensive definition and abstractionism. That abstractionism is not the way we learn to form concepts – is not primal in concept formation – no more yields that no concept can be formed by abstraction than ostensive definition is not the way we learn what words mean – is not primary in language learning – implies that no word can be ostensively defined. Consequently, all Geach shows is that we do not begin to acquire concepts by abstraction: that abstraction is neither logically nor genetically primitive in the acquisition of concepts. This claim, true or not, does not rule out the possibility of learning how to form concepts by abstraction. It would be a higher order skill, involving mental capacities and certain concepts not learned by abstraction; and it could create all sorts of concepts, such as the concept of recurrent features. On this view, the concept of abstraction would be neither without application nor incoherent. Instead, it would involve a full-fledged mental capacity, exercised not in the making of judgments, but rather in the making of concepts.

Such a defence of abstractionism raises a deeper question about Geach's theory of concepts: whether concepts are mental capacities or whether they presuppose them? Geach sums up his theory:

> We can now say something that goes for all concepts
> without exception: Having a concept never means being
> able to recognize some feature we have found in direct

experience; the mind *makes* concepts, and this concept-formation and the subsequent use of the concepts formed never is a mere recognition or finding; but this does not in the least prevent us from applying concepts in our sense-experience and knowing sometimes that we apply them rightly. In all cases it is a matter of fitting a concept to my experience, not of picking out the feature I am interested in from among other features given simultaneously (p. 40).

Does the mind make all concepts? Geach mentions Russell's analysis of universal propositions in Geach's discussion of logical concepts: '"every S is P" does mean the same as "no S is not P", and this is the negation of "some S is not P"' (p. 24). Russell's analysis is right, Geach says; and abstractionism cannot account for the concepts of all, some, not, and their relations. But the failure of abstractionism does not ensure the success of Geach's alternative that these concepts are mental capacities or made by the mind. 'Every S is P' converts to 'No S is not P' and 'No S is not P' is negated by 'Some S is not P' whether the mind exercises itself on these propositions, concepts, and relations or not. We neither recognize similarities nor make anything as we *find* the logical relations and the concepts they involve in this set of propositions. Of course, mental capacities are present, but they are necessary conditions for seeing the conceptual entailments in these propositions; they are not the concepts themselves. When I see that if A implies B and B implies C, then A implies C, and come to understand the concepts of implication or entailment, asymmetry and transitivity, even if it is true as Geach says that I do not abstract these concepts from propositions such as these or this set but that I already have these concepts before I understand this implication, it does not follow that my concepts of implication or entailment, asymmetry and transitivity are made, not found. I did not make them, nor did anyone else; they are as independent of my mind as $2 + 2 = 4$. That implication or entailment is asymmetrical and transitive is a truth about a concept if anything is. I need some mental capacity to see this. But why my mental capacity should be identified with *what* it is exercised on escapes me. Having the concept of implication may be the same as being able to perform certain tasks. But unless the having of this concept is identified (erroneously, I think) with the concept itself, the concept of implication is not the same as any ability. Geach's real target, thus, is not dispositional abstractionism – that concepts are capacities for recognition – but rather certain entity theories: that concepts are things other than mind and matter, or other than the mental and the physical. It is, I think, the ominous possibility that concepts are supersensible entities if they are not abstractions, which they are not for him; or mental capacities, which they are for him, that philosophically motivates Geach's identification of concepts with these capacities. However, as our survey shows, the affirmation of concepts as distinct from apprehension of or engagement with them need not lead to any metaphysical theory of their status. A more accurate account of traditional theories of concepts dissolves the abstractionist theories Geach takes as the major tradition into but *one* strand of abstractionism, since most abstractionists have regarded concepts to be entities in the mind, not capacities. And an even more detailed account of the history of philosophical theories of concepts offers us theories, such as that of Sextus Empiricus and perhaps Hume, which affirm the autonomy of concepts in the non-metaphysical sense of objects of discourse and thought which are not mental, physical, or supersensible. On this view, to say that there are concepts is not to assign an ontological status to them but simply to affirm their irreducibility to words, things, and mental acts or capacities. Geach, then, to conclude, gives us neither an accurate history of philosophical theories of concepts, a refutation of abstractionism, nor a correct theory. Whatever concepts are, not all of them reduce to exercises of mental capacities. And, whatever their philosopical history has been, not all theories of concepts assert, imply or reduce to concepts as recognitional capacities. It is the entity theory, not the abstractionist theory, dispositional or not, that has been dominant and pervasive. That it has been is – if anything is – the overwhelming conclusion of this whole history and survey of it. Indeed, the historical centrality of the entity theory, in all its varieties, has been one of the compelling reasons why it has been necessary to attempt our survey of the history of philosophical theories of concepts.

CHAPTER 15

Conclusion

Is there, then, a history of philosophical theories of concepts? It has been my sustained argument in this book that there is. A theory of concepts, however, is not the same as the use of concepts; nor is it the affirmation that concepts are indispensable intermediaries between words and things, irreducible to either. Rather it is a doctrine, sometimes explicit but always implicit, about the ontological status of concepts – *what* they are, not *that* they are, their assigned or established roles, the conditions for playing these roles and, most important, the logical character of the sets of conditions for functioning as they do, as the particular philosopher philosophizes about the world.

The history of these sometimes explicit but always implicit philosophical theories of concepts is a history of successive and, I believe, competitive, though not necessarily *overtly* competitive, answers to the set question: What is a concept?

Of course, the history of philosophical theories of knowledge or reality or truth, among others, including perhaps even morality or tragedy, may be said to be a history of successive and overtly competitive answers to a formulated set question: What is (the nature of) knowledge? for example. However, if an articulated set question, whether set first by Plato cr, let us allow, even as far down the line by Kant, who shifts his priority from What is knowledge? to How is it possible? is to serve as the determining criterion of whether a philosophical problem has a history, then neither the question, What is a concept? nor Kant's How is knowledge possible? has a history before the relevant question is set. From which it follows, on this view, that the problems of philosophy remain *philosophia perennis*, only some of the problems are more perennial than others!

Is What is a concept? a philosophical problem as old as Plato (and before), whose implicit or explicit answers yield a history of successive and competitive, though not necessarily or always overtly competitive, answers? Certainly, What is justice? is a philosophical problem at least as old as Plato; indeed, it was he who first *set* the problem as a philosophical one. Plato gave one definition of justice. Aristotle proposed another; and in doing so, he challenged and rejected Plato's. He thereby disagreed with Plato on the nature of justice. Plato, however, did not disagree with Aristotle – how could he have? – but we can say and we do say, without fabrication, false imputation or anachronism, that they disagree on the nature of justice. Indeed, their definitions, one might contend, not only differ, they contradict each other; for one, justice is real – a supersensible entity of sorts – more or less, but the world of states and humans being what it is, rather more than less imperfect instances of justice; for the other, justice is also real but exists solely in the world of states and humans.

Both Plato and Aristotle used the same Greek word *he dikaiosune* to talk about justice in order to define it. We may ask, as we do, did they mean the same thing by the same word? Or we may ask a different, perhaps less loaded yet appropriate, question – as legitimate as Do they disagree on the nature of justice? – Did they have the same concept of justice, since they had the same word? There are, I think, good reasons for either a negative or an affirmative answer. But there is no good reason for rejecting the question on the ground that neither Plato nor Aristotle had what no one can have, the concept of justice and that, therefore, they had neither the same concept nor different concepts. For of course they had the concept – or one could plausibly argue, the concepts – of justice. Their disagreement over the nature of justice, articulated in their different definitions of justice and of 'justice' (*he dikaiosune*) and their disputes over putatively correct meanings of 'justice,' whether expressed by Socrates against his fellow disputants or by Aristotle against Plato, point to nothing short of the concept of justice. This concept, whatever else it is taken to be, is not a (Greek) word, its meaning, a particular thought or conception, or the thing justice. Without the concept of justice, neither could have used the (same) word to talk about and eventually to define and state the nature of justice. And to say that they had this concept, conveyed by their shared Greek word, is not to say that they had some third, extra entity between the word and the thing: it is only to say that their concept of justice is neither reducible to its Greek word or non-linguistic thing nor is a controvertible projected object-meaning.

That the concept of justice, as employed by both Plato and Aristotle, conveyed by *hé dikaiosuné*, not named or denoted by the word, is a neutral intermediary between words and their meanings and things – and not an entity, neutral, sensible or supersensible – can be reinforced if we turn from the dispute between Plato and Aristotle to later philosophers who join the dispute and in such a way as to suggest a history of successive and overtly competing theories of justice. Roman and medieval philosophers, Italian, French, German, Russian, English, American and, most recently, John Rawls and Robert Nozick, also talked or talk about justice. Some of these openly disagree with Plato or Aristotle or with others; and some, perhaps most, offer brand new definitions of their own. And they use non-Greek words to do it. Thus, they had or have different words as well as different conceptions of justice, and they proffer competing theories of justice. Do all these philosophers have the same concept, different concepts, or no concept at all? Here, too, that they have the same concept may be as plausible as that they have different concepts. But that their perennial, seemingly endless, disputes over the nature of justice, or about the definition of 'justice' (or other word in a language other than English), or about the correct meaning of the relevant word involve only different words with their different or same meanings, but with nothing like the concept of justice as central in the disputes, is incoherent. The history of successive, overtly competing philosophical theories of justice is, whatever more it is, a history of variant, sometimes conflicting, conceptions of the concept of justice. Without the concept – as against its conveying word and its referred to thing – neither the theorists of justice nor we, who try to understand their theories, can distinguish the history of philosophical theories of justice from the history of philosophical theories of, say, reality, knowledge, morality, and so on. The concept of justice, then, mediates same or different words, justice, and same talk and argument about it – justice – and not something else. Without the concept, with only the words, there could have been talk about justice; but what then could ensure that there has been a kind of talk about one kind of thing? The concept of justice is precisely that which mediates different words, different utterances of the same or different words, the same (kind of) thing and the same (kind of) talk. The history of philosophical theories of justice is about justice, not about cats, dogs, or God. But, to repeat, the concept of justice, unlike the meaning of justice, is not a projected object; it is no dispensable, unnecessary entity. Nor is it a neutral something or other. It is a neutral intermediary, not an entity, neutral or not. And to say that there is such a concept, that it was employed by Plato, Aristotle, and others, and that it was conveyed or expressed by the same or different words, is to say no more than that it is irreducible to anything else; it is not to say what it is.

Well, now, if philosophers can dispute in a historical sequence about the nature of justice by employing the concept of justice, in different languages or in the same language, with different or the same meanings (as difficult as it may be to come by the meanings), why cannot they be said to dispute also over the nature of the concept itself? Neither Plato nor Aristotle, nor any one else, could have argued and disputed about justice without having the relevant concept, understood as that which is irreducible to a word or a thing; so, if they had the concept of *justice*, not just the words with its meaning, and they disputed about justice, which they did, they must have had the *concept* of justice. And they could have disagreed about that too, even though they had no Greek word for concept. It is indisputable that they had different theories of justice; and if we investigate their employment of the concept of justice – the roles and their conditions – we find, as I hope I have found, that they differ not only in their theories of justice but also in their theories of concepts. If my reading of their theories of concepts is at all correct, then, for Plato, the *concept* of justice is a skill whose various manifestations are governed by definitive sets of conditions, derived from the essential properties of the form that guarantee the measure of success of the manifestation of the concept. For Aristotle, on the other hand, the *concept* of justice is a definitional *logos*. For others, it is an innate idea, a composite image, a *species expressa*, an abstraction, a predicate, and even a platonic *eidos*, among other sensible, mental or supersensible entities. Philosophers, then, may and do have the same word or different words in the same or different languages; they may and do have the same or different theories of justice; they may and do have the same or different criteria for the correct use of their words for justice; they may and do give the same or different answers to the questions, What is justice? Is *x* just? Why is *x* just? They may and do even have the same concept of justice, however particular their individual thoughts or conceptions regarding this concept may be. And philosophers may and do also differ, sometimes radically, in their explicit or implicit views about what concepts are: their ontological status.

It is this history – of philosophical theories of concepts, not philosophical theories of particular concepts, such as those of justice, morality, knowledge, and so on – that I have surveyed in this book.

There is such a history. It is a history of successive and competing answers to the set question What is a concept? not Are there concepts? It is no more implausible to ask it of Plato even though he singled out no special word for concept, than to ask it of Aquinas or Frege, who did have words for concept; or than it is to characterize Aristotle's rejection of Plato's theory of justice as a disagreement between them on the nature of justice. Moreover, if it is true, as I am convinced it is, that philosophy is, whatever else it includes, concept-ualization in language, and that philosophers employ concepts, expressed or conveyed by the words they use, in order to talk about the world – the non-existent as well as the existent, the ought to be as well as what is – then it is of the utmost importance to try to understand what individual philosophers take concepts to be, whether they philosophize about or only with them.

Why, now, is this history of philosophical theories of concepts important in the understanding of the history of philosophy and of philosophy itself? For one thing, the history reveals an astonishing variety of theories of concepts. Ontological views range from concepts as supersensible entities, such as universals, meanings, abstract objects, definitions, and predicates and relations to concepts as mental entities or states, such as composite images, ideas, thoughts, conceptions, or innate ideas; or concepts as neutral entities between words, thoughts and things; or concepts as abstractible items from families of sentences or as extracted features of similar things; or concepts as human or animal skills or abilities, only one of which is the ability to wield linguistic expressions; or concepts as the roles of certain expressions *tout court*.

Each of these ontological doctrines, stated or implied by one or other philosopher discussed in this book, both affirms or implies that there are concepts and affirms or implies what they are. It has not been my purpose in this work to argue for or against any of these ontological doctrines. (It is, however, my conviction that none of them is true as a definitive statement of what a concept is. This failure of definition traditional theories of concepts share with traditional theories of other, perhaps all, set philosophical matters. No one has yet come up with a true theory of morality, knowledge, truth, or reality, either. Indeed, the history of philosophical theories of concepts reinforces the shattering observation that all traditional, putatively definitive, answers to philsophical set questions of the What is the nature of *x*? form are more putative than true. Whether there *can* be a true ontological theory of concepts and whether philosophy *requires* such a theory as a necessary condition for the coherence, hence truth or falsity, of philosophy, I leave for others to decide. I do not know whether there cannot be such a theory, though I am sceptical about the requirement. I discuss these two questions, Can there be such a true ontological view about concepts? and Is such a view a necessary condition for doing philosophy? in the first chapter of *The Opening Mind*.

The second thing that the history of philosophical theories of concepts shows is that the concept of a concept is more a family than it is something ambiguous, vague or gaseous. Concepts have been taken to be many differents kinds of things; whether there are these kinds of things or whether these kinds of things share generic traits or are mere family resemblances, I also leave for others to debate. What is important to me as a historian, at least in this book, is whether, as many have said, the history of philosophical theories of concepts manifests any wholesale pattern or doctrine? Mill, Ryle and Geach, whom we discussed among others, whom we have not mentioned, offer such wholesale views. However, if I am right, the history of philosophical theories of concepts is *not* a series of mistaken views of concepts as unintelligible abstract entities or as postulated mental states or as abstractions or as erroneous misreadings of the meanings of certain words or, with some eighteenth-century intimations of the contemporary true theory of concepts, as the possession of certain capacities and abilities.

The variety among the theories, both explicit and implicit, forecloses on any such wholesale formula, whether it be Mill's, Ryle's or Geach's. To be sure, the doctrine that concepts are entities of some sort, either sensible or supersensible, has been dominant, perhaps pervasive. However, that doctrine, at least on my reading of the history, starts with Aristotle, not with Plato, and continues through Frege to Russell, Moore, and the Wittgenstein of the *Tractatus*, as well as to many contemporary philosophers. In this tradition, concepts have served as mental entities with which we think about the world or as supersensible entities about which we think when we think about the world. It is this doctrine that the dispositional theory – perhaps the dominant, certainly the most articulate, view today – was designed to smash. But it is my contention that the dispositional theory is as old as Plato, is not anticipated by Berkeley, Hume or Kant, does not touch Sextus Empiricus' theory of concepts (See A1) and, most important, has difficulties of its own that defeat its claim to be the true theory of concepts and the having of them. That concepts as the having of them is being able to perform certain tasks, one of which is being able to use language correctly, is no more secure than that concepts are entities of a certain sort that we can come to possess. What is a concept? What is it to have a concept? What is the concept of x? What is it to possess the concept of x? None of these questions has received its definitive answer. So far as the ontological aspect of the theory of concepts is concerned, we are, I submit, no closer to *the* answer to What is a concept? at the end of our historical survey and, I believe, today, than was Plato, even though we have a word for concept and he did not.

The history of philosophical theories of concepts is of fundamental importance in the understanding of the history of philosophy and of philosophy itself, then, not because of any true answer to the ontological question, What is a concept? Rather, as I have tried to show, its significance lies in its answers to the more basic question of a theory of concepts: What is the logical character of the sets of conditions under which concepts function as they do?

Are concepts governed by definitive sets of necessary and sufficient properties, conditions or criteria? Is it a necessary condition of all intelligible philosophical discourse about the world that this discourse – its subjects and predicates and the concepts expressed by them – be closed: governed by definitive sets of criteria?

It is the central thesis of this book that affirmative answers to both of these questions have been given or are implied by traditional philosophical theories of concepts and have been basic in the kind of solutions traditional philosophers – from Plato to early Wittgenstein and beyond – have offered to their articulated problems. For implicit in all the ostensible variety and diversity among the entity theories and some of the recent dispositional theories is the assumption that concepts, when complex, and their conveying terms, whether of simple or complex concepts, are and must be governed by definitive sets of necessary and sufficient properties, conditions or criteria. It is this assumption, epitomized by Frege's dictum: 'A concept that is not sharply defined is wrongly termed a concept,' which I have stressed has been as pervasive as it has been (and remains) basic in philosophy. It is also this assumption about the requisite exactness of concepts in the history of philosophy that enjoins a historical survey of philosophical theories of concepts and gives such a survey its primary importance. For if it is true, as I think it is, that philosophy is conceptualizing in language, then the assumption that the concepts the philosopher employs in doing philosophy are and must be closed – 'sharply (and completely) defined' – becomes the determining factor in the *logical* kind of answer or solution he gives to his fundamental questions or problems. I am of course not suggesting that the assumption that all concepts are and must be closed if philosophy is to be coherent determines the particular doctrines or set of doctrines of an individual philosopher. No, what I have showed is that the assumption of the univocity of closed concepts is compatible with a great assortment and diversity of ontological, epistemological, moral, aesthetic, theological – philosophical doctrines. The assumption that a concept, to be a concept, must be closed, governed by definitive criteria, determines not the specific philosophical doctrine but that *the* definitive answer is required and forthcoming to whatever question, however the individual philosopher formulates it – about essences, meanings, or necessary and sufficient properties, conditions or criteria – the philosopher has raised in his philosophy; where the criteria for the correct answer correspond to and are governed by the definitive criteria of the postulated closed concept.

Concepts are and must be closed. This, then, is the doctrine or assumption that has served as the overriding, overall, second-order necessary condition for the very intelligibility of philosophical discourse and thought about the world. It is this assumption that makes a theory of concepts and the history of such theories basic in philosophy and in our understanding of philosophy and its history. It is also the primary reason why I have attempted this work at all.

Throughout, I have not asked or answered the question, Is the doctrine of closed concepts true or a necessary condition for coherent philosophy? That it is false and unwarranted, I have pursued elsewhere. In any case, all that is relevant to our history is whether or not it is true that traditional theories of concepts, as diverse as they are,

are univocal in their adherence to the logical assumption that all concepts and their conveying terms are and must be governed by definitive sets of properties, conditions or criteria?

It has of course been my overriding contention that all the great philosophers I have discussed concur in the doctrine that all concepts are and must be closed if philosophy is to secure a coherent and possibly true view of the world. Whether concepts are what we think with or what we think about, and whatever they are in their ontological nature and status, concepts are composed of or governed by definitive or essential properties or criteria. Though few, if any, philosophers, from Plato to Ryle, and beyond, echoed Frege's dictum about the exactitude of concepts, however indistinctly, who among them did or would have or could have disagreed with it? Perhaps Ryle and Geach, among the modern dispositonal theorists. But Ryle, I believe, though he had a penchant for the rejection of putatively necessary conditions supposedly governing the correct use of certain mental concepts, nevertheless persisted in what he used to call the 'hard-edgedness' of all concepts; and Geach, in spite of the aphasiac who can conceptualize without being able to use language, is still willing to settle for being able to perform certain linguistic tasks as definitive for the possession of concepts. Like other philosophers before and after them, they recognize and accommodate ambiguity and vagueness of words or phenomena; but openness of concepts, not at all.

That concepts and their conveying terms are and must be governed by definitive sets of criteria remains unchallenged in the history of philosophy until perhaps Sir Karl Popper's attack against the doctrine, which he assimilated to methodological essentialism, but certainly not before C. L. Stevenson's radical criticism of it in 'Persuasive Definitions' (*Mind*, 47 [1938]), to be followed by but not influencing the consummate demolition of it in Wittgenstein's *Philosophical Investigations*. The history of open concepts (which I tell elsewhere) is as recent as the understanding and acceptance of them is rare, even among some contemporary philosophers, including a few revolutionaries. The doctrine that at least some (important) concepts are open – governed by sets of criteria that are and must remain less than definitive if these concepts are to perform their assigned roles – is shared by few, the majority preferring to keep things neat and tidy by consigning these concept-pretenders to their deserved limbos of the ambiguous, woolly or gaseous.

Is my contention correct that the history of philosophical theories of concepts is unanimous, or almost, on the assumption that all concepts, whatever they are, are and must be closed in their logical sets of conditions?

Is Plato, to begin at the beginning, committed to this doctrine? The orthodox, traditional interpretation of concepts in Plato as mental or supersensible entities includes an unequivocal affirmative answer. Whether construed as *noemata* or *ennoiai* (thoughts), *eide* or *noeta* (forms or eternal objects of thought) – provided these are not simples, such as The Good – or as *logoi* (rational accounts) – which cannot be simple – concepts, on this interpretation, are and must be composed of properties, definitive in their necessary and sufficient character as essences. Though concepts do not have definitive criteria, their definitive properties determine the definitive criteria of the correct use of the words that name these concepts. Thus, on this view, nothing could be a thought – it might be an *eikasia* (image) instead – or a supersensible entity, that happens to be complex, or a rational account, that must be complex, and contain properties less than definitive ones.

If, on the other hand, and according to my reading, concepts in Plato are intellectual skills in moving about in the world, founded on but never identical with the forms, apprehension or assumption of them, or even with the essences of those classes for which there are no corresponding forms, such as love, these skills are also closed: governed by definitive sets of criteria.

Having the concept of x, say of piety, then, is being able to name, identify, recognise pious acts, to distinguish pious from impious acts, to collect and divide pious acts, to form true opinions about them, to define piety – to give the *logos* of its *eidos*, where being able to do these things presupposes the form piety. This presupposition is a necessary condition for having the concept; the being able in a variety of ways is a sufficient condition. Plato wavers, as some of his later dialogues show, on whether being able to do certain things, such as curing a disease, writing a terrifying speech, or striking a high rather than low note, can be a sufficient condition – a knowing how – without an apprehension of the necessary condition – for knowing what disease, tragedy, or harmony is. But he does not waver on whether any manifestation of the having of the concept can satisfy some but not all of its criteria. I might know how to be pious without knowing piety or what it is; but I could not identify pious acts, distinguish them from other acts, collect and divide them, or define piety if identifying, discriminating, defining, among other manifestations of the concept, were governed by sets of criteria that fall short of the definitive.

Thus, for Plato, to have a particular concept of x, whatever x may be, is to possess certain ranges of skills or abilities, where each of them is marked off from the others by clearly statable different sets of necessary and sufficient criteria; and where these sets determine the correct use of the words, 'naming,' 'discriminating,' 'collecting and dividing,' and 'defining.' For Plato, to have the concept of x and for this having, or for x, to be open in a variety of ways, such as being governed by necessary but not sufficient, or sufficient but not necessary, or disjunctive sets of nonnecessary, nonsufficient criteria, is as unthinkable for him as it is true (for me). That concepts are and must be closed, consequently, that the words that name them (on the entity view) or that convey them (on the dispositional view) must also be closed if our language is to be at all adequate in expressing our thoughts about the world, are as integrally Plato as is the corresponding ontological doctrine of a closed order of forms and things. The definiteness of the conceptual life reflects as it emanates from the definiteness of reality. A world without forms and essences would be as unintelligible as a concept without definitive conditions or criteria. The necessary second-order overall condition of necessary and sufficient properties or criteria for the very intelligibility of thought and talk about reality and of reality itself remains fundamental in Plato.

Aristotle, too, I have said, has a theory of concepts according to which they are definitional entities – *logoi* that are closed in their necessary and sufficient properties which serve as the governing criteria of the correct use of the concepts and terms that convey them.

Readers of Aristotle, however, may object to my wholesale attribution of closed concepts to him. There are important passages, it may be claimed, that contradict my contention that Aristotle's primary concern is with the real definitions of the essences of things. But if we examine these passages, we find that Aristotle, though he says that definitions are not always possible or required, does not reject the doctrine that the concept in question is closed. Consider, for example, the two most likely contenders against my interpretation: his substitution of analogy for definition in his discussion of actuality and potentiality in *Metaphysics*, 1048a 31ff; and his caveat that we should not expect exactitude when we go from the study of mathematics to the inquiry into politics and the good in *Nicomachean Ethics*, I, iii.

In regard to actuality and potentiality, Aristotle says: 'What we mean can be plainly seen in the particular cases by induction; we need not seek a definition for every term, but must comprehend the analogy.' He then gives analogies to illustrate his distinction, among them, 'that which is actually building is to that which is capable of building, so is that which is awake to that which is asleep.' But here is the last line of the same passage: 'Let actuality be defined by one member of this antithesis and the potential by the other.'

Are the concepts of the actual and the potential governed by conditions less than definitive here, in spite of the appeal to analogy as an acceptable alternative to definition? Of course not. In the full discussion, Aristotle does not substitute analogy for definition; rather he *defines* by analogy. These two concepts remain definitional *logoi*.

Secondly, Aristotle says at the beginning of the *Ethics*: 'Now our treatment of this science [Politics] will be adequate, if it achieves that amount of precision which belongs to its subject matter. The same exactness must not be expected in all departments of philosophy alike, any more than in all the products of the arts and crafts' (I, iii, 1). Commentators interpret this admonition as Aristotle's rejection of the search for any definition of the good. Yet, once again, a few pages on there follows as exact a definition of the good as any philosopher has given: as the exercise of reason on itself and on our appetites and emotions. Is Aristotle's expressed reservation here a rejection of real definition or is it a mere curtain raiser that diverts us, but not him, from his ever serious business at hand of finding and securing a *logos*? I stand firm in my contention that Aristotle is totally committed to the doctrine that all concepts are governed by definitive sets of conditions, that can and must be formulated into real definitions.

What about Augustine? For him, there are not only concepts – Gilson's denial notwithstanding – but they are, at least for the most part, innate ideas, implanted in our minds by God. These concepts, which range from the concept of God to that of divine illumination, and include even the concept of time which though neither innate, in that it relates the immutability of God to the mutability of the world,

Conclusion

nor defined but not thereby indefinable, are each of them governed by necessary and sufficient conditions. As concepts, they are therefore closed, where their closure derives from the definitive properties of God, time, divine illumination, or whatever; and where this closure determines in turn the definitive, correct criteria of the (Latin) words employed to express the relevant concepts. That God is less than a being 'than which nothing better can be thought;' and that the concept of God or the word 'God' (*deus*) is governed by criteria less than or other than those derived from the attributes or properties of such a being, are doctrines that are and must be false for Augustine. The concept of God, like the correct use of 'God,' is necessarily as determinate as is God Himself. Augustine's confession that he cannot explain what time is implies only that he cannot define it, not that time may not have definitive properties or that the concept of time and 'time' (*tempus*) are employed correctly under less than definitive conditions. The concept of time is closed: his confession points to his agony of not being able to state its closure, not to any heresy regarding its openness.

In Aquinas, concepts are mental entities. Both his explicit and implicit theories support that this is what concepts are for Aquinas. In my chapter on Aquinas, I raised no question about this orthodox interpretation nor about its truth or falsity. Instead, I challenged its avowed and attributed Aristotelian base that all concepts arise in and return to sense materials. Such a theory about concept formation, I argued, is incompatible with Aquinas' concepts which, as mental entities, contain more than could possibly be given in or ascertained by our senses. The concept of God, for example, unlike our knowledge of Him, cannot be known indirectly: indeed, the very intelligibility of indirect as against direct knowledge of God rests on the concept of God and our apprehension of it. This concept of God may not be innate, which Aquinas does not think it is; nor can it be empirically based either, which Aquinas and his followers wish and claim it to be. The concept of God remains a mental entity in Aquinas, but not one that arises in and returns to any phantasm or collection of them.

However, I said nothing in my chapter about Aquinas' doctrine regarding the logic of the sets of conditions that characterize his concepts in their use by him. I simply assumed that good Aristotelian as he was, and certainly on this issue, he accepted without question that all concepts are and must be closed. Aquinas certainly acknowledges the phenomena of ambiguity and vagueness. But he does not, I submit, acknowledge or imply the acceptance of the openness of concepts. In all his voluminous talk about the concept, however he variously names it – as *intentio, ratio, conceptus, conceptio, verbum mentis*, or *species expressa*, among others – and whether, as a mental entity, it is what we think with (*id quo intelligitur*) or what we think about (*id quod intelligitur*), Aquinas, I think, never questions that the concept or the particular concepts he discusses or employs lack in the essential definitive sets of criteria. Essences, concepts and real definitions; conceptual closure matching ontological closure – this is the three-in-one trinity of Aquinas' philosophic quest. The concept of God without necessary and sufficient conditions would be as incoherent as the real God without all the properties entailed by and contained in The Supreme Being. That Aquinas subscribes to the doctrine of closed concepts I offer as an hypothesis, to be submitted for refutation, not as a generalization based on cited confirming cases and no disconfirming ones. It may be that scattered in his works are certain concepts – not just ambiguous, vague or woolly words – that have conditions for their correct or assigned use which are less than definitive. But even if there are, this fact would call only for modification of my wholesale attribution of the doctrine of closed concepts to him: the pervasiveness of the doctrine remains.

Descartes, Spinoza and Leibniz, however much they differ in their ontological doctrines about concepts – for Descartes, they are irreducible supersensible entities on a par with God, mind and matter; for Spinoza, they are conceptions; and for Leibniz, they are innate ideas – concur completely in the logical doctrine that concepts, unless they are simple, are and must be composed of or governed by definitive sets of properties or conditions, whose sets or whose simple nature in turn determine the criteria of the correct use of the words that convey these concepts. Each, I have argued, assumes as an overall necessary condition of the intelligibility as well as truth of both thought and talk about God and the world definitive sets of properties, conditions or criteria. That the closure of concepts and of correct language corresponds to, manifests, and reflects the essentialist order of reality, that is, that concepts are closed, according to their theories of concepts are, I think, beyond dispute, so central are these doctrines in their philosophies. What perhaps remains in doubt and what certain readers may balk at is the 'stunning dilemma' I infer from the concept of God as closed and which I say Spinoza is the first and only philosopher in the western tradition to pose and resolve.

The dilemma I infer from the closed concept of God and from Spinoza's treatment of it is: that either God exists (and for Spinoza he does) and we do not; or we exist and God cannot. I derived this dilemma from Spinoza's conception of God: if God is all-inclusive, among His other attributes, there can be nothing except God and His attributes and modes. 'Individual things are nothing but affection or modes of God's attributes, expressing those attributes in a certain and determinate manner' (I, xxv, Corol.).

But, it may be objected, that God is all there is is not incompatible with our existence because our existence is a mode of God's omnipotence, since Spinoza also says:

> Inability to exist is impotence, and, on the other hand, ability to exist is power, as is self-evident. If, therefore, there is nothing which necessarily exists excepting things finite, it follows that things finite are more powerful than the absolutely infinite Being, and this (as is self-evident) is absurd; therefore either nothing exists or Being absolutely infinite also necessarily exists. But we ourselves exist, either in ourselves or in something else which necessarily exists...
> Therefore the Being absolutely infinite, that is to
> say...God, necessarily exists (I, xi).

Spinoza, then, does not state the dilemma I attribute to him; rather he seems to deny it by affirming our existence as a necessary manifestation of God's omnipotence. Spinoza seems to imply that if we did not exist, then God could not either, for He would be lacking in omnipotence. So we exist, but only as modes of God; so we do not exist 'in ourselves.' From which it does follow not as Spinoza says that 'either nothing exists or Being absolutely infinite also exists,' but that either we exist or God does and we do not unless we are infinite and omnipotent, in which case we are God.

Spinoza also states that there are temporal facts. He also says that God is eternal. Does this mean that God exists at no time or at all times? Although Spinoza wavers on this throughout the *Ethics* (see, for example, I, xx, Coral 2; V, xxix; V, xl), and says also that '...eternity cannot be defined by time, or have any relationship to it' (V, xxiii, Schol.) and '...eternity cannot be manifested through duration' (V, xxix), given his conception of God as immutable, that is, as non-changing, it seems difficult, if not incoherent, to accept both God as eternal and God as sempiternal, that is, existing at all times: in all temporal facts. A second dilemma presents itself, again not stated by Spinoza, indeed seemingly denied by him in his insistence on temporality in the world: Either God as eternal exists and the temporal does not; or the temporal exists and God cannot.

I cannot see how Spinoza can have it both ways: that both God and we exist; and that both God and time exist. What, then, is Spinoza's answer to these dilemmas? It must be that 'We exist' and 'There are temporal facts' are at best 'knowledge of the first kind, opinion or imagination' (II, xl, Schol. 2); in any case, neither is rational or intuitive knowledge which, once attained, reduce to error, as Spinoza understands error, the assertions 'We exist' and 'There are temporal facts.' The dilemma I attribute to, or as some will say, foist on, Spinoza stands, perhaps resolved by his distinction between imagination and reason or intuition, but nevertheless unconvincing in its implication that once (one time!) we think about it, we realize that we do not exist, even in God, but that God alone exists, even in us.

Hobbes, too, I think, has a full theory of concepts: what they are, what they do, and the conditions under which they do it. Concepts are definitions in his sense of explications of compounded names by resolution; and, as definitions, whether they serve as arbitrary or real, they are statements of necessary and sufficient conditions. The closure of concepts, explicated in definitions of them, remains as binding on our thought and talk as does the covenant on the citizens of his commonwealth.

Locke, in spite of his rejection of real for nominal essences, opts for closed concepts rather than, as he may very well have done, for open concepts. Concepts, such as his favourite concept of gold, are mental entities, implied by but not implying ideas, that are employed to name or classify (sort) substances but under disparate sets of criteria. People mean different things by the word 'gold' in the same or different languages. For Locke, this shows that we have different ideas (concepts) of gold, each with its own nominal set of criteria rather than that we have the same idea (concept) but with different, perhaps even competing, criteria. Accordingly, at least on my interpretation, the concept or idea of gold (or of anything else) as governed by criteria less than definitive gives way to concepts or ideas of gold (or of anything else), where each of these concepts is governed by necessary and sufficient – albeit nominal – criteria. Locke thus retains his subscription to the classical assumption that all concepts or ideas are and must be closed. What is new and radical in his theory of concepts is not his logical or ontological doctrines of closure of concepts as mental entities but his rejection of the classical overall ontological assumption of intelligibility of thought and talk about the world: that there is and must be an order of real essences in order to guarantee the coherence of nominal essences. It is we, not nature, that, for Locke, determine the closure of our concepts.

Does Berkeley also regard concepts as closed? In my chapter on Berkeley, I was mainly concerned to show that he presupposes that there are concepts in his attack on certain abstract ideas, such as that of a triangle without any particular qualities; in his account and defence of general ideas, such as that of a line that can serve as a representative example of all lines; and in his inventory of particular ideas, such as that of red, or of notions, such as that of oneself. These concepts, I argued, are not words or ideas or notions; nor are they abilities, as some commentators interpret the having of general ideas in Berkeley's elucidation of them. Rather, concepts function as mental entities other than and irreducible to sensations, images or notions. I also claimed that Berkeley joins his implicit ontological doctrine of concepts as mental entities with a principle of significance for all concepts: that they be governed by criteria which are verified in sense or inner experience – by particular ideas or notions. It is this principle, I said, that ensures his fundamental ontology of percepts and perceivers, by foreclosing on any purported concept of matter as material substance.

Does Berkeley, then, also accept the doctrine that all concepts are closed: governed by necessary and sufficient criteria? It seems to me that he does. Each of his concepts, whether of an idea or a notion, whether of that which is simple in its nature or complex, is governed by definitive *mental* criteria that in turn determine the meaningful use of the words that convey these concepts. That a concept of anything or its conveying term should be governed by criteria less than or more than the mental or other than the determinate and precise is as unthinkable for Berkeley as that matter is conceivable.

Berkeley's implicit theory of concepts, thus, includes both the ontological doctrine that concepts are mental entities and the logical doctrine that they (and their conveying words) function correctly only under definitive sets of empirical, verified criteria of sense and inner experience. It is this theory, to repeat, that is basic to his metaphysics, not his metaphysics that yields this theory. Both his metaphysics of a world of percepts and perceivers and his denial of matter derive from his stringent empirical version of the classical doctrine of closed concepts as this doctrine sets his overall necessary condition for intelligible, meaningful thought and talk about the world.

Hume also requires and presupposes concepts in order to promote his central doctrines that perceptions or impressions and ideas are exhaustive of the mind, that causality is a necessary connection among events, and that the self is a unity of perceptions. Without concepts, as distinct from impressions and ideas, his central doctrines are incoherent; these concepts, on Hume's own principles, are entities, but of a non-perceptual kind, and exist independently of the contemplation of them. Such is the ontological doctrine of Hume's theory of concepts I was mainly concerned to delineate in my chapter on Hume.

But now we must ask: Does Hume also accept the logical doctrine that all concepts are governed by necessary and sufficient conditions or criteria; or do some of his concepts function under sets of conditions or criteria that are less than definitive? Hume distinguishes between words, impressions and ideas. Words are or can be exact or imprecise; they mean the ideas they stand for, and when they do not, they are meaningless; their meaning, however, is not their use, rather their correct use depends on their meanings; and words can be defined, though many only by ostension. Words, at least the general terms Hume employs in his philosophical writings, whether they name the simple or complex, impression or idea, must be governed by exact criteria, derived from our definition or description of the (named) impression or idea, if these general terms are to be used correctly, to do their assigned jobs.

Impressions are simple or complex, internal or external, original or secondary, calm or violent. These cannot be inexact, nor can they, except the complex ones, be defined, only described. Complex impressions, about which Hume says little, have distinguishable parts: an apple, for example, is a complex impression; it combines this red colour, this round shape, this tart taste, etc. The particular qualities may change from apple to apple, but there is no particular apple – no complex impression of an apple – that can have qualities other than it does without being a different impression.

Consequently, that an impression, simple or complex, could be open or indeterminate, not closed or determinate is not only impossible for Hume but, as it should be for anyone, senseless.

What, now, about ideas? Hume distinguishes simple and complex ideas, imaginary and memory ideas, and particular and general or abstract ideas; and, among the complex ideas, those of relations, modes and substances. Each is an image; each is beholden to its corresponding impression or impressions. Some, such as the idea of existence and the idea of external existence are the same. Some are no ideas at all, such as the putative ideas of the infinitely divisible and a vacuum; some are ideals, such as the imaginary ideal of equal lines or of physical continuants; at least one – the idea of belief – is a lively idea, almost verging on an impression. Some, such as the geometer's ideas of a curve or a right line are vague – 'loose and undeterminate' Hume calls them (*Treatise*, I, ii, 4). And there are ideas of space, time, causality, necessary connection, substances, virtues, emotions, institutions, among those Hume discusses. As varied as they are and as difficult as it is to trace them back to their original impressions in order to secure their legitimacy, Hume never goes beyond vagueness in characterizing ideas. A 'loose and undeterminate' idea remains an idea; but an idea with no discoverable parent impression or impressions converts from a putative idea into an empty word without a meaning. Ideas may have constituent properties or conditions. They may add up to definitive conditions, as does the idea of belief; or, when simple, they may lend themselves to only descriptions. But in no case does Hume affirm or allow that ideas – even his 'vague' ones – are open.

What, now, about concepts? That Hume has concepts and that they are not reducible to words, their meanings or ideas, nor traceable to any impressions, follows from his distinctions between an impression and an idea, between causality as necessary connection among events and constant conjunction, and between the self as a unity rather than a collection of perceptions.

If we add to these concepts of an impression, idea, necessary connection, and unity – without which Hume cannot even state his central doctrines about the content of the mind, causality and the self, or begin his search for the impression-based ideas of causality and the self – as well as the many other concepts Hume introduces, are any of them governed by criteria less than the definitive?

Among these are the concepts of human nature, reason,

knowledge, number, equality, imagination, understanding, virtue, vice, passion, emotion, property, sympathy, justice, and promise. Some of these Hume refers to as ideas. Some even *he* does not. There is no mention, for example, that his central concept – the concept of human nature – is an idea; yet it is what his great *Treatise* is all about, as his full title indicates. Hume's overriding philosophical aim is to provide the first experimental science of human nature which he takes to be basic to all other sciences. Without the concept of human nature, expressed by 'human nature,' Hume could not have proceeded to realize his aim; nor could he have demolished competing theories of human nature.

His concept of human nature is not his words; nor is it an essence hidden away in human beings. It is certainly not an impression, simple or complex. Is it an idea? If it is, is it an abstract idea, like that of man or line: a particular that can serve as a general representation? But how can my idea of human nature be abstract when an abstract idea is based on a particular idea? What is a particular idea of human nature that parallels the particular ideas of a man or a line, without which no idea can be abstract? The idea of human nature is abstract from the very beginning, secured by no possible particulars, therefore, it cannot be an idea, particular or abstract, according to Hume. Nor can it be self-contradictory or vacuous, since after all he writes a treatise about human nature, not about its non-existence.

Hume, thus, has the concept of human nature. It is no word, idea, impression, or essence. Without it, all his talk of the principles of human nature makes no sense.

Some concepts in Hume are like his concept of human nature: reason, understanding, knowledge, among them; some are exemplified in ideas, others, in impressions. And now: Are any of them open or are all of them closed? If the concept of human nature – Hume's overarching concept – can serve as an example, that concept is absolutely closed: governed by necessary and sufficient criteria. It is these criteria that Hume employs throughout the *Treatise* to expound, assess and demolish competing conceptions – theories – of human nature; and to establish his own 'experimental' theory. Nowhere does Hume even intimate that the debate between his theory and others about human nature is one over the logical nature of the set of criteria for the concept of human nature. Instead, he pits one set of definitive criteria – his – against another set – his opponents. For Hume, his concept is as hard-edged, determinate, closed as is the concept for his rationalist or mystical opponents. That the concept of human nature, as the debate reveals, is essentially disputable, open-textured, or open in other ways, rather than closed, is as antithetical and unthinkable to Hume as that the impressions we have, both internal and external, are inexact.

All concepts in Hume, I submit, function under clearly statable sets of necessary and sufficient criteria. To be sure, some, as Hume says, are not definable, only discernible and describable. But even these that he does not define but rather describes because they concern simples that we can understand only by ostension, are nevertheless governed by criteria with which the relevant concept is exemplified and without which it is not. That something is a feeling of joy rather than of grief, just rather than unjust, reason rather than passion, knowledge rather than belief, impression rather than idea, cause rather than event, self rather than percept, however difficult it is to locate its relevant idea or antecedent impression, is never questioned by Hume. Our words may be ambiguous or without meaning; our ideas may be vague; but our concepts, like our impressions, cannot be but exact and determinate. Frege's dictum holds for Hume: an inexact concept is no concept at all. Hume's explicit doctrine that perceptions as impressions and ideas exhaust the content of the mind – the doctrine that is foundational in his science of human nature – may reinforce his implicit theory of concepts. But just as certain is it that his implicit theory of concepts as closed ensures that his foundational doctrine must be secured in the exactitude of all impressions and their corresponding ideas. That a necessary second-order overall condition of the intelligibility and meaningfulness of true thought and correct talk about the world is the doctrine of closed concepts, expressed by their clear and precise terms, governed by definitive sets of criteria, remains intact in Hume, his rejection of rationalism and his adherence to empiricism notwithstanding. His implicit theory of closed concepts indeed underwrites his whole science of human nature, including his implicit denotative theory of meaning which, for many of his critics, is mistakenly taken to be his major and, because it is considered to be erroneous, his most vulnerable assumption.

Concepts are avowedly central in Kant's philosophy. He also meticulously elucidates their fundamental roles in knowledge and reason: in mathematics and physics as well as in metaphysics. Although he states their nature and status, no unequivocal doctrine emerges. Rather two views compete throughout: that concepts are rules and that concepts are entities, different from yet present in phenomenal objects. In my chapter on Kant, I said that though both are articulated and supported by Kant, neither is argued convincingly, indeed, that concepts are entities seems downright inconsistent with his major doctrine of Transcendental Idealism.

However difficult it is to determine his exact theory of the nature of concepts, the roles he gives concepts in the origin and content of knowledge – in its explanation and justification – leave no doubt that concepts, whether they are construed as rules or as entities, are and must be in their *a priori* and determinant character in knowledge, definitive in their necessary and sufficient conditions. That any of his categories, for example, causality or substance, or any of his other concepts, whether called by him concepts or forms of intuition or ideas or ideals, could be governed by criteria less than exact, determinate or definitive, is as unthinkable to Kant as that there could be rules that are imprecise, flexible, vague, or not binding. Thus, that our concepts are and must be closed is, for Kant, not only a necessary overall condition of the intelligibility of thought and talk about the world, but in his terms synthetic and *a priori* as well. As a principle, this condition serves as a guarantee of all such thought and talk, including, in my judgment, Kant's fundamental transcendental unity of apperception, even though he disclaims a concept of it.

Kant, then, neither articulates nor challenges the classical doctrine of closed concepts. His silence nothwithstanding, he presupposes and implies it in his major stated doctrines and principles. Without it as his basic synthetic *a priori* transcendental principle of knowledge – as the overall condition of intelligibility of thought and talk – Kant could not have composed his version of the critique of pure reason, replete as it is with concepts, empirical, *a priori*, and synthetic *a priori*, each of which is and must be governed by necessary and sufficient conditions or criteria, in order to be and to function as concepts and without which closed concepts there could be no knowledge at all.

No one, then, I submit, before Frege questions or rejects the doctrine of closed concepts. Frege's dictum, thus, is not a departure from but the summing up of the whole classical tradition.

In Frege, the theory of concepts – of their ontology, their roles, their conditions, and the logical nature of the sets of conditions – is complete. Concepts for him are platonic *Noeta*, conveyed by their predicative expressions, governed by definitive conditions, determining the definitive criteria of their conveying expressions. '...A concept that is not sharply defined is wrongly termed a concept' is no mere exhortation to clarity and precision for him: it is the very condition of coherence of the order of true thought and perspicuous talk about the world. To deny it, or to violate it, or even to become indifferent to it, so as to accommodate the logical variety of concepts and the persistent vagaries of conceptualization, especially as these are exemplified in the humanities and in ordinary language, would be for him, as he makes abundantly clear, tantamount to abandoning the fundamental *tertium non datur* principle of the conceptual life for the morass of imprecision, inexactness and openness.

Frege not only epitomizes the classical theory of concepts as it converges on the logical doctrine that all concepts are and must be closed. He also sets the standard for later philosophers, including Russell, Moore, early Wittgenstein, and perhaps even Ryle and Geach, among many other contemporaries; who, although they pride themselves on their repudiation of either essences, real definitions or necessary and sufficient properties, nevertheless persist in their unabated quest for the necessary and sufficient conditions or criteria of our basic concepts. How else are we to explain Quine's insistence on the necessary and sufficient conditions of synonymy as an absolutely minimum condition for any acceptable distinction between the analytic and synthetic; or recent attempts by Roderick Chisholm and Keith Lehrer, among others, to secure once again and finally the necessary and sufficient conditions of knowledge that can then serve as a true, real definition of it; or equally recent efforts by Hilary Putnam and Saul Kripke to establish once again the essential properties of natural kinds; or, finally, Donald Davidson's search for a theory of meaning that is rooted in a Tarski theory of truth which provides a set of necessary and sufficient conditions for both meaning and truth?

This fixation on the traditional quest for real definition, essences or, in any case, necessary and sufficient conditions is as remarkable as any of the doctrines of contemporary philosophy. That the concepts of synonymy, knowledge, natural kind, or meaning are and must be closed is as alive today as ever it was in the past. The overall, second-order condition of coherence of intelligible thought and perspicuous talk about the world remains as necessary to these philosophers, revolutionary and innovative as they may be, as it was to Plato and all who followed. The history of philosophy, indeed, is a history of footnotes to platonic doctrine!

It is not appropriate in a work such as this to raise fundamental questions about these extremely modern attempts to sustain the doctrine of closed concepts, especially in a concluding and summary chapter. Suffice it to say that the final judgment on the truth or falsity of these recent theories of synonomy, knowledge, natural kinds, and meaning awaits their own Day of Judgment on the truth or falsity of the theory of closed concepts on which their respective theories are founded. Among so many Goliaths of closure where, one may very well ask, is there a David to challenge them? My aim, now realized, has been only to establish the dominance and pervasiveness of the doctrine of closed concepts in the history of philosophy. That its hegemony persists reflects as much its continuing history as it does on the vulnerability of much contemporary philosophy, leaning, as this philosophy does, on a theory of concepts that is as hoary as it may be fragile.

NOTES

Chapter 4   Aquinas

1   St Thomas Aquinas, *De Potentia,* q. 8, a. 1; translated by J. F.
Peifer, who also quotes the Latin text in his book, *The Concept in
Thomism* (New York, 1952), pp. 138–9.
2   St Thomas Aquinas, *Summa Contra Gentiles*, I, *Cap.* 53; translated
by J. F. Peifer, who also quotes the Latin text in *op. cit.*, pp.
139–40.
3   St Thomas Aquinas, *Compendium Theologiae, Cap.* 39; translated
by J. F. Peifer, who also quotes the Latin text in *op. cit.*, p. 157.
4   St Thomas Aquinas, *De Veritate*, q. 4, a. 2 *ad* 3; translated by J.
F. Peifer, who also quotes the Latin text in *op. cit.*, p. 184.
5   Étienne Gilson, *The Christian Philosophy of St Thomas Aquinas*
(New York, 1956), pp. 475–6.
6   *Ibid.*, p. 229.
7   Frederick Copleston, *A History of Philosophy* (Garden City, 1962),
vol. 2, Part II, p. 110.
8   *Ibid.*
9   Peifer, *op. cit.*, pp. 140–41.
10   *Ibid.*, p. 161.
11   Étienne Gilson, *The Spirit of Mediaeval Philosophy* (New York,
1940), p. 249.
12   Étienne Gilson, *The Christian Philosophy of St Thomas Aquinas*,
p. 229.
13   *Ibid.*, p. 230.
14   *Ibid.*
15   Peter Geach, *Mental Acts* (London, 1957), p. 18 (italics in
original).
16   *Ibid.*, 130.

Chapter 7 Leibniz

1 Leibniz, 'Remarques sur la lettre de M. Arnauld,' in a letter to Hessen-Rheinfels, May, 1686; in C. I. Gerhardt, ed., *Die Philosophischen Schriften von Gottfried Wilhelm Leibniz* (Hildesheim, 1960, 7 volumes), vol. 2, p. 43. (Hereinafter cited as *Gerhardt*).
2 *Gerhardt*, 7, p. 186.
3 Cited in Latin as a fragment by Louis Couturat, *La Logique de Leibniz, d'après des Documents Inédits* (Paris, 1901), pp. 87–8n.
4 *Gerhardt*, 7, p. 185.
5 Leibniz, 'Projet d'un art d'inventer,' in L. Couturat, ed., *Opuscules et Fragments Inédits de Leibniz* (Hildesheim, 1961), pp. 175–82.
6 In A. Buchenau and Ernst Cassirer, eds, *Hauptschriften zur Grundlegung der philosophie* (Leipzig, 1924, 2 volumes), vol. 2, pp. 504–6.
7 *Gerhardt*, 2, pp. 37–47.
8 *Gerhardt*, 7, p. 309.
9 *Gerhardt*, 2, p. 182.
10 *Gerhardt*, 2, p. 232.
11 *Gerhardt*, 2, p. 241.
12 *Gerhardt*, 4, p. 424.
13 *Gerhardt*, 7, p. 261.
14 *Gerhardt*, 7, p. 262.
15 Nicholas Rescher, *The Philosophy of Leibniz* (Englewood Cliffs, 1967), pp. 66–8; 152.
16 *Gerhardt*, 4, pp. 359, 406; quoted by Rescher, *op. cit.* p. 67.

Chapter 8 Hobbes

1 See J. W. N. Watkins, *Hobbes's System of Ideas: a Study in the Political Significance of Philosophical Theories* (London, 1965); Isabel C. Hungerland and George R. Vick, 'Hobbes's Theory of Signification,' *Journal of the History of Philosophy* (vol. XI; no. 4, Oct., 1973), pp. 459–82; and 'Hobbes's Theory of Names and Its Relationship to His Theory of Signification,' (forthcoming); references to this latter article are to the typescript, generously provided by the authors.
2 Hungerland and Vick, 'Hobbes's Theory of Names and Its Relationship to His Theory of Signification' (forthcoming);
3 *Ibid.*
4 Hungerland and Vick, *op. cit.*

Chapter 12 Kant

1 P. F. Strawson, *The Bounds of Sense: An Essay on Kant's Critique of Pure Reason* (London, 1966), p. 16.

2 See George Schrader, 'Kant's Theory of Concepts,' *Kant-Studien, Band* 49 (1958); reprinted in R. P. Wolff, ed., *Kant: A Collection of Critical Essays* (New York; 1967), pp. 134–55), for further doubts about empirical, sensible concepts.

Chapter 13   Some nineteenth and twentieth century theories: Frege, Russell and Moore

1 Thomas Reid, *Essays on the Intellectual Powers of Man,* edited by Sir William Hamilton, *Works,* 2 volumes, 1846; see vol. I, *Essay* iv, esp. chs 1–2.

2 Gilbert Ryle, 'Systematically Misleading Expressions,' *Proceedings of the Aristotelian Society,* 1931–32; reprinted in A. Flew, ed., *Essays on Logic and Language,* First Series (Oxford, 1951), p. 11.

3 Charles Sanders Peirce, 'How To Make Our Ideas Clear,' first published in English in *Popular Science Monthly,* 12 (Jan., 1878), pp. 286–302; reprinted in Charles Hartshorne and Paul Weiss, eds., *Collected Papers of Charles Sanders Peirce* (Cambridge, 1931–35), 6 volumes, 5. 402. Later Peirce revised his thesis:

> ... If one can define accurately all of the conceivable experimental phenomena which the affirmation or denial of a concept could imply, one will have therein a complete definition of the concept, and *there is absolutely nothing more in it* (5. 412).

4 Morris Weitz, 'Analysis and the Unity of Russell's Philosophy,' P. Schilpp, ed., *The Philosophy of Bertrand Russell* (Evanston, 1944), pp. 57–121.

5 See e.g., the essays by Nagel, Black, and Weitz in *The Philosophy of Bertrand Russell;* also Charles Fritz, *Bertrand Russell's Construction of the External World* (London, 1952).

6 Russell's acceptance is in his 'Reply to Criticisms,' *The Philosophy of Bertrand Russell,* pp. 684–6; Ayer's criticism is in Alfred J. Ayer, *Russell and Moore: The Analytic Heritage* (Cambridge, 1971), p. 11.

Chapter 14   Some nineteenth and twentieth century theories: Ryle and Geach

1 Gilbert Ryle, 'Systematically Misleading Expressions,' *Proceedings of the Aristotelian Society,* vol. xxxii, 1932; reprinted in Gilbert Ryle, *Collected Papers,* 2 volumes (New York and London, 1971). All references to Ryle's essays in the text are to this edition, with volume number, followed by page number; this essay is in II, 39–62.

2 Ryle, 'Categories,' *Proceedings of the Aristotelian Society,* vol. xxxviii, 1938; reprinted in *Collected Papers*, II, 170–93.

3 Ryle, *Philosophical Arguments* (Inaugural Lecture as a Waynflete Professor of Metaphysical Philosophy, Oxford), 1945; reprinted in *Collected Papers*, II, 194–211.

4 Ryle, 'The Theory of Meaning,' C. A. Mace, *British Philosophy in Mid-Century* (London, 1957); reprinted in *Collected Papers*, II, 350–72.

5 Ryle, 'Are There Propositions?' *Proceedings of the Aristotelian Society*, vol. xxx, 1930; reprinted in *Collected Papers*, II, 12–38.

6 Ryle, 'Plato's "Parmenides",' *Mind*, vol. xlviii, 1939; reprinted in *Collected Papers*, I, 1–44.

7 Ryle, 'Ordinary Language,' *Philosophical Review*, vol. lxii, 1953; reprinted in *Collected Papers*, II, 301–18.

8 Ryle, 'Thinking Thoughts and Having Concepts,' *Logique et Analyse*, no. 20 (*Thinking & Meaning*, Entretiens d'Oxford, Organisées par l'Institut International de Philosophie, septembre, 1962), pp. 156–71; reprinted in *Collected Papers*, II, 446–450; the Findlay question is on p. 167 of the original.

9 Ryle, 'Phenomenology Versus "The Concept of Mind",' in (French translation) 'La Philosophie Analytique,' *Cahiers de Royaumont Philosophie*, no. iv, Les Editions de Minuit, Paris, 1962, pp. 65–84; English Original text in *Collected Papers*, I, 179–96.

BIBLIOGRAPHY

Articles from periodicals referred to in the text or notes are not listed here, since the full facts of their publications are given in the notes. All other articles and all books cited in the text or notes, or articles or books that relate to the figures or topics in the text are listed here. Readers who wish more extensive bibliographies or who wish to probe further may consult those bibliographies appended to the separate articles on philosophers or philosophical problems in *The Encyclopedia of Philosophy* (8 vols, editor in chief, Paul Edwards; New York: Macmillan and Free Press; London: Collier-Macmillan, 1967).

AARON, R. I. *John Locke.* Oxford: Oxford University Press, 1937; rev. ed., 1955.
——. *The Theory of Universals.* Oxford: Oxford University Press, 1952.
ALLAN, D. J. *The Philosophy of Aristotle.* Oxford: Oxford University Press, 1952.
ALLEN, R. E. *Plato's 'Euthyphro' and Earlier Theory of Forms.* London: Routledge and Kegan Paul, 1970.
ANSCOMBE, G. E. M. and P. T. GEACH. *Three Philosophers: Aristotle, Aquinas, Frege.* Oxford: Blackwell, 1961.
ANSELM, ST. *Proslogion,* with *A Reply on Behalf of the Fool* by Gaunilo and *The Author's Reply to Gaunilo,* translated with an introduction and philosophical commentary by M. J. CHARLESWORTH. Oxford: Clarendon Press, 1965.
ARISTOTLE. *Aristotelis Opera,* ed. I. BEKKER. 5 vols. Prussian Academy Edition, Berlin: G. Reimer, 1831–70.
——. *Works.* 23 vols, eds. H. COOKE, H. TREDENNICK,

H. RACKHAM, W. K. C. GUTHRIE, E. S. FOSTER, among others; Greek and corresponding English translations. Loeb Classical Library. London: Heinemann; Cambridge, Mass.: Harvard University Press, 1926–65.

——. *The Works of Aristotle*, translated into English, ed. W. D. ROSS. 12 vols. Oxford: Oxford University Press, 1908–52.

——. *De Anima*, ed. W. D. ROSS. Oxford: Clarendon Press, 1961.

——. *Analytica Priora et Posteriora*, ed. W. D. ROSS, rev., L. MINIO-PALUELLO. Oxford: Clarendon Press, 1964.

——. *Metaphysica*, ed. W. JAEGER. Oxford: Clarendon Press, 1957.

——. *Aristotle's Categories and De Interpretatione Translated With Notes*, translated by J. L. ACKRILL. Oxford: Clarendon Press, 1963.

——. *Poetics*, translated by S. H. BUTCHER. London: Macmillan, 1895; rev., 1911.

——. *Aristotle's Metaphysics*, ed. W. D. ROSS. 2 vols. Oxford: Clarendon Press, 1924.

——. *Index Aristotelicus*, ed. H. BONITZ. Reprinted, Graz: Akademische Druck-U Verlagsanstalt, 1955.

AUGUSTINE, ST. *Opera, Patrologiae Curses Completus, Series Latina*, ed. J. P. MIGNE, vols. 32–42. Paris, 1841–42; reprinted, Turnholti, Belgium: Typographi Brepolis, 1878–90.

——. *Opera, Corpus Scriptorum Ecclesiasticorum Latinorum*, vols. 12, 25, 28, 33, 36, 40, 41–44, 51–53, 57, 58, 60, 63 . . . (in progress). Vienna: Tempsky, 1866–.

——. *Opera, Corpus Christianorum, Series Latina*. Turnholti, Belgium: Typographi Brepolis, 1953.

——. *City of God*, various editors and translators. 7 vols. Loeb Classical Library, London: Heinemann; Cambridge, Mass.: Harvard University Press, 1957–68.

——. *Confessions*, translated by W. WATTS (1631). 2 vols. Loeb Classical Library. London: Heinemann; Cambridge, Mass: Harvard University Press, 1912.

——. *The Works of Aurelius Augustine*, ed. M. DODS. 15 vols. Edinburgh: T. Clarke, 1872–76.

——. *City of God*, translated by M. DODS, G. W. WILSON, and J. J. SMITH. New York: Modern Library, 1950.

——. *Confessions*, translated by E. P. PUSEY. London: Dent, 1907.

——. *Concerning the Teacher and On the Immortality of the Soul*, translated with a preface by G. C. LECKIE. New York: Appleton-Century-Crofts, 1938.

——. *De libero arbitrio voluntatis*, translated as *On Free Choice of the Will* by A. S. BENJAMIN and L. H. HACKSTAFF. Indianapolis: Bobbs-Merrill, 1964.

——. *De doctrina Christiana*, translated as *On Christian Doctrine* by D. W. ROBERTSON, Jr. Indianapolis: Bobbs-Merrill, 1958.

AYER, A. J. *Russell and Moore: The Analytic Heritage.* Cambridge, Mass: Harvard University Press, 1971.

BENNETT, JONATHAN. *Kant's Analytic.* Cambridge: Cambridge University Press, 1966.

——. *Kant's Dialectic.* Cambridge: Cambridge University Press, 1974.

——. *Locke, Berkely Hume: Central Themes.* Oxford: Clarendon Press, 1971.

BERKELEY, GEORGE. *The Works of George Berkeley*, ed. A. C. FRASER. 4 vols. Oxford: Clarendon Press, 1871; rev., 1901.

——. *The Works of George Berkeley, Bishop of Cloyne*, eds. A. A. LUCE and T. E. JESSOP. 9 vols. Edinburgh: Nelson and Sons, 1948–57.

——. *Philosophical Works, Including the Works on Vision*, ed. M. R. AYERS. London: Dent; Towota, New Jersey: Rowman and Littlefield, 1975.

BIRD, GRAHAM. *Kant's Theory of Knowledge.* London: Routledge and Kegan Paul; New York: Humanities Press, 1962.

BOETHIUS. *Opera, Patrologiae Latina*, vols. 63 and 64.

——. *In Isagogen Porphyrii Commenta* ('Commentaries on Porphyry'), *Corpus Scriptorum Ecclesiasticorum Latinorum*, eds. G. SCHEPSS and S. BRANDT. Leipsig: G. Freytag, 1906.

——. *Theological Tractates and De Consolatione Philosophiae*, translated and edited by H. F. STEWART and E. K. RAND. Loeb Classical Library. London: Heinemann; Cambridge, Mass.: Harvard University Press, 1918.

BROAD, C. D. *Examination of McTaggart's Philosophy.* 2 vols. Cambridge: Cambridge University Press, 1933.

CAJETAN, CARDINAL (THOMAS DE VIO). *Commentaria in De Ente et Essentia*, ed. M. H. LAURENT. Turin: Marietti, 1934; translated as *Commentary on Being and Essence* by L. KENDZIERSKI and F. WADE. Milwaukee: Marquette University Press, 1964.

CARBONARA, C. 'Concetto,' *Enciclopedia Filosofica*. Florence: Sansoni, 1957.

CARNAP, RUDOLF. *Meaning and Necessity: A Study in Semantics and Modal Logic*. Chicago: University of Chicago Press, 1950.

CARRÉ, M. H. *Realists and Nominalists*. Oxford: Clarendon Press, 1946.

CHENU, M.-D. *Towards Understanding Saint Thomas*. Chicago: Henry Regnery, 1964.

CHERNISS, H. F. 'The Philosophical Economy of the Theory of Ideas,' *American Journal of Philology*, 57 (1936), 445–56.

CHURCH, ALONZO. 'A Formulation of the Logic of Sense and Denotation,' *Structure, Method, and Meaning: Essays in Honor of H. M. Sheffer*, eds. P. HENLE, H. M. KALLEN and S. K. LANGER. New York: Liberal Arts, 1951.

——. 'The Need for Abstract Entities in Semantic Analysis,' *Contributions to the Analysis and Synthesis of Knowledge, Proceedings of the American Academy of Arts and Sciences*, vol. 80, no. 1 (1951), 100–12.

CICERO. *De Natura Deorum, Academica I and II*, translated by H. RACKHAM. Loeb Classical Library. London: Heinemann; Cambridge, Mass.: Harvard University Press, 1933.

——. *Topica*, translated by H. M. HUBBELL. Loeb Classical Library. London: Heinemann; Cambridge, Mass.: Harvard University Press, 1949.

——. *Tusculan Disputations*, translated by J. E. KING. Loeb Classical Library. London: Heinemann; Cambridge, Mass.: Harvard University Press, 1927; rev. ed., 1945.

COHEN, S. MARC. 'Socrates on the Definition of Piety: Euthyphro 10A–11B,' *Journal of the History of Philosophy*, IX, 1 (1971); reprinted, *The Philosophy of Socrates: A Collection of Critical Essays*, ed. G. VLASTOS. New York: Doubleday, 1971.

'Concept,' *Grand Larousse encyclopédique*. Paris: Larousse, 1960.

'Conceptus,' *Thesaurus Linguae Latinae*. Leipzig: Teubineri, 1900.

COPLESTON, F. C. *Aquinas*. Harmondsworth: Penguin Books, 1955.

——. *A History of Western Philosophy*, vol 2, part ii. New York: Doubleday, 1962.

COUTURAT, LOUIS. *La Logique de Leibniz*. Paris: Felix Alcan, 1901.

CROMBIE, I. M. *An Examination of Plato's Doctrines*. 2 vols.

London: Routledge and Kegan Paul, 1962–3.

——. *Plato: The Midwife's Apprentice*. London: Routledge and Kegan Paul, 1964.

CROSS, R. C. 'Logos and Forms in Plato,' *Mind*, 63 (1954), 433–50.

——. and A. D. WOOZLEY. *Plato's Republic: A Philosophical Commentary*. New York: St. Martin's Press, 1964.

DAVIDSON, DONALD. 'Semantics for Natural Languages,' *Linguaggi nella società e nella tecnica*, 177–188. Milano: Edizioni di Comunita, 1970; reprinted, *The Logic of Grammar*, eds. DONALD DAVIDSON and GILBERT HARMAN. Encino, California: Dickenson, 1975.

DESCARTES, RENÉ. *Oeuvres de Descartes*, eds. CHARLES ADAMS and PAUL TANNERY. 13 vols. Paris: Cerf, 1897 – 1910.

——. *Correspondance*, eds. CHARLES ADAMS and GÉRARD MILHAUD. Paris: Felix Alcan, Presses Universitaires de France, 1936–63.

——. *The Philosophical Works of Descartes*, translated by E. S. HALDANE and G. T. R. ROSS. 2 vols. Cambridge: Cambridge University Press, 1911–12; corrected edition, 1934; paperback: New York: Dover, 1955; Cambridge: Cambridge University Press, 1967.

——. *Descartes: Philosophical Writings*, selected, translated, and edited by G. E. M. ANSCOMBE and P. T. GEACH. Edinburgh: Thomas Nelson and Sons, 1954.

——. *Discours de la méthode*, text and commentary by ÉTIENNE GILSON. 2nd ed., Paris: J. Vrin, 1930.

——. *Descartes: A Collection of Critical Essays*, ed. WILLIS DONEY. New York: Doubleday, 1967.

Descartes' Conversation with Burman, translated with introduction and commentary by JOHN COTTINGHAM. Oxford: Clarendon Press, 1976.

DIOGENES LAERTIUS. *Lives of Eminent Philosophers*, translated by R. D. HICKS. 2 vols. Loeb Classical Library. London: Heinemann: Cambridge, Mass.: Harvard University Press, 1925.

DUMMETT, MICHAEL. *Frege: Philosophy of Language*. New York: Harper and Row, 1973.

DUNS SCOTUS. *Philosophical Writings: A Selection*, edited and translated by ALLAN WOLTER. Edinburgh: Nelson, 1962.

EDELSTEIN, LUDWIG. *Plato's Seventh Letter*. Leiden: E. J. Brill, 1966.

EISLER, R. 'Begriff,' *Wörterbuch der Philosophischen Begriffe.* Berlin: Mittler, 1927.

ELSE, G. F. *Aristotle's Poetics: The Argument.* Cambridge, Mass.: Harvard University Press, 1957.

ERNOUT, ALFRED and A. MEILLET. *Dictionnaire étymologique de la langue latine: histoire des mots.* 4th ed., Paris: C. Klincksieck, 1959.

EWING, A. C. *A Short Commentary on Kant's Critique of Pure Reason.* London: Methuen, 1938.

FIELD, G. C. *The Philosophy of Plato.* Oxford: Oxford University Press, 1949.

FINDLAY, J. N. *Hegel: a Re-examination.* London: George Allen and Unwin; New York: Macmillan, 1958.

FREGE, GOTTLOB. *Die Grundlagen der Arithmetik,* translated as *The Foundations of Arithmetic* by J. L. AUSTIN. Oxford: Blackwell, 1950.

——. *Translations from the Philosophical Writings of Gottlob Frege,* translated and edited by P. T. GEACH and MAX BLACK. Oxford: Blackwell, 1952.

From Frege to Gödel: A Sourcebook in Mathematical Logic, ed. JEAN VAN HEIJENHOORT. Cambridge, Mass.: Harvard University Press, 1967.

FRITZ, CHARLES A, Jr. *Bertrand Russell's Construction of the External World.* London: Routledge and Kegan Paul; New York: Humanities Press, 1952.

GEACH, P. T. *Mental Acts: Their Content and Their Objects.* London: Routledge and Kegan Paul, 1957.

GILSON, ÉTIENNE. *L'esprit de la philosophie médievale.* 2nd ed. Paris: Vrin, 1944; translated as *The Spirit of Mediaeval Philosophy* by A. H. DOWNES. New York: Scribners' Sons, 1940.

——. *Introduction à l'étude de saint Augustin.* Paris: Vrin, 1931; 2nd ed., 1943; translated as *The Christian Philosophy of Saint Augustine* by L. E. M. LYNCH. New York: Random House, 1960.

——. *La philosophie au moyen âge des origines patristiques à la fin du XIVᵉ siecle.* 2nd ed. Paris: Vrin, 1952; translated as *History of Christian Philosophy in the Middle Ages.* New York: Random House, 1954.

——. *Le Thomisme.* Paris: Vrin, 5th ed., 1944; translated as *The Christian Philosophy of St. Thomas Aquinas* by L. K. SHOOK. New York: Random House, 1956.

HALLER, R. 'Begriff,' *Historisches Wörterbuch Der Philosophie*, ed. JOACHIM RITTER. Basel/Stuttgart: Schwabe, 1971.

HAMILTON, SIR WILLIAM. *Lectures on Metaphysics and Logic,* eds. H. L. MANSEL and JOHN VEITCH. 4 vols. Edinburgh: W. Blackwood, 1859–60.

HAMPSHIRE, STUART. *Spinoza.* Harmondsworth: Penguin books, 1951.

HARE, R. M. 'Plato and the Mathematicians,' *New Essays on Plato and Aristotle*, ed. R. BAMBROUGH. London: Routledge and Kegan Paul, 1965.

HEGEL, G. W. F. *Sämmtliche Werke*, ed. H. GLOCKNER, 26 vols. Stuttgart: F. Frommann, 1951–60.

——. *The Logic of Hegel*, translated by WILLIAM WALLACE from the *Encyclopedia of the Philosophical Sciences*, with the editor's Prolegomena. Oxford: Clarendon Press, 1873, 1892.

——. *The Science of Logic*, translated by W. H. JOHNSTON and L. G. STRUTHERS. 2 vols. London: G. Allen and Unwin, 1929.

HEMPEL, CARL G. *Aspects of Scientific Explanation and other Essays in the Philosophy of Science.* New York: Free Press, 1965.

——. *Fundamentals of Concept Formation in Empirical Science, International Encyclopedia of Unified Science*, vol II, no. 7. Chicago: University of Chicago Press, 1952.

HINTIKKA, J. 'Cogito ergo sum: Inference or Performance,' *Philosophical Review*, 71 (1962), 3–32.

HOBBES, THOMAS. *Opera Philosophica Quae Latine Scripsit Omnia*, ed. WILLIAM MOLESWORTH. 5 vols. London, 1839–45; reprinted Germany: Scientia Verlag Aalen, 1951.

——. *English Works of Thomas Hobbes*, ed. SIR WILLIAM MOLESWORTH. 11 vols. London: J. Bohn, 1839–45; reprinted Germany: Scientia Verlag Aalen, 1962.

——. *Leviathan*, ed. with an introductory essay and notes by MICHAEL OAKESHOTT. Oxford: Blackwell, 1957.

HUME, DAVID. *The Philosophical Works of David Hume*, eds. T. H. GREEN and T. H. GROSE. 4 vols. London: Longmans, Green, 1898.

——. *Hume's Enquiries*, ed. L. A SELBY-BIGGE. Oxford: Clarendon, 1894.

——. *A Treatise of Human Nature*. 3 vols. Edited in 1-volume edition by L. A. SELBY-BIGGE. Oxford: Clarendon Press, 1888.

ISHAGURO, HIDÉ. *Leibniz's Philosophy of Logic and Language.*

Ithaca: Cornell University Press, 1972.

JAEGER, WERNER. *Aristoteles: Grundlegung einer Geschicte seiner Entwicklung.* Berlin: Weidmannsche, 1923; translated with author's corrections and additions as *Aristotle: Fundamentals of the History of His Development,* by RICHARD ROBINSON. Oxford: Oxford University Press, 1934; 2nd ed., 1948; paperback, 1962.

JAMES, WILLIAM. *The Principles of Psychology.* 2 vols. New York: Holt, 1890; reprinted New York: Dover, 1950.

JOHN OF SALISBURY. *Metalogicon, Patrologiae Latina,* vol. 199; translated as *The Metalogicon,* with introductory notes, by D. D. MCGARRY. Gloucester, Mass.: Peter Smith, 1971.

JOHN OF ST. THOMAS. *Cursus Theologicus.* Paris, Rome, Tournai: Opere et studio Monachorum Solesmensium, 1933.

KANT, IMMANUEL. *Gesammelte Schriften.* 23 vols. Prussian Academy of Sciences Edition. Berlin: G. Reimer, 1902–55.

——. *Kant's Werke,* ed. ERNST CASSIRER. 10 vols. Berlin: B. Cassirer, 1912–22.

——. *Kritik der Reinen Vernunft.* Riga: J. F. Hartknoch, 1st ed., 1781; 2nd ed., 1787.

——. *Kritik der Reinen Vernunft,* Nach der ersten and zweiten Original-Ausgabe neu herausgegeben von RAYMUND SCHMIDT. Leipsig: Felix Meiner, 1926; Hamburg: Felix Meiner, 1971.

——. *Critique of Pure Reason,* translated by NORMAN KEMP SMITH. London: Macmillan, 1929.

——. *Kant's Prolegomena to any Future Metaphysics,* translated by PAUL CARUS. Chicago: Open Court, 1933.

——. *Fundamental Principles of the Metaphysics of Morals,* translated by T. K. ABBOTT. London: Longmans, Green, 1883; reissued, with an introduction by MARVIN FOX. Indianapolis: Bobbs-Merrill, 1949.

——. *Kantlexicon,* ed. RUDOLF EISLER. Reprinted Hildesheim: G. Olms, 1961.

KENNY, ANTHONY. *Descartes: A Study of His Philosophy.* New York: Random House, 1968.

——. *Wittgenstein.* Cambridge, Mass.: Harvard University Press, 1973.

KNEALE, W. and M. *The Development of Logic.* Oxford: Clarendon Press, 1962.

KNOWLES, DAVID. *The Evolution of Medieval Thought.* London: Longmans, 1962.

KÖRNER, STEPHAN. *Conceptual Thinking: A Logical Enquiry.* New York: Dover, 1959.

——. *Kant.* Harmondsworth: Penguin Books, 1955.

KRIPKE, SAUL. 'Naming and Necessity,' *Semantics of Natural Language*, eds. DONALD DAVIDSON and GILBERT HARMAN. Dordrecht: D. Reidel, 1972.

——. 'Identity and Necessity,' *Identity and Individuation*, ed. MILTON K. MUNITZ. New York: New York University Press, 1971.

LEHRER, KEITH. *Knowledge.* London: Oxford University Press, 1974.

LEIBNIZ, GOTTFRIED WILHELM. *Sämtliche Schriften und Briefe.* Prussian Academy of Sciences Edition. In Progress. Darmstadt: Reichl, 1923.

——. *Die Philosophische Schriften von G. W. Leibniz*, ed. C. I. GERHARDT. 7 vols. Berlin: Weidman, 1875–90; facsimile reprint Hildesheim: G. Olms, 1962.

——. *Hauptschriften zur Grundlegung der Philosophie*, eds. A. BUCHENAU and E. CASSIRER. 5 vols. Leipzig: F. Meiner, 1904–6; 2nd ed., 2 vols. Leipzig: F. Meiner, 1924; reprinted Hamburg: Meiner, 1966.

——. *Opuscules et fragments inédits de Leibniz*, ed. LOUIS COUTURAT. Paris: Felix Alcan, 1903; reprinted Hildesheim: G. Olms, 1961.

——. *Leibniz: Philosophical Papers and Letters*, translated by L. E. LOEMKER. 2 vols. Chicago: University of Chicago Press, 1956.

——. *Leibniz: Selections*, ed. PHILIP WIENER. New York: Charles Scribner's Sons, 1951.

——. *Discourse on Metaphysics, Correspondence with Arnauld, and Manadology*, translated by G. R. MONTGOMERY; corrected and revised by ALBERT C. CHANDLER. La Salle, Illinois: Open Court, 1924.

——. *Leibniz: A Collection of Critical Essays*, ed. HARRY FRANKFURT. New York: Doubleday, 1972.

LEWIS, C. I. *An Analysis of Knowledge and Valuation.* La Salle, Illinois: Open Court, 1946.

——. *Mind and the World-Order.* New York: Scribner's Sons, 1929.

LOCKE, JOHN. *An Essay Concerning Human Understanding.*

London, 1690; 5th ed., with additions, 1706. Reprint of 5th edition, with revisions, ed. JOHN YOLTON. 2 vols. London: Dent, New York: Dutton, 1961.

LUCRETIUS. TITI LVCRETI CARI, *DE RERVM NATVRA*, ed. with Prolegomena, Critical Apparatus, Translation and Commentary CYRIL BAILEY. 3 vols. Oxford: Clarendon Press, 1947.

MACINTYRE, A. C. *A Short History of Ethics: A History of Moral Philosophy from the Homeric Age to the Twentieth Century.* London: Routledge and Kegan Paul, 1967.

MACKIE, J. L. *The Cement of the Universe.* Oxford: Clarendon Press, 1974.

MACNABB, D. G. C. *David Hume: His Theory of Knowledge and Morality.* London: Hutchinson's University Library, 1951.

Markus, R. A. 'St. Augustine on Signs,' *Phronesis*, 2 (1957), 60–83; reprinted *Augustine: A Collection of Critical Essays*, ed. R. A. MARKUS. New York: Doubleday, 1972.

MARTIN, GOTTFRIED. *Leibniz: Logik und Metaphysik*, 1960; translated as *Leibniz: Logic and Metaphysics*, by K. J. NORTHCOTT and P. G. LUCAS. Manchester: University Press, 1963.

MATES, BENSON. *Stoic Logic.* Berkeley: University of California Press, 1953.

Medieval Philosophy: From St. Augustine to Nicholas of Cusa, eds. J. F. WIPPEL and ALLAN B. WOLTER. New York: Free Press, 1969.

MILL, JOHN STUART. *An Examination of Sir William Hamilton's Philosophy.* 2 vols. London: Longmans, Green 1865; 5th ed. 1878.

——. *A System of Logic.* 2 vols. London, 1843; 8th ed. 1872; reprinted *Collected Works of John Stuart Mill*, vols. 7 and 8, ed. J. M. ROBSON. Toronto: University of Toronto Press, 1974.

MOORE, G. E. 'The Nature of Judgment,' *Mind* VIII (1899), 176–193.

——. *Philosophical Papers.* London: Allen and Unwin, 1959.

——. *Principia Ethica.* Cambridge: Cambridge University Press, 1903.

——. *Some Main Problems of Philosophy.* London: Allen and Unwin; New York: Macmillan, 1953.

——. *The Philosophy of G. E. Moore*, ed. P. A. SCHILPP. Chicago and Evanston: Northwestern University Press, 1942.

MORRIS, C. R. *Locke, Berkeley, Hume.* Oxford: Clarendon Press, 1931.

NOZICK, ROBERT. *Anarchy, State, and Utopia.* New York: Basic Books, 1975.

O'CONNOR, D. J. *John Locke.* Harmondsworth: Penguin Books, 1952.

PARKINSON, G. H. R. *Logic and Reality in Leibniz's Metaphysics.* Oxford: Clarendon Press, 1965.

——. *Spinoza's Theory of Knowledge.* Oxford: Clarendon Press, 1954.

PASSMORE, JOHN. *Hume's Intentions.* Cambridge: Cambridge University Press, 1952.

PATON, H. J. *Kant's Metaphysics of Experience: A Commentary on the First Half of the Kritik der Reinen Vernunft.* 2 vols. London: Allen and Unwin, 1936.

Patrologiae cursus completus. Series Latina, ed. JACQUES PAUL MIGNE. 221 vols. Paris, 1844–64; reprinted Turnholti, Belgium: Typographi Brepolis, 1878–90.

PEARS, DAVID. *Bertrand Russell and the British Tradition in Philosophy.* London: William Collins: New York: Random House, 1967.

——. *Wittgenstein.* London: William Collins, 1971.

PEIFER, J. F. *The Concept in Thomism.* New York: Bookman Associates, 1952.

PEIRCE, CHARLES SANDERS. *The Collected Papers of Charles Sanders Peirce*, vols. I–IV, eds. CHARLES HARTSHORNE and PAUL WEISS. Cambridge, Mass.: Harvard University Press, 1931–35; vols. VII and VIII, ed. ARTHUR BURKS. Cambridge, Mass.: Harvard University Press, 1958.

PETERS, R. S. *Hobbes.* Harmondsworth: Penguin Books, 1956.

PHILO. *Works*, with English translations by F. H. COLSON and G. H. WHITAKER. 10 vols. 2 supplementary vols., translated by R. MARCUS. Loeb Classical Library. London: Heinemann; Cambridge, Mass.: Harvard University Press, 1929–62.

PLATO. *Platonis Opera*, ed. JOHN BURNET. 5 vols. Oxford: Clarendon Press, 1900–1907.

——. *Works.* 12 vols. Greek with English translations by H. N. FOWLER, W. R. LAMB, R. G. BURY, and PAUL SHOREY. Loeb Classical Library. London: Heinemann; Cambridge, Mass.: Harvard University Press, 1921–53.

——. *The Dialogues of Plato*, translated with analyses and introductions by BENJAMIN JOWETT; rev. ed. D. J. ALLAN and H. E. DALE. 4 vols. Oxford: Oxford University Press, 1953.

——. *Plato's Cosmology: The Timaeus of Plato*, translated with running commentary by F. M. CORNFORD. London: Routledge and Kegan Paul, 1937.

——. *Plato's Examination of Pleasure*, Translation of the *Philebus* with introduction and commentary by R. HACKFORTH. Cambridge: Cambridge University Press, 1945.

——. *Plato and Parmenides: Parmenides' 'Way of Truth' and Plato's 'Parmenides'*, translated with running commentary by F. M. CORNFORD. London: Routledge and Kegan Paul, 1939.

——. *Plato's Phaedo*, translated with introduction, notes and appendices by R. S. BLUCK. London: Routledge and Kegan Paul, 1955.

——. *Plato's Phaedrus*, translated, with commentary, by R. HACKFORTH. Cambridge: Cambridge University Press, 1952.

——. *The Republic of Plato*, translated, with introduction and notes, by F. M. CORNFORD. Oxford: Oxford University Press, 1941.

——. *Studies in the Platonic Epistles*, ed. G. R. MORROW. Urbana: University of Illinois Press, 1935; revised as *Plato's Epistles*, a translation with critical essays and notes. Indianapolis: Bobbs-Merrill, 1962.

——. *Plato's Theory of Knowledge: the Theaetetus and Sophist*, translated with running commentary, by F. M. CORNFORD. London: Routledge and Kegan Paul, 1935.

PLOTINUS. *Enneads*. Greek text and French translation, with notes, by É. BREHIER. 6 vols. Paris: Budé, 1924–38. Greek text with English translation by A. H. ARMSTRONG. 7 vols projected, 5 already published. Loeb Classical Library. London: Heinemann; Cambridge, Mass.: Harvard University Press, 1966.

——. *The Enneads*, translated by STEPHEN MACKENNA. 5 vols. London: Faber and Faber, 1930.

——. *The Philosophy of Plotinus: Representative Books from the Enneads*, translated with an Introduction by JOSEPH KATZ. New York: Appleton-Century-Crofts, 1950.

POPKIN, RICHARD H. *The History of Scepticism from Erasmus to Descartes*. New York: Humanities Press, 1964; rev. New York: Harper and Row, 1968.

POPPER, KARL. *The Open Society and Its Enemies*. 2 vols. London:

Routledge and Kegan Paul, 1945; 2nd ed. rev. and enlarged, 1952.

——. *The Poverty of Historicism*. London: Routledge and Kegan Paul, 1957.

PORPHYRY. *Isagoge* (with Boethius translation), *Commentaria in Aristotelem Graeca*, iv, i, ed. A. BUSSE. Berlin: G. Reimer, 1887.

PRICE, H. H. *Hume's Theory of the External World*. Oxford: Clarendon Press, 1940.

——. *Thinking and Experience*. London: Hutchinson's University Library, 1953.

PUTNAM, HILARY. 'Meaning and Reference,' *The Journal of Philosophy*, LXX (November 8, 1973), 699–711.

QUINE, W. VAN ORMAN. *From a Logical Point of View: Logico-Philosophical Essays*. Cambridge, Mass: Harvard University Press, 1953.

——. *Word and Object*. Cambridge, Mass: MIT Press, 1960.

RAWLS, JOHN. *A Theory of Justice*. Cambridge, Mass.: Harvard University Press, 1971.

Realism and the Background of Phenomenology, ed. RODERICK CHISHOLM. Glencoe, Illinois: Free-Press, 1960.

REID, THOMAS. *Works*, ed. SIR WILLIAM HAMILTON. 2 vols. Edinburgh: J. Bartlett, 1846–63.

RESCHER, NICHOLAS. *The Philosophy of Leibniz*. Englewood Cliffs: Prentice-Hall, 1967.

ROBINSON, RICHARD. *Definition*. Oxford: Clarendon Press, 1950.

——. *Plato's Early Dialectic*. Oxford: Clarendon Press, 2nd ed. 1953.

ROSS, W. D. *Aristotle*. London: Methuen, 5th ed. 1949.

——. *Plato's Theory of Ideas*. Oxford: Clarendon Press, 1953.

RUSSELL, BERTRAND. *The Analysis of Matter*. London: Paul, Trench, and Trubner; New York: Harcourt, Brace, 1927.

——. *The Analysis of Mind*. London: Allen and Unwin; New York: Macmillan, 1921.

——. *A Critical Exposition of the Philosophy of Leibniz, with an Appendix of Leading Passages*. Cambridge: Cambridge University Press, 1900; 2nd ed. 1937.

——. *Human Knowledge: Its Scope and Limits*. London: Allen and Unwin; New York; Simon and Schuster, 1948.

——. *An Inquiry into Meaning and Truth*. London: Allen and Unwin; New York: Norton, 1940.

——. *Introduction to Mathematical Philosophy*. London: Allen and

Unwin; New York: Macmillan, 1919.

Logic and Knowledge: Essays 1901–1950, ed. ROBERT C. MARSH. London: Allen and Unwin; New York: Macmillan, 1956.

——. 'Meinong's Theory of Complexes and Assumptions,' *Mind*, 13 (1904), 204–19; 336–54; 509–24.

——. *Mysticism and Logic*. London and New York: Longmans, Green, 1918.

——. *Our Knowledge of the External World*. Chicago: Open Court, 1914; London: Allen and Unwin, 1922.

——. *An Outline of Philosophy*. London: Allen and Unwin; New York: Norton, 1927. (American edition entitled *Philosophy*).

—— and ALFRED NORTH WHITEHEAD, *Principia Mathematica*. 3 vols. Cambridge: Cambridge University Press, vol. 1, 1910; 2nd ed, 1925; vol. 2, 1912; vol. 3, 1913.

——. *The Principles of Mathematics*. Cambridge: Cambridge University Press, 1903; 2nd ed. New York: Norton, 1937.

——. *The Problems of Philosophy*. London: Williams and Norgate; New York: Heney Holt, 1912.

——. 'Recent Work on the Philosophy of Leibniz,' *Mind*, 12 (1903), 177–201.

——. *The Philosophy of Bertrand Russell*, ed. P. A. SCHILPP. Evanston: Northwestern University Press; Cambridge: Cambridge University Press; Toronto: Macmillan, 1944.

——. *Bertrand Russell: A Collection of Critical Essays*, ed. D. F. PEARS. New York: Doubleday, 1972.

RYLE, GILBERT. *The Concept of Mind*. London: Hutchinson's University Library, 1949.

——. *Collected Papers*. 2 vols. London: Hutchinson's University Library; New York: Barnes and Noble, 1971.

——. *Dilemmas*. Cambridge: Cambridge University Press, 1954.

——. 'John Locke on the Human Understanding,' *Tercentenary Addresses on John Locke*, ed. J. L. STOCKS. Oxford: Oxford University Press, 1933.

——. 'Plato,' *The Encyclopedia of Philosophy*.

——. *Plato's Progress*. Cambridge: Cambridge University Press, 1966.

SCHRADER, GEORGE. 'Kant's Theory of Concepts,' *Kant-Studien*, 49 (1958); reprinted *Kant: A Collection of Critical Essays*, ed, R. P. WOLFF. New York: Doubleday, 1967.

Selections from Medieval Philosophy, ed. RICHARD MC KEON. 2

vols. Charles Scribner's Sons, 1929–30.

SEXTUS EMPIRICUS. *Works*. Greek text with English translation and a glossary, ed. R. G. BURY. 4 vols. Loeb Classical Library. London: Heinemann; Cambridge, Mass.: Harvard University Press, 1917–55.

SHOREY, PAUL. *Unity of Plato's Thought*. Chicago: University of Chicago Press, 1903; reprinted 1960.

——. *What Plato Said*. Chicago: University of Chicago Press, 1933; 6th imp. 1965.

SMITH, NORMAN KEMP. *A Commentary to Kant's Critique of Pure Reason*. London: Macmillan, 1918; rev. 1923.

SPINOZA, BENEDICT (BARUCH). *Spinoza Opera*, ed. CARL GEBHARDT. 4 vols. Heidelberg: Carl Winter, 1925.

——. *The Chief Works of Spinoza*, translated by R. H. M. ELWES. 2 vols. London, 1883; reprinted New York: Dover, 1951.

——. *Ethics*, translated by W. H. WHITE and A. H. STIRLING. London: H. Frowde, 1910.

——. *Spinoza: A Collection of Critical Essays,* ed. MARJORIE GRENE. New York: Doubleday, 1973.

STENZEL, JULIUS. *Plato's Method of Dialectic*, translated from 2nd German ed. by D. J. ALLAN. Oxford: Clarendon Press, 1940.

STEVENSON, C. L. *Facts and Values: Studies in Ethical Analysis*. New Haven: Yale University Press, 1963.

STRAWSON, P. F. *The Bounds of Sense: An Essay on Kant's Critique of Pure Reason*. London: Methuen, 1966.

TAYLOR, A. E. *Plato: The Man and His Work*. London: Methuen; New York: Dial, 1927.

THOMAS AQUINAS, ST. *S. Thomae Aquinatis, Opera Omnia*. Leonine edition. *Summa Theologiae*, with Cajetan's *Commentary*, vols. iv–xii; *Summa Contra Gentiles*, vols xiii–xv. Rome: Apud Sedem Commissionis *Leoninae*, 1982-; reprinted Turin: Marietti, 1934-.

——. *Opera Omnia*. 25 vols. Parma: Fiaccadori, 1852–73; reprinted New York, 1948–50.

——. *Opera Omnia,* eds, É. FRETTÉ and P. MARÉ. 34 vols. Paris; Vivès, 1872–80.

——. *De Ente et Essentia*, ed. LUDWIG BAUR. Münster, 1933; translated as *On Being and Essence* by ARMAND MAURER. Toronto: Pontifical Institute of Mediaeval Study, 1949.

——. *Quaestiones Disputatae de Veritate*, ed. R. M. SPIAZZI. Turin:

Marietti, 1954; translated as *Truth* by R. W. MULLIGAN *et al.* 3 vols. Chicago: Henry Regnery, 1954.

———. *Thomas-Lexicon*, ed. LUDWIG VON SCHÜTZ. Stuttgart: Fr. Frommanns, 1958.

———. *Basic Writings of Saint Thomas Aquinas*, translated by ANTON C. PEGIS. 2 vols. New York: Random House, 1944.

———. *St. Thomas Aquinas, Philosophical Texts*, selected and translated by THOMAS GILBY. Oxford: Oxford University Press, 1951.

THOMSON, J. F. 'Berkeley,' *A Critical History of Western Philosophy*, ed. D. J. O'CONNOR. New York: Free Press, 1964.

URMSON, J. O. *Philosophical Analysis: Its Development Between Two World Wars*. Oxford: Clarendon Press, 1956.

———. 'Polymorphous Concepts,' *Ryle: A Collection of Critical Essays*, eds. D. P. WOOD and G. PITCHER. New York: Doubleday, 1970.

WALSH, W. H. *Reason and Experience*. Oxford: Clarendon Press, 1947.

WARNOCK, G. J. *Berkeley*. Harmondsworth: Penguin Books, 1953.

———. *English Philosophy Since 1900*. London: Oxford University Press, 1958.

WARRENDER, HOWARD. *The Political Philosophy of Hobbes: His Theory of Obligation*. Oxford: Clarendon Press, 1957.

WATKINS, JOHN W. N. *Hobbes's System of Ideas: A Study in the Political Significance of Philosophical Theories*. London: Hutchinson's University Library, 1965.

WATLING, JOHN L. *Bertrand Russell*. Edinburgh: Oliver and Boyd, 1970.

WEITZ, MORRIS. *The Opening Mind: A Philosophical Study of Humanistic Concepts*. Chicago and London: The University of Chicago Press, 1977.

WELDON, T. D. *Introduction to Kant's Critique of Pure Reason*. Oxford: Clarendon Press, 1945.

WELLS, RULON. 'Frege's Ontology,' *Review of Metaphysics*, IV (1951), 557–73.

WHITE, A. R. *G. E. Moore: A Critical Exposition*. Oxford: Blackwell, 1958.

WILLIAM OF OCKHAM. *William of Ockham: Philosophical Writings: A Selection*, ed. and translated by P. BOEHNER. Edinburgh: Nelson, 1957.

WITTGENSTEIN, LUDWIG. *The Blue and the Brown Books.* Oxford: Blackwell, 1958.

——. *Tractatus Logico-Philosophicus*, translated by C. K. OGDEN. London: Routledge and Kegan Paul, 1922; newly translated by DAVID PEARS and B. F. MC GUINNESS. London: Routledge and Kegan Paul, 1961.

——. *Philosophical Investigations*, translated by G. E. M. ANSCOMBE. New York: Macmillan, 3rd ed. 1968.

——. *Wittgenstein: The Philosophical Investigations: A Collection of Critical Essays*, ed. G. PITCHER. New York: Doubleday, 1966.

WOLFF, ROBERT P. *Kant's Theory of Mental Activity.* Cambridge, Mass.: Harvard University Press, 1963.

WOLFSON, HARRY A. *Philo: Foundations of Religious Philosophy in Judaism, Christianity and Islam.* 2 vols. 3rd ed. rev. Cambridge, Mass.: Harvard University Press, 1962.

——. *The Philosophy of Spinoza.* 2 vols. Cambridge, Mass.: Harvard University Press, 1958.

——. 'The Terms TASAWWUR and TASDIQ in Arabic Philosophy and their Greek, Latin and Hebrew Equivalents,' *The Moslem World*, 33 (1943), 114–28.

WULF, MAURICE DE. *History of Mediaeval Philosophy.* 2 vols. London: Longmans, Green, 1935.

301

PUBLICATIONS BY MORRIS WEITZ

Books

Philosophy of the Arts. Russell and Russell, 1964.

Philosophy in Literature: Shakespeare, Voltaire, Tolstoy and Proust. Wayne State University Press, 1963.

Hamlet and the Philosophy of Literary Criticism. University of Chicago Press, 1974.

The Opening Mind: A Philosophical Study of Humanistic Concepts. University of Chicago Press, 1977.

Theories of Concepts: Routledge & Kegan Paul, 1988.

Problems in Aesthetics, Second Edition, 1970.

Twentieth Century Philosophy: The Analytic Tradition, Free Press, 1966.

(Edited by Morris Weitz) E. Hanslick, *The Beautiful in Music*, Library of Liberal Arts, 1957.

Articles

'Does Art Tell the Truth?' *Philosophy and Phenomenological Research*, 1943, pp. 338–48.

'Analysis and the Unity of Russell's Philosophy,' *The Philosophy of Bertrand Russell*, Library of Living Philosophers, vol. 5, pp. 55–121, 1944.

'The Logic of Art,' *Philosophy and Phenomenological Research*, 1945, pp. 378–84.

'Philosophy and the Abuse of Language,' *Journal of Philosophy*, 1947, pp. 533–46.

'Analysis and Real Definition,' *Philosophical Studies*, 1950, pp. 1–8.

'Art, Language and Truth,' in Vivas and Krieger (eds) *The Problem of Aesthetics*, 1951.

'Professor Ryle's Logical Behaviorism', *Journal of Philosophy*, 1951, pp. 297–301.

'T. S. Eliot: Time as Mode of Salvation,' *Sewanee Review*, 1952; reprinted in B. Bergonzi, ed., *T. S. Eliot: Four Quartets*, Macmillan, 1969.

'Criticism Without Evaluation,' *Philosophical Review*, 1952.

'Oxford Philosophy,' *Philosophical Review*, 1953, pp. 187–233.

'Art and Symbolism,' *Review of Metaphysics*, 1954, pp. 466–81.

'Analytic Statements,' *Mind*, 1954, pp. 487–94.

'Truth in Literature,' *Revue internationale de philosophie*, 1955.

'The Role of Theory in Aesthetics,' *The Journal of Aesthetics and Art Criticism*, 1956. (Matchette Prize Essay)

'The Philosophy of Criticism,' *Proceedings* of the III International Congress of Aesthetics, 1956.

'Aesthetics,' *Chroniques de philosophie*, 1958. (Written for UNESCO.)

'Reasons in Criticism,' *Journal of Aesthetics and Art Criticism*, 1962.

'The Form-Content Distinction,' in W. Kennick, ed., *Art and Philosophy*, St. Martin, 1964.

'Tragedy,' *Encyclopedia of Philosophy*, Macmillan, 1967.

'Analysis, Philosophical,' *Encyclopedia of Philosophy*, Macmillan, 1967.

'Marcel Proust,' *Encyclopedia of Philosophy*, Macmillan, 1967.

'The Nature of Art,' in D. Ecker and E. Eisner, eds, *Philosophies of Art Education*, Blaisdell, 1966.

'Knowledge in Art,' *Proceedings*, Interamerican Congress of Philosophy, 1967.

'The Organic Theory,' in Tillman and Cahn, eds, *Readings in Aesthetics*, Harper and Row, 1968.

'Purism and the Dance,' in L. Jacobus, ed., *Aesthetics and the Arts*, McGraw-Hill, 1968.

'Genre and Style,' *Proceedings*, XIV International Congress of Philosophy, 1968.

'Genre and Style,' *Contemporary Philosophic Thought*, vol. 3., State University of New York Press, 1970, pp. 183–218.

'Professor Goodman on the Aesthetic,' *Journal of Aesthetics and Art Criticism*, 1971, pp. 485–7.

303

'The Coinage of Man: *King Lear* and Camus' *Stranger*,' *Proceedings*, Brockport Centre for Philosophic Exchange 1970; *Modern Language Review*, January 1971, pp. 33–9.

'The Content of Form,' *New Literary History*, vol. II, 2, pp. 351–6.

'Aby Warburg,' *The Art Bulletin*, March, 1972 (Review essay of E. H. Gombrich, *Aby Warburg: An Intellectual Biography*), pp. 107–10.

'Open Concepts,' *Revue internationale de philosophie*, 172, pp. 86–110.

'What is Aesthetic Education?' *Education Theatre Journal*, 1972, pp. 1–4.

'The Concept of Human Action,' *Philosophic Exchange*, 1972, pp. 201–37.

'Wittgenstein's Aesthetic,' *Language and Aesthetics*, University of Kansas Press, 1973, pp. 7–20.

'The Grounds of Sense: The Philosophy of Everett J. Nelson,' *Philosophy and Phenomenological Research*, 1973, pp. 455–71.

'Interpretation and the Visual Arts,' *Theoria*, 1973, pp. 101–12.

'Literature Without Philosophy: *Antony and Cleopatra*,' *Shakespeare Survey*, 28 (1975), pp. 29–36.

'Art: Who Needs It?' *Journal of Aesthetic Education*, 1976, pp. 19–28.

'Research on the Arts and in Aesthetics: Some Pitfalls, Some Possibilities,' *Art and Aesthetics: an Agenda for the Future*, Cemrel and National Institute for Education, 1975, pp. 29–37.

'Literature and Philosophy: Sense and Nonsense,' *Yearbook of Comparative Criticism*, 1982.

'Descartes' Theory of Concepts,' *Midwest Studies in Philosophy*, vol. 8, 1983.

'Making Sense of the Tractatus,' *Midwest Studies in Philosophy*, vol. 8, 1983.

'On Criticism,' *Sonus*, vol. 2, no. 1, 1981.

Reviews

About 70 or so, in *Philosophical Review, Ethics, Mind, Journal of Philosophy, American Scholar, Virginia Quarterly Review, Partisan Review*, etc.

INDEX

absolute possibility, 164
abstraction, 48–9, 54, 56, 119; and
    Frege, 189
abstractionism, 251–5
acts of judgment, 249–52
Adam, Charles, 61
Alciphron, 125
Analysis of Matter, The, 208
Analysis of Mind, The, 208, 213,
    238
analytic philosophy, vii
anamnesis, 17
Anselm, 36, 93
antinomies, 170–1
Aquinas, Thomas, xiv, xvi, 260, 268;
    abstraction, 48–9, 54, 56; *The
    Christian Philosophy of St
    Thomas Aquinas, 53;
    Compendium Theologiae*, 43, 45,
    50; Copleston, 51–2; *De Potentia*,
    43; *De Veritate*, 45; Geach, P., 54–
    5; God, 52, 55–8; *History of
    Philosophy*, 57; intellect, 43–53,
    56, 58; intelligible *species*, 44–5,
    50; knowledge, 50–2; Peifer on,
    52–3; phantasm, 49–51; *Summa
    Contra Gentiles*, 43–4, 46
Aristotle, xvi, xviii, 1, 18, 34, 50, 58,
    60, 84, 142, 248, 257–61, 266–7;
    character of, 29; conception, 22–
    6; *De Anima*, 22; definitional
    entity, 30–2; intuition, 20–1, 24–
    5; knowledge, 20, 23–5; *Medea*,

30; *Nicomachean Ethics*, 24, 26;
    Oedipus Rex, 28, 30; *On
    Interpretation*, 19; *Physics*, 23;
    and Plato, 20, 22, 31; *Poetics*, 27–
    9; *Posterior Analytics*, 20–1;
    Topics, 22; tragedy, 27–31;
    universals, 20–2
arithmetic, 186–91; *see also*
    mathematics
Arnauld, 84, 87–8
Augustine, xix, 34–42, 267–8; and
    Anselm, 36; *Confessions*, 38; *De
    libero arbitrio voluntatis*, 37; *De
    Trinitate*, 40; divine illumination,
    40–2; faith, 35–6; God, 36–42;
    time, 38–40
Austin, J., 189

Bacon, Francis, 85
Begriff, 148
Berkeley, 18, 123, 124–33, 136, 262,
    272; *A New Theory of Vision*,
    128; on ideas, 124, 128–9; and
    Locke, 126; matter, 130–2;
    mental entities, 129, 132–3;
    nominal essence, 126; notions,
    124, 128–9; *Philosophical
    Commentaries*, 126
*Bertrand Russell, Logic and
    Knowledge: Essays*, 204
Bradley, 215–16, 217–19
Bread, C. D., 186
Brentano, 185, 221